DANTE AND THE GREEKS

DUMBARTON OAKS MEDIEVAL HUMANITIES

Series Editor
Jan M. Ziolkowski

DANTE AND THE GREEKS

Edited by

JAN M. ZIOLKOWSKI

Dumbarton Oaks Research Library and Collection
WASHINGTON, D.C.

Printed in the United States of America

22 21 20 19 18 17 16 15 14   1 2 3 4 5

Library of Congress Cataloging-in-Publication Data

Dante and the Greeks / edited by Jan M. Ziolkowski.
pages cm.—(Dumbarton Oaks Medieval Humanities)
Includes index.
ISBN 978-0-88402-400-2 (first)
1. Dante Alighieri, 1265-1321—Criticism and interpretation.
2. Dante Alighieri, 1265-1321—Knowledge—Classical literature.
3. Philosophy, Ancient—Influence.
I. Ziolkowski, Jan M., 1956– editor.
PQ4390.D275 2014
851'.1—dc23
2014014301

www.doaks.org/publications

Series design: Barbara Haines
Cover and text composition: Melissa Tandysh

CONTENTS

Introduction

JAN M. ZIOLKOWSKI

The cultures that Byzantinists and medievalists explore share much common ground. In particular, both sets of experts occupy themselves with roughly the same chronological span, more or less from the fifth through the fifteenth century. Yet the two fields split geographically. Although the designation "medieval studies" can be taken to subsume Islamic, Byzantine, and Judaic studies,[1] it is generally restricted more narrowly to the interdisciplinary investigation of Western Europe, whereas "Byzantine studies" pertains to the similar exploration of Byzantium. In this usage—and it was devised only in the sixteenth century—Byzantium serves as shorthand for the Byzantine Empire and its civilization. Byzantium must be distinguished from Byzantion, a toponym for an ancient city that stood on the same site where Constantinople (or Constantinopolis Nova Roma, to use its full name) was eventually founded. In turn, Constantinople became the seat of what is commonly known as the Byzantine Empire. A conceptual break, corresponding to the physical divide of the Bosphorus, has been imposed between what is considered Byzantine, concentrated heavily in the Near or Middle East, especially Asia Minor (or Anatolia), and what is Western medieval.[2]

Both medievalists and Byzantinists have had motivations and incentives for understating the frequency and intensity of contacts and exchanges in the Middle Ages between the cultures of Western Europe and the Byzantine Empire. As with the study of the Crusades, scholars have shown greater interest, on the whole, in military, political, and ideological confrontations between the two worlds than in instances or patterns of cultural engagement. Furthermore, no one can deny the divisions that have run between the Latin and Greek worlds since antiquity. For every case of Philhellenism or Graecomania among the ancient Romans, we can uncover one of condescension

1 The broader sense is followed in *Handbook of Medieval Studies: Terms, Methods, Trends*, ed. A. Classen, 3 vols. (Berlin, 2010).

2 R. S. Nelson, "Living on the Byzantine Borders of Western Art," *Gesta* 35 (1996): 3–11.

or disapprobation.[3] These reservations were complexly mutual: Romans sometimes referred to the Greeks disparagingly as *Graeculi,* "little Greeks," while Greeks, in turn, regarded the Romans as barbaric or, at least, uncouth.[4] The term Romanophilia refers to the attraction of present-day people to ancient Rome and may never have been taken to describe an inclination toward Romanness among ancient or Byzantine Greeks. Its rarity in this context speaks to the relative paucity of evidence for expressly pro-Roman sentiment among ancient native speakers of Greek.

In the medieval or Byzantine period, the tensions between East and West (or Greek and Latin) modified but did not diminish, as the ownership of Romanness itself came under dispute between the two linguistic, cultural, and political regions, and differing theological positions on various issues pulled them into conflict. Just as in considering occasional cultural tensions between any two nations today, the question is whether shared characteristics and interests between seemingly opposed groups exceed the perceived differences.

In a syndrome loosely related to broader cultural frictions, modern-day experts do not always search for commonalities that tie their specializations to others, nor do they uniformly display particular eagerness to perceive and acknowledge likenesses. On the contrary, rather than strive for mutual recognition and exchange, they sometimes focus on the disparities that allow them to maintain their branches of study as separate.[5] At the same time, such scholars may feel that their specialty is underappreciated by the general public and other professionals in comparison to other fields and disciplines. The recognition and resources available to humanists are meager by most measures, but human nature being what it has always been, researchers are still tempted to begrudge or envy their peers in related fields of study for what they possess, and suspect that they have been granted more advantages and rewards than are their due. Intensifying these nearly universal predispositions are exceptional features specific to the two cultures under consideration here.

The Latin West and Greek East have been defined as "sibling cultures," and scholarship devoted to them suffers from the rivalries often associated with sisters and brothers.[6] Classicists often self-identify as either Hellenists or Latinists,[7] and Byzantinists and medievalists (of whom Dantists are one highly evolved subset) divide similarly according

3 Most generally, see N. Petrochilos, *Roman Attitudes to the Greeks*, S. Saripolos's Library 25 (Athens, 1974). For the Roman response to Hellenism, see E. S. Gruen, *Culture and National Identity in Republican Rome*, Cornell Studies in Classical Philology 52 (Ithaca, NY, 1992).

4 On *Graeculus* (and *Graeculio*), see *Oxford Latin Dictionary*, ed. P. G. W. Glare, 2nd ed., 2 vols. (Oxford, 2012), 1:846. A. Henrichs, "Graecia Capta: Roman Views of Greek Culture," *Harvard Studies in Classical Philology* 97 (1995), 243–61.

5 In this regard, I agree wholeheartedly with E. D. Karampetsos, *Dante and Byzantium* (Boston, 2009), 7.

6 D. J. Geanakoplos, *Interaction of the "Sibling" Byzantine and Western Cultures in the Middle Ages and Italian Renaissance (330–1600)* (New Haven, 1976).

7 For an amusing description of how the two groups differ, see D. Wender, *Roman Poetry: From the Republic to the Silver Age* (Carbondale, IL, 1980), ix.

to the principal scriptural language—Greek in the first case, Latin in the second—of the cultures on which they focus. Viewed from a distance, the languages and literatures with which they grapple reveal many superficial resemblances, since in both cases the languages and literatures were built upon a classical substratum that was overlaid with a Christian layer that took shape in antiquity and late antiquity. Both strata were not immune to the dynamics (known as *diglossia*) between the learned and the fully living tongues. But up close, Byzantine and medieval cultures reveal many discrepancies, owing to the nuances of the classical traditions upon which they drew, the distinct theologies of the two brands of Christianity upon which they rested, and much more.

Medieval and Byzantine studies each place heavy demands on their followers. The study of Byzantium or the Western Middle Ages alone could demand a lifetime (or more) of learning, even without imposing the obligation of becoming versed in the other domain, too. Both areas require the mastery of challenging ancient and medieval languages, extensive primary sources, and sprawling secondary literature in several modern languages, and the temptation to justify a concentration on only one of the areas while ignoring the other is strong.

Furthermore, the number of high school, college, or even graduate students who are equipped linguistically to pass the basic requirements for immersion in a topic such as "Dante and the Greeks" has plummeted from a century ago. Greek and Latin are both dead languages that demand substantial effort to master. Fewer students enter college or even leave graduate school with as much exposure to Greek, Latin, and Italian as in the times when elite secondary education had the reading of ancient classics in the original Latin and Greek as a central objective. Medievalists, who steep themselves in the cultures of Western Europe, are often required to learn not only Latin but also medieval vernacular as well as modern languages, and many begin this study later in life than was once the case. Byzantinists face a similar but often more daunting linguistic challenge, as Slavic, Turkic, Coptic, and Semitic tongues (such as Arabic and Syriac), among others, enter the picture. Yet the continuing global ascent of English means that correspondingly less heed is paid to other modern research languages. Despite the persistence of emigration, immigration, and exile in the present day, the particular brands of serendipitous polyglottism that the military and political conflicts of the mid-twentieth century created within European and American academic settings have vanished.

Against this backdrop, it has been convenient to exaggerate the divisions, mutual distrust and disinterest, and unintelligibility, admittedly great, between the Latin and Greek worlds. Under the circumstances, it has made sense to overstate the divide between Rome (the Old, or original, Rome) and Constantinople (the New, or Second, Rome), as well as between the Latin and the Western European vernaculars, on the one hand, and Greek, Syriac, Arabic, Turkish, Old Church Slavonic, and other such languages, on the other. No one, not even a linguistic prodigy, could gain facility in all the languages involved in the two spheres and so, consequently, it may come as a relief to be reassured that the people who lived from 500 to 1500 were, themselves, partitioned into two discrete groups in their use of language and their cultural preferences.

Yet the sense of an iron curtain—or at least an iron portcullis—between what happened on one side of the Adriatic and the other is misleading. Even more erroneous is an impression of a "clash of civilizations" between the Latin West and Greek East.[8] A seductive but false analogy would be to ring a change on the celebrated saying, ascribed to various celebrities of the nineteenth and twentieth centuries, that characterizes the special relationship between the United States and Britain as "two cultures separated by a common language": thus, we would be oversimplifying to speak of "two cultures separated by a common religion."

The relative neglect of the Hellenic, and especially the Byzantine, components in Western European culture may be gauged by how long it took for even the roughest Greek equivalent to Ernst Robert Curtius's *European Literature and the Latin Middle Ages* (German 1949; English 1953) to be produced.[9] Walter Berschin's *Greek Letters and the Latin Middle Ages: From Jerome to Nicholas of Cusa* (German 1980; English 1988) was itself published nearly forty years after Albert Siegmund's monograph on the transmission of Greek Christian literature in the Latin Church up to the twelfth century (1949).[10] On the other side of the equation—the Byzantine reception of ancient and medieval Western culture—the failings are no less and may be even greater, since to date no corresponding book exists for Byzantium: no one has written *Latin Letters and the Greek Middle Ages* or *Latin Literature and Byzantium*, although Elizabeth Fisher, represented by a very clear stocktaking in this volume, has published most of the requisite prolegomena for such a synthesis.

Communication between scholars of Byzantine and medieval studies (again, encompassing Dante studies) ought not remain static or dwindle but instead intensify: for such grand intellectual endeavors to survive, and even to thrive, in the twenty-first century, we can no longer afford (if ever we could) the luxury of splendid isolation. We must uphold the integrity of our specialties while simultaneously crossing the boundaries of our fields and disciplines, nurturing the consequent intellectual growth within them (and ourselves), and in the process maintaining public awareness and appreciation of them. Failure to attain such success would have costs none of us can afford. But the difficulties in acquiring the requisite background and scope to make a responsible contribution to a topic such as "Dante and the Greeks" are enormous.

8 The phrase and concept "clash of civilizations" originated with a short working paper that was followed a few years later by a book, both by S. P. Huntington: *The Clash of Civilizations?*, working paper / Project on the Changing Security Environment and American National Interests 4 (Cambridge, MA, 1993), and *The Clash of Civilizations and the Remaking of World Order* (New York, 1996).

9 E. R. Curtius, *Europäische Literatur und lateinisches Mittelalter* (Francke, 1948); *European Literature and the Latin Middle Ages*, trans. W. R. Trask, Bollingen Series 36 (New York, 1953).

10 A revised and expanded edition of Berschin's book was translated into English by J. C. Frakes (Washington, DC, 1988). Siegmund's book is *Die Überlieferung der griechischen christlichen Literatur in der lateinischen Kirche bis zum zwölften Jahrhundert*, Veröffentlichung des Byzantinischen Instituts Scheyern, Abhandlungen der Bayerischen Benediktiner-Akademie 5 (Munich, 1949).

Beyond the obstacle of achieving competency in even just one of the three fields, let alone all three, we must weigh the possibility that the closetful of preconceptions known as Orientalism may have prompted, long ago, the drawing of more rigid boundaries between the Latin West and the Greek East than was warranted.[11] Associating the Greek East with the Orient may look problematic, because ancient Greece is often posited as the foundation of what would eventually emerge as the West. But the place of Greece between East and West has always been, and remains, a cultural conundrum as much as a geographical reality. The understanding Dante would have had of the Greek Mediterranean is analyzed with a special cartographic twist in Theodore Cachey's essay in this volume.

In a world that trains its sights heavily and even, in my view, unwisely on the present and future to the exclusion of earlier times, the devotees of Byzantium and the Middle Ages (including, of course, Dante) are best qualified for mediating what can be discovered about their respective pasts for the education, edification, and entertainment of our contemporaries. On a planet that supposedly witnesses the extinction of languages at the rate of one every two weeks, we count ourselves among the protectors of already dead as well as still-living tongues.[12] And in a world that idolizes new devices and products, we can convey the excitement of an old and seemingly superseded technology, since the civilizations we all scrutinize rested largely on texts preserved and transmitted through the vehicle of the manuscript codex.

Dante lived in an age in which authority held true to the etymology it presupposes: it rested upon the command of earlier, authoritative authors.[13] The great Italian poet ranks high among authors who have staked their authenticity on dialogue with earlier writers. At the same time, he was anything but detached from the distinguishing characteristics of the late thirteenth- and early fourteenth-century world that surrounded him. On the contrary, he was rooted deeply in the specificities of life and events in his own day.

The poet of the *Commedia* is an ideal candidate for intensive scholarly examination that relies upon digital or conventional research methods. No medieval author can be plumbed more searchingly through digital philology with a broader array of tools for digitized texts and images,[14] but by the same token none can be read more attractively in printed books, while deliberately refraining from any electronic distraction except perhaps artificial lighting. No medieval author—and perhaps no author, period—is more

11 Karampetsos, *Dante and Byzantium*, xv.

12 A cardinal exposition of the once-every-two-weeks extinction rate is provided by A. Dalby, *Language in Danger* (London, 2002).

13 For a setting of the stage, see J. M. Ziolkowski, "Cultures of Authority in the Long Twelfth Century," *Journal of English and Germanic Philology* 108 (2009): 421–48. For a book on the topic that is geared to Dante in particular, see A. R. Ascoli, *Dante and the Making of a Modern Author* (Cambridge, 2008).

14 "Digital Dante," http://dante.ilt.columbia.edu (accessed 16 July 2013).

profoundly intertextual in his interaction with both predecessors and successors, but likewise none more richly deserves to be set in a historicizing context thanks to his connections with the politics, polemics, and personages of his lifetime.

The symposium in which this volume originated was cosponsored by the Dante Society of America, founded in 1881, in conjunction with its annual meeting. The event took place fittingly under the auspices of the Dumbarton Oaks Research Library and Collection, which was bequeathed to Harvard University in stages between 1940 and 1969 for the furthering of Byzantine studies. The name of Dumbarton Oaks is familiar to the musically inclined owing to compositions commissioned for performance there, not only the *Dumbarton Oaks Concerto* (Concerto for Chamber Orchestra in E Flat Major) by Igor Stravinsky (1882–1971), but also the later *Nonet for Solo Strings* by Aaron Copland (1900–1990) and *Dumbarton Quintet* by Joan Tower (1938–). To history buffs, Dumbarton Oaks calls to mind the negotiations among Allied Powers that took place on its premises as the world lay in the ruins of the Second World War in 1944: the "Dumbarton Oaks Conversations" led ultimately to the formation of the United Nations. But the overriding aim of the founders was not to further musical composition or diplomacy: it was to foster advanced research in the humanities, and the field for which it was established, to repeat, was Byzantine studies.

Flanking (and even protecting) what became the primary entrance to the main building of Dumbarton Oaks as the mansion of Robert and Mildred Bliss was expanded to render it suitable for service as a research institute are inscriptions that offer insight into the values that guided them in making their donations. The Blisses wished for this institute to be a paradise for scholars, above all for Byzantinists, and for their gardens and museum to be accessible on a regular basis to a cultured public. They intended the institution they founded to be, in their words, "a home of the humanities."[15]

My mission as director of the institution, as organizer of the symposium, and as editor of this volume has been to undergird as vigorously as possible the subjects that Dumbarton Oaks was established to promote. Anyone who steps across the threshold of the main building treads upon a mosaic from ancient Antioch that contains in the Greek alphabet the noun *apólausis*, meaning "enjoyment." The Blisses' appropriation of this inscription was a signal from them: all the erudition and culture that the research library and collection purvey are supposed to be suffused with a spirit and ambience of joy. The person who proceeds into the Byzantine courtyard gallery in the museum that lies beyond the entrance foyer finds on a lintel a longer Greek inscription, taken from Menander.

Strikingly, the gardens that surround most of the main building contain not a word of Greek (a language too little known, even in the well-cultured set of the donors,

15 *A Home of the Humanities: The Collecting and Patronage of Mildred and Robert Woods Bliss*, ed. J. N. Carder, Dumbarton Oaks Museum Publications 1 (Washington, DC, 2010).

relatives, and friends) but rather inscriptions in Latin, English, Middle English, and Italian. Significantly, the two Italian inscriptions are drawn from the *Commedia*. The Blisses were evidently fond of Dante (and of the canonicity he embodied), as were others in their circle of friends and associates. The Music Room, the hall in which the symposium lectures were delivered, was constructed in 1929 from a design by the storied American architectural firm of McKim, Mead, and White. Lawrence Grant White (1887–1956), son of the founding partner Stanford White (1853–1906), was a senior partner when the Music Room was built in 1923 and may have had a passion for Dante already at the time, seeing that he published a translation into English blank verse of the entire *Divine Comedy* a quarter-century later (in 1948). These tidbits of information, when put together, leave little doubt that the Blisses would have approved heartily of an exploration devoted to Dante and the Greeks, bringing together as it does not only Dante and Byzantium but also scholars and the public.

The symposium "Dante and the Greeks" took place in 2010. By happenstance, that year marked the thirty-fifth anniversary of the 1965 Dumbarton Oaks symposium on "The Byzantine Contribution to Western Art of the Twelfth and Thirteenth Centuries," in which such luminaries of art history as the German- and Austrian-born émigrés Kurt Weitzmann (1904–1993), Ernst Kitzinger (1912–2003), Otto Demus (1902–1990), and Hugo Buchthal (1909–1996) participated.[16] All four of these art historians—and various others could be identified as well, such as André Grabar (1896–1990)—plied their trade on both sides of the academic aisle, as Byzantinists and medievalists. Although their willingness and ability to cross the gulf between the two areas of studies owe something to superior grounding that training in classical gymnasia imparted to them in their youth, they may also reflect the circumstance that these men achieved intellectual maturity long before the growth of higher education and the entrenchment of a "publish or perish" ethos that encouraged scholars to specialize and even to overspecialize. The sense of common ground that existed among art historians for decades in the mid-twentieth century bespeaks perspectives that may have come closer to the truth than do the fault lines and even rifts that opened as scholarly specialization became ever more the norm and necessity in the years after the Second World War.

The end of the twentieth century and beginning of the twenty-first have not lacked efforts at bridging the gaps that have persisted in scholarship on the Latin West and the Greek East, but we can do far more to span the divide. In the hopes of helping others to create the necessary trestles rather than inflicting my own pontifications, I will invoke one long quotation:

16 E. Kitzinger, "The Byzantine Contribution to Western Art of the Twelfth and Thirteenth Centuries: Report on the Dumbarton Oaks Symposium of 1965," *DOP* 20 (1966): 265–66. Otto Demus wrote a book that he acknowledged was inspired by the symposium: *Byzantine Art and the West*, Wrightsman Lectures 3 (New York, 1970).

> To the historian of Western culture in the Middle Ages, the Greek East is a subject of ever increasing importance. Long considered an alien . . . civilization, Byzantium has now come to be regarded as a great reservoir of material from which the less civilized West continued to draw throughout the mediaeval period. The channels of communication between East and West, however, often ran beneath the surface, and many of the contacts were occasional or accidental, so that the process of transmission often eludes us. Again and again our only evidence is a fine piece of craftsmanship, an obviously Byzantine type in art, a sacred relic from Constantinople, or a Latin translation of Greek hagiography or science, with no indication of how these came westward. Under such conditions the story of Byzantine influence must be built up by the slow accumulation of individual detail.

The author of this passage was the erstwhile Harvard professor of medieval history, Charles Homer Haskins (1870–1937), in an essay devoted to "Contacts with Byzantium" that was published in 1929, about the time when the setting of the symposium, the Music Room of Dumbarton Oaks, took shape.[17] The Music Room has at its east end two large sixteenth-century marble arches, reportedly from Ravenna, where Dante was buried after his death in 1321.

Enough has now been said about Byzantium and Dumbarton Oaks, with a nod to medieval studies in general. Fairness demands that we devote equal time to Dante. It would be wrong to suggest that the topic of Dante and the Greeks has gone utterly unexamined. Every contributor to this volume has established a track record relating to one or another aspect of the complex relationship between Dante and the Greeks, who comprehend not merely ancient Hellenes but early Christians and Byzantines, as well. Entries on relevant topics appear in the six-volume *Enciclopedia Dantesca* (1970–78).[18] A wide-ranging book devoted to *Dante and Byzantium* was published by E. D. Karampetsos in 2009, a topic on which the most comprehensive study theretofore had been a single Italian essay.[19] Last but not least, the title *Dante and the Greeks* acknowledges an article by Glenn Most that has been disseminated in English (2006), French (2005), and Italian (2006).[20] Most set for himself the goal of answering the question: "Who are the Greeks for Dante?"[21] At the same time, despite these groundbreaking contributions, the topic has not been treated

17 *Studies in Mediaeval Culture* (Oxford, 1929), 160.

18 *Enciclopedia Dantesca,* 6 vols. (Rome, 1970–78).

19 See above, n. 5. The essay was Antonio Carile, "Dante e Bisanzio," *Studi Medievali,* ser. 3, 40, no. 2 (1999), 535–58.

20 G. W. Most, "Dante's Greeks," *Arion* 13, no. 3 (winter 2006): 15–47. This was an expanded version of an essay originally published in French under the title "Les Grecs chez Dante," in *Colloque: La Grèce antique sous le regard du Moyen âge occidental; Actes*, ed. J. Leclant and M. Zink, Cahiers de la Villa Kerylos 16 (Paris, 2005), 95–117. The Italian version is "I Greci di Dante," *Belfagor: Rassegna di varia umanità* 61, no. 2 [362] (2006): 181–201.

21 Most, "Dante's Greeks," 18.

as fully as one would expect. Dante's attitudes toward Islam and possible indebtedness to ultimately Arabic sources have been probed far more often and intensively than his attitudes and indebtedness to Greek culture.[22] Revealingly, *The Dante Encyclopedia* contains an entry on "Islam and Islamic Culture" but no corresponding one on "Byzantium and Byzantine Culture," the Greek Orthodox Church, or Constantinople.[23] The comparatively brief entry on "Greeks" is restricted to ancient Greeks.

As a gambit for opening this consideration, let us evaluate what can be gleaned from Dante's texts. To begin with the matter of language, Dante recognized the linguistic prominence of Greek.[24] In *De vulgari eloquentia* (On Eloquence in the Vernacular; 1.8.2) he recounts how people who came westward after the fall of the Tower of Babel brought with them the original "threefold idiom" (*ydioma tripharium*) that gave rise to the three main families of European spoken languages: proto-Romance in the south (itself eventually tripartite), proto-Germanic in the north, and Greek in the east of Europe and in Asia Minor. Thus, he indicates that the Greeks, by whom he means the people we now subsume as the Byzantines, are one of the three groups that together constitute the whole of the linguistic world.

Yet despite acknowledging the foundational importance of Greek, Dante himself had scant exposure to the language or its literature. Unlike humanists of a few decades later, he resembled most educated Western Europeans of his day in his inability to speak, read, or write Greek. The prolonged Byzantine presence in parts of Italy caused a few words to be nativized throughout Italian and others to become rooted in particular regions, but its effects may well have been less pronounced than those of the Arabic occupation of Sicily and southern Italy. The origins of linguistic islands formed by Greek speakers in such venues as Calabria and Terra d'Otranto have been much debated.[25] Whenever the archipelago of such enclaves formed, it has had little or no impact on the evolution of Italian.

Yes, a few common words can be pinpointed in modern Italian that seeped into the vernacular in the Middle Ages either directly from Byzantine Greek or indirectly via the local reflex of medieval Latin. The premiere case in point would be *gondola*, first attested in 1094, perhaps by way of a hypothetical regional Latin form **condua*, from the Byzantine Greek neuter plural *kondya* and its diminutive *kondylion*, "vessel."[26] Yet such lexical items are rare by any measure. Many more Grecisms in Italian are due to the

22 J. Ziolkowski, issue editor, *Dante Studies* 125 (2007), revised as *Dante and Islam* (New York, forthcoming).

23 *The Dante Encyclopedia*, ed. R. Lansing, Garland Reference Library of the Humanities 1836 (New York, 2000).

24 M. Tavoni, "'Ydioma Tripharium' (Dante, De Vulgari Eloquentia, I 8–9)," in *History and Historiography of Linguistics, Papers from the Fourth International Conference on the History of the Language Sciences (ICHoLS IV), Trier, 24–28 August 1987*, ed. H.-J. Niederehe and K. Koerner, 2 vols. (Amsterdam, 1990), 1:233–47.

25 B. Migliorini, *The Italian Language*, ed. T. Gwynfor Griffith (London, 1984), 40.

26 C. Battisti and G. Alessio, *Dizionario etimologico italiano*, 5 vols. (Florence, 1950–57), 3:1843.

robust presence of Greek in both classical and medieval Latin than to the ramifications of any Byzantine occupation or Greek exilic communities from any period.[27]

From Latin sources, Dante gleaned etymologies for some Greek words, but he manifested no grasp of the distinctive workings of the language. The furthest he could go was to neologize by extrapolating from a rudimentary grasp of Greek etyma, as in coining the noun *teodìa,* "song directed to God" (*Par.* 25.73), by analogy with such words as *com(m)edìa,* "comedy"; *melodìa,* "melody"; and *tragedìa,* "tragedy."[28] One of his main wellsprings was Huguccio of Pisa's *Derivationes* (*Derivations,* 1197–1201), which contains clues that its author had contact with contemporary Greek speakers.[29] Dante credited Huguccio as his source in *Convivio* 4.6.5 when considering the origins of the word *auctor* and may have relied on him for information about various other words and allusions.[30] Dante's limited exposure to Greek is examined in this collection by Réka Forrai in her scrutiny of the place Greek learning held in Italian culture during his life.[31]

To turn from language to culture, Dante demonstrates a degree of acquaintance with ancient and medieval Greece typical of an educated medieval Westerner of his era. Since Dante epitomizes the medieval Western—medieval Latin—ambience, it is not surprising to find that he crystallizes much of the complementarity and friction between it and Greek culture in his writings. The positive side of his vantage point can be gauged from his approving nods to Greek myth, literature, and history, as well as to Greek attainments in the arts and sciences, and, above all, to the archetypically Greek innovation of philosophy.[32]

Put simply, Dante's familiarity with the highlights of ancient Greek culture means that he can drop names, as is evident from a roster that contains Aristotle, Socrates, Plato, Democritus, Diogenes, Anaxagoras, Thales, Empedocles, Heraclitus, Zeno, Dioscorides, Orpheus, Linus, Euclid, Ptolemy, Hippocrates, and Galen.[33] At *Inferno* 23.4–6, Dante mentions one of Aesop's fables. In *Purgatory* 22, he touches upon three tragedians—Euripides, Antiphon, and Agathon—and the lyric poet Simonides. But the names do not imply intimacy with the works of these figures. After all, many major

27 Migliorini, *Italian Language,* 55.

28 P. Manni, *Il Trecento toscano: La lingua di Dante, Petrarca e Boccaccio* (Bologna, 2003), 155–56. Manni points out that *antomata* in *Purgatorio* 10.128, once thought to have been a calque of the same sort, is, in fact, a borrowing via Latin translations of Aristotle. An alternative explanation of *teodìa* would relate it to *psalmodìa*: E. Moore, *Studies in Dante, First Series: Scripture and Classical Authors in Dante* (Oxford, 1896), 66.

29 H. D. Austin, "Notes on the Greek in Dante's Latin Dictionary," *Studies in Philology* 44 (1947): 477–82, at 480–81.

30 P. Toynbee, "Dante's Obligations to the *Magnae Derivationes* of Uguccione da Pisa," *Romania* 26 (1897): 537–54.

31 The fullest consideration of Dante's knowledge of Greek is G. M. Gianola, "Il greco di Dante," in *Memorie (Istituto veneto di scienze, lettere ed arti. Classe di scienze morali, lettere ed arti)* 37, no. 3 (1980).

32 Most, "Dante's Greeks," 21.

33 T. Hudson-Williams, "Dante and the Classics," *Greece and Rome* 20, no. 58 (1951): 38–42.

authors, even philosophers, are omitted: Pindar, Aeschylus, Sophocles, Aristophanes, Demosthenes, and Pythagoras. Furthermore, Dante's exposure, both direct and indirect, came solely through Latin sources. Partly for this reason, he privileges Aristotle far over Plato: the only Platonic dialogue familiar to Dante is the *Timaeus*, as translated into Latin by the fourth-century Calcidius (or Chalcidius).[34]

Views diverge on the specific aspects of Aristotle that mattered most to Dante. In her essay for this volume, Réka Forrai argues that the Aristotle who holds sway over Dante is not so much the metaphysician or logician as the practical philosopher. As Teodolinda Barolini elucidates in her contribution to this volume, the Aristotelianism that pervades the Italian poet's oeuvre is evident even in his canzone on true nobility, *Le dolci rime*. Marcia Colish, in her essay, admits the sway that Aristotle exercised upon Dante's thinking about actions taken against conscience, but points out that, in the main, it does not stem from the specific Aristotelian passages that have been customarily flagged as sources and that, in addition, the Italian poet may have been conditioned by various classical and medieval Latin authors. Filippo Naitana takes a similar tack, by arguing that in the *Convivio* Aristotelianism is above all a science of happiness, which Dante understands as mediated through Cicero's *De finibus bonorum et malorum* (On the Ends of Good and Evil). Michele Trizio gives a special spin to the issue of Dante's Aristotelianism by demonstrating that Western debates on Aristotle's *Nicomachean Ethics*, specifically those that influenced Dante, were rooted in Byzantine commentaries.

As a principle, we may state that Dante knew nothing of ancient Greek culture except as transmitted through either the works of canonical Latin authors or the prodigious gloss and commentary tradition upon them.[35] Thus, in *Inferno* 4.94–96 (compare *Purg.* 22.101–2), he is welcomed first by Homer, who is distinguished by his sword to betoken his associations with the martial genre of epic. The Greek bard is accorded preeminence, walking before the major Latin poets—Virgil, Horace, Ovid, and Lucan—who are introduced with him in limbo. Yet Dante's knowledge of Homer comes only secondhand, and he recognizes this shortcoming. His assertion in *Convivio* 1.7.93–100 that no Latin translation of Homer exists may signal his awareness that *Homerus Latinus* (Latin Homer), also known as the *Ilias Latina* (Latin Iliad), does not correspond exactly to the Greek *Iliad*. In *Vita Nuova* 2.8, Dante quotes a bit of Homer's *Iliad* (24.258–59) but via a Latin translation of Aristotle's *Nicomachean Ethics* (7.1.1145a). Likewise, in *Vita Nuova* 25.9, he gives the opening of the *Odyssey* but as borrowed from Horace's *Ars poetica* 141–42. Beyond such testimony (and other scraps can be found) for Dante's indirect exposure to Homer, there is no evidence that he had read other Greek

34 For quick orientation in the major phases of philosophical exchange between the Latin West and the Greek East during late antiquity and the Middle Ages, see S. Ebbesen, "Greek-Latin Philosophical Interaction," in *Byzantine Philosophy and Its Ancient Sources*, ed. K. Ierodiakonou (Oxford, 2002), 15–30.

35 Most, "Dante's Greeks," 24.

belles-lettres even in translation.[36] In *Vita Nuova* 25, Dante seems to lend credence to the notion that Greek love lyric existed in antiquity, but he names no lyricists to substantiate this view.

In limbo, Dante parades many personages before us. Of the non-Christians, the Greeks are usually first, followed by ancient Romans, and finally Muslims. He imbues his underworld in Greek myth and especially Greek mythic geography, but mostly by way of Virgil. Thus, in his underworld we meet Hades, Minos, Phlegyas, Charon, Cerberus, Pluto, and the infernal rivers of Acheron (*Inf.* 3), Styx (*Inf.* 7), Phlegethon (*Inf.* 12), and Cocytus (*Inf.* 32–34), as well as Lethe (*Purg.* 28–33), in the earthly paradise atop Mount Purgatory, where it is twinned with a river whose name, Eunoë, he coined from the Greek elements *eu,* "good," and *noe,* "mind."[37] George Dameron, in his essay for this volume, focuses upon the treatment of the hybrid Geryon in *Inferno* 16. Elsewhere, in cantos 20 and 30 of the *Inferno,* Dante draws an example from Greek myth more than once, but at least partly to signify that it impresses him less than something more closely contemporary with him. From the Trojan War he singles out Helen, Dido, Sinon, Tiresias, Achilles, and Diomedes.

Central to the puzzle of Dante's stance toward the ancient Greeks is the Ulysses episode in canto 26 of the *Inferno,* which has spawned a bibliography more limitless than the briny seas the Ithacan adventurer allegedly sailed.[38] In this collection, our helmsman through the turbulent interpretative waters is Piero Boitani. In this canto of the *Divine Comedy,* Virgil asks Ulysses how he died, to which the wanderer replies by explaining that before capsizing and drowning, he and his crew navigated from the Mediterranean beyond the pillars of Heracles—the promontories that flank the Strait of Gibraltar—into the Atlantic Ocean and the Southern Hemisphere.[39] For reasons that have been disputed, Virgil does not allow Dante to converse directly with the Homeric hero, so the poet must rely on Virgil as mediator.[40] Whatever the explanation for Virgil's intervention, it signals Dante's Roman, and hence Trojan, perspective that his Odysseus goes by the Latinized and Romanized name of Ulysses. In this same canto, Dante qualifies the Trojan race as being "the noble seed" of the Roman people chosen by God to rule the world (*Inf.* 26.60).

36 The most efficient approach to the bits and pieces of Homer is through G. Martellotti, *Enciclopedia Dantesca* 4:145–48, s.v. "Omero."

37 Charles Singleton pointed out that Dante followed the analogy of Protonoè, presumably by way of Huguccio's *Derivationes,* glossed in *Convivio* 2.3.11 as "the first mind": see Dante, *The Divine Comedy,* trans. C. S. Singleton, Bollingen Series 80 (Princeton, NJ, 1970–75).

38 J. C. Hirsch, "Dante among the Greeks: *Paradiso* XXVII, 82–84," *Neophilologus* 56 (1972): 162–63.

39 Most, "Dante's Greeks," 34.

40 The scholarship is vast. For a clear presentation of the episode, see D. Donno, "Dante's Ulysses and Virgil's Prohibition: *Inferno* XXVI, 70–75," *Italica* 50 (1973): 26–37.

All the Greek sages and heroes imported by Dante into the *Commedia* belong within a single stage in world history or, rather, in salvation history. The medieval Western commonplaces of *translatio studii* (transfer of knowledge) and *translatio imperii* (transfer of power) held that both learning and empire passed from ancient Greece to ancient Rome and again from ancient Rome to medieval Europe, in particular France (and still more specifically Paris).[41] By this way of thinking, the Greeks of old were vanquished by the Romans so that Rome could become Christian and thus prevail as the seat of Christianity. When the Romans embraced Christianity, those Roman Christians inherited, in accordance with providence, the birthrights of learning and rulership that had formerly belonged to the Greeks and Romans of antiquity.

Determining who the true Roman Christians or Christian Romans were was an unending bone of contention and anxiety. Were they Holy Romans, Roman Catholics, both, or neither? Perhaps the greatest jolt is to discover that the overarching issue was whether they were Westerners within the purview of the Latin Church or Easterners within the Greek one. To a degree that may be at first astonishing and even paradoxical, it is impossible to consider the nexus of Dante and the Greeks without taking into account Dante's outlook on Rome and Romanness.[42] To him, Rome was not so much the commune as the seat and symbol of universality in both empire and Church. The Rome that bestowed peace upon the world was even the model for the eternal peace of heaven, which is why Beatrice could assure Dante that they would be citizens of the City of God, the new Jerusalem. This heavenly Rome has as its foremost citizen—as its emperor—Christ himself: "quella Roma onde Cristo è romano" (that Rome in which Christ is a Roman; *Purg.* 32.102). Thus, Rome was less a specific location than a more pervasive idea. But in fundamental ways it was also not merely one place—and the concepts of Romanness, Roman Empire, and Roman Church were disputed between Rome in Italy and an ancient, or at least late antique, rival. Not without very good cause, the Eastern Romans, who have been called the Byzantines since the sixteenth century, regarded themselves as heirs to ancient Greek culture, Roman government, and the faith of the Christianized Roman Empire.[43]

The original city of Rome, itself legendarily a New Troy that gave a new home to the human remnants transplanted from a city destroyed in the East, was and is in Latium, in Italy. Across the Mediterranean—or, more specifically, across the Adriatic, Ionian, and

41 The locus classicus that presents the two concepts in tandem is Chrétien de Troyes, *Cligés*, lines 25–42, ed. A. Micha (Paris, 1957). For background and context on each in the pairing, see W. Goez, *Translatio imperii: Ein Beitrag zur Geschichte des Geschichtsdenkens und der politischen Theorien im Mittelalter und in der frühen Neuzeit* (Tübingen, 1958), and M. A. Freeman, *The Poetics of* translatio studii *and Conjointure: Chrétien de Troyes's* Cligés, French Forum Monographs 12 (Lexington, KY, 1979).

42 C. T. Davis, *Dante and the Idea of Rome* (Oxford, 1957).

43 Geanakoplos, *Interaction of the "Sibling" Byzantine and Western Cultures*, 113.

Aegean Seas—stood the New Rome of Constantinople in Asia Minor, the seat of the Eastern Roman Empire, what Dante labeled the "imperial city" (*civitade imperatrice; Conv.* 4.4.13). But though Constantinople explicitly recreated and incorporated elements of the city after which it was modeled, Dante had no truck with identifying the people we call the Byzantines with the idealized Romans he wished to have in power as peace-givers.[44]

From Dante's perspective, how distinct from the *ur*-Rome was Constantinople? We are afforded a glimpse into his thinking when Justinian (482–565; r. 527–565) comes on the scene in *Paradiso* 6, a canto extraordinary and even unique in being delivered by a single speaker, who happens (not that Dante would have known) to have been the last Latin-speaking emperor of Constantinople, and the Byzantine emperor in whose reign the famous churches in Ravenna and Classe, which Dante must have experienced in all their glittering splendor, since he spent his last years living there, were completed.[45] In fact, during his residence in Ravenna, Dante could not have failed to see Justinian as represented in the mosaics nearby. Dante was deeply conversant with Justinian's legal corpus. In the preamble to the *Corpus iuris civilis,* the emperor had written that the text had been perfected by the grace of God.[46] In the *Commedia,* Justinian, in telling of the Roman Empire and its providential history, emphasizes that when Constantine (272–337; r. 306–337), the first Christian emperor of Rome, transplanted the seat of the empire eastward from Rome and founded the new capital that took his name, he moved against the nature of the sun and the providential westward course of empire and culture, in the opposite direction—the wrong direction—from the trajectory Aeneas traversed while en route to Latium.[47]

Far beyond the borders of either city stretched the status of citizenship and the style of life that constituted *Romanitas,* "Romanness." Romanness became something tied not to the city Rome but rather more broadly to the political power of the Roman Empire and the culture of Roman civilization. This expansion helps to account for the Romanness of peoples spread throughout the Western Roman Empire who became Romanized to the point of speaking Latin, and who later became speakers of the Romance languages, the designation for which pays tribute to the Roman citizenship (and language and culture) to which those speakers laid claim.

44 W. Caferro, "Dante and the Problem of Byzantium," in *The Unbounded Community: Papers in Christian Ecumenism in Honor of Jaroslav Pelikan*, ed. W. Caferro and D. G. Fisher (New York, 1996), 93–111.

45 G. Arnaldi, "Il canto di Giustiniano," in *Liber largitorius: Etudes d'histoire médiévale offertes à Pierre Toubert par ses élèves*, ed. D. Barthelemy and J.-M. Martin, Hautes études médiévales et modernes 84 (Geneva, 2003), 3–14, and P. Sabbatino, "La felicità di raccontare: Lettura del canto VI del Paradiso," in *Miscellanea di Studi Danteschi in memoria di Silvio Pasquazi*, ed. A. Paolella, V. Placella, and G. Turco, 2 vols. (Naples, 1993), 2:769–800.

46 L. M. Valterza, "Infernal Retainers: Dante and the Juridical Tradition" (Ph.D. diss., Rutgers, State University of New Jersey, New Brunswick, 2010), 11.

47 Sabbatino, "La felicità di raccontare," 772.

The Romance languages famously comprehend such far-flung and isolated members as Romansh, in southeastern Switzerland, and Romanian, spoken in the region bordering the Black Sea. Romansh and Romanian, as well as the very term Romance, all originated ultimately in aspirations to Romanness. In one of the major Latin-derived Romance languages, Old French, were written the medieval narratives that became known as romances (because of the language in which they were composed). The ethos of such narratives included attitudes toward women and love that are associated with what we call romance, romantic, and romanticism when referring to relationships connected with love. The architecture of the early Middle Ages, with features that emerged from the state architecture associated with ancient Roman imperial constructions, came to be known as Romanesque. Those who revived and adapted the earlier attitudes of medieval romance in the nineteenth century belonged to the movement we call romanticism. All these phenomena go back ultimately to Romanness or in claims to it, even if their derivation remains unknown to many.

The Western pretension to a monopoly on Romanness hardly went undisputed, as the Eastern Romans likewise called themselves Roman. In his contribution to this collection, William Caferro, through analysis of Italian chronicles contemporary with the illustrious Italian poet, sets forth problems in the implications that Dante's idea of Rome held true for the New Rome of Byzantium. Dante's outlook could not have differed more radically than it did from that of Eastern Romans. Because Romanness and Latinness were separate matters, the Byzantines went so far as to label their language, Greek, as "Roman" and to call themselves *Rhomaioi*, meaning "Romans" in the sense of "citizens of the Roman Empire" or "upholders of Roman civilization" (against barbarism). As a result, both the Byzantine Empire and Greek Christianity were known to neighboring cultures, such as the Arabs, as Rome (*Rūm*) and their people as Romans. Thus, a companion of the prophet Muhammad was called Suhayb ar-Rūmī (born ca. 587), after his origins as a slave in the Byzantine Empire and his fair-haired appearance. Coins that resembled the denarii produced by the Eastern Roman Empire were termed *rūmī*, "Roman."

The designation *Rūmī*, transferred gradually from the people to the heartland of the territory they once occupied, continued to be applied even to non-Byzantine (non-Greek-speaking and non-Christian) inhabitants of Anatolia, as the region had belonged so long to the Byzantine Empire. For example, the thirteenth-century Persian Muslim poet and mystic Jalāl ad-Dīn Muhammad Rūmī is often called in English Rumi (commonly written without any diacritical marks). Furthermore, the Christian inhabitants of al-Andalus were sometimes designated as *Rūmī*. But in general, Arabic speakers (and speakers of other languages in countries such as Ethiopia) labeled Western Europeans in the first instance with an Arabic word *Faranji*, "Frankish," which constitutes a further piece of evidence that the West was not irrefutably Roman. The Byzantines labeled the Western Romans *Italikoi*, "Italians." The lesson to be drawn? To civilizations neighboring the Byzantine Empire, for most of the Middle Ages only the Greeks—the Rhomaioi—were Romans (*Rūmī*), though as the Byzantine Empire contracted, those who occupied the parts of Asia Minor that had been Byzantine were often called "Roman," too.[48]

In the fifth century, the Western half of the Roman Empire disintegrated into a patchwork of Germanic kingdoms. In contrast, the Eastern half remained alive—despite being diminished greatly by Islam and perhaps even more by the Western European assault of the Fourth Crusade—until 1453, when it succumbed to the Ottoman Turks under Sultan Mehmed II the Conqueror (1432–1481).

When in the fifth century the Roman Empire collapsed, the bishop of Rome was subject at least theoretically to the authority of the Christian emperor in the New Rome of Constantinople. Later emperors in the West endeavored to affirm their authority over the bishops of Rome—the popes—even to the point of deposing them. But in the second half of the eleventh century, shortly after what turned out to be the enduring schism between Rome and the Eastern Church, Pope Gregory VII (r. 1073–1085) decreed that the pope had sole right to imperial authority (in the form of insignia) and that papal supremacy extended even to the power to depose emperors.[49] In Dante's time, Boniface VIII (r. 1294–1303) reaffirmed the supremacy of the pope as spiritual power over the emperor as temporal power, and even enlarged the pope's authority by asserting papal privilege to shift at will the control of the empire from the Romans to the Franks or elsewhere. Thus, one part of the picture in the balance between Rome and Constantinople related to what could be called Church-State relations, and it was an issue of surpassing urgency to Dante, who in the third book of the *De monarchia* (On Monarchy) refuted the pope's claim over *translatio imperii*.

Another element in the equilibrium between Rome and Constantinople pertained to primacy among the chief bishoprics of the Church. Pope Leo I (r. 440–461) laid claim to dominion over all Christians. Rome had been one of four episcopal sees, with the others being Jerusalem, Antioch, and Alexandria. The bishop of Constantinople was elevated to similar status in 381, and afterward the other three cities fell under Muslim domination. The Roman Church, which became the Roman Catholic Church, placed increasing emphasis on its preeminence—on the primacy of the bishop of Rome.

Should we accept as a sign of ignorance or disinterest the absence in Dante's entire oeuvre of overt references to "Byzantium" and the "Byzantines"?[50] Hardly, since no one in the Eastern Roman Empire referred to Constantinople as Byzantium or called their empire

48 Many of the Crusaders were indeed Franks or French, but the overarching category to which they belonged was Latin. *Omnis Latinitas* was a phrase that enfolded all Latin Christendom, both Western Europe and Crusader states: see R. J. Hexter, "Medieval Latin: Horizons and Perspectives," in "*Latinitas*: The Tradition and Teaching of Latin," *Helios* 14 (1987): 69–92.

49 For full information, see H. E. J. Cowdrey, *Pope Gregory VII, 1073–1085* (Oxford, 1998).

50 Most, "Dante's Greeks," 25.

Byzantine. The toponym Byzantium was an archaism, pressed into use by Westerners in papal propaganda in the late eighth century so as to deprive the city known officially as Constantinopolis Nova Roma of both its onomastic association with a Roman emperor (and the first Christian Roman Emperor, at that) and, more importantly, of its official Romanness.[51] The adjectival derivative "Byzantine" is an exonym, not a self-designation that the Romans of the East ever used. Furthermore, it is an anachronism that came into use only after the people and their empire had ceased to exist.

To those who ruled and inhabited the Eastern Roman Empire in the Middle Ages, the realm was Roman, plain and simple. To Westerners it was Greek. But in the mid-sixteenth century it was felt necessary to devise a term that could disambiguate the post-antique afterlife of the Eastern Roman Empire from both ancient Greece and ancient Rome. Thus was spawned the adjective Byzantine.

The neologism, at least in this sense, was first employed in reference to the Eastern Empire in 1557. Hieronymus Wolf (1516–1580), a German humanist who founded the discipline of Byzantine studies, used the word when he published the *History* of Niketas Choniates (ca. 1140–1213).[52] Since the adjective was first used by Wolf, Byzantine has carried a heavy freight of political and ideological associations.[53] With it, Westerners have had a ready means of refuting the assertions of those who inhabited the Eastern Roman Empire that they were the more authentic Romans: the Romans of the West have stripped the Easterners of their Romanness by deploying in place of any word related to Rome the term Byzantine to denote them and their civilization during the period from the Arabic conquests of the seventh century until the fall of Constantinople in 1453.[54] Byzantine is thus a final and definitive attempt to sort out the whole tangle about Romanness to the disadvantage of the Eastern Romans, by de-Romanizing them once and for all. From an Eastern Roman vantage point, it is the insult that stripped them of their identity after they had endured the mortal injury of losing their city, their land, and their empire. And it must have stung that when the end came, it arrived partly thanks to the systemic damages inflicted by the Fourth Crusade, partly owing to the unwillingness of the Westerners to come to their aid when they were in the final throes of their collapse. Coincidentally, but still tellingly, the terminological expropriation of their Romanness from the Eastern Romans occurred at the same time as the Church of Rome became the Roman Catholic Church: the seesaw of religion and power landed

51 On *Constantinopolis Nova Roma*, see A. Carile, "Costantinopoli Nuova Roma," in *La città e il sacro*, ed. F. Cardini (Milan, 1994), 203–42.

52 Hieronymus Wolf's autobiography, composed in Latin and first printed in 1773, can be found in *Der Vater der deutschen Byzantinistik: Das Leben des Hieronymus Wolf von ihm selbst erzählt*, trans. H.-G. Beck, Miscellanea Byzantina Monacensia 29 (Munich, 1984).

53 The scholarship on the political and ideological freight of the term Byzantium has become vast. For full information, see *Byzantium: Identity, Image, Influence, Index of Colloquia as of July 15, 1996; Abstracts of Communications; Index of Authors: XIX International Congress of Byzantine Studies, University of Copenhagen, 18–24 August 1996*, ed. K. Fledelius (Copenhagen, 1996).

54 *OED*, s.v. "Byzantine."

heavily on the western side of the Mediterranean for the first time since before Emperor Constantine I the Great.

The Western outlook upon the Eastern Roman Empire during the Byzantine period was often unfavorable even during the Middle Ages. For instance, Dante questioned the legitimacy of the Eastern Roman Empire, since in his view (*Mon.* 3.11; *Par.* 6.94–96), the authority underlying it had been transferred to the West in the time of Charlemagne, who saved the Western continuation of the Roman Empire from the Lombard invasion. Dante was approximately correct in his understanding, although in *De monarchia* 3.10.18 he put the crowning of Charlemagne by Pope Hadrian I—actually by Pope Leo III—during the reign of Emperor Michael in the East. (In this same passage, he makes his only explicit reference to Constantinople. His only implicit reference to the city is in *Paradiso* 6.5, where he accentuates the geographical marginality of its location vis-à-vis Europe: "ne lo stremo d'Europa.") At the same time—when the Eastern Roman Empire fell in northern Italy—the Western Church embarked upon the twin processes of redesignating Constantinople as Byzantium and thereby depriving it of its onomastic attachment to the first Christian emperor.

Just when Westerners dissociated Constantinople from Constantine, they linked the city of Rome powerfully to the same emperor—the Christianizer of the Roman Empire. The same crucial stretch of time, the second half of the eighth century, saw the the papal chancery's production of the forgery known as the *Constitutum Constantini* (Donation of Constantine), a supposed Roman imperial decree by which Constantine had in 314 allegedly transferred to the pope authority over Rome and the Western part of the Roman Empire, including, of course, the cities of Italy.[55] Dante, who referred to the Donation five times, accepted it (although with regret) as genuine, as did Western Christians until the fifteenth century, when the humanist Lorenzo Valla (ca. 1400–1457) proved it to be inauthentic.[56]

Attitudes toward the "Byzantine" have remained negative in the modern period, perhaps sharpened by the legacy of the historian Edward Gibbon (1737–1794), whose views on Byzantine culture as expressed in the supremely influential six-volume *The History of the Decline and Fall of the Roman Empire* (1776–88) have continued to hold sway.[57] However bad the connotation of the adjective *medieval* in modern English, *Byzantine*,

55 For broad context surrounding the Donation, see A. Linder, *The Myth of Constantine the Great in the West: Sources and Hagiographic Commemoration,* Estratti dagli "Studi medievali" 7 (Spoleto, 1987).

56 See G. Puletti, "La 'Donazione di Costantino' nei primi del '300 e la 'Monarchia' di Dante," *Medioevo e Rinascimento* 7, n.s. 4 (1993): 113–35.

57 The groundbreaking exploration of Gibbon's expertise in and effects upon the Church history of Byzantium was D. J. Geanakoplos, "Edward Gibbon and Byzantine Ecclesiastical History," *ChHist* 35 (1966): 170–85. More recently, Geanakoplos's foray has been ramified in multiple essays in *Edward Gibbon and Empire,* ed. R. McKitterick and R. Quinault (New York, 1997): J. Matthews, "Gibbon and the Later Roman Empire: Causes and Circumstances," 12–33; Av. Cameron, "Gibbon and Justinian," 34–52; J. Howard-Johnston, "Gibbon and the Middle Period of the Byzantine Empire," 53–77; J. Shepard, "Byzantine Soldiers, Missionaries and Diplomacy under Gibbon's Eyes," 78–100; and A. Bryer, "Gibbon and the Later Byzantine Empires," 101–16.

meaning "Reminiscent of the manner, style, or spirit of Byzantine politics; intricate, complicated; inflexible, rigid, unyielding," arguably suffers from a worse odor.[58]

Alongside the contempt that medieval Westerners harbored for the Eastern Romans lurked respect, and alongside the envy, awe. For much of the Middle Ages, the material culture of Constantinople was held in high regard. Ivories, metalwork, enamels, relics and reliquaries, manuscripts, silks, gems, and coins from the great city were and are valued, and imports seem to have arrived in the West at an even faster rate in the thirteenth century than they had previously.[59] The intimate trade relations between the New Rome and Italy meant that Constantinople hosted communities of Italian merchants, in addition to ecclesiastic legations, brides and their attendants, and travelers and residents of other sorts. From encounters with these visitors, the Eastern Greeks formed impressions of Western Europeans, and through such sojourns, in turn, stereotypes of the Byzantines were transported back to Italy and other Western lands. In her chapter for this volume, Elizabeth Fisher conjures up fascinating pictures for such intersections.

The gold coins minted in Constantinople were particularly esteemed and were commonly called *bezants*, after Byzantion, the original Greek name of the city. The words *Byzantius, Byzantinus,* and *Byzanticus,* and a multitude of orthographic variants, surface in Latin texts from the second half of the eleventh century.[60] The French *besant* is attested in the twelfth century, and the Italian *bisante* in the thirteenth.[61] But it speaks to the strengthened economy of Italian municipalities that in 1260 the city of Florence began minting gold coins that became known as florins, which eventually displaced the bezants. Dante nowhere uses outright the name of either the Greek or the Florentine coins, but he does make two indirect references to the florin. In *Paradiso* 9.130 the phrase *il maledetto fiore* ("the cursed flower") plays on the lily that appeared on one side of the florins, while in *Inferno* 30.74 he alludes to the image of Saint John the Baptist stamped on the other side of the coins.[62]

While composing important stretches of the *Commedia,* Dante would have been surrounded by the splendors of early Byzantine achievements in art and architecture: in Ravenna at the latest from 1318 to 1320, when working on the *Paradiso*, he was under the patronage of Guido Novello da Polenta (d. 1333; *podestà* or mayor of the city, 1316–1322). Yet although Dante's poetry incorporates recollections of Ravenna (*Inf.* 5.97 and 27.40;

58 On the connotations, see F. C. Robinson, "Medieval, the Middle Ages," *Speculum* 59 (1984): 745–56. For the specific definition cited, see *OED,* s.v. "Byzantine A.2."

59 See W. D. Wixom, "Byzantine Art and the Latin West," in *The Glory of Byzantium: Art and Culture of the Middle Byzantine Era AD 843–1261*, ed. H. C. Evans and W. D. Wixom (New York, 1997), 435–507.

60 *Mittellateinisches Wörterbuch bis zum ausgehenden 13. Jahrhundert* (Munich, 1959–), 1:1637–38.

61 Battisti and Alessio, *Dizionario etimologico italiano* (above, n. 26), 1:529.

62 For an image of both sides of a florin, see P. Grierson, *The Coins of Medieval Europe* (London, 1991), 110, fig. 250.

Par. 6.61), he makes no explicit reference to the Byzantine edifices and artworks of the municipality, not even the famed mosaics in the sixth-century basilica of Sant'Apollinare Nuovo or to the Byzantine Christian artists who fabricated them. Nonetheless, scholars have assumed that the glittering splendor of the mosaics affected his portrayal of heaven in *Paradiso* 20, even if he did not indicate Ravenna overtly as a source of inspiration, and that the iconography of the *Commedia* corresponds somehow to the city's mosaics.[63]

Similarly, Dante would have had occasion to gaze upon many Italian paintings and other works of art deeply informed by Byzantine style. Italy has been called "an artistic province of Byzantium."[64] Although such a conception of Italian art requires nuances that are being achieved only gradually, it would be misguided to deny that centuries of interaction failed to leave a mark.[65] But what imprint would such exposure have made? Dante's contemporary, the artist Giotto di Bondone (ca. 1267–1337), was praised subsequently in the *Lives of the Most Excellent Painters, Sculptors, and Architects* by Giorgio Vasari (1511–1574) for having rejected the *maniera greca* ("Greek manner") in art and thus having enabled Italian art to progress beyond the Byzantine style. For Vasari, the "Greek manner" was as much of a pejorative as foreign designations have often been in assigning names to diseases or disapproved practices. Vasari delimited Byzantine art as what preceded rather than accompanied the medieval and Renaissance art that were closely contemporary with Dante. This legacy of attraction to the art of Byzantium in tandem with distaste for much else that has been regarded as typical of broader Byzantine culture has held true even in recent times.

At many points in history, the notion of Greekness has had complex linguistic, cultural, and geographic dimensions. In the Middle Ages, Greek constituted not only past languages and cultures, but also a present (and often rival) religious and political entity. To each of these layers the inhabitants of the Latin West related somewhat differently. Doctrine, politics, linguistics, culture, and education all played important roles in shaping attitudes, as did travel and diplomacy. As a consequence of the Fourth Crusade, Latin rulers occupied Constantinople from 1204 to 1261, and lingered until 1291 in the Crusader state of Jerusalem. They held much of Greece, especially the Peloponnesus

63 E. Vance, "Images and the Mediation of Power: Dante's *Paradiso* and the Byzantine Art of S. Apollinare Nuovo," in *The Growth of Authority in the Medieval West: Selected Proceedings of the International Conference, Groningen 6–9 November 1997*, ed. M. Gosman, A. Vanderjagt, and J. Veenstra, Mediaevalia Groningana 25 (Groningen, 1999), 332–53; L. Pasquini Vecchi, "Riflessi dell'arte ravennate nella *Commedia* dantesca," in *Corso di cultura sull'arte ravennate e bizantina: Seminario internazionale sul tema; Ricerche di archeologia cristiana e bizantina; Ravenna, 14–19 maggio 1995, in memoria del prof. Giuseppe Bovini* 42 (Ravenna, 1995), 699–719, at 719; and L. Pasquini, *Iconografie dantesche: Dalla luce del mosaico all'immagine profetica* (Ravenna, 2008).

64 Geanakoplos, *Interaction of the "Sibling" Byzantine and Western Cultures* (above, n. 6), 84.

65 L. Safran, "'Byzantine' Art In Post-Byzantine South Italy?: Notes on A Fuzzy Concept," *Common Knowledge* 18 (2012): 487–504.

(known to them as Morea) and Greek islands such as Rhodes and Cyprus.[66] Yet these Crusader occupations go utterly unremarked by Dante in his writings, as do the negotiations and strategies of Emperor Michael VIII Palaiologos (r. 1258–1282) and his immediate successors in their relations with the Latin West.[67]

Also omitted are details about the Greek Church. The Eastern and Western churches had doctrinal polemics with each other. These emerged over such matters as the primacy of the bishop of Rome—the papacy; the dating of holidays, notably Easter; and the use of leavened or unleavened bread for the Host. Also relating to the Eucharist is the *epiclesis*, an invocation of the Holy Spirit at the moment of Transubstantiation that was once made in all Christian liturgies but has been maintained only in Eastern Churches. Additional friction arose from differing views on clerical celibacy and beards, as well as on whether menstruating women could be allowed Communion and when infants could be baptized.[68]

The Eastern and Western Churches diverged as well in their attitudes toward images, with the intense contest between iconoclasts (those who supported the destruction of icons) and iconodules (those who revered such images). The first iconoclastic period in the East (730–787) concluded with the Second Council of Nicaea (787). The findings of that council in regard to images prompted Charlemagne, in turn, to commission (ca. 790) the drafting of the treatise *Opus Caroli regis contra synodum* (The Work of King Charles against the Synod), known also as *Libri Carolini* (The Books of Charles), to refute what Westerners understood of the Second Council.

Among other controversies between the Churches, an important one took place in the second half of the ninth century over the so-called double procession of the Holy Spirit. This contention arose because in the West the key word *filioque* ("and the Son") was added to the Nicene Creed to explain that the Holy Spirit proceeds from the Father "and the Son." Another doctrinal altercation came about later, when the doctrine of purgatory took hold in the West but was not accepted in the East.[69]

The final straw for the East came in the claim to universal jurisdiction of the papacy—the bishop of Rome—over all other seats of Christianity, including the Church of the Rhomaians. This claim was made by Pope Leo IX (r. 1049–1054) and presented on his behalf by the papal legate to Constantinople, Cardinal Humbert of Silva Candida (d. 1061), to the ecumenical patriarch of the city, Michael I Cerularius (Keroularios, r. 1043–1059). The rejection of this claim resulted in the East-West schism of 1054, the consequences of which remain today.

Dante lived between the time of the church councils of Lyons in 1274 (which he neglected to remark upon in any of his extant writings) and Florence in 1439 (only little

66 D. Jacobi, "The Latin Empire of Constantinople and the Frankish States in Greece," in *The New Cambridge Medieval History*, vol. 5, *c. 1198–c. 1300*, ed. D. Abulafia (Cambridge, 2008), 525–42.

67 D. J. Geanakoplos, *Emperor Michael Palaeologus and the West, 1258–1282: A Study in Byzantine-Latin Relations* (Cambridge, MA, 1959).

68 On all these issues contributing to the schism, see A. Louth, *Greek East and Latin West: The Church, AD 681–1071*, Church in History 3 (Crestwood, NY, 2007), 305–18.

69 Karampetsos, *Dante and Byzantium* (above, n. 5), 23–24.

more than a decade before the final defeat and collapse of Constantinople). Neither council led to the rapprochement it sought to achieve. Indeed, the tale of the repeated attempts to reconcile the two Churches and empires ends tragically, as the final mass celebrated in Hagia Sophia was conducted in Latin in the presence of the last reigning emperor, Constantine XI Palaiologos (1404–1453). Constantine's conversion to Catholicism, if intended to secure the allegiance of his Christian brethren in the West in a joint defense against the Ottoman Turks, failed.

Thus, Dante's lifetime unfolded in a breach between two periods of close engagement between Latin Christians and Orthodox Greeks. Both earlier and later than him, the tallies of both ecclesiastics and lay people with knowledge of Greek might well have ranged higher. Of course, the occasional friar contemporary with the great poet may have spent sufficient time abroad to attain fluency in Greek. Additionally, the same small Greek settlements remained entrenched in southern Italy and Sicily as had been there before. Finally, the Italian merchants from municipalities such as Venice who traded in the eastern Mediterranean would have persisted in doing so. In an essay entitled "Greeks in Italy at the time of Dante (1265–1321)," Vera von Falkenhausen gathers adroitly what can be discerned of merchants, diplomats, and other travelers from the Greek East in the Italy of Dante's day. Furthermore, Dante chanced to live at the same time as—although halfway across the Mediterranean from—Maximos Planoudes (ca. 1260–ca. 1305), a Byzantine who translated much patristic Latin and perhaps even texts of Thomas Aquinas into Greek. But a permeation of Italian culture by Greek immigrants as happened after the downfall of Constantinople or the steady exchange that can be traced during the era of the Crusades and Latin Kingdoms cannot be detected in the time of Dante.

Dante manifests relatively meager awareness of holy men from the Greek East. True, in a letter written after 20 April 1314 to the Italian cardinals in conclave at Carpentras, he touches upon, in a fairly long list of notable theologians, John of Damascus (d. 754), a Byzantine who lived in the city associated with his name.[70] According to Dante, John is a theologian whose works had come to be almost wholly neglected. Apart from John, all the figures Dante mentions in the *Commedia* come from the heroic early days of late antiquity, not from his own time. The two saints from the Greek East he names there are both fourth century, to wit, Macarius (*Par.* 22.49—whether the Elder, also called the Egyptian, or the Younger, of Alexandria, is uncertain) and Nicholas of Myra, a bishop in Asia Minor (*Purg.* 20.32), whose legends lead eventually to that of Santa Claus.[71] Among the multitude of Greek writers from the patristic period, Dante

70 *Epistola* 11.16, in Dante Alighieri, *Opere minori*, 2 vols., ed. D. De Robertis and G. Contini, Letteratura italiana: Storia e testi 5 (Milan, 1979–88), 2:580–83, at 586–87.

71 A. Pertusi, "Cultura greco-bizantina nel tardo medioevo nelle Venezie e suoi echi in Dante," in *Dante e la cultura veneta: Atti del convegno di studi organizzato dalla Fondazione "Giorgio Cini" in*

singles out only two: prolific Greek Church Father, Archbishop John Chrysostom of Constantinople (John "golden-mouthed," 345–407), cited by Saint Bonaventure (1221–1274; *Par.* 12.136–37), and Pseudo-Dionysius the Areopagite, who was converted in Athens by Saint Paul and martyred there in 95, discussed by first Saint Thomas Aquinas and then Beatrice (*Par.* 10.115–17 and 28.130–32).[72]

Pseudo-Dionysius was of great importance already in the twelfth century and only more so for scholastic theology from the thirteenth century onward.[73] His works had been translated repeatedly into Latin, especially in the thirteenth century by Robert Grosseteste (1175–1253), but the Latinization of Albertus Magnus (Albert the Great; d. 1280) is likeliest to have reached and affected Dante.[74] Dante may have gained a direct awareness of the so-called *Corpus Dionysiacum* only during his stay in the Lombardy and the Veneto.[75]

Whatever the specific source of transmission, Dante was profoundly beholden to the Neoplatonism of Pseudo-Dionysius. He distributes the nine angelic hierarchies in accordance with the order followed in Dionysius's *Celestial Hierarchy*, and he shows indebtedness to Dionysius in his understanding of theophany. Diego Sbacchi, in his chapter for this volume, looks into the influence of Pseudo-Dionysius on the presence and elements of light in Dante's *Paradiso*. Sbacchi finds parallels between Dante's conception of light and the treatment of it in icons, a situation he explains by hypothesizing their shared debt to Pseudo-Dionysius. Yet, in many ways, Pseudo-Dionysius stands out in his isolation as a postclassical Greek writer who left a deep imprint on Dante's thought. No Byzantine text has been proven to have exercised a similarly far-reaching influence on him.[76]

Not too long after Dante, Greek-speakers such as Michael Apostoles (ca. 1420–after 1474) and Demetrios Chalkokondyles (1423–1511) arrived in the West and expressed

collaborazione con l'Istituto universitario di Venezia, l'Università di Padova, il Centro scaligero di studi danteschi, e i comuni di Venezia, Padova, Verona; Venezia, Padova, Verona, 30 marzo–5 aprile 1966, ed. V. Branca and G. Padoan (Florence, 1966), 157–97, at 177. Pertusi's article was later reprinted in A. Pertusi, *Saggi veneto-bizantini*, ed. G. B. Parente (Florence, 1990).

72 Pertusi, "Cultura greco-bizantina," 177.

73 J. Leclercq, "Influence and Noninfluence of Dionysius in the Western Middle Ages," in *Pseudo-Dionysius: The Complete Works*, trans. C. Luibheid (New York, 1987), 25–32, at 25–29, and D. Poirel, *Des symboles et des anges: Hugues de Saint-Victor et le réveil dionysien du XIIe siècle*, Bibliotheca Victorina 23 (Turnhout, 2013).

74 D. Sbacchi, *La presenza di Dionigi Areopagita nel "Paradiso" di Dante*, Biblioteca di "Lettere italiane," ST 66 (Florence, 2006).

75 Pertusi, "Cultura greco-bizantina," 189.

76 The anonymous or pseudonymous Byzantine treatise *De virtutibus et passionibus* (On Virtues and Vices) was definitely written and circulating widely well before Dante. It has been argued that in adumbrating the moral order of the *Inferno*, Dante drew upon a Latin translation of a Byzantine Greek treatise on vice and virtue based on the Platonic threefold division of the soul. See C. A. Trypanis, "Dante and a Byzantine Treatise on Virtues and Vices," *Medium Aevum* 19 (1950): 43–49. But this proposition has been refuted by Pertusi, "Cultura greco-bizantina," 179–82.

an acute appreciation for the humanistic culture of Latins (and Italians).[77] The respect of the Greeks was more than reciprocated by the admiring attitudes of the humanists toward the ancient Greeks. Yet the cultural engagement between the Italian (or Latin) humanists and the Byzantine (or Greek) humanists took hold too late, and was too intellectual and not political enough to help motivate an alliance between the Latin and the Greek Churches that could have saved Byzantium from the final collapse of 1453. In 1463, Chalkokondyles delivered an inaugural address to launch the study of Greek at the University of Padua. At the end of the address, he drew a distressing comparison between the state of his countrymen under the Turkish occupation and the plight of the damned in Dante's *Inferno*.[78]

Sufficient room existed for interaction between the two worlds to warrant the title of a book by a Byzantinist, *Interaction of the "Sibling" Byzantine and Western Cultures in the Middle Ages and Italian Renaissance (300–1600)*. The same author emphasized the debt Dante owed to Aristotle and Pseudo-Dionysius, offsetting the apparent obliviousness of the Italian poet to the literature and theology of Byzantium. But even this Byzantinist took pains to describe how much the Westerners and the Byzantines diverged in their outlook on the literary cultivation of spoken and vernacular languages. And he made a point of conceding the consequent uniqueness of Dante in comparison with Byzantine literature: "Dante's great *Divine Comedy*, to take but one example, reaches creative heights never approached, I believe, by any Byzantine literary work."[79]

The collection that follows brings together the fruits of two distinct and distinguished fields, Byzantine and medieval studies, with the admixture of Dante studies, as well. My hope is that assembling exponents of three such heterogeneous fields to share their findings and perspectives in regard to a large and radically underexplored topic might open new vistas, resolve old controversies, and perhaps even kindle new debates. Fields can have the solidity but rigidity of railroad tracks in enabling efficient transportation at the cost of freedom and autonomy. The endeavor of this investigation was to encourage not only developing an awareness of other tracks—the rails conventional in other fields—but also to leave behind the ferrous rigidity. To the readers of this collection I can only invoke the spirit intended by the Blisses' installation of the Antiochene mosaic, already described, with its verbal noun *apólausis*: read, learn, and enjoy.

77 On Apostoles, see D. J. Geanakoplos, *Greek Scholars in Venice: Studies in the Dissemination of Greek Learning from Byzantium to Western Europe* (Cambridge, MA, 1962), 73–110.

78 Geanakoplos, *Interaction of the "Sibling" Byzantine and Western Cultures* (above, n. 6), 112, 248–49.

79 Ibid., 116.

Greeks in Italy at the Time of Dante (1265–1321)

VERA VON FALKENHAUSEN

To begin, let me place Dante's life in the framework of Byzantine history. He was born four years after the reconquest of Constantinople by the Byzantine emperor Michael VIII Palaiologos (r. 1259–1282), which put an end to the so-called Latin Empire (1204–1261) but not to the massive Latin and, in particular, Italian presence and influence in Byzantium. In April 1265, about the time of Dante's birth, a synod in Constantinople deposed the patriarch Arsenios, who had dared to excommunicate Michael VIII because he had blinded the legitimate emperor John IV Laskaris (1250–ca. 1305; emperor of Nicaea, 1258–1261).[1] The deposition of Arsenios caused the so-called Arsenite schism, which created a disruptive element in the Byzantine Church for almost fifty years.[2] In June of 1265, Michael VIII concluded a treaty with Venice that restored that city's former commercial and political privileges in the empire after they had been reduced in favor of Genoa, Byzantium's ally during the reconquest.[3] In 1274, when Dante was still a child in Florence, the Second Council of Lyons was held, where the Union of the Latin and the Greek Churches was officially concluded only to end in failure. In 1289, Dante fought on the Guelph side in the battle of Florence against Arezzo at Campaldino between the Guelphs and Ghibellines; in the same period, the Byzantine emperor Andronikos II Palaiologos (1259–1332) fought against the emperor of Epirus to recover the Adriatic coast for Byzantium; in 1302, when Dante was expelled from Florence, the Byzantine emperor was again forced by the Venetians to restore their former commercial privileges and

1 A. Failler, "Chronologie et composition dans l'Histoire de Georges Pachymère," *REB* 39 (1981): 155–64.

2 D. M. Nicol, *The Last Centuries of Byzantium, 1261–1453*, 2nd ed. (Cambridge, 1993), 96–105.

3 L. Pieralli, *La corrispondenza diplomatica dell'imperatore bizantino con le potenze estere nel tredicesimo secolo (1204–1282),* Collectanea Archivi Vaticani 54 (Vatican City, 2006), no. 9, 185–204; F. Dölger and P. Wirth, *Regesten der Kaiserurkunden des oströmischen Reiches von 565–1453*, 2nd ed. (Munich, 1977), pt. 3: no. 1934.

pay enormous indemnities.[4] In the same year, the Turks won a decisive battle in Bithynia, which would eventually give them access to Constantinople and eastern Europe. Dante died in 1321, in the first year of the civil war between Andronikos II and his homonymous grandson, Andronikos III.[5]

Throughout Dante's life, Italy had an enormous impact on Byzantine politics and, likewise, Byzantium was an important factor in the politics of Italy. Charles of Anjou, king of Sicily since 1266, forcefully defended his political interests in Epirus, the Balkans, and the eastern Mediterranean and, chiefly because of his close relationship with the former emperor Baldwin II, became the main promoter for a revival of the Latin Empire.[6] The popes tried in various ways to reimpose their supremacy on the Byzantine Church, reestablish their ecclesiastical dominion over the territory of the former Latin Empire, and organize—with or without Byzantine assistance—a crusade to liberate the Holy Land. Genoa and Venice, which actually controlled the economy of the eastern Mediterranean, pursued their wars for dominance in the territory or, better, on the waters of the Byzantine Empire and in the city of Constantinople. Even after the fall of the Latin Empire, thousands of Italians continued to live and work in Constantinople, on the Greek islands, and in Trebizond, particularly as merchants, traders,[7] clerics, monks, and friars;[8] officials in the imperial administration;[9]

4 F. Dölger, *Regesten der Kaiserurkunden des oströmischen Reiches von 565–1453* (Munich and Berlin, 1960), pt. 4: no. 2247.

5 U. V. Bosch, *Andronikos III. Palaiologos* (Amsterdam, 1965), 7–27; Nicol, *Last Centuries*, 151–66.

6 G. L. Borghese, *Carlo I d'Angiò e il Mediterraneo: Politica, diplomazia e commercio internazionale prima dei Vespri,* Collection de l'École Française de Rome 411 (Rome, 2008).

7 N. Oikonomidès, *Hommes d'affaires grecs et latins à Constantinople (XIIIe–XVe siècles),* Conférence Albert-le-Grand 1977 (Montréal, 1979); *Les Italiens à Byzance: Édition et présentation de documents,* ed. M. Balard, A. E. Laiou, and C. Otten-Froux, Byzantina Sorbonensia 6 (Paris, 1987); C. Verlinden, "Encore la traite des esclaves et les traitants italiens à Constantinople," *Bulletin de l'Institut Historique Belge de Rome* 59 (1989): 101–20; S. P. Karpov, "Les empereurs de Trébizonde, débiteurs des Gênois," in *Chemins d'outre-mer: Études sur la Méditerranée médiévale offertes à Michel Balard,* ed. D. Coulon et al., vol. 2, Byzantina Sorbonensia 20 (Paris, 2004), 489–94.

8 R. Loenertz, O.P., *La Societé des frères pérégrinants,* Études sur l'Orient dominicain 1 (Rome, 1937); M. Roncaglia, O.F.M., *Les Frères mineurs et l'église grecque orthodoxe au XIIIe siècle (1231–1274)* (Cairo, 1954); G. Matteucci O.F.M., *Un glorioso convento francescano sulle rive del Bosforo: Il S. Francesco di Galata in Costantinopoli, c. 1230–1696,* Biblioteca di Studi Francescani 7 (Florence, 1967), 54–64; R. Janin, *La Géographie ecclésiastique de l'empire byzantin,* vol. 1, *Le Siège de Constantinople et le patriarcat oecuménique,* pt. 3, *Les Églises et les monastères,* 2nd ed. (Paris, 1969), 569–93; M.-H. Congourdeau, "Notes sur les Dominicains de Constantinople au début du 14e siècle," *REB* 45 (1987): 175–81; eadem, "Frère Simon le Constantinopolitain, O.P. (1235?–1325?)," *REB* 45 (1987): 165–74; C. Delacroix-Besnier, *Les Dominicains et la Chrétienté grecque aux XIVe et XVe siècles,* Collection de l'École Française de Rome 237 (Rome, 1997).

9 Such as the Genoese notary Ogerius Boccanegra, active in the imperial chancery at least during the years 1272–86, whose career from *sacri imperii et comunis Ianue notarius et ipsius comunis cancellarius* in 1261 to *prothonotarius interpretum Latinorum curie domini mei sanctissimi imperatoris Romanie* in 1278 has been reconstructed by Pieralli, *La corrispondenza* (above, n. 3), 88–95.

and soldiers in the Byzantine army.[10] George Pachymeres quite often mentions the Italians or Genoese of Constantinople (κατὰ τὴν πόλιν or κατὰ τὴν μεγαλόπολιν).[11]

But despite all this, Byzantium is absent from the *Commedia*. We do find the emperor Justinian in paradise: *Cesare fui e son Giustiniano, / che per voler del primo amor ch'i' sento, / d'entro le leggi trassi il troppo e 'l vano* (*Par.* 6.10–12). On Theodora, there is discreet silence. Nor is there any mention of Constantinople, except for a vague *nello stremo d'Europa* (*Par.* 6.5), and this is probably not simply because of metrical difficulty. If we look at the *De monarchia,* when Dante discusses the imperial coronation of Charlemagne, he gets the names of the pope and the Byzantine ruler wrong: it was not Hadrian but Leo III who crowned the Western emperor, and the contemporary Byzantine sovereign was not Michael I but Empress Irene. Concerning this event, the treatise contains a sentence that would have pleased any learned Byzantine citizen who read it: *usurpatio enim iuris non facit ius* (the usurpation of a right does not create right).[12] It is as if Dante had doubts about the legitimacy of the Western Roman Empire.

This, however, is not the topic of this essay, which, in dealing with the Greeks in Italy in the time of Dante, focuses on four apparently unconnected aspects, although the political issues and events mentioned above provide a common background. First, the declining Greek communities in Sicily and southern Italy, particularly Calabria and the Terra d'Otranto. Second, Greek ambassadors and agents who were sent for various reasons to Italian states and courts, especially to the papal curia to promote the unification of the two Churches before and after the Council of Lyons. Third, Greeks, such as traders or artists, who came to Genoa and Venice for commerce and work. Fourth, and finally, dynastic connections, as when Theodore Palaiologos, the second son of Andronikos II and Yolanda of Montferrat, became marquis of Montferrat in 1306 at the age of fourteen. Thus, I invite you to follow me on a trip in search of Greeks in Dante's Italy. Let us begin with the south.

Greek Communities in Sicily and Southern Italy

In the time of Dante, the Greek communities in southern Italy, especially in Calabria, Sicily, and the Terra d'Otranto, were in decline. They had survived long after the Norman conquest in the second half of the eleventh century. The Norman knights who conquered southern Italy were valiant warriors, but they did not have any administrative experience, and that conquest, unlike the contemporary conquest of England, was not a dynastic but a private military affair. Thus, they were not accompanied by clerics capable of running the government of the new country in which half the population

10 M. C. Bartusis, *The Late Byzantine Army: Arms and Society, 1204–1453* (Philadelphia, 1992), 78, 140, 196, 209.

11 Georges Pachymeres, 9.1, ed. A. Failler, vol. 3, CFHB 24.3 (Paris, 1999), 219; 11.14, 12.6, 12.9, 13.27, vol. 4, CFHB 24.4 (Paris, 1999), 437, 535, 541, 687.

12 Dante Alighieri, *Monarchia,* ed. and trans. G. Vinay (Florence, 1950), 3.11, p. 256.

spoke non-Romance, foreign languages, that is, Greek and Arabic. In this respect, the conquerors depended entirely on local collaborators. During the first decades after the conquest the Normans did not really trust their Arab subjects, so for more than fifty years the Norman administration in Calabria and Sicily was run by members of an educated, or at least literate, Greek middle class. Most of the private documents and most of the charters of counts Roger I (r. 1062–1101) and Roger II (r. 1105–1154; king from 1130) for recipients in Calabria and Sicily were issued in Greek.[13] As in Byzantium, most of the Greek notaries in Calabria and Sicily were priests or at least belonged to the lower orders of the church, as subdeacons or deacons.[14] We may compare this Greek middle class with the families of the Protestant ministers or vicars in eighteenth- and nineteenth-century northern Europe, who had such an important impact on the cultural life of those countries. These families recognized themselves as being in the Greek religious rite. After the Norman conquest, the Greek dioceses of southern Italy and Sicily, which since the eighth century had belonged to the ecclesiastical jurisdiction of the patriarcate of Constantinople, returned to Roman obedience. Latin bishops were installed in all Sicilian and in the more important Calabrian bishoprics, but other dioceses, such as Rossano, Crotone, and Gerace, were held by Greek bishops, sometimes until the fourteenth century.[15] However, the Greek religious rite was preserved throughout the territory, and part of the lower clergy remained Greek for centuries.[16]

With the foundation of the Norman kingdom in 1130, things began to change, for by now most of the population in the kingdom as a whole, which included Campania,

13 For the charters of Roger I: *Documenti latini e greci del conte Ruggero I di Calabria e Sicilia: Edizione critica*, ed. J. Becker, Ricerche dell'Istituto Storico Germanico di Roma 9 (Rome, 2013); the regent Adelasia: V. von Falkenhausen, "Zur Regentschaft der Gräfin Adelasia del Vasto in Kalabrien und Sizilien (1101–1112)," in *ΑΕΤΟΣ: Studies in Honour of Cyril Mango Presented to Him on April 14, 1998*, ed. I. Ševčenko and I. Hutter (Stuttgart and Leipzig, 1998), 98–99, 105–15; King Roger II: eadem, "I diplomi dei re normanni in lingua greca," in *Documenti medievali greci e latini: Studi comparativi; Atti del seminario di Erice (23–29 ottobre 1995)*, ed. G. De Gregorio and O. Kresten, Incontri di studio 1 (Spoleto, 1998), 255–62; for the private documents in Sicily: eadem, "La presenza dei Greci nella Sicilia normanna: L'apporto della documentazione archivistica in lingua greca," in *Byzantino-Sicula 4, Atti del I Congresso internazionale di archeologia della Sicilia bizantina*, ed. R. M. Carra Bonacasa, Istituto Siciliano di Studi Bizantini e Neoellenici, Quaderni 15 (Palermo, 2002), 42–70; in English trans., eadem, "The Greek Presence in Norman Sicily: The Contribution of Archival Material in Greek," in *The Society of Norman Sicily*, ed. G. A. Loud and A. Metcalfe (Leiden, Boston, and Cologne, 2002), 262–87.

14 V. von Falkenhausen, "La tecnica dei notai italo-greci," in *La cultura scientifica e tecnica nell'Italia meridionale bizantina*, Atti della sesta Giornata di studi bizantini (Arcavacata di Rende, 8–9 febbraio 2000), ed. F. Burgarella and A. M. Ieraci Bio (Soveria Mannelli, 2006), 17–30.

15 P. Herde, "The Papacy and the Greek Church in Southern Italy between the Eleventh and the Thirteenth Century," in *Society of Norman Italy*, 220–24; T. Hofmann, "Papsttum und griechische Kirche in Süditalien in nachnormannischer Zeit (13.–15. Jahrhundert): Ein Beitrag zur Geschichte Süditaliens im Hoch- und Spätmittelalter" (Ph.D. diss., University of Würzburg, 1994), 28–30.

16 Hofmann, "Papsttum," 119–21; V. von Falkenhausen, "I Greci in Calabria fra XIII e XIV secolo," in *Petrarca e il mondo greco: VII Centenario della nascita di Francesco Petrarca (2004)*, Quaderni petrarcheschi 12–13 (2002–3) (Florence, 2007), 42–43.

Apulia, and the Abruzzi, was Latin. Thus, Latin notaries from Campania and Apulia, and even immigrants from England and France, took over, while experienced Arab administrators ran the central administration in Palermo. Greek officials became redundant, unless they were bi- or trilingual. After Roger II's death, the royal chancellery issued only a few Greek charters,[17] but throughout the twelfth century most of the private documents in Calabria and Sicily continued to be written in Greek.

In the thirteenth century, during the reign of Frederick II, the Greek impact was reduced still further, most probably for the following reasons. First, in this period, the more important positions in the administration were held by those who had an academic degree, and schools and universities taught only in Latin. After studying in Latin, it was but a small step to become entirely Latinized. Second, Frederick II had issued a decree that excluded the clergy from the notarial professions. As most of the Greek notaries belonged to the clergy, they were automatically excluded from their former profession.[18] Moreover, the Greeks of Calabria and Sicily lived in a cultural diaspora, far from the intellectual life of Byzantium, in a period when intellectual life in the West was particularly stimulating, with, for example, the beginning of the universities in Italy and France, and the foundation of the mendicant orders. Finally, after the fall of Constantinople in 1204, the status of Greeks in Latin society also fell, so that Latinization offered the easier path. To give one telling example, I know of 140 Greek documents issued in Calabria during the thirteenth century, most from the first half, but for the fourteenth century there are only six.[19] Likewise, in Sicily, I know of some fifty Greek documents from the thirteenth century but of fewer than ten from the fourteenth.[20] In the same period, members of the leading Greek families, such as the Logothetes or the Graffeo, became canons of the church of Reggio or entered the mendicant orders and were elected Latin bishops of, for example, Cefalù

17 H. Enzensberger, "Utilitas regia: Note di storia amministrativa e giuridica e di propaganda politica dell'età dei due Guglielmi," *Atti della Accademia di Scienze, Lettere e Arti di Palermo,* ser. 5a, 2 (Lettere), 1 (1981–82): 48–54; G. A. Loud, "The Chancery and Charters of the Kings of Sicily (1130–1212)," *The English Historical Review* 124 (2009): 781–83; V. von Falkenhausen, "Un diploma greco di Guglielmo II (marzo 1168)," in *Storie di cultura scritta: Studi per Francesco Magistrale,* ed. P. Fioretti (Spoleto, 2012), 377–89.

18 V. von Falkenhausen, "Friedrich II. und die Griechen im Königreich Sizilien," in *Friedrich II: Tagung des Deutschen Historischen Instituts in Rom im Gedenkjahr 1994,* ed. A. Esch and N. Kamp, Bibliothek des Deutschen Historischen Instituts in Rom 85 (Tübingen, 1996), 255–60.

19 von Falkenhausen, "I Greci in Calabria," 47–48; G. Russo, "Un'inedita pergamena greco-latina di Rossano del XIV secolo," *Archivio storico per la Calabria e la Lucania* 67 (2010): 55–85.

20 von Falkenhausen, "La presenza dei Greci" (above, n. 13), 70; eadem, "Greek Presence" (above, n. 13), map VI. The following 14th-century documents must be added to those mentioned in my article of 2002: Cod. Vat Lat. 8201, fol. 366 (Messina 1303); A. Guillou, *Les actes grecs de S. Maria di Messina: Enquête sur les populations grecques d'Italie du Sud et de Sicile (XIe–XIVe s.),* Istituto siciliano di studi bizantini e neoellenici, Testi e monumenti 8 (Palermo, 1963), no. 23, 173–75 (Rometta, 1304); H. Penet, *Le chartier de S. Maria di Messina: Il tabulario di S. Maria di Messina (1250–1500),* vol. 1, *Actes latins conservés à la Bibliothèque Nationale de Paris (1250–1429)* (Messina, 1998), nos. 93–94, 345–50 (Rometta, 1315).

and Patti.[21] Others used their linguistic skills as translators of classical or scientific texts into Latin, as in the case of Nicholas de Deoprepio.[22] On the whole, one can say that by the end of the thirteenth century, the former Greek upper class of Calabria and Sicily was Latinized. The peasantry, however, remained Greek in language and religion. In a marginal note of the redaction of the *Roman de Troyes* in old French, one can read that in Calabria the peasants speak only Greek,[23] and these peasants were passionately atttached to their Greek religious rite.[24]

In his *Istoria del Regno di Romania*, Marino Sanudo Torsello, a Venetian diplomat some two decades younger than Dante, and a convinced supporter of the Union of the Churches and a fervent promoter of a crusade,[25] wrote:

> *Sonvi anco molti Greci in Calabria ed in Terra d'Otranto, che ubbidiscono alla Santa Chiesa Romana, ma forse non così devotamente, come farianno, se l'imperator sior Michiel Paleologo detto e il Patriarca Costantinopolitano ed il figlio del detto imperatore Sior Andronicus fossero fermi e ubbidienti alla Chiesa romana e non in contumacia, onde segue danno immenso.*[26]
>
> There are also many Greeks in Calabria and in the Land of Otranto who are in obedience to the Holy Roman Church, though perhaps not so devotedly as they would

21 N. Kamp, *Kirche und Monarchie im staufischen Königreich Sizilien,* vol. 1, *Prosopographische Grundlegung: Bistümer und Bischöfe des Königreichs,* vol. 3, *Sizilien,* Münstersche Mittelalter-Schriften 10 (Munich, 1975), 1063–66; V. von Falkenhausen, "I logoteti greci nel regno normanno," in *Dentro e fuori la Sicilia: Studi di storia per Vincenzo D'Alessandro,* ed. P. Corrao and E. I. Mineo (Rome, 2009), 116–23; R. Starrabba, *I diplomi della cattedrale di Messina raccolti da Antonino Amico,* Documenti per servire alla storia di Sicilia pubblicati a cura di della Società siciliana di storia patria, s. 1, 19 (Palermo, 1888), no. 178, 179–80; V. von Falkenhausen, "I funzionari greci nel Regno normanno," *Byzantino-Sicula V: Giorgio di Antiochia; L'arte della politica in Sicilia nel XII secolo tra Bisanzio e l'Islam,* Atti del Convegno Internazionale (Palermo, 19–20 aprile 2007), ed. in M. Re and C. Rognoni, Istituto siciliano di studi bizantini e neoellenici "Bruno Lavagnini," Quaderni 17 (Palermo, 2009), 191, 194–96,198–201.

22 R. Weiss, "The Translators from the Greek at the Angevin Court of Naples," *Rinascimento* 1 (1950): 218–26, repr. in *Medieval and Humanist Greek Collected Essays,* Medioevo e Umanesimo 8 (Padua, 1977), 125–32, 134–41; von Falkenhausen, "I Greci in Calabria," 39–41 (above, n. 16).

23 *Le Roman de Troie en prose,* ed. L. Costans and E. Faral (Paris, 1922), 1: 4; G. Rohlfs, "L'antico ellenismo nell'Italia di oggi (sostrati e riflessi)," in *Le iscrizioni pre-latine in Italia: Colloquio, Roma, 14–15 marzo 1977,* Atti dei Convegni Lincei 39 (Rome, 1979), 8; G. Fiaccadori, "Umanesimo e grecità d'Occidente," in *I Greci in Occidente: La tradizione filosofica, scientifica e letteraria della collezione della Biblioteca Marciana; Catalogo della mostra,* ed. G. Fiaccadori and P. Eleuteri (Venice, 1996), xxiii–xxiv.

24 G. Garitte, "Deux manuscrits italo-grecs (Vat. gr. 1238 et Barber. gr. 475)," in *Miscellanea Giovanni Mercati 3,* ST 123 (Vatican City, 1946), 31–40.

25 C. J. Tycrman, "Marino Sanudo Torsello and the Lost Crusade: Lobbying in the Fourteenth Century," *Transactions of the Royal Historical Society,* 5th ser., 32 (1982): 57–73; A. Leopold, *How to Recover the Holy Land: The Crusade Proposals of the Late Thirteenth and Early Fourteenth Centuries* (Aldershot, 2000), 2, 38–40, 45–50.

26 M. Sanudo Torsello, *Istoria del Regno di Romania,* in *Chroniques gréco-romanes inédites ou peu connues,* ed. C. Hopf (Berlin, 1873; repr. Brussels, 1966), 143–44; Marinos Sanoudos Torsello, *Ἱστορία τῆς Ρωμανίας,* ed. Eu. Papadopoulou (Athens, 2000), 169.

be if the emperor Lord Michael Paleologos as well as the patriarch of Constantinople and the son of the said emperor, Lord Andronikos, were strict in their obedience to the Roman Church and not in contumacy, whence great harm ensues.

This statement has been thought to indicate that Greeks in southern Italy might have been a kind of Byzantine fifth column during the Sicilian Vespers,[27] but I doubt that this was so. After more than two hundred years of Latin rule, they did not nurture any feeling of loyalty toward the distant Byzantine Empire. Moreover, the Greeks belonged to the wrong section of society to organize a revolt against the new French rulers. The rebellion was staged by local barons in Sicily and not in the Terra d'Otranto, where Greek language and culture was far livelier and survived longer.[28] Apparently, no Greek from Sicily or southern Italy was involved in the negotiations between Byzantium, Peter of Aragon, and the Sicilian rebels before and during the Vespers. The chief negotiators seem to have been Genoese businessmen and John of Procida from Salerno.[29] Furthermore, in my opinion, it is quite significant that in a period when the Greek language was practically unknown at the Roman curia,[30] no Greek cleric or theologian from southern Italy was involved in the theological discussions on the Union of the Churches between the papal curia and Byzantium before or after the Second Council of Lyons. In fact, the learned and bilingual bishop of Crotone, *magister* Nicholas, who, in 1261–65, had been the main theological mediator between Rome and Byzantium, was a Greek from Durazzo (Albania), had lived at the court of Nicaea and in Constantinople, and had probably never taken possession of his Calabrian bishopric.[31] It would seem that no well-educated Greek theologian from southern Italy was available to take part in the discussions.

27 D. J. Geanakoplos, "The Greek Population of South Italy and Sicily and Its Attitudes toward Charles of Anjou and Michael Palaeologus before and during the Early Phase of the Sicilian Vespers (1282)," in *Constantiople and the West: Essays on the Late Byzantine (Palaeologan) and Italian Renaissances and the Byzantine and Roman Churches (*Madison, 1989), 9: 189–94.

28 A. Jacob, "Culture grecque et manuscrits en Terre d'Otrante," in *Atti del III° Congresso Internazionale di Studi Salentini e del I° Congresso Storico di Terra d'Otranto, Lecce 22–25 ottobre 1976* (Lecce, 1980), 53–77; idem, "Testimonianze bizantine nel Basso Salento," in *Il Basso Salento: Ricerche di storia sociale e religiosa* (Galatina, 1982), 49–69; idem, "Une bibliothèque mediévale de Terre d'Otrante (Parisinus Gr. 549)," *RSBN,* n.s. 22–23 (1985–86): 285–315. Many very important articles about the survival of the Greek language and culture in Terra d'Otranto in the post-Byzantine period have been published by this author, most of which are mentioned in A. Peters-Custot, *Les Grecs de l'Italie méridionale post-byzantine: Une acculturation en douceur,* Collection de l'École Française de Rome 420 (Rome, 2009), 551–56, 649–51; S. Lucà, "Il libro bizantino e postbizantino nell'Italia meridionale," in *Scrittura e libro nel mondo greco-bizantino,* Atti del corso, Ravello, Villa Rufolo, 6–9 Novembre 2007, ed. C. Casetti Brach, *Il futuro del passato* 4 (Ravello, 2012), 25–76.

29 Bartholomaeus de Neocastro, *Historia Sicula ab anno MCCL ad annum MCCXCIII,* ed. G. Paladino, Rerum Italicarum Scriptores 13.3, 2nd ed. (Bologna, 1922), 36; D. J. Geanakoplos, *Emperor Michael Paleaeologus and the West, 1258–1282: A Study in Byzantine-Latin Relations* (Cambridge, MA, 1959), 344–67.

30 Roncaglia, *Les Frères mineurs* (above, n. 8), 140, n. 3; Pieralli, *La corrispondenza* (above, n. 3), 83–85.

31 Kamp, *Kirche und Monarchie* (above, n. 21), 958–963; T. M. Kolbaba, "Repercussions of the Second Council of Lyon (1274): Theological Polemic and the Bounderies of Orthodoxy," in *Greeks,*

Greek Ambassadors and Agents

For the period between 1265 and 1321, the *Regesten der Kaiserurkunden des oströmischen Reiches* mention more than sixty embassies sent by the emperors Michael VIII and Andronikos II to Italy, most to the pontifical curia and to Venice and Genoa, but also to the kings of Sicily and to Pisa, Ancona, and Montferrat. Thus, almost every year, several representatives of the Byzantine emperors came to Italy to discuss highly delicate political questions, such as the Union of the Churches, dynastic marriages, commercial treaties, and piracy, with the leaders of the most important Italian states. But who were these Byzantine ambassadors? Unfortunately, we know only a few names.

As the Greek language was not well known in Italy, and Byzantine subjects might experience problems traveling through the territory of the hostile king of Sicily to reach their final destination, the emperors sometimes used their Italian officials—often Genoese—on diplomatic missions, such as the *protonotarios* Ogerius Boccanegra, who was sent as *ambaxator illustrissimi imperatoris* to Genoa in 1272,[32] or Benedetto Zaccaria to Peter of Aragon in 1282.[33] Even the delivery of Byzantine money to the king of Aragon to finance the Sicilian Vespers was probably organized by Genoese businessmen.[34] Maximus Aloubardes may also have been Italian by birth, if we accept Franz Dölger's convincing interpretation of the name as *a Lombardis.* Michael VIII sent him to Rome just after the conquest of Constantinople in 1261, where he was nearly killed as a traitor. Despite this, he was brave enough to return to Italy the following year with a new imperial embassy.[35]

It appears that the emperor sometimes sent officials with a mixed Greco-Italian family background; at least this would seem to be suggested by names such as George Tzimiskes Visconti from Berroia, *familiaris secretarius maiestatis ipsius Imperatoris* and *magnus interpres* of Michael VIII, who was sent to Venice in 1268 and died in a shipwreck on his way to the Second Council of Lyons in 1274,[36] or Obertus Dokeianos, *pansebastus sebastus* and *familiaris* of the emperor, who was sent on an embassy to Genoa in 1262.[37] Obertus was a common name in Genoa. On other occasions, Andronikos II used Greeks from the Venetian territories in the eastern Mediterranean for diplomatic

---

Latins and Intellectual History: 1204–1500, ed. M. Hinterberger and C. Schabel, Bibliotheca 11 (Leuven, 2011), 47, is mistaken in describing him as "a Latin prelate who had mastered the Greek language."

32 *Regesten,* no. 1990; Pieralli, *La corrispondenza,* 92.

33 R. Sabbatino Lopez, *Genova marinara nel Duecento: Benedetto Zaccaria, ammiraglio e mercante* (Messina and Milan, 1933), 256–57; É. Malamut, "De 1299 à 1451 au coeur des ambassades," in *Bisanzio, Venezia e il mondo franco-greco (XIII–XV secolo),* Atti del Colloquio Internazionale organizzato nel centenario della nascita di Raymond-Joseph Loenertz, O.P., Venezia, 1–2 dicembre 2000 (Venice, 2002), 101–2.

34 C. N. Tsirpanlis, "The Involvement of Michael VIII Palaeologus in the Sicilian Vespers (1279–1282)," *Βυζαντινά* 4 (1972): 320–25.

35 *Regesten,* no. 1901a; *PLP,* no. 689; Pieralli, *La corrispondenza* (above, n. 3), 173–74, n. 34.

36 *Regesten,* nos. 1960, 2007, 2009, 2009a; Pieralli, *La corrispondenza,* 224, n. 5, 253.

37 *Regesten,* no. 1914; Pieralli, *La corrispondenza,* 153–57.

missions to Venice, such as Nikephoros, the archbishop of Crete, in 1296,[38] or the interpreter George of Koron in 1302.[39]

Some ambassadors were dispatched several times to the same destination, as for instance Stephanos Syropoulos, who went to Venice four times. In 1303, as junior translator *(de interpretibus nostris),* he was a member of the imperial delegation together with the *hetaireiarches* Alexios Komnenos Diplovatatzes and the *interpres Imperii nostri* Constantine Fiscomalo;[40] in 1319, he accompanied the marquis of Montferrat, Theodore Palaiologos, from Constantinople via Venice to his marquisate,[41] and in 1324 and 1332, with the title of *pansebastos sebastos,* he served as ambassador to Venice.[42] He was apparently considered to be an expert on Venice or northern Italy, but nothing more is known about him.

Among the ambassadors were some who were highly educated, such as Gregory Kleidas, from 1313 *dikaiophylax* of Hagia Sophia. Andronikos II sent him to Venice in 1319 und used him twice in 1327 as a mediator with his grandson Andronikos III. But soon Kleidas made an arrangement with the younger emperor, who promoted him to be general judge (καθολικὸς κριτὴς τῶν Ῥωμαίων) and archdeacon of Hagia Sophia, and sent him again on mission to Venice in 1332, together with Syropoulos. In 1337, all the members of the high court of justice were accused of corruption, removed from their position, and exiled. During his exile, Kleidas wrote his eloquent *apologia* of the condemned judges.[43] The *orphanotrophos* Leo Bardales, an elegant writer and poet and later *protasekretis* and Kleidas's colleague as a judge, had been sent as ambassador to Venice in 1296,[44] but also to other destinations in Asia Minor, including, in 1321, the first year of the civil war, to Andronikos III, who then marched toward Constantinople.[45] He was clearly a clever and much-appreciated diplomat. Removed from his position in the high court together with Kleidas, he, too, wrote an *apologia.*[46] Both corresponded with the elite of contemporary Byzantine intellectuals.

It is obvious why legal experts should have been indispensable during the complicated discussions in Venice on the renewal of, or modifications to, the treaties with Byzantium, or on the calculation of indemnities, but one wonders why the monk and distinguished Latin scholar Maximos Planoudes, a renowned professor, poet, and translator of classical and patristic Latin literature, should have been sent on diplomatic

38 *Regesten,* no. 2193.

39 Ibid., no. 2247.

40 G. M. Thomas, *Diplomatarium Veneto-Levantinum sive acta et diplomata res Venetas Graecas atque Levantis illustrantia, a. 1300–1350* (Venice, 1880), no. 46, 83; *Regesten,* no. 2250.

41 *Regesten,* nos. 2417–18.

42 *PLP,* no. 27218; *Regesten,* nos. 2510, 2787.

43 *PLP,* no. 11781; G. J. Theocharides, "Die Apologie der verurteilten höchsten Richter der Römer," *BZ* 56 (1963): 69–100.

44 *Regesten,* no. 2197.

45 Ibid., no. 2463.

46 I. Ševčenko, "Léon Bardales et les juges généraux ou la corruption des incorruptibles," *Byzantion* 19 (1949): 247–59; *PLP,* no. 2183.

missions to Venice in 1296/97 together with Leo Bardales, and again in 1302; and why the bilingual monk Sophonias, a paraphraser of Aristoteles, should have been sent to the king of Sicily in 1294.[47] Was it really only because of their linguistic skills? Planoudes may have gone for his own reasons—to find and acquire Latin manuscripts—but a passage in Nikephoros Gregoras may suggest another answer. In his account of the embassy of Theodore Metochites and the later patriarch John Glykys to Cyprus and Armenia to organize a dynastic marriage for Michael IX, Gregoras comments that ambassadors to foreign countries were chosen not only for their experience in political matters but also for their exquisite theological and classical education, which gave them the upper hand in discussions on all subjects and enabled them to impress foreign courts with the erudite eloquence of their speech.[48]

The ambassadors sent to Rome to discuss the Union of the Churches had to be well-trained theologians and ardent Unionists. Thus, the bilingual and well-educated *magister* Nicholas of Durazzo,[49] a Greek from Albania who was familiar with the imperial courts of Nicaea and Constantinople, and who after a short career at the curia had been appointed bishop of Crotone by Innocent IV, must have seemed an excellent choice. He was praised as an active and fervent promoter of the union in the years between 1262 and 1266, but apparently he lacked diplomatic skills and thus ran into trouble with both parties. In 1266/67, he was condemned in Rome for *haeresia Graecorum* and deposed from his bishopric. He fled from the papal prison to Byzantium, but after a while, Michael VIII, for unknown reasons, exiled him to Herkleia Pontica.[50] He reappeared in Italy in 1275 and, on his death in Viterbo (1276), left an interesting library of biblical, patristic, and liturgical books in Latin and Greek.[51]

The second intermediary between Byzantium and the papal curia was again a Roman Catholic of Greek origin, the Franciscan friar John Parastron, a Constantinopolitan by birth and bilingual in word and script.[52] He served on several embassies between Rome and Constantiople, and was a member of the imperial delegation to the Council of

47 Pachymeres 9.21, vol. 3:269–71; *Regesten*, nos. 2197, 2247, 2156a; Congourdeau, "Notes sur les Dominicains" (above, n. 8), 175–81; A. Failler, "La mission du moine Sophonias en Italie et le mariage de Michael IX Palaiologos," *REB* 60 (2002): 151–66; D. M. Searby and A. Sjörs, "A Rhetorical Declamation of Sophonias the Monk and Paraphrast," *BZ* 104 (2011): 147–82.

48 *Nicephori Gregorae Byzantina Historia* 6.8, ed. L. Schopen (Bonn, 1829), 1:193–94: μὴ μόνον δι᾽ ἣν τῶν πραγμάτων ἐτύγχανον ἔχοντες πεῖραν, ἀλλὰ καὶ διὰ τὸ πόλλῳ τῶν ἄλλων προέχειν συνέσεως ἐμβριθείᾳ καὶ σοφίας περιουσίᾳ, ὅση τε περὶ τὰ θεῖά τε καὶ ἡμέτερα δόγματα καὶ ὅση περὶ τὸν Ἕλληνα λόγον ἠσχόληται. τοιούτους γὰρ εἶναι ἀνάγκη τοὺς πρὸς ὑπερόρια πρεσβεύοντας ἔθνη, ἵνα πανταχόθεν οὑτωσὶ τὴν γλῶτταν ἔχοντες ὡπλισμένην κἀν ταῖς διαλέξεσιν ἀριστεύωσιν, ὁποῖαί ποτ᾽ ἂν εἶεν.

49 Pachymeres 5.8, vol. 2:463: ἄνδρα λόγιον ὄντα καὶ διγλωσσοῦντα κατ᾽ ἐπιστήμην τὴν θείαν.

50 Pachymeres' explication is vague (5.8, vol. 2:463): φωραθεὶς ἐκεῖνος εἰς δύσνοιαν καὶ τῶν ἡμετέρων βλάβην.

51 Kamp, *Kirche und Monarchie* (above, n. 21), 958–63; P. Sambin, *Il vescovo cotronese Niccolò da Durazzo e un inventario di suoi codici latini e greci (1276)* (Rome, 1954), 16–27.

52 P. Radiciotti, "Episodi di digrafismo grecolatino a Costantinopoli: Giovanni Parastro ed i codici Coislin 200 e Parigino greco 54," *Römische historische Mitteilungen* 39 (1997): 181–86.

Lyons.[53] In contrast to Nicholas of Crotone, he was apparently well liked on both sides: Pachymeres' judgment of him is definitely positive,[54] and it is said that after his death in 1275 Byzantium tried to promote his canonization.[55]

The Union of the Churches was extremely unpopular among the Byzantine people and clergy. This is easy to understand if we consider that for more than fifty years, the supremacy of the Roman Church had been imposed on the Byzantine Church and population. Nevertheless, for Michael VIII, union was the only expedient to save the empire, by preventing the pope from preaching a crusade against Byzantium and assisting Charles of Anjou in his attempt to reconquer the East. Thus, the emperor insisted on concluding the union in spite of the opposition of the patriarch and most of the clergy. It is quite revealing that among the members of the Byzantine delegation at the Second Council of Lyons in 1274 who officially accepted the reconciliation of the two churches, there was no representative of the patriarch of Constantinople. The imperial ambassadors were the learned *logothetes* George Akropolites, the ex-patriarch Germanos, and the archbishop of Nicaea, all personal friends or relatives of Michael, and three Franciscans, among them the Greek-born Parastron. We do not know whether the Latin Fathers of the Council were aware that no official delegate of the Constantinopolitan Church was present; in any case, his absence was not mentioned.[56]

In the following years, the emperor sent almost annual delegations with gifts to Rome to convince the pope of his good will and religious obedience, and to be kept informed about political goings on there. Some of Michael's delegates, qualified Greek theologians such as George Metochites and Constantine Meliteniotes,[57] were committed Unionists. George Metochites, the father of the more famous Theodore, was sent to Rome twice, in 1275 and 1278, and describes his cordial conversations with Pope Gregory X and his successor about a common crusade to liberate the Holy Land and a projected meeting between the pope and the emperor either in Brindisi or Valona.[58] George was on friendly terms with the Franciscan friar Jerome of Ascoli, the later pope Nicholas IV (r. 1288–1292), who

53 Roncaglia, *Les Frères mineurs* (above, n. 8), 140–42, 173–74; B. Roberg, *Die Union zwischen der griechischen und lateinischen Kirche auf dem II. Konzil von Lyon (1274),* Bonner Historische Forschungen 24 (Bonn, 1964), 67, 70, 83–85, 100–104, 114, 125–28, 145, 159–61, 262; D. J. Geanakoplos, "Bonaventura, the Two Mendicant Orders, and the Greeks at the Council of Lyons (1274)," in *Constantinople and the West* (above, n. 27), 198–99, 205–8; Pieralli, *La corrispondenza* (above, n. 3), 84, 230, 331, 344, 379, 388.

54 Pachymeres, 5.11, vol. 2:475–79; 7.6, vol. 3:31.

55 Roncaglia, *Les Frères mineurs* (above, n. 8), 174.

56 Roberg, *Die Union,* 121–28.

57 R.-J. Loenertz O. P., "Théodore Métochite et son père," *Archivum Fratrum Praedicatorum* 23 (1953): 184–94; H.-G. Beck, *Kirche und theologische Literatur im byzantinischen Reich,* Byzantinisches Handbuch im Rahmen des Handbuchs der Altertumswissenschaften 2.1 (Munich, 1959), 684; E. de Vries-van der Velden, *Théodore Métochite: Une réévaluation* (Amsterdam, 1987), 31–51.

58 C. Giannelli, "Le récit d'une mission diplomatique de Georges le Métochite (1275–1276) et le Vat. gr. 1716," in M.-H. Laurent O.P., *Le bienheureux Innocent V (Pierre de Tarentaise) et son temps,* ST 129 (Vatican City, 1947), 435–39.

knew some Greek and had twice been sent as an ambassador to Constantinople.[59] He even wrote a treatise on the procession of the Holy Spirit, accepting the theological position of the Latins.[60] Thus, until the election in 1281 of French Pope Martin IV, Charles of Anjou received no papal support for a war against Byzantium.

But then things changed. The new pope encouraged the king of Sicily to proceed in his intentions against Byzantium and, on 3 July in Orvieto, then the papal residence, a treaty was signed

> *inter . . . Philippum, in Christo fidelissimum Imperatorem, Romanie moderatorem semper augustum, et Karolum, Regem Hierusalem, Sicilie, Ducatus Apulie . . . per se ipsos ex parte una; et magnificum virum dominum Joannem Dandulo, Dei gratia Venetorum, Dalmatie atque Chroacie ducem . . . de galeis et teridis mittendis et tenendis in mari per septem menses in anno usque ad illud tempus, quo fiet per ipsos passagium in Romaniam contra Paleologum et alios, qui tenent et occupant Imperium Romanie. . . . ad faciendam guerram et dompnificandum Paleologum et alios, qui occupant et detinent occupatum Imperium Romanie.*[61]

> [B]etween . . . Philip the most faithful emperor in Christ, the ruler of Romania, eternal augustus, and Charles, king of Jerusalem, Sicily, the duchy of Apulia . . . for themselves on one side and the magnificent ruler Lord Johannes Dandulo, by the grace of God dux of Venice, Dalmatia, and Croatia . . . concerning the dispatch and maintenance of galleys and cargo barges at sea for seven months in the year, until such time as to afford them passage to Romania against Paleologos and the others who hold and occupy the Roman empire. . . . to wage war upon and bring to submission Paleologos and the others who occupy and hold the Roman empire.

On 18 November, the pope excommunicated the Byzantine emperor,[62] but Michael VIII's delegates continued to frequent the papal court. There is an interesting note in a manuscript, now preserved in the library of Saint Catherine's Monastery on Mount Sinai (Sinait. gr. 50, fols. 262v–263v), recording that "The writing of this psalter has been

59 Giannelli, "Le récit," 441–43; M. P. Roncaglia, "Les Franciscains et les langues grecques et orientales au XIIIe siècle," in *Die islamische Welt zwischen Mittelalter und Neuzeit: Festschrift für Hans Robert Roemer zum 65. Geburtstag,* ed. U. Haarmann and P. Bachmann, Beiruter Texte und Studien 22 (Wiebaden, 1979), 540–42; A. Franchi, "Girolamo d'Ascoli: Origini e formazione culturale e religiosa," in *Niccolò IV: Un pontificato tra Oriente ed Occidente,* ed. E. Menestò, Atti del convegno internazionale di studi in occasione del VII centenario del pontificato di Niccolò IV, Ascoli Piceno (14–17 dicembre 1989) (Spoleto, 1991), 37; G. Barone, "Niccolò IV," in *Enciclopedia dei Papi* (Rome, 2000), 2:455–59.

60 Up to now only some fragments of the text have been published: PG 141:1405–20.

61 G. L. F. Tafel und G. M. Thomas, *Urkunden zur älteren Handels- und Staatsgeschichte der Republik Venedig mit besonderer Beziehung auf Byzanz und die Levante vom neunten bis zum ausgehenden fünfzehnten Jahrhundert,* vol. 3, *(1253–1298),* Fontes rerum austriacarum 2.14.3 (Vienna, 1857; repr. Amsterdam, 1964), no. CCCLXXIV, 296–98.

62 S. Cerrini, "Martino IV," in *Enciclopedia dei Papi,* 2:447.

finished by me the cleric John Drosinos from Constantinople, of Saint Anthony's Square, son of Drosinos Protos and Protena. It was written in Tuscany in the city of Orvieto at the court of the holy pope, the 25th of March, the day of the Holy Trinity in the year 6790,"[63] that is, 1282. Nothing more is known of John Drosinos.[64] He must have been pro-union, because he speaks of the "holy pope," and he had probably taken part in the last imperial embassy to the pope, although he and his colleagues could not convince Martin IV to change his mind.

On 31 March 1282—a few days after John Drosinos had finished the copy of his psalter at Orvieto—the rebellion of the so-called Vespers exploded in Palermo: Charles of Anjou was thrown out of Sicily by local barons and the navy of Peter of Aragon. Thus, the projected French crusade against Byzantium failed, and Byzantium was saved. In his autobiography, Michael VIII says that the Sicilians owed their freedom to God, but that he, Michael, had been God's tool.[65] Nikephoros Gregoras remarks: εἰ μὴ τηνικαῦτα τοιοῦτος βασιλεὺς [Michael VIII] τοῖς Ῥωμαίων ἐπεστάτει πράγμασι, ῥᾳδίως ἂν ὑπὸ τῷ ῥηγὶ τῆς Ἰταλίας Καρούλῳ ἡ Ῥωμαίων ἡγεμονία ἐγεγόνει ("If at the time such an emperor [Michael VIII] had not been in charge of the affairs of the Romans, the state of the Romans would have come easily under the power of King Charles of Italy").[66] The Sicilian Vespers eliminated the Angevin danger; thus, the Union of the Churches, which was highly unpopular in Byzantium, became redundant. After Michael VIII's death, Andronikos II exiled the more prominent pro-Unionists. George Metochites remained under arrest until his death in 1328; Constantine Meliteniotes had died in 1307.[67] We do not know what happened to John Drosinos of Saint Anthony's Square in Constantinople.

Greeks in Genoa and Venice

My third point regards the Greeks in Genoa and Venice. The Genoese, who had helped Michael VIII to reconquer Constantinople, were the principal winners of the revival of the Byzantine Empire in the old capital. They were rewarded with access to the Black Sea and the main commercial routes to the Far East. But Venice, which was well established on the Greek shores and islands, could not be ousted. Moreover, the Venetians had common geopolitical interests with Byzantium, as they could not allow access to the Adriatic Sea, that is, the western and the eastern shores of the Adriatic, to be controlled by one state. Thus, just as the Venetians had been the natural allies of Byzantium

63 + Ἐτελειώθη τὸ παρὸν ψαλτήριον διὰ χειρὸς ἐμοῦ τοῦ ἁμαρτωλοῦ Ἰωάννου τοῦ Δροσίνου τοῦ ἀπὸ Κοσταντινουπόλεως πλησίον τοῦ ἁγίου Ἀντωνίου τῆς πλατέας στράτας υἱοῦ τοῦ Δροσήνου τοῦ καὶ Πρώτου καὶ μητέρος τῆς Πρώτενας· ἐγράφη εἰς τὴν Τοσκάναν ἔνδοθεν κάστρου τοῦ Ὁρμπεβέτου εἰς τὴν κόρτην τοῦ ἁγίου πάπα, μηνὶ μαρτίῳ κε' ἡμέρα ἁγία τε καὶ μεγάλη Τριάδα ὥρα θ' ἔτους ,ςψϙ' ἰνδικτιῶνος ι'· εἰ μὲν χεὶρ ἡ γράψασα μέλλει σίπεσθαι τάφῳ, γραφὴ δαὶ μενῒ εἰς χρόνους πληρεστάτους +. H. Husmann, "Die datierten griechischen Sinai-Handschriften des 9.–16. Jahrhunderts," *OKS* 27 (1978): 151, reads "Drosimos."

64 *PLP*, no. 5856.

65 H. Grégoire, "Imperatoris Michaelis Palaeologi *De Vita sua*," *Byzantion* 29–30 (1959–60): 461.

66 Gregoras, 5.6 (1:144–45); Tsirpanlis, "Involvement" (above, n. 34), 312.

67 Giannelli, "Le récit" (above, n. 58), 425–26.

against the eastern expansion of the Normans, so they now joined temporarily with Byzantium against Charles of Anjou. During the second half of the thirteenth and throughout the fourteenth century, many truces and treaties between Byzantium and Genoa and between Byzantium and Venice were concluded, broken, redefined, and renewed. In the meantime, the two major sea powers of the Mediterranean fought their wars for predominance on Byzantine shores and waters, and blackmailed the emperor, who was never able to create a navy of his own for lack of money and nautical know-how. Thus, he tried more or less successfully to play Genoese against Venetians, and vice versa. Most of the treaties contain a paragraph on the rights of Byzantine merchants in the ports of Genoa[68] and Venice.[69] But these merchants rarely appear in the local documentation of our period.[70] The *logia Grecorum* at Genoa is not mentioned before the second half of the fourteenth century and apparently was not run by Greeks but Genoese.[71]

There is, however, some evidence for Greeks living in Venice and Genoa. After the Byzantine recovery of Constantinople, some Greeks and their families had moved to Venice, apparently with the assistance of Venetian authorities. In fact, in the summer of 1271, the major council deliberated about the status and rights of long-term Greek residents in Venice: they were free to move wherever they chose, but those who left the commune could not claim any financial support.[72] As for Genoa, in one of his vernacular poems, the so-called Anonimo Genovese, active in the period between 1283 and 1311,[73] gives a rather unkind description of a Greek living in his neighborhood (*contrada*): "In general every Greek is a mischief-maker, bad and arrogant, but the one in

68 14 March 1261: Pieralli, *La corrispondenza* (above, n. 3), 138: *Item quod omnes mercatores et singuli, qui sunt de terra nostri imperii, possint ire Ianuam et facere mercanciam et per totum districtum eius, quem habet et de cetero acquisierit, et extrahere de Ianua et districtu eius de omnibus mercimoniis et armis et equis libere sine aliqua dacita vel comergio et quod sint liberi et franchi in Ianua et districtu eius, quem habet et acquisierit, eundo et redeundo et quod custodiri debeant sani et naufragi.* 22 March 1308: L. T. Belgrano, "Prima serie di documenti riguardanti la colonia di Pera," *Atti della Società Ligure di Storia Patria* 13, no. 2 (1877): 112–13.

69 18 June 1265: Pieralli, *La corrispondenza*, 190: Ἵνα οἱ πραγματευταὶ τῆς χώρας τῆς βασιλείας μου οἱ μέλλοντες ἀπέρχεσθαι εἰς Βενετίαν ποιῶσι τὰς δοκούσας αὐτοῖς πραγματείας καὶ διδῶσι τὸ κομμέρκιον κατὰ τὴν συνήθειαν τῆς Βενετίας καὶ ἐξωνῶνται τὰ δοκοῦντα αὐτοῖς ἀνεμποδίστως, and ibid., 286, 298–99 (1277); M. Pozza and G. Ravegnani, *I trattati con Bisanzio 1265–1285,* Pacta Veneta 6 (Venice, 1996), 64 (1268), 104 (1277), 145 (1285).

70 For Venice, B. Imhaus, *Le minoranze orientali a Venezia, 1300–1510* (Rome, 1997), 435; D. Jacoby, "I Greci e altre comunità tra Venezia e oltremare," in *I Greci a Venezia: Atti del convegno internazionale di studio, Venezia, 5–7 novembre 1998*, ed. M. F. Tiepolo and E. Tonetti (Venzia, 2002), 44–48.

71 C. Otten-Froux, "Deux consuls des Grecs à Gêne à la fin du XIVe siècle," *REB* 50 (1992): 243–48; S. Origone, "La comunità e la loggia dei Greci a Genova," *Rivista di studi liguri* 71 (2005): 177–84.

72 Jacoby, "I Greci e altre comunità," 45–46; *Deliberazioni del Maggior Consiglio di Venezia,* vol. 2, ed. R. Cessi (Bologna, 1931), 153 (60): *Fuit capta pars quod de illis Grecis, qui sunt et steterunt longis temporibus in Veneciis, illi, qui vuluerint, tam masculi quam femine, habeant libertatem eundi, quo voluerint, et illi, qui ibunt, non debeant ullo tempore habere a Comuni aliquod pro expensis vel pro sallario.*

73 Anonimo Genovese, *Poesie,* ed. L. Cocito (Rome, 1970), 15–28.

our neighborhood is even worse than the others. If I do not treat him with the utmost politeness, he does not stop insulting me." In the end, the exasperated poet who compares his neighbor to an aggressive dog, prays to God that the devil should take him away.[74] Although the Anonimo Genovese does not mention Greeks in his other verses, this rimed invective is perhaps proof that Greek neighbors were not particularly rare in Genoa in this period.

Moreover, there must have been lower-class Greek immigration to Venice and Genoa of sailors and artisans.[75] A paragraph in the treaty of 1308 deals with young Byzantine subjects who had been convinced by Genoese citizens to move to the West and make their fortune in Genoa, where they were then sold as slaves.[76] Few cases are documented or published, but Greek slaves bought in *Romania*, especially females, are mentioned in Genoese and Venetian documents.[77]

In his *De itinere Terrae Sanctae,* written in about 1340, Ludolph de Suchem records of Athens: "This was once an exceeding noble city, but now is almost deserted; for there is scarce anywhere in Genoa a marble column or piece of good hewn stone which has not been brought thither from Athens, even as Venice is built of the stones of Troy."[78] We do not know where he got this information, which is not mentioned in other Genoese sources;[79] moreover, at least today, no marble *spolia* from Greece are visible in the town. His remark about Venice can be explained by the Venetian legend that the town was founded by refugees from Troy.[80] There is, however, evidence from Venetian documents

74 Anonimo Genovese, *Poesie,* no. 26, 208; Anonimo Genovese, *Rime e ritmi latini,* ed. J. Nicolas, Collezione di opere inedite o rare pubblicate dalla Commissione per i testi di lingua 149 (Bologna,1994), no. 26, 93: *Quasi ogni greco per comun / è lairaor, necho, e soperbo; / e in nostra contrá n'è un / chi de li aotri è pu axerbo. / Ché e' no l'alosengo tanto / che mai so crior se stagne; / semper m'aaguaita in calche canto / per adentarme le carcagne. / Doncha, se semper dè star re'/ e no mendar le overe torte, / e' prego l'aotissimo De'/ che ma<r> lovo ne lo porte./ Amen.*

75 Jacoby, "I Greci e altre comunità," 47; M. Balard, "Le minoranze orientali a Genova (secc. XIII–XV)," in *La Storia dei Genovesi,* vol. 3, Atti del Convegno Internazionale di Studi sui Ceti dirigenti nelle Istituzioni della Repubblica di Genova, Genova, 10–12 giugno 1982 (Genoa, 1983), 78–80; S. A. Epstein, *Speaking of Slavery: Color, Ethnicity, and Human Bondage in Italy* (Ithaca, 2001): 85–86.

76 Belgrano, "Prima serie" (above, n. 68), 113: *Item dicunt et exponunt quod aliqui Ianuenses induzerunt aliquos pueros et puellas grecas de Constantinopoli et de aliis terris Romanie, promittentes eis multa bona facere, ut cum eis Januam venirent; et multi et multe venerunt et cum fuerunt in civitate Janue vendiderunt eos et eas pro sclavis, quod est iniquum.* Origone, "La comunità e la loggia dei Greci," 173.

77 C. Verlinden, *L'esclavage dans l'Europe médiévale,* vol. 2, *Italie—Colonies italiennes du levant—Levant latin—Empire byzantin* (Ghent, 1977), 463–65, 554–65; Balard, "Le minoranze orientali," 74; idem, "La femme-esclave à Gêne à la fin du Moyen Âge," in *La femme au Moyen Âge,* ed. M. Rouche and J. Heuclin (Maubeuge, 1990), 299–310; Epstein, *Speaking of Slavery,* 82, 92–93.

78 *Ludolph von Suchem's Description of the Holy Land and the Way Thither, Written in the Year A.D. 1350,* trans. A. Stewart (London, 1895), 28.

79 R. Müller, *"Sic hostes Ianua frangit": Spolien und Trophäen im mittelalterlichen Genua,* Marburger Studien zur Kunst- und Kulturgeschichte 5 (Weimar, 2002), 105, n. 322.

80 A. Carile, "Le origini di Venezia nella tradizione storiografica," in *Storia della cultura veneta dalle origini al Trecento* (Vicenza, 1976), 1:147–52.

that during the thirteenth and early fourteenth century marble columns and slabs from Greece were exported to Venice.[81]

Greek artifacts[82] and artists were clearly most welcome in Venice and Genoa. Otto Demus wrote about Venice after 1261: "A new wave of Byzantine influence seems to have reached Venice, namely the impact of the renascent art of Byzantium,"[83] and Greek artisans worked in the glass factories of Murano.[84] Robert Nelson has attributed to a Greek painter the fresco of the Last Judgment in the cathedral of Genoa, which he dates to the first decade of the fourteenth century,[85] and mentions a Greek painter, *magister Marchus Grecus pintor qui fui de Constantinopoli,* who is attested in a Genoese document of 1313.[86] Greek painters were working in the Latin churches in Pera,[87] so it is easy to presume that some of them had additional commissions in Genoa.

81 A. Lombardo, *Pasquale Longo: Notaio in Corone 1289–1293,* Monumenti storici pubblicati dalla Deputazione di Storia Patria per le Venezie, n.s. 6 (Venice, 1951), 42–43, no. 55 (1291); F. Thiriet, *Délibérations des assemblées vénitennes concernant la Romanie* (Paris and La Haye, 1966), 1:122–23 (1309).

82 The *Inventarium paramentorum* of the cardinal Luca Fieschi († 1336) mentions a number of precious textiles, though not the most expensive ones, said to have been produced in Cyprus, Romania, or Greece:

> *una planeta de samito cremesino laborata in Cipro ad aquilas aureas cum frisio et stellis et perlis, due gramite laborate ad aurum et aves cum acu facte in Romania, due gramite cum pectorali facte in Grecia et laborate de auro cum imaginibus apostolorum et domini nostri, unum par de pugnalibus cum mediis imaginibus factis in Grecia sutis in tela alba, stola et manipulus de opere Grecie laborati ad medias imagines fodrate de sindone rubeo, una stola et duo manipuli de seta cum compassibus et foiaciis laborati in Cipro, domus de opere de Grecia cum figura domini nostri stantis in cruce et ex alia parte domine nostre iacentis in partu, una mitra facta in Grecia cum perlis et esmaltis de vitro, unum pluviale antiquum suprasanutum azurrinum laboratum in Grecia ad angelos et imagines cum coronis.*

A. Sisto, *Genova nel Duecento: Il capitolo di S. Lorenzo,* Collana storica di Fonti e Studi diretta da Geo Pistarino 28 (Genoa, 1979), 195, 197–200.

83 O. Demus, *The Church of San Marco in Venice: History, Architecture, Sculpture,* DOS 6 (Washington, DC, 1960), 146.

84 C. Maltézou, "Un artisan verrier crétois à Venise," in *Chemins d'outre-mer: Études sur la Méditerranée médiévale offertes à Michel Balard,* ed. D. Coulon et al., Byzantina Sorbonensia 20 (Paris, 2004), 2:539–40.

85 R. S. Nelson, "A Byzantine Painter in Trecento Genoa: The Last Judgement at S. Lorenzo," *ArtB* 67 (1985): 548–66.

86 Ibid., 555; C. Di Fabio, "Bisanzio a Genova fra XII e XIV secolo: Documenti e memorie d'arte," in *Genova e l'Europa mediterranea: Opere, artisti, committenti, collezionisti,* ed. P. Boccardo and C. Di Fabio (Milan, 2005), 42, 54–62; R. S. Nelson, "Byzantine Icons in Genoa before the *Mandylion,*" in *Intorno al Sacro Volto: Genoa, Bisanzio e il Metiterraneo (secoli XI–XIV),* ed. A. R. Calderoni Masetti, C. Dufour Bozzo, and G. Wolf (Venice, 2007), 79–92.

87 S. Westphalen, "Pittori greci nella chiesa domenicana dei Genovesi a Pera (Arap Camii): Per la genesi di una cultura figurativa levantina nel Trecento," in *Intorno al sacro Volto,* 51–62; idem, "Die Dominikanerkirche der Genuesen von Pera (Arap Camii): Griechische Maler—Lateinische Auftraggeber," in *Austausch und Inspiration: Kulturkontakt als Impuls architektonischer Innovation,* ed. F. Pirson and U. Wulff-Rheidt (Mainz, 2008) 281–89; H. Çetinkaya, "Arap Camii in Istanbul: Its Architecture and Frescoes," *Anatolia Antiqua* 18 (2010): 169–88.

In his first treaty with Genoa, Michael VIII had promised to send *palium unum deauratum* to the archbishop of the town each year.[88] One is displayed in Genoa in the Museo di Sant'Agostino; until 1633, it had been preserved in the treasury of the local cathedral. In ten scenes the *pallio* illustrates the life and martyrdom of Saint Lawrence, Genoa's holy patron, including one of the emperor Michael Palaiologos being guided by the saint to the church of Genoa with the Latin inscription: *S(anctus) Laur(entius) induce(n)s Altissimum Imp(er)atorem Gr(a)eco(rum) D(omi)n(u)m Mich(ae)l(em) Duca(m) Ang(e)l(um) Co(m)nenu(m) Paleologu(m) in ecc(les)iam Jan(uae) or Juan(uensium).*[89] All the embroidered captions on the pallium are in Latin and are original, not interventions by a later restorer. In an encomium addressed to Michael VIII, the Byzantine rhetorician Manuel Holobolos in fact describes this πέπλος, dedicated by the emperor to Genoa, which displays as in a book "οἱ τοῦ καλλινίκου μάρτυρος Λαυρεντίου καὶ τῶν σὺν αὐτῷ περιφανεῖς ἐνεχαράχθησαν ἀγῶνες καὶ τὰ μέχρι θανάτου διὰ Χριστὸν σκάμματα . . . ὧν ἕκαστον καὶ ἐπιστήμασι δι' Ἰταλικῶν γραμμάτων ἐνεσημαίνετο . . . οὐ πέπλος ὁ πέπλος ἦν, ἀλλὰ βίβλος" (the splendid struggles and trials to the death of the glorious martyr Laurence and those with him . . . each of which was depicted in figures with Latin letters . . . the robe was not a robe, but a book).[90]

A pallium with similar iconography but apparently with some captions in Greek is described in the inventory of the treasure of Pope Boniface VIII (1295):

> *Item, unum pannum pro dorsale, totum laboratum de argento tractitio, et in aliquibus partibus et figuris de argento tractitio non deaurato, in quo est imago Salvatoris deaurata cujus vestimenti plicature distincte sunt cum pernis et est in quodam circulo oblongo de argento albo et precedunt due vites cum foliis viridibus et uvis de pernis minutis: que vites quasi extendunt per totum dorsale: super imagine Salvatoris est quedam pars ad modum celi de argento albo tractitio in quo est quedam manus desuper benedicens, iiij. cherubini et in medio eorum quedam avis et a quolibet latere dictorum cherubinorum sunt ij. angeli majores quasi extra celum; in pede Salvatoris est media imago Virginis in quodam throno habens quasdam imagines sanctorum a latere cum libris in manibus; et subtus dictas figuras est imago B. Petri, coram quo est imago domini Gregorii tenentis per manum Paleologum et presentat eum beato Petro reconciliatum, cum litteris grecis et latinis; et per pannum sunt multe historie apostolorum, prout predicaverunt et battizaverunt, cum litteris grecis et latinis, in provinciis eis decretis; in circuitu vero dicti panni sunt littere grece et*

88 Pieralli, *La corrispondenza* (above, n. 3),136.

89 P. Johnstone, "The Byzantine 'Pallio' in the Palazzo Bianco at Genova," *GBA* 87 (1976): 99–108; C. J. Hilsdale, "The Imperial Image at the End of Exile: The Byzantine Embroidered Silk in Genoa and the Treaty of Nymphaion (1261)," *DOP* 64 (2010): 150–99; I. Toth, "The Narrative Fabric of the Genoese *Pallio* and the Silken Diplomacy of Michael VIII Palaiologos," in *Objects in Motion: The Circulation of Religion and Sacred Objects in the Late Antique and Byzantine World,* ed. H. G. Meredith, BAR International Series 2247 (Oxford, 2011), 91–109.

90 X. A. Siderides, "Μανουὴλ Ὁλοβώλου ἐγκώμιον εἰς τὸν αὐτοκράτορα Μιχαὴλ Η΄ τὸν Παλαιολόγον," *Ἐπ.Ἑτ.Βυζ.Σπ.* 3 (1926): 186–89; Toth, "Narrative Fabric," 96–99.

latine, et perne per circuitum dicti panni; et per diademata sanctorum et imaginum et per plicaturas vestium sunt perne; et est dictus pannus foderatus de xamito rubeo et habet dictus pannus v. annulos argenti deauratos a quolibet latere.

Item, a cloth for a dossal, entirely worked in silver thread, and in various places and figures with silver thread, ungilded, among which is the figure of Christ in gold thread, the folds of whose garments are picked out with pearls. He is within a mandorla of white silver from which run two vines with green leaves and grapes formed of seed pearls: the vines cover almost the whole dossal. Above Christ is an area representing heaven, embroidered with white silver in which appear a blessing hand above four cherubim and in the center a certain bird (!), and on either side of the cherubim are two archangels almost outside of heaven. At Christ's feet, in the center, is the Virgin enthroned, with saints holding books on either side. Beneath these figures appears the lord Gregory, holding the Palaeologus by the hand and presenting him to Saint Peter in token of reconciliation with inscriptions in Greek and Latin. And there are many scenes of the Apostles preaching and baptizing in their respective regions with Greek and Latin inscriptions. Greek and Latin inscriptions run around the border of the panel and pearls. For the haloes of the saints and the folds of the robes, pearls are used. The frontal is lined with red samite and it has five gilt silver rings at each side.[91]

Obviously, not only the diplomats and some theologians but also the imperial silk manufactury worked for the Union of the Churches.

Dynastic Connections

The last stage of our journey in search of Greeks in Dante's Italy takes us to the marquisate of Montferrat in present-day Piedmont. As we have already noted, the fourteen-year-old Theodore Komnenos Doukas Angelos Palaiologos became marquis of Montferrat in 1306 and ruled that state until his death, in 1338. Theodore was the second son of Andronikos II and Yolanda of Montferrat, the emperor's second wife. Since the Komnenian period it was common, if not the rule, for Byzantine emperors to marry princesses from Western Europe and to give their daughters or nieces in marriage to Western princes. In 1261, Michael VIII had given Eudokia, one of the daughters of Theodore II Laskaris, in marriage to the Genoese count William Peter of Ventimiglia, who had been prisoner of war in Constantinople; after the wedding the couple was sent back to Liguria.[92] The marquises of

91 É. Molinier, "Inventaire du Trésor du Saint Siège sous Boniface VIII (1295): (Suite[1])," *Bibliothèque de l'École des Chartes* 46 (1885): no. 811, 18–19; the translation is from J. Gardner, *The Roman Crucible* (Rome, 2013), 332–33; Johnstone, "Byzantine 'Pallio'," 100–101.

92 L. T. Belgrano, "Cinque documenti genovesi-orientali," *Atti della Società ligure di storia patria* 17 (1885): 227–29; S. Origone, "Oriente e Occidente: Bisanzio e i Lascaris di Ventimiglia," in *La Storia dei Genovesi,* Atti del Convegno di studi sui ceti dirigenti nelle istituzioni della Repubblica di Genova, Genova, 10–11–12 Giugno 1987 (Genoa, 1988), 427–38.

Montferrat had had strong ties with the Byzantine Empire since the reign of Manuel I.[93] After 1204, Boniface of Montferrat became king of Thessalonike, the city where, after her marriage, Yolanda resided for many years. When, in 1305, Yolanda's brother, the marquis of Montferrat, died childless, she became his legal heir and appointed one of her sons as his successor. Her firstborn, John, was too close in the line of imperial succession, as there was only one elder brother from Andronikos's first marriage, Michael IX. Therefore, his father, as well as the patriarch Athanasios, opposed John's nomination out of fear that such a young man might not be able to preserve his faith while living "in a foreign land, inhabited by barbarians, by an utterly arrogant and most insolent nation which has lost all sense." Should he have succeeded his father on the throne of Constantinople, he would have been spiritually contaminated by this exposure to a Latin environment.[94] The third son, Demetrios, was still a child. Thus, Theodore was chosen. He was at once married to Argentina, daughter of Opizzino Spinola, member of one of the leading Genoese families. In Byzantium this marriage was considered a misalliance,[95] but without the assistance of the Genoese fleet Theodore would have never reached his marquisate. We do not know how well the young prince was prepared for his new job: whether he knew the language of the foreign country to which he was sent, or whether he was accompanied by Greek officials from the emperor's entourage to help him with the government. Most likely he was not and was guided and helped by his father-in-law and the latter's Genoese allies. There is no evidence of a Greek court at Chivasso or Trina, the towns where he resided, and the officials mentioned in his documents are local *iurisperiti* or members of the feudal aristocracy of the marquisate.[96] As for his religion, he must have converted to Roman Catholicism on his political appointment and marriage.

Apparently, Theodore did not consider his Italian position to be permanent. Twice he returned to Byzantium, each time for a period of about two years: in 1317, when, after the birth of his daughter, the legitimate succession in Montferrat was guaranteed, and then in 1326, after the birth of his son and the death of his elder brother in Constantinople.[97] In a brief autobiographical note, Theodore states the main reason for his two trips home was a desire to employ his advice and experience to help his father,

93 P. Magdalino, *The Empire of Manuel I Komnenos, 1143–1180* (Cambridge, 1993), 100–101.

94 A. E. Laiou, "A Byzantine Prince Latinized: Theodore Palaeologus, Marquis of Montferrat, *Byzantion* 38 (1968): 386–410; *The Correspondence of Athanasius I, Patriarch of Constantinople: Letters to the Emperor Andronicus II, Members of the Imperial Family and Officials,* ed. A.-M. M. Talbot, CFHB 7 (Washington, DC, 1975), no. 84, 220–26.

95 Gregoras, 7.5 (1:237–44).

96 P. Grillo, "Il governo del Marchesato," in *"Quando venit marchio grecus in terra Montisferrati": L'avvento di Teodoro I Paleologo nel VII centenario (1306–2006),* ed. A. A. Settia, Atti del convegno di studi, 14–15 ottobre 2006, Casale di Monferrato, Moncalvo, Serralunga di Crea (Casale Monferrato, 2008), 103–17.

97 A. Kiesewetter, "Markgraf Theodoros Palaiologos von Monferrat (1306–1338), seine *Enseignements* und Byzanz," *Medioevo greco* 3 (2003): 145–56, 160–68.

the emperor, against his enemies, the Turks and Tartars;[98] but this may have been only a pretext. He was probably looking for a more promising imperial position in the East. When, in 1319, Theodore returned to Italy from his first trip, he was accompanied by the *nuntius* Stephanos Syropoulos, one of his father's trusted officials who was apparently considered an expert on northern Italy.[99] In the parliament of Montferrat, Syropoulos declared that Andronikos II, *imperator et moderator Romanorum,* considered the marquisate a part (*membrum*) of his empire, and that he promised help on the condition that his subjects showed *constantiam, fidem perfectam, obedientiam debitam erga imperium nostrum et carissimum filium imperii nostri.*[100] This can be little but mere rhetoric when we consider that the Eastern Roman emperor, in all his dealings with Western European countries, was completely dependent on the ships of Venice and Genoa.

In Byzantium, however, Theodore was not at all welcome. According to Nikephoros Gregoras, he was too Latinized: "in his judgment, in his faith, in his manners, and with his shaved beard he was a pure Latin."[101] Moreover, he was considered a political troublemaker who had come just to extort money from his father. No one trusted him, and he was not given any commission.[102] There is, however, no evidence that he tried to influence his father in favor of the Union of the Churches. In his autobiographical note, Theodore says that he returned to Italy in 1328 for three reasons: first, because he understood that things in the empire were going from bad to worse (*praefatum imperium male fore dispositum*) and there seemed to be no remedy; second, because he had heard about a rebellion in his marquisate; and third, because of the *invidia aliorum Graecorum magnatum,* especially of Theodore Metochites, whom he describes as an omnipotent, vain, evil, and corrupt minister of his father.[103] Byzantines love to mention "envy," φθόνος, whenever anything goes wrong.[104] This is a real topos in Byzantine literature. In this respect, Theodore was a real Byzantine. In the West he was considered a Greek in the traditional pejorative sense: an ambassador from Aragon describes him as *magnus et potens in Ytalia set miser et nullius audacie sive strenuitatis, sicut qui est naturaliter et a progenitoribus suis Grecis.*[105]

98 C. Knowles, *Les Enseignements de Théodore Paléologue,* Texts and Dissertations 19, French series (London, 1983), 36–38.

99 See above, nn. 40–42.

100 W. Haberstumpf, "Tra Monferrato e Bisanzio: un testamento del 1338 di Teodoro Paleologo," *Quaderni Medievali* 19 (1985): 37.

101 Gregoras, 9.1 (1:396): καὶ γνώμῃ καὶ πίστει καὶ σχήματι καὶ γενείων κουρᾷ καὶ πᾶσιν ἔθεσιν Λατῖνος ἦν ἀκραιφνής.

102 Ibid.; Knowles, *Les Enseignements,* 39–40.

103 Knowles, *Les Enseignements,* 40–41; de Vries-van der Velden, *Théodore Métochite* (above, n. 57), 240–47.

104 M. Hinterberger, "Phthonos als treibende Kraft in Prodromos, Manasses und Bryennios," *Medioevo greco* 11 (2011): 83–106.

105 H. Finke, *Acta Aragonensia* (Berlin and Leipzig, 1908), 1: no. 266, p. 403; Haberstumpf, "Tra Monferrato," 43; idem, "Cartario dei documenti latini editi riguardanti i Marchesi di Monferrato per l'Oriente (quinta e ultima parte)," *Monferrato Arte e Storia* 11 (1999): 163.

Theodore was, however, a well-educated Greek. Like many Byzantine princes and emperors, but unlike most of his contemporary Western European rulers, he was a writer. During his last stay in Constantinople he wrote a treatise on military tactics, Ποίημα περὶ πριγκίπων ἀναγωγῆς καὶ πολεμικῆς τέχνης, to demonstrate, as he remarks, his potential in words, as he had not been allowed to prove himself by deeds.[106] The treatise is a strange mixture of a *speculum principis* and military strategical treatise. Back in Montferrat, he translated the text into Latin, for by now the treatise was addressed to Western readers who did not understand Greek, and he added a short autobiography as an introduction. The original Greek text is lost. Parts of the Latin translation have been preserved in the chronicle of Benvenuto da Sangiorgio, but the entire treatise exists only in a French translation by Jean de Vignay under the title *Enseignements et ordenances pour un seigneur qui a guerres et grans gouvernemens a faire.*[107] A second treatise, also preserved only in the French translation of Jean de Vignay, is entitled *Divisions sur la maniere des richeces et povretez de ce monde.*[108] Theodore probably wrote this last text at the end of his life; it reveals a rather disillusioned view of the world and humanity.

Although in 1328 Theodore had returned from Byzantium disappointed in his expectations and skeptical about the future of the Eastern Roman empire—*praefatum imperium male fore dispositum*—he persisted until his death in 1338 in the hope that he or his descendants might eventually be reestablished in Constantinople. In his will, he mentions the possibility that his son might return to *partes ultramarinas.*[109] Similarly, the popes, in particular John XXII, and various pretenders in Italy to the throne of the Latin Empire, considered Theodore and his offspring as useful links for an eventual revival of the Latin Empire in Constantinople.[110] As late as 1372, Theodore's son, the marquess John II, claimed in his testament that *cumque Imperium predictum Graecorum, videlicet Constantinopolitanum et Romaniae de iure pertineret ad eundem D. Theodorum filium dicti D. Imperatoris per testamentum factum per dictum Imperatorum Andronicum.*[111]

But now I have overstepped my chronological limit: Dante died in 1321 and Theodore in 1338. It is significant that, despite the frequent contacts with Byzantium and the continuous arrival of educated and even learned Greeks, interest in and

106 Knowles, *Les Enseignements,* 40–41.

107 Ibid., 23.

108 M. Di Branco and A. Izzo, *L'Elogio della sconfitta: Un trattato inedito di Teodoro Paleologo, marchese di Monferrato* (Rome, 2014), 22–29, 60–80. I am grateful to the authors, who allowed me to read their text before publication.

109 W. Haberstumpf, "Due documenti inediti di Teodoro I Paleologo marchese di Monferrato," *Bollettino storico-bibliografico subalpino* 83 (1985): 215–17.

110 U. V. Bosch, "Ein 'Testament' des Kaisers Andronikos II. Palaiologos," *Zbornik radova Vizantinološkog instituta* 12 (1970): 57–59; Kiesewetter, "Markgraf Theodoros Palaiologos" (above, n. 97), 168–80.

111 Benvenuto di San Giorgio, *Historia Montisferrati,* in Muratori, *Scriptores Rerum Italicarum* 23 (Milan, 1733), 576; Bosch, "Ein 'Testament'," 56.

reception of Greek language and culture in Dante's Italy was apparently minimal, with the possible exception of some Franciscans.[112] Only in the following decades did new generations of Italian writers and scholars, taught by Byzantine immigrants such as Leontius Pilatus[113] and Manuel Chrysoloras, or by Greeks from southern Italy who had studied in Constantinople and other cities of the empire, such as Barlaam, transform the intellectual climate of the country. But they may be the protagonists of another essay.

112 Roncaglia, "Les Franciscains" (above, n. 59), 540–42; C. M. Mazzucchi, "Un testimone della conoscenza del greco negli ordini mendicanti verso la fine del Duecento (Ambr. Q 74 sup.) e un codice appartenuto al Sacro Convento d'Assisi (Ambr. E 88 inf.)," *Νέα Ῥώμη* 3 (2006): 355–59.

113 A. Rollo, in *Petrarca e il mondo greco: Leonzio lettore dell'Ecuba nella Firenze di Boccaccio,* Quaderni petrarcheschi 12–13 (Florence, 2007), 10–19, has presented convincing arguments that Leontius Pilatus was born and received his early education in Thessalonike.

Change and Continuity

Italian Culture and Greek Learning in the Age of Dante

RÉKA FORRAI

William of Moerbeke, the last great medieval translator, famous for his rendering of Aristotle's works, died in 1286. In 1342, Petrarch began studying Greek with Leontius Pilatus, the translator of Homer. These two dates, coinciding roughly with Dante's lifetime (1265–1321), mark the end and the beginning of two eras. By the end of the thirteenth century, the medieval canon of Greek lore had solidified only to be replaced by the new humanist trends in the fourteenth and fifteenth centuries. Greek learning in the West underwent a crucial change in scope and content. The list of Latin translations was expanded and reevaluated, as the medieval interest in Christian Greek literature and Aristotelian philosophy faded in favor of works by the classical pagan poets, orators, and historians preferred by the humanists. As Greek teachers and, with them, grammars, arrived in the West, the study of Greek became systematic, institutional, and much more popular. The agents involved in this new field also had a different social status than their medieval counterparts; the monopoly on Greek learning shifted from clerics to lay intellectuals, and patronage from the Church to political leaders. Moreover, this new culture of Greek learning took shape not in Rome, formerly a key area for Greek-Latin contacts, but in Dante's hometown: while Moerbeke accomplished many of his translations at Viterbo, Leontius was giving his Greek courses in Florence.[1]

For learning Greek, therefore, Dante was born in the right place but perhaps not the right time. His acquaintance with the Greek language and Greek books remains superficial and hard to document. Yet discussing his exposure to Greek matters will be informative: Dante, extraordinary as he was, was also ordinary insofar as he was a representative figure of an emerging social stratum, that of lay intellectuals.[2] While he

1 R. Weiss, "Gli inizi dello studio del Greco a Firenze," in *Medieval and Humanist Greek* (Padua, 1977), 227–54.
2 R. Imbach, *Dante, la philosophie et les laïcs* (Paris, 1996).

was never to become a main protagonist in the great transformation sketched above, placing him in the context of Greek learning of the thirteenth and fourteenth centuries may help us to understand the problems of accessibility and availability of Greek in late medieval Europe.

In trying to position him in this linguistic landscape, I will deal with the Greek knowledge of the historical Dante, not Dante the literary character,[3] and his interest in texts rather than his vision of Greek culture,[4] his awareness of the language, and his acquaintance with Greek works in translation. From the peripheral view of Dante's Greek I will then move toward an overview of the characters who played a central role in producing and disseminating translations. Viewed on its own, Dante's scattered knowledge of Greek culture might perhaps be disappointing, but placed in context, it will help illuminate the changes and continuities in the dramatically transforming late medieval Italian cultural landscape.

A myth in Dante's biography has him teaching Greek to a young man from Gubbio during his exile. "Happily for him [i.e., the young man], this was before the days of examinations!" remarked Edward Moore in his work on Dante's biographers.[5] The origin of this myth is found in an apocryphal Dante sonnet, addressed to a certain Bosone da Gubbio,[6] congratulating him on his son's progress in the study of French and Greek:

Ponti sera e mattin contento al desco,
Poichè del car figliuol vedi presente
Il frutto che sperasti e si repente
S'avaccia nello stil greco e francesco.[7]

From the early commentators on, the received wisdom has been that Dante did not know Greek. Still, contrary opinions have sprung up every now and then, particularly in the eighteenth and nineteenth centuries. Those who take the above-quoted sonnet as fact cite as corroborating evidence a manuscript from the Bibliotheca Laurenziana (Florence, Bibliotheca Laurenziana, Plut. 13.16), which contains the *Liber de Teleutelogio* of one Sebastiano Eugubino. There Dante is mentioned as the author's teacher.[8] Sebastiano's family ties with Bosone were merely conjectures, and the passage does not mention any Greek tutoring, but this did not stop further speculation. Bandini's catalogue entry

3 See G. Most, "Dante's Greeks," *Arion* 13, no. 3 (2006): 15–48.

4 See P. Renucci, *Dante: Disciple et juge du monde greco-latin* (Paris, 1954).

5 E. Moore, *Dante and His Early Biographers* (London, 1890), 89.

6 Cf. P. Bertolini, "Bosone da Gubbio," in *Dizionario Biografico degli Italiani* (Rome, 1971), 13:274–77.

7 P. Fratricelli, *Opere minori di Dante Alighieri*, vol. 1, *Il canzoniere di Dante Alighieri* (Florence, 1894), 282.

8 Fol. 209v: "Dantem Alighierii . . . tuae a teneris annis adolescentiae praeceptorem."

also suggests that Sebastiano might be the erudite son of Bosone, who was well versed in Latin and Greek.[9]

Baldassare Lombardi, in his commentary to the *Commedia* published in 1791–92, speculated that although Dante did not know Greek while composing the *Convivio*, he must have learned it before writing the *Commedia* or he would not have understood Virgil's allusions:

> *nella Commedia ne dà il Poeta moltissimi contrassegni di perizia del Greco linguaggio; massimamente, come già avvisai* Inf. *XIV, 134 e seg., ove fa da Virgilio pretendersi che dal Greco nome "Flegetonte" dovesse Dante di per se intendere, che il così appellato fiume fosse appunto quel medesimo in cui vedeva "il bollor dell'acqua rossa."*[10]
>
> The poet, in his Comedy, gives many indications of his competence in Greek; most importantly, as I have already noted, in *Inferno* 14.134 and below, where he makes Virgil expect that from the Greek word "Flegetonte" Dante must understand that the river with this name is the same in which he saw the "red and seething water."

Giuseppe Pelli, an early nineteenth-century *dantista*, devoted five pages to the question "se Dante avesse alcuna tintura della lingua greca." (He also summarizes opinions on the subject by his contemporaries.) Pelli's main argument is an anachronistic, rhetorical question that presupposes Dante to have behaved according to citation standards of modern times: "E come poteva conoscere di quali encomi era degno il Padre della Greca Eloquenza, Omero, e con tanta venerazione e lode nominarlo nella sua Commedia, se la feconda poesia di questo non avesse gustata nella lettura de' suoi Poemi?"[11] (How could he have known what praises Homer, the Father of Greek Eloquence, was worthy of, if he could not have tasted his prolific poetry by reading his works?)

Antonio Lubin, another nineteenth-century Dante scholar, argued along the same lines in his edition of the *Commedia* but from a moral standpoint; he was incapable of imagining Dante faking knowledge of Greek:

> *E qui mi cade opportuno il dire, che Dante dovea avere conoscenza del greco; altrimenti non avrebbe egli usato nelle sue opere tante parole greche; e meno poi sarebbesi arrogato l'ufficio di maestro col darne l'etimologia di parecchie, e se composte, darne il significato di ciascuna componente. Questa sarebbe stata peggio che saccenteria: una impostura, indegna di Dante.*[12]

9 "qui in Grecis Latinisque litteris, prout ea ferebat aetas, mirificos progressus fecerat." A. M. Bandini, *Catalogus codicum manuscriptorum Bibliothecae Mediceae Laurentianae varia continens Opera Graecorum Patrum*, vol. 1 (Florence, 1764), col. 62, note 2.

10 Text available online via the Dartmouth Dante Project: http://dante.dartmouth.edu/biblio.php?comm_id=17915 (accessed 20 July 2013).

11 G. Pelli, *Memorie per servire alla vita di Dante Alighieri ed all storia della sua famiglia* (Venice, 1758; 2nd rev. ed. Florence, 1823), 85–89.

12 A. Lubin, *Commedia di Dante Alighieri preceduta dalla vita e da studi preparatori illustrativi* (Padua, 1881), 88.

> It seems proper to say here that Dante must have had knowledge of Greek, otherwise, he wouldn't have used so many Greek works in his writings—and he certainly wouldn't have taken on the role of teacher, giving the etymologies of any Greek words, and explaining the components of words formed from Greek roots. That would have been worse than presumptuous: it would have been a fraud, unworthy of Dante.

Hoping to close a futile debate, the Italian philologist Gino Funaioli wrote:

> *Il greco, è naturale, non lo seppe; e vanamente si affaticò questo o quel dantista sopra un problema che non esiste per chi sa quali furono le sorti di questa lingua nel Medio Evo occidentale e particolarmente nel centro e nel nord d'Italia. Fantasticare di greco sulla voce chioccia e informe di Pluto "papé Satàn, papé Satàn" è ingenua oziosaggine.*[13]
>
> Naturally, he didn't know Greek, and one Dante scholar after another has worn himself out in vain over a problem that doesn't even exist for those who really know about the vagaries of this language in the medieval West—especially in central and northern Italy! Speculating on Pluto's harsh and ill-formed words (Pape Satan Pape Satan) is an ingenious pasttime.

Readdressing the problem is a bit more than ingenious pastime. Even if Dante's own Greek was minimal, we should not underestimate the presence of Greek in central and northern Italy during the Middle Ages. Besides, arguing that *papé* is Greek is not the wildest possibility: there is a Latin interjection *papae,* which derives from the Greek *παπαί*. It features in a Latin dictionary that Dante was using, that of Huguccio of Pisa (d. 1210): "pape—interjectio admirantis."[14]

A few additional, more meaningful Greek words appear in Dante's work, mainly in the *Commedia* and *Convivio*. The databases of The Princeton Dante Project list thirteen occurrences of the terms *greco* and *Greci*, usually to mark a Greek concept in the text.[15] Paget Toynbee, in his work on Dante's Latin dictionary, notes seventeen Greek terms used by Dante.[16] Two major types occur: Greek technical (scientific or philosophical) terms, and etymological explanations of the components of Latin neologisms of Greek origins. These occasional usages do not point to Dante's *further* knowledge of Greek; rather, they constitute the complete range of his *actual* knowledge of Greek.

An example of his use of scientific vocabulary is in the *Convivio,* where he uses the term *hormen* and defines it as "il appetito d'animo naturale."[17] Dante probably had in

13 G. Funaioli, "Dante e il mondo antico," in *Medioevo e Rinascimento: Studi in onore di Bruno Nardi* (Florence, 1955), 323–38.

14 See P. Toynbee, "Dante's Latin Dictionary," in *Dante Studies and Researches* (London, 1902), 112.

15 http://etcweb.princeton.edu/dante/index.html (accessed 20 July 2013).

16 Toynbee, "Dante's Latin Dictionary," 101–8.

17 It appears twice in the text: "l'appetito de l'animo, lo quale in greco e chiamato hormen" (*Conv.* 5.21); "che li Greci chamano hormen, cioe appetito d'animo naturale" (*Conv.* 4.12).

mind the Greek word ὁρμή, meaning "impulse" or "impetus," but his use of the accusative betrays the source as Cicero's *De finibus*, where the term is also used in the accusative case to mean "an impulse of desire, what in Greek is called hormen."[18]

Another technical term, *antomata* (*Purg.* 10.124–29),[19] has long vexed commentators. Some suspected it to be *entomon*, neuter of ἔντομος, "to be cut off," and concluded that Dante used the word to signify an insect. Lorenzo Minio-Paluello demonstrated that it is, instead, αὐτόματον, a technical term from the biological works of Aristotle, denoting spontaneous, involuntary action.[20]

Greek etymologies for Latin words (mostly compounds) appear often in the *Convivio*. For instance, Dante explains the words *autore* and *autoritade* with reference to the Greek term *autentin*, probably αὐθεντήν from αὐθεντέω, "to have power, authority" (*Conv.* 4.6). Here, he also quotes his source as Huguccio of Pisa's *Derivationes*. He also delights in offering simple explanations of the derivation of such terms as peripatetics, "Peripatetici che tanto vale quanto deambulatori" (*Conv.* 4.6), and philosophy, "amatore di sapienza chiamato, cioe filosofo, che tanto vale in greco philos, com'e a dire amore in latino, e quindi dicemo noi philos quasi amore, e sophia quasi sapienza" (*Conv.* 3.11).

In these cases, Dante's Greek words derive from Latin dictionaries and philosophical writings. This was not unusual. In very few cases can one find what we would call a "genuine" knowledge of Greek in the Latin Middle Ages. Few could understand, read, speak, write, and translate the language, but most intellectuals of the time had a rudimentary knowledge of Greek vocabulary, chiefly philosophical or technical terms gleaned from Latin works or bilingual editions of biblical texts, most often the Psalms. The standard education in Latin made use of a large group of texts with lexical content. Huguccio of Pisa's *Derivationes*, mentioned above, is a major lexicographical treatise from the end of the twelfth century. Many of the grammatical works of John of Garland (ca. 1190–1270) make frequent mention of Greek expressions. Guilelmus Brito's (ca. 1165–1226) *Brito metricus* is a poem of some 2,000 leonine hexameters on Greek and Hebrew words.

18 Cicero, *De finibus* 5.6.17: "appetitum animi, quem ορμεν Graeci vocant."

19 *non v'accorgete voi che noi siam vermi*
nati a formar l'angelica farfalla,
che vola a la giustizia sanza schermi?
Di che l'animo vostro in alto galla,
poi siete quasi antomata in difetto,
sì come vermo in cui formazion falla? (*Purg.* 10.124–29)

Do you not see that we are born as worms
though able to transform into angelic butterflies
that unimpeded soar to justice?
What makes your mind rear up so high?
You are, as it were, defective creatures,
like the unformed worm, shaped from the mud.

(trans. R. Hollander and J. Hollander)

20 L. Minio-Paluello, "'*Antomata' Purg.* 10.128 e i testi latini della biologia di Aristotele," in *Luoghi cruciali in Dante*, ed. F. Santi (Spoleto, 1993), 71–109.

Eberhard of Béthune's *Graecismus* (ca. 1212), a didactic poem on Latin grammar, has an ample section on Greek names. In about 1275, the English friar William of Mara composed a treatise on the Greek alphabet. The Flemish Franciscan Gerard of Huy's so-called *Triglossos* was a verse guide to the study of the three sacred languages.[21] From this group of texts, three were available in Florence at the turn of the century: the Santa Croce library possessed the works of John of Garland, William of Mara, and Huguccio of Pisa. Dante made use of Huguccio's *Derivationes* on more than the one occasion he referenced.[22] The method of learning Greek from Latin dictionaries was also familiar to Petrarch, who used not only Huguccio's work but also that of Gerard of Huy and the *Graecismus* of Eberhard of Béthune. From his glosses on his translated Homer, it is clear that Petrarch used medieval grammatical works to learn some Greek vocabulary.[23]

For someone unacquainted with the language, the only way to become familiar with Greek authors was by way of translations. According to Leonardo Bruni (1370–1444), Dante was not interested in anything but "molestia" and failed to read even the few available classics: "Dante quodlibeta fratum atque eiusmodi molestia lectitasse, librorum autem gentilium, unde maxime ars sua dependebat, nec eos quidem qui nobis reliqui sunt, attigisse."[24] Defenders of Dante, such as the poet Domenico da Prato (ca. 1389–1433), maintained that it was not necessary to know the ancients to surpass them. Indeed, he argued, many who knew them could not surpass them; translators are dead in their graves, anonymous, forgotten by all.[25]

21 O. Weijers, "Lexicography in the Middle Ages," in *Viator* 20 (1989): 139–53.

22 Toynbee, "Dante's Latin Dictionary," 101–8.

23 R. Weiss, "Per la storia degli studi greci del Petrarca: Il *Triglossos*," in *Medieval and Renaissance Greek* (Padua, 1977), 136–49; P. de Nolhac, "Les scholies inédites de Pétrarque sur Homère," *Revue de philologie, de littérature et d'histoire anciennes* 11 (1887): 97–118. Cf. Walter Berschin:

> All these works belong to the history of Latin language instruction of the Middle Ages. Their purpose is not to teach Greek or Hebrew, but rather to expand the expressive capacity of Latin by means of "exotic" finesse. If scholars allowed themselves to be deterred from sensibly learning Greek as a foreign language, that was not alone the fault of the authors of these fantastic works. In practice, however, those factitious lexicographical books determined the image of Greek in the Late Middle Ages, especially since the possibility of a control on these works by Greek grammatical treatises was lacking, and the old glossaries had fallen into obscurity.

W. Berschin, *Greek Letters and the Latin Middle Ages*, rev. ed., trans. J. C. Frakes (Washington, DC, 1988), 254.

24 Leonardo Bruni, *Dialogi ad Petrum Histrum* 1.44, ed. S. Ugo Baldassarri (Florence, 1994), 255–56.

25 Tu non hai adunque lette le traduzioni che delle opere greche d'Aristotele e di Plutarco ho fatte in latino?—Al quale in fino da ora rispondo averne lette e vedute alcune . . . imperò che la fama è delli inventori delle opere e non delli traduttori, né truovo per li passati che alcuna stima se ne facesse, né per essi, che anticamente tradussono tante e sì maravigliose opere, quante e quali si leggono al presente, furono in altri intitulate che solo in quelli alli quali s'appartenevano, occultando essi traslatatori li nomi loro, con ciò sia cosa che tali traduzioni facevano caritativamente e non

No evidence helps the historian do justice to either of these opinions. Nothing is known of Dante's library or, for that matter, whether his life of exile even allowed him to have one.[26] Thus, conjectures about his reading practices can be made only by studying the books available in Florence during his life. At that time, the two main city libraries belonged to religious orders. Successful attempts have been made to reconstruct the contents of the Franciscans' library at Santa Croce[27] and the Dominican convent's holdings at Santa Maria Novella[28] at the turn of the thirteenth–fourteenth centuries. Although no demonstrable direct link between the manuscripts and Dante exists, the holdings do illustrate the reading practices of a community with which he had contact. Dante was not only exiled from a civic community, but also an intellectual and textual one that boasted prominent scholars such as Peter John Olivi and Remigio dei Girolami. The oral nature of the educational process leaves little evidence of teachers' sharing their reading experiences. But while Dante may not have been a regular reader of the friars' books, he could have learned about these texts in other ways, such as attending lectures or, indeed, listening to sermons.[29]

From a group of forty-six codices that entered the Santa Croce library between 1246 and 1350, a few would have been particularly relevant for someone interested in Greek

---

> per vanità di pompa, acciò che alli latini fussero noti li essempli ed ammaestramenti greci ed ebraici. Sarebbono adunque da vituperare li poeti e li filosofi grechi che non hanno avuto il latino, e li poeti e filosofi latini che 'l greco non hanno avuto secondo la oppinione di questi bilingui o trilingui che siano. Ma quelli insuppati nella dottrina lasciano questi appuntatori sterili e nelli luoghi aridi ed asciutti; e quelli vivono ancora, e questi sempre son morti. . . . dicono sé aver greco e latino, e Dante e gli altri prenominati le lettere greche ignorare, e che questi, vanagloriandosi d'avere la scienzia delle lettere, vituperino coloro, li quali hanno avuta la sapienzia intellettuale e vera speculazione inventrice della posizione litterale.

Lirici toscani del quattrocento, ed. A. Lanza, 2 vols. (Rome, 1973), 1:511–12.

26 C. T. Davis, "Education in Dante's Florence," *Speculum* 40 (1965): 415–35. Idem, "The Florentine Studia and Dante's Library," in *The Divine Comedy and the Encyclopedia of Arts and Sciences*, ed. G. C. Scipio and A. Scaglione (Amsterdam, 1988), 339–66. Cf. M. Mulchahey, "Education in Dante's Florence Revisited: Remigio de' Girolami and the Schools of Santa Maria Novella," in *Medieval Education*, ed. R. B. Begley and J. W. Koterski (New York, 2000), 143–81.

27 C. T. Davis, "The Early Collection of Books of Santa Croce in Florence," *American Philosophical Society* 107, no. 5 (1963): 399–414. On the library of Sante Croce, see also C. Mazzi, "L'inventario quattrocentistico della biblioteca di S. Croce in Firenze," *Rivista delle biblioteche e degli archivi* 8–9 (1897–98): 16–31, 99–113; F. Mattesini, "La biblioteca francescana di S. Croce e Fra Tedaldo della Casa," *Studi francescani* 57 (1960): 254–316; R. Manselli, "Due biblioteche di *Studia* Minoritici: Santa Croce di Firenze e il Santo di Padova," in *Le scuole degli ordini mendicanti (secoli XIII–XIV)* (Todi, 1978), 353–72.

28 S. Orlandi, *La Biblioteca di Santa Maria Novella in Firenze dal sec. XIV al sec. XIX* (Florence, 1952); G. Pomaro, "Censimento dei manoscritti della Biblioteca di S. Maria Novella, Parte I: Origini e Trecento," *Memorie Domenicane* 11 (1980): 325–470, and "Parte II: Sec. XV–XVI," *Memorie Domenicane* 13 (1982): 203–353. Idem, "Firenze: Biblioteca Nazionale Centrale; Fondo Conventi Soppressi (Santa Maria Novella)," in *Catalogo di manoscritti filosofici nelle biblioteche italiane*, vol. 3, *Firenze, Pisa, Pistoia* (Florence, 1982), 3–75.

29 For an imaginative reconstruction, see S. Piron, "Le poète et le théologien: Une rencontre dans le *studium* de Santa Croce," *Picenum Seraphicum: Rivista di studi storici e francescani* 19 (2000): 87–134.

learning. Among them, of foremost importance, are the works of Aristotle in Latin translation (*Metaphysics, Ethics, Politics, Rhetorics*), as well as a number of works from the Pseudo-Aristotelian corpus (*Economics, De mundo, De coloribus*).[30] The library also had Aquinas's commentaries on some of Aristotle's works (*Super libros x ethicorum ad Nichomachum, Super librum de causis, Super libros iv de anima*).[31] From the Greek Church Fathers, the Franciscans had John of Damascus's *De fide orthodoxa*;[32] John Chrysostom's *Homilies in Matthew* in Burgundio's version;[33] Basil the Great's *In Hexaemeron,* in the old translation;[34] Didymus of Alexandria's *De Spiritu Sancto,* translated by Jerome, and Athanasius's *De fide et spiritu,* translated by Burgundio;[35] and Hugh of Saint Victor's commentary on Pseudo-Dionysius the Areopagite's *De coelesti hierarchia,*[36] based on John Scotus Eriugena's translation. The library also possessed Hugh Etherianus's *De haeresibus graecorum*, a rich resource for Greek patristic lore.[37] It also had a few Latin dictionaries and glossaries, which could be searched for exotic Greek items: Huguccio's *Derivationes,*[38] John of Garland's *Opus synonymorum,*[39] and William of Mara's *Tractatus de litteris et vocabulis hebraeis et graecis.*[40]

The Dominicans at Santa Maria Novella also had an extensive library. Its mid-fourteenth-century catalogue mentions, among other works, *Papias, Bricto, Ughuccio ... Barlaam et legende quorumdam sanctorum ... Damascenus et quedam naturalia et postille super Matheum.*[41] Its identifiable early possessions include the following translations from Greek: Eusebius (*Historia Ecclesiastica*),[42] Euclid (*De speculis,*[43] *De geometria*),[44] Pseudo-Galen (*Experimenta*),[45] Pseudo-Dionysius (*Epistola ad Timotheum*),[46] and Aristotle (*Physica, De caelo, De generatione, Meteorologica, De anima, De sensu, De memoria, De somno, De motu animalium, De longitudine, De iuventute, De respiratione, De morte, De progressu*).[47]

30 Plut. 13. sin. 6, from the 13th century.
31 Plut. 29. dext. 10, 13th century.
32 Plut. 13. dext. 6, late 13th century.
33 Plut. 14. dext. 4, 13th century.
34 Plut. 13 dext. 9, 13th century.
35 Both texts in Plut. 14. dext. 7, 13th century.
36 Plut. 22. dext. 4, 12th century.
37 Plut. 23. dext. 3, late 12th–early 13th century.
38 Plut. 27. sin. 5, 13th century.
39 Plut. 25. sin 5, 13th century.
40 Plut. 25. sin 4, late 13th century.
41 BNF Conv. Soppr. F.3.565, edited in G. Pomaro, "Censimento, Parte I," 326–29. The last group might have been a selection of Burgundio of Pisa's work: he translated John Damascenus, John Chrysostom's homilies on Matthew, and scientific works by Galen and Nemesius Emesenus.
42 BNF Conventi Soppresi, A.1.450; Pomaro, "Censimento, Parte I," 337–38.
43 BNF Conventi Soppresi, S.B.3.18; Pomaro, "Censimento, Parte I," 357–58.
44 BNF Conventi Soppresi C.1.448; Pomaro, "Censimento Parte I," 364–65.
45 BNF Conventi Soppresi S.D.3.849; Pomaro, "Censimento, Parte I," 384–85.
46 BNF Conventi Soppresi C.8.1173; Pomaro, "Censimento, Parte I," 374–75.
47 BML Conventi Soppresi 612; Pomaro, "Censimento, Parte I," 462–63.

A historian, a mathematician, a philosopher, a few theologians, and a tale about an Eastern sage: these are the Greeks one could have encountered had one had full access to the mendicant libraries of Florence at the turn of the thirteenth–fourteenth centuries. While he probably had not studied them, Dante was certainly aware of many; Euclid's epithet *geomètra* shows up in several of his works.[48] He also knew of John Chrysostom and Pseudo-Dionysius the Areopagite; they are the only Greek Christian writers to appear in the circles of wise men in *Paradiso* (each circle has only one wise Greek). While he demonstrated greater familiarity with Pseudo-Dionysius,[49] he referred to Saint John Chrysostom laconically as *metropolitano*.[50] This qualifier, however, seems to indicate unfamiliarity with his qualities as a writer or, indeed, a golden-mouthed orator. John Chrysostom's entry to the medieval West was ensured through two major waves of translations, one in late antiquity and the other during the High Middle Ages. Anianus of Celeda, in the fifth century, and Mutianus, in the sixth century, translated many treatises and homilies, though the latter, unfortunately, are lost. In the 12th century, Burgundio of Pisa translated two more sets of homilies on the Gospels of Matthew and John, and Angelo Clareno also translated one of his letters. Burgundio's version of the homilies of Matthew was also available in the Santa Croce library.

The question of Dante's knowledge of the Aristotelian corpus has already received wide attention.[51] A point often emphasized is that familiarity with Aristotelian thought is distinct from familiarity with Aristotelian texts, whether in translation or original versions. One often finds that medieval readers of Aristotle were actually readers of Aquinas. The same holds true for readers of Pseudo-Dionysius. Hugh of Saint Victor's commentary, written in the early twelfth century, was available in thirteenth-century Florence. Dante seems to have been more aware of Greek authors whose texts had Latin commentaries, which would explain his references to Aristotle and Pseudo-Dionysius but not Basil and other authors.

48 *Inf.* (4.142); *Conv.* (2.13.26); *Mon.* (1.1.4).

49 See the chapter by Diego Sbacchi in this volume.

50 *Par.* 12.136–37. Dante calls Plato *un uomo excellentissimo* (*Conv.* 2.21–22). Plato was, like Homer, still awaiting his translators at this time (there was one 12th-century attempt by Henricus Aristippus, who translated the *Meno* and *Phaedo*, but these texts never achieved wide circulation). Dante could be familiar only with his name and some of his ideas as survived in varieties of Christian Neoplatonism.

51 A. H. Gilbert, "Had Dante Read the *Politics* of Aristotle?" *Publications of the Modern Language Association* 43, no. 3 (1928): 602–13; B. Nardi, *Saggi di filosofia dantesca* (Florence, 1967; orig. ed., 1930); L. Minio-Paluello, "Dante's Reading of Aristotle," in *The World of Dante*, ed. C. Grayson (Oxford, 1980), 61–80; idem, *Luoghi cruciali in Dante*, ed. F. Santi (Spoleto, 1993); S. Gentili, "Il fondamento aristotelico del programma divulgativo dantesco (*Conv.* I)," in *Le culture di Dante: Studi in onore di Robert Hollander*, ed. M. Picone, T. J. Cachey, and M. Mesirca (Florence, 2004), 179–97; S. Gentili, *L'uomo aristotelico alle origini della letteratura italiana* (Rome, 2005); M. C. de Matteis, "Aristotele," *Enciclopedia Dantesca* 1:372–77; E. Berti, "Etica," in *Enciclopedia Dantesca* 2:756–58; idem, "Fisica," *Enciclopedia Dantesca* 2:933–34; idem, "Metafisica," *Enciclopedia Dantesca* 3:924–26; idem, "Politica," *Enciclopedia Dantesca* 4: 585–87.

Thus, at the turn of thirteenth–fourteenth centuries, the average Florentine's access to a library was limited and training in the Greek language was virtually nonexistent. The few who acquired Greek sometimes did so by unconventional means. Dante's contemporary Angelo Clareno (1247–1337), a Franciscan friar from Cingoli, was reported to have received his knowledge of Greek from the Holy Spirit, while spending Christmas in a Greek monastery:

> *Et cantandosi l'ufficio et dicendosi le lectioni de' frati greci, subitamente sentendosi frate Agnolo infondere nell'animo per divino miracolo la notitia della lingua greca, andò al padre suo frate Liberato, et dimandòli licentia di dire una lettione in quella lingua, et dicendo benedicite. Della qual cosa maravigliandosi frate Liberato, considerando la sanctità sua, li concedette che andasse a dire. Et così lesse quella lettione, come se fusse nato et sempre nutricato in quella lingua greca, et da indi inançi seppe liberamente parlare in greco.*[52]
>
> While singing the Office and reading the Lessons of the Greek Brothers, Brother Agnolo suddenly felt the knowledge of the Greek language take root within him, through divine miracle. He went to his Superior, Father Liberato, and asked permission to recite a lesson in that language. Father Liberato was marveled at this and, considering his holiness, allowed him to go and recite [the lesson]. Thus, he read the lesson as if he had been born and raised with the Greek language, and from then on knew how to speak fluently in Greek.

Clareno, like Dante, spent a considerable part of his life in exile. Due to conflicts with the minister general of the Franciscan order, Giovanni Minio da Morrovalle, Clareno spent two long periods in Greece, one in the Corinthian bay (1295–97) and one in eastern Thessaly (1298/99–1304/5). While there, he translated much Greek spiritual literature, including the *Scala paradisi* of John Climacus, a number of writings of Basil the Great (including the Rule, letters, and prologues to several of his ascetic pieces), and a letter of Saint John Chrysostom to Cyriacus.[53]

The late thirteenth century was also the period of peak activity for William of Moerbeke (1215–1286). Though of Flemish origin, he had strong ties to Italy. He often visited the papal court at Viterbo, where he completed some of his translations. Unlike Clareno, William was exclusively interested in the philosophy and science of classical Greece, and he rendered works of Proclus and Archimedes into Latin. He also

52 *Expositio Regulae Fratrum Minorum auctore Angelo Clareno,* ed. L. Oliger (Grottaferrata, 1912), xxxv.

53 See G. L. Potestà, *Angelo Clareno: Dai poveri eremiti ai fratricelli* (Rome, 1990), 23–25, 315–23; P. Varalda, "Per la conoscenza di Giovanni Climaco nell'Occidente Latino fra Trecento e Quattrocento," in *Padri greci e latini a confronto (secoli XIII–XV),* ed. M. Cortesi (Florence, 2004), 37–61.

(re)translated most of the works of Dante's dear Philosopher, and it was on these translations that Thomas Aquinas would write his commentaries to Aristotle.[54]

Peter of Abano (ca. 1250–1316/17), a Paduan physician and contemporary of Dante's,[55] seems to have contributed substantially to the medical literature of the period, completing two of Burgundio of Pisa's translations of Galen.[56] He commented on Aristotle's *Problemata physica* and seems to have translated the so-called *Problemata inedita*. Moreover, he translated two other sets of *Problemata*, attributed to Cassius Iatrosophista and Alexander of Aphrodisias.[57] His commentary, together with Bartholomew of Messina's Latin translation of the *Problemata,* was translated into French in about 1380 by Évrart de Conty.[58]

As this last case exemplifies, Greek culture was traveling not only through Greek-Latin translations; more complicated routes existed. Another physician from Padua, Taddeo Alderotti (1215–1295), shared an interest in Aristotle's moral philosophy with Brunetto Latini (ca. 1220–1294), a Florentine notary and politician with whom Dante was well acquainted. Both Alderotti and Latini prepared partial translations of Aristotle's *Nicomachean Ethics,* into Italian and French, respectively. The textual history of their translations is complicated, and the close correspondence between them has given rise to different hypotheses. One of the most plausible of these holds that both translations were, in turn, based on a Latin translation of an Arabic variant, translated by Herman the German in about 1243. Latini included his translation in his *Trésor,* but when the *Trésor* was translated into Italian, the relevant Aristotelian passages were replaced with Alderotti's Italian rendering.[59]

54 L. Minio-Paluello, "Moerbeke, William of," in *Dictionary of Scientific Biography* (New York, 1974), 9:434–40; *Guillaume de Moerbeke: Recueil d'études à l'occasion de 700e anniversaire de sa mort (1286),* ed. J. Brams and W. Vanhamel (Leuven, 1989).

55 On Abano and Dante, see B. Nardi, "Dante e Pietro d'Abano," *Nuovo Giornale Dantesco* 4 (1920): 1–15.

56 M. T. d'Alverny, "Pietro d'Abano, traducteur de Galien," *Medioevo* 11 (1985): 19–64; M. McVaugh, "The Lost Latin Galen," in *The Unknown Galen*, ed. V. Nutton, *Bulletin of the Institue of Classical Studies Supplement* 77 (London, 2002), 153–68.

57 P. de Leemans, "Was Peter of Abano the Translator of Pseudo-Aristotle's *Problemata physica*?" *Bulletin de Philosophie Médiévale* 49 (2007): 103–18. Cf. G. Federici Vescovini, "L'expositio succinta problematum Aristotelis de Pierre d'Abano," in *Aristotle's* Problemata *in Different Times and Tongues*, ed. P. de Leemans and M. Goyens (Leuven, 2006), 55–69; L. Olivieri, *Pietro d'Abano e il pensiero neolatino: Filosofia, scienza e ricerca dell'Aristotele greco tra i secoli xiii e xiv* (Padua, 1988).

58 J. Ducos, "Lectures et vulgarisation du savoir aristotélicien: Les gloses d'Évrart de Conty," in de Leemans and Goyens, *Aristotle's* Problemata, 199–225; P. De Leemans and M. Goyens, "La transmission des savoirs en passant par trois langues: Le cas des *Problemata* d'Aristote traduits en latin et en moyen français," in *La transmission des savoirs au Moyen âge et à la Renaissance,* vol. 1, *Du XIIe au XVe siècle*, ed. Pierre Nobel (Besançon, 2005), 231–57.

59 N. G. Siraisi, *Taddeo Alderotti and His Pupils: Two Generations of Italian Medical Learning* (Princeton, NJ, 1981), 77–82; J. Bolton Holloway, *Twice-Told Tales: Brunetto Latino and Dante Alighieri* (New York, 1993); I. Maffia Scariati, ed., *A scuola con Ser Brunetto: Indagini sulla ricezione di Brunetto Latini dal Medioevo al Rinascimento* (Florence, 2008); S. Gentili "Destini Incrociati:

Translation into the vernacular from a Latin version of a text originally composed in Greek was a phenomenon that originated in Dante's time.[60] Apart from Brunetto's *Trésor*, other early French renderings of Aristotle included the *Meteorology* of Mahieu le Vilain, in about 1290, which was accompanied by a commentary that was, in turn, inspired by Alexander of Aphrodisias's *Meteorology* commentary. The translation was based on the Latin version of William of Moerbeke.[61]

The emergence of science and philosophy in vernacular is a field of research only recently opened and partially mapped.[62] In any case, translations were its core elements, and while they were done exclusively from Latin or another vernacular into vernacular Italian, some of those Latin texts were originally written in Greek. This is, perhaps, the single most important fact about Greek culture in Dante's time: it became accessible, through vulgarizations, to the emerging lay readership. It was still the same scholastic medieval canon, but in the vernacular the emphasis shifted from theology and metaphysics to science and practical philosophy.

The thirteenth century was the last, but perhaps the most glorious, century of the medieval Latin-Greek translations. William of Moerbeke and Angelo Clareno, the clerical scholars, represent its most important protagonists. Both were mendicants (one a Dominican and the other a Franciscan friar) who translated into Latin from Greek originals. They propagated a canon of ancient philosophy and Christian patristics, the two major interests of the Latins throughout the Middle Ages. Both men probably learned their Greek while traveling in Byzantium. Their works were very popular, but at the same time, voices criticizing the common methodology of the translators—the literary (*verbum e verbo*) rendering—were rising. Roger Bacon not only called the medieval translators (except for his own teacher Robert Grosseteste) liars (*mendici translatores*) who corrupt and pervert the texts, but he was ready to take more radical steps:

> If I had power over the books of Aristotle (as at present translated), I would burn them all; for to study therein is but lost time, and a source of error and a

Taddeo Alderotti docente allo studio bolognese e la letteratura volgare delle orgini," in *Bologna nel Medioevo, Atti del convegno, Bologna, 28–29 ottobre 2002,* Quaderni di Filologia Romanza della Facoltà di Lettere dell'Universita di Bologna 17 (2004): 169–210; A. Cornish, "The Treasure of the Translator: Dante and Brunetto," in *Vernacular Translation in Dante's Italy: Illiterate Literature* (Cambridge, 2011), 126–57. See also R. Imbach, "La philosophie d'un notaire: Brunetto Latini et son Trésor," in *Dante, la philosophie* (above, n. 2), 37–41. F. Mazzoni, "Latini, Brunetto," in *Enciclopedia Dantesca*, 3:579–88.

60 With the notable exception of the translations of Notker Labeo from the monastery of Saint Gall at the turn of the tenth-eleventh centuries: he rendered the Latin translation of Boethius of Aristotle's *Categoriae* and *De interpretatione*.

61 J. Ducos, "L'oeuvre de Mahieu le Vilain: Traduction et commentaire des Météorologiques," in *Les traducteurs au travail: Leurs manuscrits et leurs méthodes*, ed. J. Hamesse (Turnhout, 2001), 285–309.

62 Cf. Imbach, *Dante* (above, n. 2).; S. Lusignan, *Parler vulgairement: Les intellectuels et la langue française au XIIIe et XIVe siècles* (Paris, 1986); *Filosofia in volgare nel Medioevo,* ed. N. Bray and L. Sturlese (Louvain-la-Neuve, 2003). M. Goyens, P. de Leemans, and A. Smets, eds., *Science Translated: Latin and Vernacular Translations of Scientific Treatises in Medieval Europe* (Leuven, 2008).

multiplication of ignorance beyond all human power to describe. . . . Whosoever will glory in Aristotle's science, he must needs learn it in its own native tongue, since false translations are everywhere, in theology as well as in philosophy.[63]

Peter of Abano, Alderotti, and Brunetto belong to a more progressive group. They were laymen, interested in philosophy and science (and the more practical aspects of each), as reflected in their choice to translate medical works and Aristotle's *Ethics*. Most importantly, Alderotti and Brunetto translated into vernacular languages, and they did not translate directly from Greek. The choice of language reflects a shift in their respective audiences, and they seem to have been targeting other laymen. Dante's *Convivio* is, in important respects, a project comparable to those of Alderotti and Brunetto. It is the translation of a scholarly genre into a popular one, trying out in vernacular a discourse that has scholastic Latin as its conventional environment. In both cases, philosophy, whether the actual text of Aristotle or the very genre of the philosophical commentary, is given both new means (vernacular) and new readership (laymen).[64] It is interesting to note, however, that although himself a writer in vernacular, Dante placed Brunetto in hell;[65] he also mentioned Alderotti in Paradise only as a negative counterexample to Saint Dominic and explicitly condemned Alderotti's rendering as *laido* in his *Convivio*.[66] Being a translator in general did not bode well in the *Divine Comedy*: Michael Scot, the famous Arab-Latin translator, also ends up in hell among diviners and witches.[67]

The general trend of Greek-Latin and Latin-vernacular scientific translation was diverted by the next generation in an episode that epitomizes the imminent change in the history of Greek learning in the West: the acquaintance of Petrarch (1304–1374) and Boccaccio (1313–1375) with Homer, through the help of two southern Italian Greeks, Barlaam of Calabria (1290–1348) and Leontius Pilatus (d. 1366).

Before this celebrated moment, very little was known about Homer in the medieval West. He was considered just one of the many writers who told the history of the Trojan War. Medieval people were acquainted with the core of the narrative through Virgil ("translator" of Homer insofar as telling partially the same story),[68] the so-called *Ilias*

63 *Si enim haberem potestatem super libros Aristotelis ego facerem omnis cremari, quia non est nisi temporis amissio studere in illis, et causa erroris et multiplicatio ignorantiae ultra id quod valeat explicari. . . . Quicumque vult gloriari de scientia Aristotelis, oportet quod eam addiscat in lingua propria et nativa, cum ubique est falsitas translationum, tam in theologia quam in philosophia.*

R. Bacon, "Compendium studii philosophiae," in *Opera Quaedam Hactenus Inedita*, ed. J. Sherren Brewer (London, 1859), 469; English translation G. G. Coulton, *Life in the Middle Ages* (Cambridge, 1967), 60–61.

64 Cf. Cornish, in *Vernacular Translations* (above, n. 60), 3.

65 Cf. Cornish, "Treasure" (above, n. 59), 126–47.

66 Cf. D. Pietropaolo, "Dante on Translation," in *Lost in Translation? The Medieval Translator*, ed. D. Renevey and C. Whitehead, Traduire au Moyen Age 12 (Turnhout, 2009), 87–92.

67 Cf. R. Key, "The Spare Ribs of Michael Scot," in *Dante Studies* 103 (1985): 1–14.

68 A 12th-century *Accessus Homeri*, for example, uses Homer almost as a pretext to talk about

Latina,[69] the *De excidio Troiae historia* of Dares the Phrygian,[70] and the *Ephemeridos belli Troiani libri* of Dictys of Crete.[71] These last two were said to be translations from Greek of two eyewitness accounts from the opposing armies by Cornelius Nepos and Lucius Septimius, respectively. In 1160, a French vernacular poet, Benoît de Sainte-Maure, combined the two texts of Dares and Dictys into a vernacular *Le Roman de Troie*, which, in turn, was translated back into Latin by a contemporary of Dante, the Sicilian poet Guido delle Colonne, in his *Historia destructionis Troiae* of about 1287.[72] While interest in the narrative was significant—all these texts enjoyed wide circulation throughout the Middle Ages— there seemed to be no awareness of the importance of the Homeric "variant" of the story.

Petrarch, on the other hand, venerated the text even before being able to understand it. His affection toward his Greek copies of the *Iliad* and Plato is well known. In 1342, he first tried to learn Greek with Barlaam, who offered a series of Greek lessons at the Avignon curia. It is impossible to estimate how far Barlaam's lectures took him. After Barlaam left the papal court, Petrarch had no further opportunity to study Greek until he met Leontius, Barlaam's former student, in Padua in 1359. By now, he had given up on his ambition to learn Greek. Instead, he convinced Leontius to prepare a translation of Homer for him. Leontius at first prepared a draft of the first five books of the *Iliad* and only later, while he was in Florence, did he complete the task.[73] He was in Florence from 1360 to 1362, teaching Greek. His move to Florence was arranged by Boccaccio, who managed to convince the town leaders to employ Leontius as a Greek teacher. There, by 1362, he had almost completed his translation of the entire epic. The result, however, was far from the cathartic aesthetic experience Petrarch had been eagerly anticipating. Leontius copied out the Greek text with large spaces between the lines. In these he wrote his translation in an interlinear fashion, word for word, or rather word above word, and added marginal glosses. It was the standard medieval technique of translating scientific, philosophical, and theological texts, but it was not the method that would conserve poetic beauty.

Virgil: *Homerus in greco sermone fecit duos libros, Odissam et Iliadem, in quibus imitatur eum Virgilius*, ed. R. B. C. Huygens, *Accessus ad auctores* (Brussels, 1954), 20–21.

69 M. Scaffai, *Baebii Italici Ilias Latina* (Bologna, 1982).

70 Dares Phrygius, *De excidio troiae historia,* ed. F. Meister (Leipzig, 1873).

71 Dictys Cretensis, *Ephemeridos belli Troiani libri*, ed. W. Eisenhut (Leipzig, 1973).

72 Guido delle Colonne, *Historia destructionis Troiae*, ed. N. E. Griffin (Cambridge, MA, 1936).

73 A. Pertusi, *Leonzio Pilato fra Petrarca e Boccaccio* (Venice and Rome, 1964); R. Weiss, "Notes on Petrarch and Homer," and "Petrarca e il mondo greco," in *Medieval and Renaissance Greek* (Padua, 1977), 150–65 and 166–92; M. Pade, "The Fortuna of Leontius Pilatus's Homer: With an Edition of Pier Candido Decembrio's 'Why Homer's Greek Verses are Rendered in Latin Prose'," in *Classica et beneventana*, ed. F. T. Coulson and A. A. Grotans (Turnhout, 2008), 149–72; idem, "Un nuovo testimone dell'Iliade di Leonzio Pilato," in *Posthomerica* 3, ed. F. Montanari and S. Pittaluga (Genoa, 2001); T. Rossi, *Il codice parigino latino 7880: Il Iliade di Omero tradotta in Latino de Leonzio Pilato con le Postille di Petrarca* (Milan, 2003); M. Feo, et al., eds., *Petrarca e il mondo greco*, 2 vols., *Quaderni Petrarcheschi* 12–13 (Florence, 2002).

The failure of Petrarch and Boccaccio to learn the language and read their Homer can only partially be blamed on their teachers. If divine intercession is any indication, learning Greek was extraordinary during these centuries. There were no Greek textbooks, grammars, or dictionaries. There were only inconvenient ways to learn Greek. One could travel to Byzantium, like William of Moerbeke, Peter of Abano, and Angelo Clareno. One could hope to meet a southern Italian or a Byzantine Greek in northern Italy, as did Petrarch and Boccaccio. Or one could hire Greek assistants, like the Englishman Robert Grosseteste, who attempted to compile his own Greek-Latin dictionary.[74] All these options required substantial financial means (for manuscripts and scribes, travel, and teachers) or the support of an institution (like the mendicant orders, the papacy, or the city government). For an average medieval intellectual, not to mention an exiled poet, the desire to learn Greek would not have been enough. And we cannot be sure that Dante possessed even this desire. Without extraordinary financial or institutional support, one could pick up the scant Greek scattered across a variety of sources.

The initiatives of Petrarch and Boccaccio and the responses of Barlaam and Leontius testify to many new developments. First, already with Alderotti and Brunetto, knowledge of Greek was exiting the narrow circle of elite clerics. While Barlaam still taught at the papal court, Leontius was paid by the city government. Second, they were interested in establishing a different canon: not religious and scientific literature, but poetry. They turned to Homer first. They approached him, however, with the techniques of the scholastics, that is, word-for-word translation, supplemented by marginal notes that functioned as additional sets of keys to the texts. Even if the literary genre and author was an unusual and innovative choice, the method of translation was genuinely medieval.

Walter Berschin remarked that Petrarch remained typically medieval in his approach to the learning of the Greek language, but he foreshadowed humanism in his choice of which Greek authors to read.[75] Dante, seen from this perspective, remains utterly medieval. He used Greek as an "ornament to Latin," knew more about Aristotle

74 A. C. Dionisotti, "On the Greek Studies of Robert Grosseteste," in *The Uses of Greek and Latin*, ed. A. C. Dionisotti, A. Grafton, and J. Kraye (London, 1988), 19–39; idem, "Robert Grosseteste and the Greek Encyclopaedia," in *Rencontres de cultures dans la philosophie médiévale: Traductions et traducteurs de l'antiquité tardive au XIVe siècle*, ed. J. Hamesse and Fattori (Turnhout, 1990), 337–53; M. Holland, "Robert Grosseteste's Greek Translations and College of Arms MS Arundel 9," in *Robert Grosseteste: New Perspectives on His Thought and Scholarship*, ed. J. McEvoy (Turnhout, 1995), 121–47.

75 Petrarch thought of himself as a Janus figure, and that he certainly was in his Greek interests. They are typically medieval in several senses: he lacked the necessary élan to make use of the (few) aids and opportunities for the grammatical acquisition of the language. Greek remained a kind of ornament to Latin. In other ways, however, he also went beyond the Middle Ages. The Greek books that Petrarch embraces are no longer the Psalter, the Gospels, the theological works, but rather Plato and Homer. Ecclesiastical Greek recedes, antiquity stays in the foreground. The humanistic shift of axes has begun in Western consciousness—away from theology and philosophy, toward poetry, history, the epistolary art, rhetoric; away from all despicable Scholastic scholarship, toward the artistic freedom of the individual; away from the Middle Ages, toward Antiquity!

Berschin, *Greek Letters* (above, n. 23), 270.

than Plato or Homer, and he was satisfied with second hand access to these texts. He did not have the urge to consult the Greek originals the way Petrarch would try to do. He was, however, more interested in the practical philosophy of Aristotle than in his logic or metaphysics. He was probably learning about it in both Latin and vernacular, but commenting in vernacular. If anything was momentous during Dante's lifetime in Greek studies, it was the laicization of both interpreters and readership, which went hand in hand with the vernacularization of science and philosophy. From the point of view of the source language, it is an insignificant element in the history of Greek translations, but from the point of view of the cultural milieu of the target language, it was an important phase in the transmission of knowledge.

Homo Byzantinus and *Homo Italicus* in Late Thirteenth-Century Constantinople

ELIZABETH A. FISHER

THIS CHAPTER WILL APPROACH the general topic "Dante and the Greeks" by adopting Byzantium as its point of reference; I shall examine the areas of contact between Greeks and Westerners—or "Italikoi," as the Byzantines called them in generic terms—and consider the image of Greeks possibly transmitted to the West between the mid-thirteenth century and approximately 1320 by Westerners residing in or visiting Constantinople.[1] Although this is the period of Dante's lifetime, I do not presume to know what information Dante personally encountered about the Greeks of Constantinople or how he used such an image of contemporary Byzantine Greeks in his writings. Accordingly, my observations about reports to the West regarding the character of Byzantine Greeks will be consistently expressed in very tentative, subjunctive terms. In addition, my insights into the interactions between Westerners and Greeks in Constantinople are very selective in that they depend upon the fragmentary and limited evidence available. Occasionally, specific comments and explicit documents emerge, but more often only potential channels of communicating attitudes and information can be suggested. As I assembled material for this study, I felt like a silent observer peering into a large room through a rather small keyhole. The room seems to be full of people, all maintaining complicated relationships, coming and going at will, and speaking to one another in their own language, in an acquired second language, or through an interpreter. I can observe only what passes in front of my keyhole, and I can hear only parts of long and detailed conversations that sometimes continue *sotto voce* beyond my observation point. For convenience, I will examine the insights gained through the keyhole in several categories: the experiences of Western brides and their retinues at the imperial court; Western traders in the city;

1 I am grateful to Jan Ziolkowski for suggesting this topic to me and to participants in the symposium "Dante and the Greeks" for their interest, encouragement, and stimulating observations. I also wish to thank Denis Sullivan for his help and support throughout this project and two anonymous readers for their helpful suggestions.

Westerners serving in the Byzantine chancery; various Catholic religious institutions and legations in Constantinople and Pera/Galata; and, finally, Byzantines educated in the Latin language and literature who interacted with Western scholars in the city. Beyond this room there are other voices. As an informative prelude to our discussion, we may note the comments recorded by George Pachymeres (1242–1310) about Western mercenaries, "a bellicose race"; the army of William of Achaea, "stupid, cowardly, and effeminate"; and Western "superciliousness," a cliché known since the twelfth century.[2]

Western Brides in the Imperial Family

Several Western women of noble, if not royal, lineage married into the Byzantine imperial family and took their place in the court life of Constantinople during the late thirteenth and early fourteenth centuries. Such mixed marriages continued a practice dating from at least the ninth century in Byzantium and especially pursued by Komnene rulers of the twelfth century. These marriages were evidently the result of intense (if delicate and confidential) negotiations between Byzantium and various Western powers, for they were vehicles for the political, economic, and military ambitions of both parties. Western states, in particular, were motivated by competition among themselves and by uneven relations with the papacy to promote their own trade privileges, secure advantages against their rivals, and gain the prestige of an imperial connection. The prospect of such benefits led the Italians, especially, to seek increased influence at the Byzantine court through marriage alliances. After the Latin conquest of Constantinople in 1204, the Latin emperors at Constantinople and the Byzantine imperial line in Nicaea briefly entertained a vision of a combined Latin-Byzantine dynasty that would both validate the Latin Kingdom and also offer the Byzantine emperor in exile the prospect of reclaiming the city by right of succession.[3] Two Byzantine emperors at Nicaea pursued such an advantage by marrying female relatives of the Latin emperors of Constantinople: Theodore I Laskaris married Maria of Courtenay, sister of the emperor Robert, and John III Vatatzes married Constance of Hohenstaufen, daughter of Frederick II. Following the expulsion of the Latin Kingdom from Constantinople, the Byzantines hoped to collect and neutralize Western claims to imperial lands established during the Crusader kingdom and forestall further

2 A. E. Laiou, "Italy and the Italians in the Political Geography of the Byzantines (14th Century)," *DOP* 49 (1995): 73–98, esp. 73–74.

3 D. M. Nicol, "Mixed Marriages in Byzantium in the Thirteenth Century," *Studies in Church History* 1 (1964): 160–72, esp. 161–62, and M. Angold, "The Latin Empire of Constantinople, 1204–1261: Marriage Strategies," in *Identities and Allegiances in the Eastern Mediterranean after 1204*, ed. J. Herrin and G. Saint-Guillain (Burlington, VT, 2011) 47–67, esp. 50–62. Various motives for mixed marriages in Byzantium are discussed by R. J. Macrides, "Dynastic Marriages and Political Kinship," in *Byzantine Diplomacy: Papers of the Twenty-Fourth Spring Symposium of Byzantine Studies, March 1990*, ed. S. Franklin and J. Shepard (Brookfield, VT, 1992) 263–80, repr. in R. J. Macrides, *Kinship and Justice in Byzantium 11th–15th Centuries* (Burlington, VT, 1999).

Western expansionist adventures by cultivating advantageous political alliances with sympathetic Western powers. Michael VIII Palaiologos, who regained Byzantine control of the city, negotiated a marriage for his son and successor Andronikos with Maria of Hungary. Upon her death, Andronikos II, in 1284, married Yolanda of Montferrat, a descendant of Boniface, leader of the Fourth Crusade. Andronikos's grandson Andronikos III later reinforced Palaiologan connections with Italian noble families by marrying first Adelheid of Braunschweig-Grubenhagen, a relative of the house of Montferrat, in 1318, and later Constance of Savoy, in 1326.[4]

The introduction of a socially well-placed Western bride at the imperial court of Constantinople provided an ideal opportunity to advance the interests of her state and family through the Western advisers, protectors, and confidants sent with a young woman abruptly transplanted into a land of alien customs, unfamiliar language, and "schismatic" religious beliefs. Carefully chosen members of the bridal retinue could insert Western interests and perspectives into Byzantine court circles through the bride and her new imperial connections, and supply through their own personal and political connections a conduit to the West for inside information about the court. Unfortunately, little information about the individuals included in such retinues and their subsequent activities in Constantinople survives; the kind of information they reported in Italy that might have affected the impression Italians formed about the Greek court and Greeks in general at the time of Dante is also unknown. We can, however, examine surviving evidence of the advantages secured by both Western and Byzantine parties through marriage, some details of a bridal retinue, and Byzantine court gossip that might have been conveyed to the West. Let us begin by looking at the evidence, however meager.

In 1284, the emperor Andronikos II Palaiologos married Yolanda, the eleven-year-old daughter of the marquis William VII of Montferrat, who was second in his line of succession.[5] Yolanda, who followed traditional Byzantine practice by taking the Greek name Irene, brought to Byzantium an alliance with the Italian Ghibellines and also the renunciation of her family's claims on Thessalonike, inherited from her grandfather Boniface I; Andronikos, in return, promised to supply soldiers and financing to the Ghibellines in northern Italy.[6] The terms of this marriage settlement surely made clear that the Byzantine imperial house intended to influence the internal politics of Italy. Three Genoese galleys conveyed the bride and her retinue to Constantinople; significantly for Genoese interests, that retinue contained two additional Genoese ambassadors

4 Nicol, "Mixed Marriages," 164–70, and U. V. Bosch, *Kaiser Andronikos III Palaiologos: Versuch einer Darstellung der byzantinischen Geschichte in den Jahren 1321–1341* (Amsterdam, 1965), 10 and 26.

5 William VII of Montferrat designated Yolanda to succeed her brother should he die without an heir. See A. E. Laiou, "A Byzantine Prince Latinized: Theodore Palaeologus, Marquis of Montferrat," *Byzantion* 38 (1968): 386–410, esp. 387–88; D. M. Nicol, *The Byzantine Lady: Ten Portraits, 1250–1500* (Cambridge, 1994), 48–58, esp. 48–56.

6 See S. Origone, "Marriage Connections between Byzantium and the West in the Age of the Palaiologoi," *Mediterranean Historical Review* 10 (1995): 226–41, esp. 237 and 234.

as well as, one would assume, advisers provided by Yolanda's family in support of the young bride.[7] The arrival of such a contingent must have been impressive; information regarding the marriage of Giovanna of Savoy (Anna) to Andronikos III in a slightly later period (1326) confirms the substantial Latin presence expected at the time in a Western bridal retinue while offering more specific information about some of the persons accompanying her from Italy and suggesting the nature of their subsequent activities.

As a bride of nineteen, Anna brought to Constantinople a further connection with the Genoese/Ghibelline orbit, personified magnificently in her minicourt of sixty individuals. Among her retinue were four Franciscan friars to press papal ambitions regarding ecclesiastical union, as well as entire Italian families (e.g., the family of Isabella of Ronchette) to maintain her connection with Italy and represent Italian concerns within Byzantine court life. Members of Anna's minicourt who returned to Italy could be replaced by others. Her contacts with relatives and friends in Pera, including the Franciscan bishop Arego, are also known and represent potential sources both of Western influence upon the empress and information about Greeks and the Byzantine court to interested parties in the West.[8]

Court gossip surrounding Yolanda of Montferrat (Irene) was evidently petty and vicious, indicating that a Western-born empress was subject to close and skeptical scrutiny by her Byzantine subjects who distrusted alien Western ideas and Catholic connections. The example of Irene provides sharp insight into the defensive, conservative, and xenophobic attitudes of some Greeks that might well have generated court gossip of a sort particularly offensive to any Westerners who heard it. In 1305, Irene wished to designate her eldest son, John, as marquis of Montferrat when she inherited the title after her brother died without issue.[9] John, who was second in line to the imperial throne of Byzantium, would have been obliged to reside in Montferrat as its ruler, a prospect that prompted the patriarch Athanasios I to write Irene's husband Andronikos II in some alarm. In the course of counseling the emperor against sending John to Montferrat, Athanasios cited the spiritual perils inherent in such a course of action and articulated the sorts of prejudice held in Byzantium against Westerners: "Who can ... guarantee that he (John) will be able to keep his faith intact, he, such a young man, in an alien land, inhabited by barbarians, by a most arrogant and most irrational people?"[10] At a single stroke, the patriarch insulted Irene's son John as irresolute in his commitment to his Orthodox faith, Irene's homeland as "an alien land," and her countrymen as uncultured and "barbarian," "arrogant," and "most irrational." He then continued by counseling that John should not defy his mother's wishes, "Because if he does not obey her, respecting her as a mother or as Empress, he will cause her great grief. And if, because

7 Origone, "Marriage," 233.

8 Ibid., 230 and 239–40.

9 Laiou, "Byzantine Prince," 392.

10 See ibid. for the Greek text (404–6) and English translation (407–10) of this letter; I quote from 408–9.

of meanness of heart, or because of wicked suggestions, she should speak more rudely, or even curse him, this would be unprofitable to both." In the view of the patriarch, Irene was petty, dependent upon the opinion of bad (probably Western) advisers, and vindictive. In addition to this negative view of Irene's character as faulty, her judgment as flawed, and her temper as uncontrolled, an insult regarding her social status was evidently current at the time. The historian Nikephoros Gregoras (*Historia romana* 1.237–38) dismisses her as a commoner as well as a foreigner, complaining that she "was not of illustrious parentage, or she would not so easily have been sent to marry among the Romans [that is, the Byzantines]. For she was the descendant of a marquis, and the class of marquis is not an important one among the Latins. Among the Latins, a marquis is like to a man who carries the imperial standard in the army."[11] Such statements indicate a Byzantine sense of superiority over Latins of the upper classes that could not have failed to find expression in subtle or overt slights to individuals associated with Irene and the West, rousing resentment in those Westerners who experienced dismissive behavior from Greeks in Constantinople and encouraging a general dislike of insolent Greeks among Latins in the West who heard reports of a scornful and condescending population ready to insult Italians of high social status.

Western Merchants and Byzantine Translators

When Michael VIII Palaiologos entered Constantinople in 1261, the city once again became the Byzantine imperial capital, although much reduced in the territory and prestige it had commanded in previous centuries. The roles of Greeks and Latins as subjects and overlords suddenly reversed under a Byzantine government. Commercial and informal interaction between these two groups continued, but evidently not without friction and dislocation.

Trading privileges and concessions remained in the hands of the Italian, French, and German colonies firmly established in Constantinople in a process that began with the Komnene treaty with Venice in 1082 and eventually placed Byzantine traders at a significant competitive disadvantage. As a result, a tense and unpleasant commercial climate apparently dominated trading activities in Constantinople. It seems likely that Italian merchants used their favored tax status to bring into Constantinople not only their own goods but also those of merchants not entitled to the privilege, leading to suspicion and probably confiscations by Byzantine customs officials. The same officials frequently disregarded legal exemptions both as a matter of overzealous enforcement as well as personal aggrandizement, and took the opportunity to extort bribes, perhaps targeting Italians, in particular, and reflecting a general resentment of Byzantines against privileged foreign merchants.[12] After the reconquest of Constantinople, Genoese domination of the grain

11 Translation by Laiou, op. cit., 396.

12 See D. Jacoby, "The Byzantine Outsider in Trade (c. 900–c. 1350)," in *Strangers to Themselves: The Byzantine Outsider (Papers from the Thirty-Second Spring Symposium of Byzantine Studies, University of Sussex, Brighton, March 1998)*, ed. D. C. Smythe (Aldershot, 2000), 129–47, esp. 134–41;

trade prompted the fiery patriarch Athanasios I to inveigh publicly against the hoarding of grain in the warehouses of Pera and Constantinople during a severe famine in the capitol (1306), further inflaming anti-Latin sentiments in the Byzantine population and endangering Western commercial interests in the city.[13] Evidence of Western displeasure with the business climate in Constantinople emerges from Roger Bacon's Greek grammar, composed in 1270 with a secular as well as religious purpose. Bacon explains that learning Greek would not only enable his Franciscan brothers to preach the true faith effectively to the schismatic Greeks but would also prevent Latin-speaking traders from being cheated by wily Greek translators in commercial dealings.[14] One can only imagine the complaints of embarrassed and infuriated Western merchants that motivated Bacon's pedagogical enterprise. Sharp dealings designed to damage the commercial position of unsuspecting Western traders and expedited by Greek (mis)interpreters would have supported a persistent image among Westerners of shifty and devious Byzantines ready to exploit any foreign businessmen who could not deal with them directly in their own language.

Western Churches and Monasteries in Constantinople

The Latin Church made its first modest appearance in Constantinople in the late tenth century to serve the spiritual needs of Western traders conducting business in the city; with the growth of Western trading colonies over the next two centuries, the presence of Latin religious foundations grew as well.[15] After the fall of the city in 1204, the papacy could act aggressively to convert the schismatic Greeks. Western religious institutions rapidly integrated into the fabric of life in Constantinople during the years of Crusader domination, not only serving the Latin Catholic population but also dedicated to missionary activities. Especially prominent in this endeavor were the Franciscans and Dominicans. Both maintained houses in the city and left tangible evidence of their efforts to instruct and convert the Greeks. Members of these communities had regular, close contacts with the Greeks of Constantinople and formed impressions of Greeks that could reach the West in oral reports carried by traders, travelers, and religious and secular messengers; for instance, Andres de Longjumeau (1238) and a papal delegation en route to the Byzantine court at Nicaea (1242) are known to have stayed in the Dominican house during their visits to Constantinople.[16] Although the substance

repr. in D. Jacoby, *Latins, Greeks and Muslims: Encounters in the Eastern Mediterranean, 10th–15th Centuries* (Aldershot, 2009).

13 J. L. Boojamra, "Athanasios of Constantinople: A Study of Byzantine Reactions to Latin Religious Infiltration," *ChHist* 48 (1979): 27–48, esp. 45–46.

14 Roger states, "interpretes . . . rarius inveniuntur fideles." Roger Bacon's career and views are discussed by G. Golubovich, *Biblioteca bio-bibliografica della Terra Santa dell' Oriente francescano,* 2 vols. (Florence, 1913), 2:404–11.

15 R. Janin, *La géographie ecclesiastique de l'Empire byzantin,* vol. 1, *Le siège de Constantinople et le partiarchat oecuménique,* 2nd ed. (Paris, 1969), 570–79.

16 C. Delacroix-Besnier, "Les precheurs, du dialogue à la polémique (XIIIe–XVe siècle)," in *Greeks, Latins and Intellectual History 1204–1500*, ed. M. Hinterberger and C. Schabel (Leuven, 2011), 151–67, esp. 151.

of any such news reported in the West is lost, it is possible to examine evidence of the activities of Dominicans and Franciscans and infer the impression of Greeks that they might have communicated to Italy during the thirteenth century.

Proselytizing involved active engagement with Greeks in their own language. Two undated Greek versions of Latin texts useful for the instruction of Greek converts survive from the thirteenth century and may have originated in the early missionary efforts of the mendicant orders. The first is a fragment of the Latin Mass translated into Greek and based upon the *Ordo Romanus antiquus*.[17] The second is also fragmentary, preserving portions of the Franciscan Rule that would especially concern an initiate into the order. A native Greek speaker evidently translated the Latin original, for the translation is correct and idiomatic in its use of Greek grammar (e.g., the case of a noun object is determined by the first verb in a series) and vocabulary (e.g., φρεμενουρίων = *Fratres minores*, adopted from contemporary usage), and consistent with the usages of the Greek liturgy (e.g., εἰς τὴν βασιλείαν).[18]

The Franciscan community used images as well as words to instruct visitors to their house in the Franciscan perspective on the contemporary Church. The earliest images of Saint Francis so far identified survive in badly damaged fresco panels dating from the Franciscan occupation of the Orthodox church of Christos Akataleptos (the Church of the Mother of God Kyriotissa; Turkish, Kalenderhane Camii); after being restored to the fullest extent possible, these frescoes are now displayed in the Istanbul Archaeological Museum. The frescoes vividly portray events from the life of Saint Francis, and on the arch surrounding the images of the saint are two almost life-size figures of Greek Church Fathers, one identified in a Latin inscription as John Chrysostom, the other without a surviving caption. Both wear Greek liturgical vestments perfect in detail, and both are slightly different in technique from the main program; perhaps a Greek artist painted these figures.[19] They bear silent witness by their presence to the link between the new Western monastic tradition of the Franciscans and the Orthodox Church by referring visually to the early heritage they shared. On the arch of the chapel's apse was the Latin inscription *Domine, dilexi decorum domus tuae et locum habitationis tuae* (Lord, I have loved the beauty of your house and the place where you dwell; Ps. 25:8). A curtain wall, constructed after 1261 at a date not possible to determine with precision, eventually concealed the frescoes.[20] As long as these Western adornments to the church remained visible, however, they provided a powerful statement about Latin religious culture for all who visited the building, whether

17 J. Darrouzès, "Conference sur la primauté du Pape à Constantinople," *REB* 19 (1961): 76–85, esp. 81 and n. 3. I am grateful to Manolis Patedakis for this intriguing reference.

18 S. Salaville, "Fragment inédit de traduction grecque de la Règle de saint François," *EO* 28 (1929): 167–72, esp. 168 n. 2, 170 n. 1 and n. 3.

19 C. L. Striker and D. Kuban, *Kalenderhane in Istanbul: The Buildings* (Mainz, 1997), 128–42, and plates 155–70. See also http://www.qantara-med.org/qantara4/public/show_document.php?do_id=716&lang=en (accessed June 2012).

20 Janin, *La géographie*, 506.

Catholic or Orthodox, and expressed Unionist sentiments in visual terms that Greeks would readily comprehend.

Franciscan reports received in the West concerning Greeks might well have been fairly positive, reflecting their attitude toward the Greeks they were attempting to convert. The Dominicans, however, were less conciliatory than the Franciscans in their dealings with the Greeks of Constantinople, as is evident in discussions conducted by each order beginning in the 1240s over the question of whether to follow the Western practice of using unleavened bread in the Mass or to require the Orthodox use of leavened bread. Dominicans took an increasingly uncompromising and confrontational stance on the question in comparison to that of the Franciscans.[21] The anonymous *Tractatus contra graecos* of 1252, composed in the Dominican community at Constantinople and promulgated both in Latin and in Greek, illustrates the order's combative attitude toward Greeks in the city and testifies to the order's preoccupation with aggressively preaching conversion to the Orthodox.[22] This document certainly reached Dominicans in the West, for Thomas Aquinas (ca. 1225–1274) cited parts of it in his *Contra errores graecos* and *Summa theologiae*.[23]

Although Michael VIII pursued ecclesiastical union as a practical policy to protect his fragile rule, Latin religious institutions gradually relocated to areas outside the city proper after 1261. The twenty churches and thirteen monasteries in Constantinople that Catholics appropriated from Byzantine clergy and monks during the Latin Kingdom returned to Orthodox control, and the Latins who had inhabited these institutions became much less conspicuous.[24] Both the Latin patriarch of Constantinople and the Dominican community moved to Negroponte near the eastern coast of Greece; Dominican monks and Latin clergy nevertheless continued their activities very close to Constantinople in the Genoese enclave of Pera, where Latin Rite churches and monasteries remained.[25] Six such churches established before 1300 are attested in Pera, among them the Dominican Church of Saint Dominic and Saint Paul dating from the 1260s.[26] Guillaume Adam notes that Michael's son and anti-Unionist successor Andronikos II expelled the Dominicans and Franciscans from the city at some unspecified date after he became sole emperor in 1282, because they were successful in proselytizing among the Greeks.[27] Undoubtedly this action aroused resentment in the West. It is by no means certain, however, that all Latin religious orders had ceased to reside in Constantinople

21 C. Schabel, "The Quarrel over Unleavened Bread in Western Theology, 1234–1430," in Hinterberger and Schabel, *Greeks, Latins* (above, n. 16), 85–127, esp. 105–11.

22 A. Dondaine, "'Contra Graecos': Premiers écrits polémiques des dominicains d'Orient," *AFP* 21 (1951): 321–30.

23 Schabel, "Quarrel," 111.

24 Janin, *La géographie*, 579.

25 T. M. Violante, *La provincia domenicana di Grecia* (Rome, 1999), 84.

26 Janin, *La géographie*, 587–91.

27 G. Adae, *Recueil des historiens des croisades*, vol. 2, *Documents Arméniens*, ed. E. Dulaurier (Paris, 1906), 548.

or had broken off contact with Greeks in the city during the early period of Andronikos's reign. The Franciscans apparently closed their house for a short time but reopened it after 1274; by 1296, the Franciscan house hosted King Aitone (Hetoum) II of Armenia during his stay in Constantinople.[28]

After the Dominicans removed their community to Negroponte in 1261, a few brothers apparently remained among the Greeks of Constantinople, but they lacked the structure of a formal monastery. In 1299, Guillaume Bernard de Gaillac stayed among them and negotiated with Andronikos II for the purchase of a property to be used by Dominicans.[29] The community in Negroponte remained well informed about events and personalities in Constantinople, perhaps by communicating with these brothers in the city. From Negroponte the Dominican Simon of Constantinople corresponded with members of the imperial and patriarchal bureaucracy, including the emperor Andronikos II, concerning issues of ecclesiastical union.[30] A native of Constantinople, Simon was born about 1235, probably to a Latin family, and enjoyed a high reputation for his learning both in Latin and Greek. His letters to members of the Byzantine elite express the Catholic understanding of the procession of the Holy Spirit in an elegant Greek style adapted to the interests of each recipient. For the emperor Andronikos, Simon invoked the memory of his father's uniate efforts; for the grammarian and rhetorician Holobolos, he provided a grammatical exegesis; and for the Aristotelian commentator Sophonias, he cited Aristotle. Simon's correspondence implies current knowledge of the activities of these recipients and also suggests that messengers conveyed letters and news between the Dominican community in Negroponte and individuals in Constantinople. News gathered from this exchange may have indirectly reached the order in the West as well.

Guillaume Bernard de Gaillac spent the first years after his arrival in Constantinople perfecting his Greek language skills and forming acquaintances with Greeks in the city before founding a formal Dominican house in Pera (ca. 1307).[31] He confided his experiences with Greeks in two Latin treatises, perhaps intended for his Dominican brothers in the West. In 1305, he wrote from Constantinople of a seemingly peaceful climate that allowed for theological discussion; however, by 1307 the situation had deteriorated. Guillaume Bernard wrote from Pera that John the "praetor and chief translator at the imperial court" (*Ioanni, praetori et magno interprete imperialis palatii*) rather peremptorily countered his complaints of mistreatment by Greeks in the city with the assurance that "No cultured or educated Greek would insult Latins, unless concerning the single Procession of the Holy Spirit" (*Nullus, inquit, sapiens seu litteratus Graecus*

28 R.-J. Loenertz, "Les établissements dominicains de Péra-Constantinople," *EO* 34 (1935): 332–49; cited from repr. in *Byzantina et Franco-Graeca*, ed. P. Schreiner (Rome, 1970), 209–26, esp. 213 n. 4.

29 M.-H. Congourdeau, "Note sur les Dominicains de Constantinople au début du 14e siècle," *REB* 45 (1987): 175–81, esp. 176, and Boojamra, "Athanasios" (above, n. 13), 33.

30 For a full discussion of Simon's life and writings, see M.-H. Congourdeau, "Frère Simon le constantinopolitain, O.P. (1235?–1325?)," *REB* 45 (1987): 165–74.

31 Congourdeau, "Note," 176–78; translations from this text are my own after Congourdeau.

calumniatur Latinos nisi de sola processione Spiritus Sancti); further, Guillaume Bernard mentions the plight of the Greek monk Sophonias, learned in Greek and Latin, who endured persecution because of his adherence to the Catholic faith and adds that he himself sometimes experienced exclusion from Greek churches and dinner parties. If Guillaume Bernard's treatises reached the West and circulated there, they would support an impression of Greeks as rude, vindictive, and whimsical, as well as schismatic and doctrinally unsound.

Papal Legates in Constantinople

The gulf between the interests of Rome and Constantinople in the thirteenth century required the presence of papal legates both during the Latin Kingdom and after the return of the Byzantines. Papal legates in crusader Constantinople acted to protect papal authority against the ambitions of the Latin patriarch controlled by Venice and also secure and monitor progress toward ecclesiastical union. A series of papal legates (Peter Capuano, Benedict of Saint Susanna, Pelagius of Albano, and John Colonna) took decisive and aggressive action to establish and protect the primacy of the pope in matters of ecclesiastical regulation and property, until the offices of legate and patriarch merged under Gregory IX (1231).[32] In the course of this prolonged contest, an exasperated Pope Honorius complained in 1218 that the patriarch Gerasius took independent actions that challenged the authority of the papacy, compromised ecclesiastical unity, and even resembled the insubordinate behavior of schismatic Greek patriarchs, an insult that relied upon a negative image of Greeks held in the West and consistent with their reputation at the time of Dante.[33]

In the years after Michael VIII restored Greek rule to Constantinople, and as he pursued ecclesiastical union, papal legations sent to Constantinople to negotiate the Union of Lyons and assess its success would have been a significant source of information in the West about Greeks and their affairs. Evidence concerning a sequence of events commencing in 1278 during the papacy of Nicholas III allows us to observe the extent to which the internal affairs of the Byzantine Empire might have become known and disparaged in the West. The Byzantine historian George Pachymeres claims that the Franciscan community of Constantinople informed the pope that the Union of Lyons carried no credibility in Byzantium and was, in fact, considered a joke (γέλως; Pachymeres 4.20).[34] Although Pachymeres does not say when this report reached Rome, measures taken by Nicholas III suggest that he considered such news credible, for in 1278 he dispatched a permanent delegation to Constantinople to observe and report

32 For a full treatment of this subject, see R. L. Wolff, "Politics in the Latin Patriarchate of Constantinople, 1204–1261," *DOP* 8 (1954): 225–303, esp. 272–84 and 288–92.

33 Ibid., 275.

34 *Relations historiques Georges Pachymeres*, ed. A. Failler, trans. V. Laurent, CFHB 24, 5 vols. (Paris, 1984) 2:381.22. See D. M. Nicol, "The Greeks and the Union of the Churches: The Report of Ogerius, Protonotarius of Michael VIII Palaeologos, in 1280," *Proceedings of the Royal Irish Academy* 63, section C (1962): 1–16, esp. 2 n. 3.

on progress toward ecclesiastical union. Bartolomeo, bishop of Grosseto, headed the group, consisting of Bartolomeo of Siena; Filippo, lector of Perugia; and Angelo, lector of Orvieto.[35] When Nicholas's permanent mission to Constantinople arrived in the autumn of 1278, Michael attempted to create an illusion of harmony in the Church by prohibiting the Byzantine clergy from engaging in any anti-Unionist discussions and even ordered many forged signatures to satisfy Nicholas's demand for an oath accepting the beliefs and primacy of Rome from "the Patriarch, the Prelates, the Clergy of the State, of every fortress, of every town, and of every place."[36] Michael did not, of course, admit to any such activities in the formal report he sent to the pope but rather presented himself as the fervent supporter of union and victim of unreasonable resistance to his policy. He detailed specific measures he had taken to punish those opposing ecclesiastical union, including members of the nobility and of his own family; in 1279, Michael reinforced this imperial image by arranging for the papal legates to tour the prison where some of his prominent enemies were held in chains.[37] Despite Michael's efforts, the presence of the permanent papal legation in Constantinople provided openings for unofficial information to reach the West, confirming a negative image of devious and duplicitous Byzantines consistent with the reports from Western traders, courtiers, and monastic houses, and presenting Michael VIII as an ineffective leader unable to control even his own family. If Nicholas's legates in Constantinople managed to gain any sense of the intrigues and intimidation surrounding ecclesiastical union in Byzantium, their reports would have been extremely damaging to the Western estimation of the Greeks' capacity for honorable conduct. In any case, Nicholas's successor, Martin IV, excommunicated Michael in 1281.

The Byzantine Imperial Chancery

The bilingual chancery of the Byzantine emperors apparently lapsed under Latin overlords, although they initially forced Theodore Tornikes, head of the Byzantine translation bureau, to serve them until he escaped. While some Franks of the second generation knew Greek (e.g., William de Villehardouin, Geoffrey d'Aulnay, Phillip and Anselm de Toucy) and evidently learned the language in Constantinople, there is no evidence that the Latins felt the need for an imperial translation bureau that included Greeks.[38] In general, Greeks had a poor reputation among the Frankish emperors and their Western connections. The exchange in 1243 between Blanche of Castile and her son Baldwin, Latin emperor of Constantinople, is instructive. Blanche faulted the emperor for relying upon the advice of two Greeks, prompting him to swear solemnly "that we have never in the past taken the advice of any Greeks, nor do we now, nor shall we; rather whatever we

35 *PLP*, fasc. 8, 160–61.

36 J. M. Hussey, *The Orthodox Church in the Byzantine Empire* (Oxford, 1986), 240–42.

37 D. M. Nicol, "The Byzantine Reaction to the Second Council of Lyons, 1274," *Studies in Church History* 7 (1970): 113–46, esp. 131–32; repr. in D. M. Nicol, *Studies in Late Byzantine History and Prosopography* (London, 1986).

38 P. Lock, *The Franks in the Aegean, 1204–1500* (New York, 1995), 295–98.

do is done on the advice of the noble and good men of France who are with us."[39] Their exchange provides background for attitudes among Western nobility toward the Greeks of Constantinople that apparently persisted at the time of Dante.

Under Michael VIII, an entirely different linguistic and cultural climate prevailed in the new imperial court at Constantinople, for Michael's survival depended upon successful negotiations with the Italian city-states, the papacy, and Western courts. Such negotiations required that the terms of treaties and other documents originating in Michael's imperial court be expressed without risk of misunderstanding or misconstruction by Western parties who received imperial documents. Accordingly and consistent with the practice in Constantinople of his Byzantine predecessors, Michael maintained an official translation bureau within his chancery and employed both Westerners and Byzantines as translators in the Latin section and as imperial envoys.[40] The most prominent of these Westerners was Ogerius Boccanegra, member of a prominent Genoese family who authenticated the Treaty of Nymphaion (1261).[41] Ogerius later appeared as the Latin translator of an imperial agreement with Genoa that he personally carried to the Commune (1272), presumably conveying as well an oral message from Michael VIII and his own informal report of news from the city.[42] Ogerius had risen professionally to become chief of the translation bureau (*protonotarios*) by 1278, when he drafted the official memorandum in Latin to the papal legates Marco and Marchetto detailing the emperor's oral message they were to deliver to Pope Nicholas; in this, Michael described the dangerous rebellion against his rule led by several members of his own family and supported by various Latin rulers in Greece.[43] This highly sensitive document survives in the Vatican archives and provides evidence of treachery within the Byzantine imperial family that would support a Western view of Byzantines and their government as unstable and dishonorable. Ogerius was evidently present at the interview between the emperor and the papal legates, probably as translator, and he endorsed the official instructions to the legates by asserting at the close of the memorandum he drafted:

> These are the words that my most sacred Emperor spoke in your presence, which you should report faithfully, just as you heard them, to his Apostolic Holiness. And I, Protonotarios of the Latin translators at the court of my most sacred Emperor of the Romans, have signed these words in surety. I am Ogerius,

39 Quoted from K. Setton, *The Papacy and the Levant, 1204–1571,* 4 vols. (Philadelphia, 1976), 1:65–66.

40 N. Oikonomides, "La chancellerie impériale de Byzance du 13e au 15e siècle," *REB* 43 (1985): 167–95, esp. 168–73.

41 L. Pieralli, "I rapporti diplomatici tra Roma e Costantinopoli negli anni 1274–1279 attraverso le varianti introdotte nel testo della professione di fede imperiale," in *Documenti medievali greci e latini: Studi comparativi*, ed. G. de Gregorio and O. Kresten (Spoleto, 1998), 395 n. 31.

42 F. Dölger and P. Wirth, *Regesten der Kaiserurkunden des oströmischen Reiches von 565–1453*, 2nd ed., pt. 3 (Munich, 1977), 59–60, no. 1990.

43 R.-J. Loenertz, "Mémoire d'Ogier, protonotaire, pour Marco et Marchetto nonces de Michel VIII Paléologue auprès du pape Nicolas III. 1278, printemps–été," *OCP* 31 (1965): 374–408.

Protonotarios, who have written the above in my own hand and signed it with my own signature.[44]

This interesting and unusual document illustrates the extent to which a Westerner like Ogerius Boccanegra could take a central role in the internal affairs of Byzantium; it also establishes that Westerners were trusted by Michael VIII to carry sensitive information written in Latin to Rome. Ogerius remained in the Byzantine chancery under Michael's son and successor Andronikos II until at least 1286, when the Latin text of an imperial letter to Genoa can be attributed to him.[45] Over the course of his long career, did Ogerius convey inside information about Byzantine affairs to his Genoese connections? He could have done so either independently or under instructions from the Byzantine court. In any case, Andronikos II evidently found the use of Western translators in the chancery satisfactory, for imperial documents of 1303 and 1304 survive from the hand of one Nicholas of Parma.[46] A few years later, a bilingual treaty renewal with Venice (1310) was drafted cooperatively in the imperial chancery by two scribes, the Byzantine Theodoros Phialites, who transcribed the Greek portion of the document, and Stefano Giordano (= Stephanus Zordanes), who transcribed the Latin text under special authorization of the emperor.[47] Nicholas of Parma, Stefano Giordano, and other Western scribes otherwise undocumented in the surviving sources may have provided to their connections in Italy not only personal impressions of life in the imperial capital but also information about imperial affairs. We know nothing, however, about such individuals beyond two names and the fact of their association with the imperial court.

How did Western scribes and ambassadors used by the Byzantine court affect the public image of Greeks in Dante's Italy? Ogerius, in particular, presents an interesting case. Although associated with a prominent Genoese family, Ogerius seemingly "went native" among the Greeks of Constantinople, assuming the role of Latin spokesman for Michael VIII in 1272 and becoming a sort of naturalized Byzantine in his interactions with the West. A second figure of ambiguous ethnic identity is the bilingual Franciscan monk John Parastron or Parastos, prominent in Michael VIII's efforts to gain Western support for his reign through ecclesiastical union. The surname Parastron suggests that John came from the mixed Greco-Venetian community in Constantinople, where he might have served as *barastron* or councilor, while the surname Parastos suggests a

44 "Hec sunt que locutus est uobiscum dominus meus sanctissimus imperator, que debetis sicut tenemini <denunitiare> summe apostolice sanctitati. Et subsignaui hec ego prothonotarius interpretum Latinorum curie domini mei sanctissimi imperatoris Romanie ad cautelam. Ego Ogerius prothonotarius que supra manu propria scriptsi et meo signo signaui." Cited from Loenertz, "Mémoire d'Ogier," 393, §19.

45 F. Dölger, *Regesten der Kaiserurkunden des oströmischen Reiches von 565–1453*, pt. 4 (Munich, 1960), 9–10, no. 2117; Pierelli, "I rapporti," 395 n. 31.

46 Dölger, *Regesten*, 4:40 no. 2251 and 4:41–42 no. 2261.

47 Ibid., 4:55 no. 2325; Oikonomides, "La chancellerie," 172.

family origin in the town of that name across the Bosphorus from Constantinople.[48] Although his early life is undocumented, John's fluency both in Latin and in Greek earned him the high regard of Michael VIII and an appointment in 1270 as the imperial envoy from Michael to Louis IX of France and as envoy to the papal court to negotiate the Union of Lyons. In this latter mission, he was accompanied by Nicholas of Durazzo, a Franciscan like John who also enjoyed a reputation at Constantinople as learned in both Latin and Greek.[49] In 1272, John Parastron returned to Constantinople from the West with the pope's invitation to Michael VIII to attend the Council of Lyons. John himself attended the council and died a year later in 1275. In recognition of his services, Michael VIII and his uniate Byzantine clergy pressed the pope to canonize John but without success, despite the three hundred miracles they credited to him.

The eventful career of this Franciscan imperial envoy and unsuccessful candidate for sainthood raises interesting questions about the effect his presence in the West may have had upon Western perceptions of Byzantines. Were figures like Ogerius Boccanegra and the two Franciscans John Parastron and Nicholas of Durazzo regarded as Westerners flourishing in the East, or as Byzantines parading in Western garb? Were they received in the West as skillful and reliable "go-betweens" in negotiations with Byzantines or as ambiguous "in-betweens" of indeterminate origins and loyalties?[50] The uncertain ethnic identity of these individuals might leave Westerners with an ambivalent and mistrustful impression of the bilinguals who served the Byzantine chancery and represented official Byzantine interests in the West.

Byzantine Latinists

During the long and close association of Ogerius with the imperial chancery, two Byzantines accomplished in Latin also served the court. Both Manuel Holobolos (1245–after 1310) and Maximos Planoudes (ca. 1255–ca. 1305) were premier products of the traditional form of Byzantine education centered on grammar in the broadest sense of the word and including the disciplines of the quadrivium; this system had ensured a well-trained cadre of talented young men for administrative service in Church and State over the centuries.[51] Holobolos, the older of the two by some ten years, was the first Byzantine scholar since late antiquity known to have learned Latin and to have translated Latin literary works into Greek. He evidently joined the imperial translation bureau before 1261, when he would have been a very young colleague of Ogerius.[52] In

48 For the life and career of John Parastron/Parastos, see G. Matteucci, *La missione francescana di Constantinopoli,* vol. 1, *La sua antica orgine e primi secoli di storia (1217–1555)* (Florence, 1971), 111–36.

49 Pachymeres 5.8 (ed. Failler 2:463.13–14).

50 Sylvia Molloy enunciated this provocative distinction in her paper "Reading Bilingual: An Uneasy Reflection on Cultural Encounters" (delivered at George Washington University, 27 April 2007), illustrating the ambivalent position of translators by citing G. Packer, "Betrayed: The Iraqis Who Trusted America the Most," *The New Yorker* (26 March 2007), 52–73.

51 "Education," *ODB* 1:677–78.

52 E. A. Fisher, "Manuel Holobolos and the Role of Bilinguals in Relations Between the West and

this early period of his career, Holobolos apparently made his first translations of Latin literary works as practical aids for rhetoricians in training. He produced Greek versions of Boethius's *De hypotheticis syllogismis* and *De topicis differentiis*, explaining in a rare example of a translator's preface that these works were not meant to replace the already more than adequate rhetorical resources of the Greek literary tradition but rather to supplement it in a useful way.[53] He also mentions contemporary Latin scholars approvingly and describes Boethius's career in some detail, expressing open admiration for the Latin author, his vivid portrayal of Lady Philosophy in the first book of *De consolatione philosophiae*, and his success as a commentator on Aristotle. The scholarly writings of Boethius had a profound effect on Holobolos's own activities, for he used Boethius's commentary on Porphyry's *Isagoge* to study Aristotle, a startling choice for a Byzantine trained in the Greek tradition. It is evident, however, both from Holobolos's remarks on the process of translation and from his practices in translating from Latin to Greek that he knew Boethius's Second Preface and followed the Latin scholar's recommendations for successful translation.[54] Holobolos evidently worked with Latin scholars at Constantinople and came to respect them,[55] although in some of the extensive notes that supported his translation of Boethius's *De topicis differentiis*, he expressed an ambivalent and occasionally hostile attitude toward the Latins and their language. At the conclusion of the manuscript, Holobolos sternly and metrically enjoins the reader, "Throttle the Italians and their proud ways, friend, by mastering them with these coils of syllogism."[56] These anti-Latin sentiments may reflect Holobolos's interactions with Latin officials of Church and State that he encountered in the course of his chancery duties. He was an outspoken opponent of ecclesiastical union and suffered public humiliation and imprisonment at the hands of Michael VIII for his opposition to the emperor. In an often-cited episode, Holobolos was forced to lead nine other anti-Unionists in a Parade of Infamy through the streets of Constantinople while carrying fetid sheep's entrails and suffering blows with the sheep's liver; such a disgusting public spectacle was a traditional means of humiliating enemies of the emperor and was vastly enjoyed and appreciated by the general population and surely noted by any Westerners in Constantinople at the time.[57] However, like Ogerius, Holobolos continued in imperial service under both Michael VIII and Andronikos II; he also demonstrated his interest in Latin literature

---

Byzantium," in *Knotenpunkt Byzanz*, ed. A. Speer, *Miscellanea Mediaevalia* 36 (2012): 210–22, esp. 211–12.

53 P. Canart, "À propos du Vaticanus Graecus 207," *ICS* 7 (1982): 271–98, esp. 271, 283.

54 Fisher, "Holobolos and Bilinguals," 218–22.

55 E. A. Fisher, "Manuel Holobolos, Alfred of Sareshal, and the Greek Translator of ps.-Aristotle's *De Plantis*," *Classica et Mediaevalia* 57 (2006): 189–213, esp. 200–202.

56 D. Z. Nikitas, *Boethius De topicis differentiis καὶ βυζαντινὲς μεταφράσεις τῶν Μανουὴλ Ὁλοβόλου καὶ Προχόρου Κυδώνη* (Athens, 1990), cvi–cix.

57 Pachymeres 5.20 (Failler 2:503–5). Michael VIII staged three such Parades of Infamy; see also Pachymeres 3.25 (Failler 1:301–13) and 6.33 (Failler 2:649–53). For a general discussion of Parades of Infamy, see L. Garland, "Street Life in Constantinople: Women and the Carnavalesque," in *Byzantine Women: Varieties of Experience 800–1200*, ed. L. Garland (Burlington, VT, 2006), 169–71.

and translations throughout his public career. In his capacity as public "Rhetor of the Rhetors," Holobolos publicly delivered a panegyric for Michael in which he quoted Virgil (*Aen.* 4.473ff) in Greek and identified him as the Latins' Homer.[58] Under Andronikos II, Holobolos translated the Latin text of Pseudo-Aristotle's *De plantis* and served as ambassador to Venice during the Byzantine-Venetian treaty renewal of 1302.[59] Did his demeanor toward the Latin speakers he encountered throughout his long association with the Byzantine court reflect Holobolos's early vehement dislike of offensive Westerners and prompt a similarly negative Western response to him? Or did Holobolos acquire a veneer of diplomatic courtesy sufficient to leave his Western contacts with a positive impression of a Greek well educated in the Latin language? The question must remain unresolved, as no evidence survives to answer it.

Like Holobolos, Planoudes served in the Byzantine chancery early in his career and translated Latin texts into Greek. Apparently under commission from Michael VIII, Planoudes produced a Greek version of Augustine's *De trinitate* in support of the Unionist position during debates in Constantinople surrounding the Union of Lyons.[60] Planoudes came to regret his association with this controversial translation but continued to translate such major works of Latin literature as Ovid's *Metamorphoses*, his *Heroides*, and Boethius's *De consolatione philosophiae* and serve the imperial court as a sort of public intellectual. In the early 1290s, he delivered an imperial panegyric for Andronikos II to an audience that included the Western diplomat Pierre Surie, envoy from the court of Charles of Anjou.[61] Did Pierre Surie know of Planoudes' translations and carry an informal report of this remarkable Byzantine scholar to the West? Sadly, as in the case of many earlier examples, we have no evidence to support a suggestion that he did. During the same period, Planoudes also led an imperial delegation to Venice (1296), probably because of his fluency in Latin.[62] The awkward political situation between Venice and Byzantium caused the delegation to be detained for a year; one can only wonder what his Venetian captors knew of the scholarly activities of this learned Latin-speaking scholar in their midst, and Planoudes, unlike the outspoken Holobolos, gives no hint in his writings of his attitude toward Westerners he encountered as a diplomat or scholar. When Planoudes died about 1305, however, the Dominicans who hosted Guillaume Bernard de Gaillac in Constantinople regarded his translation of Augustine's *De trinitate* as a deliberate falsification; Bernard describes Planoudes as "operating as a forger and not as a translator, telling a lie not only to mankind but even

58 D. Angelov, *Imperial Ideology and Political Thought in Byzantium, 1204–1330* (Cambridge, 2007), 94.

59 C. N. Constantinides, *Higher Education in Byzantium in the 13th and early 14th Centuries (1204–ca. 1310)* (Nicosia, 1982), 58.

60 E. A. Fisher, "Planoudes' *De trinitate*, the Art of Translation, and the Beholder's Share," in *Orthodox Readings of Augustine*, ed. G. Demacopoulos and A. Papanikolaou (Crestwood, NY, 2008), 41–61.

61 Angelov, *Imperial Ideology*, 173.

62 C. Wendel, "Planudes, Maximos," in *RE* 20.2:2202–53, esp. 2205–6.

to God."[63] Planoudes' *De trinitate* as it survives is an accurate translation, so this charge is unjustified and bears witness not to Planoudes' character and abilities as a translator but rather to the sort of calumny about him that circulated among the Latins of Constantinople and Pera and that may have reached the West.[64]

Latin-Greek Scholarly Relations

The careers of Holobolos and Planoudes permit some inferences regarding productive scholarly interactions between Westerners and Greeks in Constantinople. Since both Byzantine scholars used Latin and made translations from Latin texts early in their scholarly lives, they evidently learned Latin and obtained Latin manuscripts to translate in Constantinople in the 1260s. Where were these Latin manuscripts, and who were these Latin scholars living in Constantinople? They may have been Dominicans and Franciscans still resident in the city after 1261 who continued to act upon the papal recommendation issued by Innocent III in 1205 that the Greeks of Constantinople should be instructed in Latin culture.[65] The Dominicans, in particular, considered the study of Greek language and culture important for the preparation of effective missionaries in the East, as Humbert of Romans, former Dominican general, emphasized in his *De eruditione praedicatorum* (1266), reiterated in his *Opus tripartium,* and reasserted at the Dominicans' Chapter General in 1310 and again in 1312.[66]

The structure of a Dominican monastery as prescribed by the order provided an environment where promising young Greek scholars such as Planoudes and Holobolos might have found Latin books and learned Latin from Greek speakers willing to cultivate a Byzantine's interest in Western language and culture. An authorized Dominican monastery comprised at least twelve monks, a prior, and a doctor of theology, and required a library to support the monks and their missionary work (in contrast, a mission house like one in Constantinople that may have hosted Guillaume Bernard de Gaillac in 1299 would have had fewer than twelve monks and would have required no library).[67] Boethius's commentary on the *Isagoge* of Porphyry used by Holobolos and the rhetorical texts of Boethius that he translated would reasonably have been part of a Dominican library, as would Papias's popular exegesis of Boethius used by Holobolos in his scholia to *De topicis differentiis* and the Latin text that Planoudes used in translating Augustine's *De trinitate.*[68] With the relocation of the Dominicans' monastery to Negroponte, their books were evidently dispersed, and Guillaume Bernard de Gaillac

63 Congourdeau, "Note" (above, n. 29), 176; text from Dondaine, "Contra graecos" (above, n. 22), 421–22; translation from Fisher, "Planoudes' *De trinitate,*" 41–61, esp. 59.

64 Dondaine, "Contra graecos," 422 n. 26; Fisher, "Planoudes' *De trinitate,*" 59.

65 D. Z. Nikitas, *Eine byzantinische Übersetzung von Boethius "De hypotheticis Syllogismis,"* Hypomnemata 69 (Göttingen, 1982), 170–74.

66 C. Delacroix-Besniers, *Les Dominicains et Chrétienté grecque aux XIV*[e] *et XV*[e] *siècles* (Rome, 1997), 203–4.

67 Violante, *La provincia domenicana* (above, n. 25), 64–68.

68 Nikitas, *Boethius De topicis differentiis* (above, n. 56), cviii and cxxxvi.

found it necessary to replace its books when he arrived to reestablish the house at Pera.[69] While most of the Dominicans' library probably accompanied the community to Negroponte, it is also possible that some Latin books remained in the city, cared for by Greeks like Holobolos or by any Dominican brothers left behind in a small community as missionaries. The interactions between Western scholars connected with a monastery or missionary house and Greek scholars who worked with them would have been quite different from the experiences of Western merchants, courtiers, or ambassadors and legates who encountered Greeks. If reports of scholarly Byzantines who seriously studied the Latin language and who translated Latin literature into Greek reached the West, these reports would have brought a new and more positive dimension to the Western image of Byzantine Greeks in Constantinople.

In the more than half a century between 1261 and 1320, the approximate period of Holobolos's scholarly life, Planoudes' career, and Dante's life, relations between the Greeks of Constantinople and Latins in the city varied with the volatile politics of the time. A climate of cooperation among Byzantine and Western scholars at Constantinople apparently continued, however, allowing the Dominicans to enlarge the repertoire of Greek texts useful for debating the schismatic Orthodox that are included in *Contra graecos* (1252) and Philip of Pera's *De oboedientia ecclesiae romanae* (1358).[70] Political and doctrinal conflict between Greeks and Latins in Constantinople evidently did not discourage Western scholars from visiting the city in search of Greek texts. For example, Peter of Abano (Peter of Padua, ca. 1250–ca. 1310) visited Constantinople sometime between 1270 and 1290, obtained a copy of Aristotle's *Problemata*, translated the text from Greek to Latin, and finished a commentary on the work in 1310 while on the faculty of the University of Padua.[71] Nancy Siraisi has characterized Peter's *Expositio Problematum Aristotelis* as "the principal attempt to incorporate Greek problemata literature into the corpus of natural scientific knowledge generally accepted by medieval scholars in the West."[72] Roughly contemporary with Peter of Abano's visit to Constantinople, an unnamed Western scholar obtained a Greek text of Plutarch's *Moralia* annotated by Planoudes, either from Planoudes himself or from a member of his circle.[73]

Finally, an extraordinary testimonial to cooperation among Greek and Western scholars at Constantinople comes from Holobolos. In his translator's preface to the Greek version of Pseudo-Aristotle's *De plantis*, a curious work lost in Greek and preserved only in Arabic and Latin, Holobolos describes his own devotion to the writings of the Stagirite and his frustrated attempts to obtain a copy of the Latin version he had

69 Dondaine, "Contra graecos," 404–5.

70 Delacroix-Besniers, "Les precheurs" (above, n. 16), 152–66.

71 L. Thorndike, *A History of Magic and Experimental Science,* 2 vols. (New York, 1923), 2:877–79.

72 N. G. Siraisi, "The *Expositio Problematum Aristotelis* of Peter of Abano," *Isis* 61 (1970): 321–39, esp. 321.

73 P. A. Stadter, "Planudes, Plutarch, and Pace of Ferrara," *Italia medioevalia e umanistica* 16 (1973): 137–62, esp. 157–59.

heard touted in the boasts of Latin scholars.[74] After years of searching for the work in vain, Holobolos describes unexpected success:

> For a certain Latin from someplace or another suddenly appeared to us, a man of considerable literary education and learning; he enters our room, greets us pleasantly, chats in a friendly fashion, then places in our hands the book we longed for! I was delighted at this event, like a gift from God! I took the book with a burning heart; I became wholly engrossed in it. I read its contents with care. (814b20–25)[75]

It is frustrating to us that Holobolos gives no further identification of his benefactor than these cryptic words; although he uses the Greek word "Italikos" to describe him, this term designates "Latin-speaking" or "Western" as well as "Italian" at the time of Holobolos.[76] Did Holobolos use this generic term to protect a benefactor who, for some reason, wished to remain anonymous? Or might this scene be a piece of rhetoric simply invented by Holobolos to create an intriguing and dramatic vignette?

With this mysterious but affecting anecdote of respectful scholarly cooperation in Constantinople near the close of the thirteenth century, the evidence fades and my view through the keyhole comes to an end. I have caught—or think I have caught—a few snatches of Latin conversations in offended and hostile tones: "The Greeks call us barbarians. . . ." "They insult the noble Yolanda. . . ." "They cheat honest traders, especially if they can't speak Greek. . . ." "They stubbornly defend their unsound views about the Holy Trinity. . . ." "Their government is chaotic and their emperor is. . . ." A mild scholarly voice seemed to emerge from the jumble of complaints, "But Greek scholars are excellent and are helpful to Western scholars. . . ." With the exception of this last observation, the Latin comments that I may have detected reinforce a negative stereotype of the Greeks of Constantinople but permit no firm conclusions about what Dante knew about them, only suggesting what he might have known. Although incomplete and often inconclusive, my rather dismal report provides a glimpse into a crowded room where Greeks and Westerners shared an atmosphere of mutual distrust and disparagement that unfortunately seems to have predominated over the occasional episode of scholarly support, cooperation, and shared respect between the two communities.

74 For a comprehensive study of this work, see H. J. Drossaart Lulofs and E. Poortman, *De Plantis: Five Translations* (Amsterdam, 1989).

75 Text in Drosaart Lulofs and Poortman, *De Plantis*, 590; translation from Fisher, "Manuel Holobolos, Alfred of Sareshal" (above, n. 55), 199.

76 See E. Trapp, ed. *Lexikon zur byzantinischen Gräzitat* (Vienna, 2001) s.vv. Ἰταλός and Ἰταλικῶς, and Laiou, "Italy and the Italians" (above, n. 2), 74–80.

Acting against Conscience

Dante and the Aristotelian, Stoic, and Christian Traditions

MARCIA L. COLISH

As a thinker deeply concerned with moral questions, Dante knew that we can act against conscience. In addressing this theme in the *Commedia,* he could have drawn on a range of teachings from the Greek, Latin, and medieval Christian traditions. Of the ancient Greeks, Aristotle, "the master of those who know" (*'l maestro di color che sanno*; *Inf.* 4.131)—especially as reprised by Thomas Aquinas, his leading medieval commentator—is generally awarded the palm by Dante scholars. Stoicism, as personified by "moral Seneca" (*Seneca morale; Inf.* 4.141), receives less attention. And, while Bernard of Clairvaux, "that man of contemplation" (*quel contemplante*; *Par.* 32.1), is honored as the pilgrim's final guide, his star billing, for Dantists, derives mainly from his role as a mystic and devotee of the Virgin Mary; Bernard is rarely treated as an authority on the will or the psychodynamics of moral choice. Also bypassed by Dante scholars are treatments of conscience in scholastic texts informed by sources other than Aristotle. A fuller appreciation of Dante's ancient and medieval sources will help us to locate Dante in relation to those on which he could have drawn and those he may have chosen to apply, or ignore, in placing his own stamp on the topic of acting against conscience.

Aristotle calls the problem *akrasia* and its *locus classicus* is in book 7 of his *Nicomachean Ethics*. Medieval translators and commentators rendered akrasia as *incontinentia*; modern scholars also call it weakness of will. Both terms are unfortunate. Incontinence suggests unchastity, a limited if immoral behavior. But it also denotes the inability to control one's excretory organs, a dysfunction lacking in moral significance. Weakness of will suggests a full-blown mental faculty, an idea that postdates Aristotle. For Aristotle, akrasia involves a flawed relationship between intellect, the seat of our ethical principles, and spirit or passion, the other two parts of the soul. This disturbance is temporary and can occur in either passion or spirit. In either case, the immediate result is a physical reaction that overwhelms us, interfering with our ability to process sense-data correctly and to infer valid conclusions when we apply our principles to concrete cases. Thus, we act wrongly or fail to act rightly. Once we realize what we have done, we regret it.

This leads Aristotle to discuss different kinds of akratic behaviors and how they may be cured. Akrasia stemming from spirit is less culpable, because it is more rational and more easily healed than that arising from passion.[1]

While Aristotle notes that we can act impulsively or on the basis of soft knowledge, his real point is that akratics possess the same grasp of correct first principles as the habitually virtuous. He contrasts akratics sharply with the habitually vicious, those whose first principles are wrong and who act consistently with those principles. True, making good applications of valid principles is not always easy. For, while first principles are unchanging and can be known with certitude, particular situations always involve contingencies and cannot be known with certitude. For Aristotle, this fact complicates akratic decisions, but he views akrasia primarily in terms of the physical dysfunctions it causes, interfering with our normal cognitive operations. As for the cure, he says, "We must refer here to the natural scientists."[2] Physical problems need to be cured by specialists in physiology.

Aristotle on akrasia has received much attention from scholars who read him in the light of modern *problemata* and enlist him and his medieval commentators to their side.[3] As is well known, revisions of Robert Grosseteste's first complete translations of the *Nicomachean Ethics* served as the basis for commentators on the text in the second half of the thirteenth century. The *Nicomachean Ethics* was also read in university arts faculties. Notwithstanding Aristotle's own understanding of the somatic effects of akrasia, medieval and modern interpreters both tend to treat it as a problem in fallacious

1 The edition of the *Commedia* cited in this paper is that by G. Petrocchi (Milan, 1966–67; 2nd ed. 1994). The translation is Dante, *Inferno, Purgatorio, Paradiso*, trans. R. Hollander and J. Hollander, 3 vols. (New York, 2000–2007). Aristotle, *Nicomachean Ethics* 7.1–14, ed. and trans. R. Crisp (Cambridge, 2000), 119–42. Hereafter cited as *NE*.

2 *NE* 7.3, 7.5–10 (Crisp ed. 124–25, 127–36); quotation at 7.3 (125).

3 Without exhausting these debates, useful guides are provided by D. Wiggins, "Weakness of Will, Commensurability, and the Object of Desire," in *Essays on Aristotle's Ethics*, ed. A. Oksenberg Rorty (Berkeley, 1980), 241–65; C. Toner, "*Akrasia* Revisited: An Interpretation and Defense of Aristotle," *Southern Journal of Philosophy* 41 (2003): 283–306; A. W. Price, "Akrasia and Self-Control," in *The Blackwell Guide to Aristotle's Nicomachean Ethics*, ed. R. Kraut (Oxford, 2006), 234–54; M. Sultana, *Self-Deception and Akrasia: A Comparative Conceptual Analysis*, Analecta Gregoriana 300, Series Facultatis Philosophiae, B.21 (Rome, 2006), 142, 239–41, 244–52, 305–54; T. Hoffmann, J. Müller, and M. Perkams, "Die mittelalterliche Beitrag zum Problem der Willensschwäche," in *Das Problem der Willensschwäche in der mittelalterlichen Philosophie*, ed. T. Hoffmann, J. Müller, and M. Perkams (Leuven, 2006), 5–11; T. H. Irwin, "Aristotle Reads the *Protagoras*," in ibid., 22–41; P. Destrée, "Aristotle on the Causes of *Akrasia*," in *Akrasia in Greek Philosophy from Socrates to Plotinus*, ed. C. Bobonich and P. Destrée (Leiden, 2007), 139–65; M. Zingaro, "*Akrasia* and the Method of Ethics," in ibid., 167–91; D. Charles, "Aristotle's Weak *Akrasia*," in ibid., 193–214; T. Hoffmann, "Introduction," in *Weakness of Will from Plato to the Present*, ed. T. Hoffmann (Washington, 2008), ix–xii; N. O. Dahl, "Aristotle on Action, Practical Reason, and Weakness of Will," in *A Companion to Aristotle*, ed. G. Anagnostopoulos (Oxford, 2009), 498–511; and J. Müller, *Willensschwäche in Antike und Mittelalter: Eine Problemgeschichte von Sokrates bis Johannes Duns Scotus* (Leuven, 2009), who sees Christian thinkers before the reception of Aristotle as concerned mainly with the will as corrupted by original sin.

reasoning: correct, ethical first principles provide the major premise of a practical syllogism, but we draw faulty conclusions because of errors we make in the minor premise. The therapist needed is a logician not a physiologist.[4]

Although some expositors find Aristotle hard to defend, they do not attack him with the weapons provided by the Stoics, the leading ancient critics of akrasia.[5] The

4 On the medieval textual tradition of the *NE* as well as a dating of the commentary of Thomas Aquinas, placing its composition in Italy between 1261 and 1264 rather than during his second regency in Paris between 1269 and 1272, or 1271 and 1272, as is more standard, see V. J. Bourke, "The *Nicomachean Ethics* and Thomas Aquinas," in *St. Thomas Aquinas, 1274–1974: Commemorative Studies*, 2 vols. (Toronto, 1974), 1:239–59. Without exhausting treatments of medieval thinkers on *akrasia*, important contributions include R. Saarinen, *Weakness of the Will in Medieval Thought from Augustine to Buridan* (Leiden, 1994); idem, "Aristotle's *Akrasia* in Medieval Ethics," in *Les philosophies morales au moyen âge*, Actes du IXe congrès international de philosophie médiévale, Ottawa, 17–22 août 1992, ed. B. C. Bazán, E. Andújar, and L. G. Sbiocchi, 3 vols. (Ottawa, 1995), 2:922–31; idem, "Weakness of the Will: The Plurality of Medieval Explanations," in *Emotions and Choice from Boethius to Descartes*, ed. H. Lagerlund and M. Yrjönsuuri (Dordrecht, 2002), 85–97; Müller, *Willensschwäche*, 290–301, 381–698. Aquinas has been the favored focus, as in B. Kent, "Transitory Vice: Thomas Aquinas on Incontinence," *Journal of the History of Philosophy* 27 (1989): 199–223; eadem, *Virtues of the Will: The Transformation of Ethics in the Late Thirteenth Century* (Washington, DC, 1995); eadem, "Aquinas and Weakness of Will," *Philosophy and Phenomenological Research* 77 (2007): 70–91. See also E. Stump, "Aquinas's Account of Freedom: Intellect and Will," *The Monist* 80 (1997): 276–97; T. H. Irwin, "Will, Responsibility, and Ignorance: Aristotelian Accounts of Incontinence," in Hoffmann et al., *Das Problem der Willensschwäche* (above, n. 3), 39–58; T. Hoffmann, "Aquinas on the Moral Progress of the Weak Willed," in ibid., 221–47; D. J. M. Bradley, "Thomas Aquinas on Weakness of Will," in Hoffmann, *Weakness of the Will* (above, n. 3), 82–114. For this topic in other scholastics who would have been available to Dante, see M. J. Tracey, "Albert on Incontinence, Continence, and Divine Virtue," in Hoffmann et al., *Das Problem der Willensschwäche*, 197–220; T. Hoffmann, "Henry of Ghent's Voluntaristic Account of Weakness of Will," in Hoffmann, *Weakness of the Will*, 15–37; M. W. F. Stone, "Henry of Ghent on Freedom and *Human Action*," in *Henry of Ghent and the Transformation of Scholastic Thought: Studies in Memory of Jos Decorte*, ed. G. Guldentops and C. Steel (Leuven, 2003), 201–25 (but see Stone's unacknowledged borrowings as noted by M. V. Dougherty, P. Harsting, and R. L. Friedman, "40 Cases of Plagiarism," *Bulletin de philosophie médiévale* 51 [2009]: 368–69); T. Hoffmann, "L'*akrasia* selon Duns Scot," in *Duns Scot à Paris, 1302–2002*, Actes du colloque de Paris, 2–4 septembre 2002, ed. O. Boulnois et al. (Turnhout, 2004), 487–516; T. Noone, "Duns Scotus on *Incontinentia*," in Hoffmann et al., *Das Problem der Willensschwäche*, 285–305; G. Alliney, "L'akrasia secondo Duns Scoto: Autonomia della volontà e disordine della passione," in *Giovanni Duns Scoto: Studi e ricerche nel VII centenario della sua morte in onore di P. César Alarcón*, ed. M. Carbajo Núñez, 2 vols. (Rome, 2008), 1:429–49. A post-Aquinas *NE* commentary (dated 1289–95/96) with a brief treatment of *akrasia* is found in Radulfus Brito, *Le questione di Radulfo Brito sull' "Etica Nicomachia"* q. 158–59, ed. I. Costa (Turnhout, 2008), 528–32, with editor's discussion at 106–55.

5 B. Guckes, "Akrasia in der älteren Stoa," in *Zur Ethik der älteren Stoa*, ed. B. Guckes (Göttingen, 2004), 94–122, refuting R. Joyce, "Early Stoicism and Akrasia," *Phronesis* 40 (1995): 315–35. Also in line with Guckes are J. Gosling, "The Stoics and ἀκρασία," *Apeiron* 20 (1987): 179–202, and Müller, *Willensschwäche*, 155–93. Confirming that Stoics throughout the history of the school rejected akrasia, with a detailed doxography, is J.-B. Gourinat, "*Akrasia* and *Encrateia* in Ancient Stoicism: Minor Vice and Minor Virtue," in *Akrasia in Greek Philosophy* (above, n. 3), 215–47. S. Bartsch, *The Mirror of the Self: Sexuality, Self-Knowledge, and the Gaze in the Early Roman Empire* (Chicago, 2006), 230–55

Stoics are physical and psychological monists. There is no mind-body problem for them. There are no infrarational faculties in the soul. The soul is a fragment of the divine *logos*. The sage makes the rational law of the cosmos the law of his own being. Virtue is life in accordance with reason, and vice is the irrational; all else is a matter of indifference. Passions leading to vice stem from false intellectual judgments about the pleasure and pain we experience or the fear and desire we anticipate. When a fool acts, having misjudged things indifferent or irrational to be goods, his will operates at full strength. From this perspective, Aristotle's akrasia is a non-event. At the same time, the radical intellectualizing of ethics makes how we can act against conscience a real Stoic conundrum. Seneca is the only Stoic to address it.

While Seneca notes the existence of what he calls weak assent, found in pre-adult or sick adult minds, his focus is on normal adults capable of rational judgment and choice. He is not the first Latin author to use the term *conscientia* to denote the moral norms guiding ethical choices, although he develops it richly.[6] Seneca offers aversion therapy to discourage bad conscience, cognitive therapy to encourage good conscience, and both nightly examination of conscience and morning *praemeditatio futurorum malorum* to keep us on message. He uses various metaphors for conscience. Conscience is our judge, censor, and interrogator. It is our pilot through the stormy sea of life. It is medicine for the soul, whether as an analgesic, an antibiotic, a palliative, a prophylactic, an upper, a downer, or a performance-enhancing drug.[7]

---

passim and esp. 242 n. 16, errs in equating akrasia with choosing the lesser of two goods or the worse of two evils in Seneca.

6 E.g., Seneca, *De tranquillitate animi* 1.4–17, 2.1–15, in *L. Annaei Senecae Dialogorum libri duodecimo*, ed. L. D. Reynolds (Oxford, 1977); *Ep.* 95.37–41, 95.57–64, 102.28–29 in Seneca, *Epistulae morales*, ed. L. D. Reynolds, 2 vols. (Oxford, 1965). These editions of Seneca's moral works and letters will be cited unless otherwise noted. On weak assent in Seneca, see J. Wildberger, "Seneca and the Stoic Theory of Cognition: Some Preliminary Remarks," in *Seeing Seneca Whole: Perspectives on Philosophy, Poetry, and Politics*, ed. K. Volk and G. D. Williams (Leiden, 2006), 89–99. On the term *conscientia,* see P. Grimal, "Le vocabulaire de l'intériorité dans l'oeuvre philosophique de Sénèque," in *La langue latine, langue de philosophie*, Actes du colloque organisé par l'École française de Rome avec le concours de l'Université de Rome "La Sapienza," Rome, 17–19 mai 1990, Collection de l'École française de Rome 161 (Rome, 1992), 144, 157–59. A. Borgo, *Lessico morale di Seneca* (Naples, 1998), does not include *conscientia* among the terms she studies.

7 From an extensive literature, of greatest utility are P. Courcelle, *Connais-toi toi même de Socrate à Saint Bernard*, 3 vols. (Paris, 1974–75), 1:49–64; R. J. Newman, "*Cotidie meditare*: Theory and Practice of the *meditatio* in Imperial Stoicism," in *Aufstieg und Niedergang der römischen Welt*, ed. W. Haase (Berlin, 1989), 2.36.3:1473–1517; A.-J. Voelke, *La philosophie comme thérapie de l'âme: Études de philosophie héllenistique* (Fribourg, 1993), 73–106; H. Cancik, "Persona and Self in Stoic Philosophy," in *Self, Soul, and Body in Religious Experience*, ed. A. I. Baumgarten, J. Assmann, and G. G. Strousma (Leiden, 1998), 434–44; B. Inwood, "Stoic Ethics," in *The Cambridge History of Hellenistic Philosophy*, ed. K. Algra et al. (Cambridge, 1999), 675–738; M. Armisen-Marchetti, "Imagination and Meditation in Seneca: The Example of *Praemeditatio*," in *Seneca*, ed. J. G. Fitch (Oxford, 2008), 102–13. Much has also been written recently on the applicability of Michel Foucault's "care of the self" in this connection. For guides to this literature, see D. Cohen and R. Saller, "Foucault on Sexuality in Greco-Roman Antiquity," in *Foucault and the Writing of History*, ed. J. Goldstein (Oxford, 1994), 35–59; A. I. Davidson, "Ethics as Ascetics: Foucault, the History of

Seneca on examination of conscience in his *De ira* has received a consensus reading, but there is much more to the story.[8] Few, alas, possess a good conscience. He often describes people who know full well the difference between right and wrong but who give themselves a pass, shirking duties whether filial, marital, personal, professional, or civic. They retain a conscience but flee from it because it condemns these evasions. They may also perform these duties but for bad reasons. Acts against conscience include not only bad deeds but also bad intentions manifested in externally good deeds.[9]

Seneca paints a vivid picture of the psychic ills afflicting those who act against conscience. Entangled in hypocrisy, they incur self-deception, shame, worry, and fear. They find no peace or security. They are their own victims and worst enemies. As he observes to his correspondent Lucilius, in describing such wrongdoers, "Let us agree: Evil deeds are flagellated by conscience, and their conscience suffers the greatest torment because perpetual anxiety whips and drives them, so that they cannot trust in any guarantees of their own safety."[10]

Yet, how can Seneca square this outcome with Stoic rationalism?[11] He accepts that the will can be divided against itself: "Men both love and hate their vices at the same

---

Ethics, and Ancient Thought," in ibid., 63–80; S. Bartsch and D. Wray, "Introduction: The Self in Senecan Scholarship," in *Seneca and the Self*, ed. S. Bartsch and D. Wray (Cambridge, 2009), 4–6, 8–9; A. A. Long, "Seneca on the Self: Why Now?" in ibid., 20–36.

8 Seneca, *De ira* 3.36.1–3. Standard readings of this passage include P. Hadot, *Philosophy as a Way of Life: Spiritual Exercises from Socrates to Foucault*, ed. A. I. Davidson, trans. M. Chase (Oxford, 1995), 81–125; G. Reydams-Schils, *The Roman Stoics: Self, Responsibility, and Affection* (Chicago, 2005), 10, 18, 20, 98. Cf. J. Ker, "Seneca on Self-Examination: Rereading *On Anger*," in *Seneca and the Self*, 160–87. For Seneca's background, see J. Fillion-Lahille, *Le De ira de Sénèque et la philosophie des passions* (Paris, 1984), passim and esp. 2, 242, 263, 271; W. V. Harris, *Restraining Rage: The Ideology of Anger in Classical Antiquity* (Cambridge, MA, 2001), 220–23, 229–63. For other *loci*, see Seneca, *De ira* 3.36.4–38.1; *De beata vita* 1.19, 17.3–4, 20.4–5; *De beneficiis* 4.12.4, 4.21.5, ed. F. Préchac, 2 vols. (Paris, 1926–29); De *brevitate vitae* 10.2, 10.5; *De clementia* 1.1.1–4, ed. F.-R. Chaumartin (Paris, 2005); *De tranquillitate animi* 6.1; *Ep.* 3.4, 16.2, 23.7, 24.12, 28.16, 118.2–3.

9 Seneca, *De brevitate vitae* 10.2, 10.5.

10 Seneca, *Ep.* 97.15, 2:404–5: "hic consentiamus, mala facinora conscientia flagellari, et plurimum illi tormentum esse eo quod perpetua illam sollicitudo urget ac verberat, quod sponsoribus suae non potest credere" (my translation). See also *Ep.* 43.4.5, 105.7–8, 122.14.

11 Seneca, *Ep.* 95.8–9, 95.37–41, 95.43–45, 95.57–62. There is considerable debate on the relative importance of intellect and will in Seneca's ethics. R. Zöller, *Die Vorstellung vom Willen in der Morallehre Senecas* (Munich, 2003), looks ahead to later theories of intellectualism and voluntarism and tends to oversystematize Seneca. B. Inwood, *Reading Seneca: Stoic Philosophy at Rome* (Oxford, 2005), 102–56, stresses the multivalence of *voluntas* in Seneca and warns against anachronistic readings. A.-J. Voelke, *L'Idée de la volonté dans le Stoïcisme* (Paris, 1973), 17–18, 30–49, 90–95, 131–39, 161–70, 174–79, 184–99; S. Bobzien, *Determinism and Freedom in Stoic Philosophy* (Oxford, 1998), 250–313; Hadot, *Philosophy as a Way of Life* (above, n. 8), 84; and P. Veyne, *Seneca: The Life of a Stoic*, trans. D. Sullivan (New York, 2003), 64–65, argue for the primacy of intellect over will. Accenting the primacy of will is Zöller, *Die Vorstellung des Willen*, 90–93, 130–53, 179–89, 232–45; reducing the self as such to will in Seneca is R. Sorabji, *Self: Ancient and Modern Insights about Individuation, Life, and Death* (Chicago, 2006), 44–45, 178, 181–85. A more balanced view is offered by P. Impara, *Seneca e il mondo del volere* (Rome, 1986).

time."[12] To explain how good will and bad will can inhabit the same psychic space, he reframes a metaphor of Chrysippus, second head of the Stoic school, to show that contingency can exist in a world governed by inexorable if rational laws. Of necessity, a rolling cylinder describes a circular motion going downhill if it is pushed. But whether or not it is pushed is a matter of contingency.[13] Shifting this metaphor from physics to ethics, Seneca yokes it to another Chrysippian image that he also modifies. A runner cannot come to an abrupt stop at the end of his course, although he wants to do so. This outcome is not a consequence of passions overcoming rational choice. Rather, "just as one who, running downhill, cannot stop when he wills to stop, but whose body impels him onward, its momentum carrying him farther than he wills," so ingrained bad will continues to motivate, overlap with, and override both reason and good will.[14]

Seneca the psychologist deserves more attention from Dantists. True, Seneca's taste for packaging ideas as pithy aphorisms made him popular with florilegists. Aside from noting a few citations to his natural philosophy and the poet's remarks on two souls who appear in the *Commedia,* Dantists have left Seneca at that.[15] But Seneca's ethical works *in extenso* remained available; they were copied in the ninth and again in the twelfth century, and referenced widely.[16] The final book of Roger Bacon's *Opus maius* (1266) nicely illustrates that fact.[17] Bacon quotes lengthy chunks from Seneca's works as basic and

12 Seneca, *Ep.* 112.4, 2:472: "Homines vitia sua et amant simul et oderunt." My translation. This possibility in Seneca has also been noted by Voelke, *L'Idée de la volonté*, 172–75; Zöller, *Die Vorstellung vom Willen*, 44–45; T. Bénatouïl, *Faire usage: La pratique du Stoïcisme* (Paris 2006), 100–105, 109–12.

13 The standard ancient *testimonia* to this Chrysippian metaphor are Cicero, *De fato* 18.42–19.43, and Aulus Gellius, *Noctes atticae* 7.2.11–12. An outstanding treatment of this topic is provided by Bobzien, *Determinism and Freedom*. See also M. R. Graver, *Stoicism and Emotion* (Chicago, 2007), 63–64.

14 Seneca, *Ep.* 40.7, 1:106: "Quemadmodum per proclive currentium non ubi visum est gradus sisitur, sed incitatio corporis ponderi servit ac longius quam voluit effertur. . . ." My translation. Graver, *Stoicism and Emotion*, 68–70, discusses the ancient report of Chrysippus on the runner, given by Galen, but does not flag the difference in Seneca's handling of this theme, one which Bénatouïl, *Faire usage*, 100–105, 109–12, reports accurately.

15 Typical is *Enciclopedia Dantesca*, s.v. "Seneca, Lucio Anneo." Little or nothing more is added by S. Debenedetti, "Dante e Seneca filosofo," *Studi danteschi* 6 (1923): 5–24; G. Marzot, "Dante e Seneca 'morale'," *Atti del convegno di studi su Dante e Roma*, Roma, 8–16 aprile 1965 (Florence, 1965), 263–82; G. Mezzadioli, *Seneca in Dante: Dalla tradizione medievale all'officina dell'autore* (Florence, 1990); E. Pasquini, "Presenza di Seneca in Dante," in *Seneca nella coscienza dell'Europa*, ed. I. Dionigi (Milan, 1999), 111–36; E. Fenzi, "Seneca e Dante: Da Alessandro Magno a Ulisse," in *Studi sul canone letterario del trecento: Per Michelangelo Picone*, ed. J. Bartuschat and L. Rossi (Ravenna, 2003), 67–78; A. Setaioli, "Seneca and the Divine: Stoic Tradition and Personal Development," *International Journal for the Classical Tradition* 13 (2007): 343–44, 356, 362–63.

16 For earlier literature on the transmission of Seneca in the Middle Ages, see M. L. Colish, *The Stoic Tradition in the Early Middle Ages*, 2 vols. (Leiden, 1985; 2nd ed. 1990), 1:16–19; the most recent study of Seneca's medieval reception is D. Carron, "Sénèque, exemplarité et ambiguïté exemplaire (IV–XIVe siècle)," in *Exempla docent: Les exemples des philosophes de l'Antiquité à la Renaissance*, ed. T. Ricklin et al. (Paris, 2006), 307–33.

17 Roger Bacon, *Philosophia moralis* d. 1.3.12–14, d. 5 proemium 4, d. 5.3.3–4, d. 6.3.12, ed. E. Massa (Zurich, 1952), 58–59, 133, 138–39, 155. On this work, see E. Massa, *Ruggero Bacone: Etica e poetica*

acknowledged guides to the moral life, including passages in which Seneca comments on acts against conscience and the sufferings they entail. Bacon mentions his own use of a manuscript containing the full Senecan canon—no rarity, he suggests; it is also a corpus he sees as fully compatible with Christian ethics.

Trawling for parallels between the works of Seneca and the New Testament has a long history, but the two differ on the matter of conscience. Central here is Saint Paul. For Paul the key is not reason but the heart, on whose fleshy tablets the moral law is inscribed. Other biblical authors also find ethical values in the heart, frequently lamenting how our sins besmirch it and praying for its repristination. They agree that a clean heart requires God's aid as well as human effort, and obedience not just to the natural law but to a divine law that may or may not coincide with it. While good conscience is craved, for Paul conscience generally exposes our shortcomings. Its basic role is to alert us to our sins so that we can repent and do better. We can call on God's grace, but in so doing we also labor under the effects of original sin.[18]

The Church Father who draws most attention in this regard is Augustine. While he accepts Paul's notion of conscience as the mirror of sin, Augustine, in his late anti-Pelagian works, limits free will absent grace to any but vicious choices. He dismisses the norm of reason in ethics and with it the idea that all passions lead to vice. He redefines the norm as *caritas,* or rightly ordered love. Such being the case, his doctrine of the divided self is ultimately neither Pauline nor Senecan. As Augustine famously prays in the *Confessions,* "Give me chastity and continence, but not yet"; he presents himself as a Hercules at the crossroads, attracted metaphorically to two desirable women at the same time.[19] The conflicting loves which this image bespeaks will remain in tension during our life *in via*, in both individuals and societies.

---

nella storia dell'Opus Maius, Uomini e dottrine 3 (Rome, 1955), 81–110. At 86 and 97, Massa notes that Bacon thinks Seneca is divinely inspired and that the apocryphal Seneca–Paul correspondence is authentic. But Bacon introduces this point only as an afterthought at the very end of *Opus maius*, book 7, at d. 7.8.5, 181.

18 A useful survey citing the pertinent biblical *loci* is P. Delhaye, *Christian Conscience*, trans. C. U. Quinn (New York, 1968), 42–49, 66–99. Delhaye also sees a carryover of the idea of conscience from Stoicism to Christianity, and reviews the literature to his date of publication. Later literature is cited by G. Verbeke, *The Presence of Stoicism in Medieval Thought* (Washington, DC, 1983), 67 n. 97. For the medieval survival of the heart as the locus of sin and conscience, see S. Vecchio, "Peccatum cordis," in *Il cuore* = *Micrologus* 11 (2003): 325–42. The possible influence of Stoicism on Saint Paul has engendered a lengthy debate dominated by confessional, political, and disciplinary agendas. See the survey by M. L. Colish, "Stoicism and the New Testament: An Essay in Historiography," in *Aufstieg und Niedergang der römischen Welt*, ed. W. Haase and H. Temporini (Berlin, 1992), 2.26.1:334–79. An update on this controversy through the end of the 1990s, also one that argues for Stoic influence on Paul, is provided by T. Engberg-Pederson, *Paul and the Stoics* (Edinburgh, 2000), 1–31. With the marginal exception of Roger Bacon (above, n. 17), the apocryphal correspondence between Seneca and Saint Paul had no influence on the topics with which this paper is concerned. On that text in the Middle Ages, see G. G. Meerseman, "Seneca maestro di spiritualità nei opuscoli apocrifi dal XII al XV secolo," *Italia medioevale e umanistica* 16 (1973): 43–135.

19 Augustine, *Confessiones* 8.7.17, ed. L. Verheijen, CCSL 27 (Turnhout, 1981), 124: "Da mihi castitatem et continentiam, sed noli modo." My translation. On this evocation of Hercules, see E. TeSelle,

If Augustine looms large as a possible basis for Dantean psychodrama, a less expected yet critical patristic source is Jerome. Jerome introduces a problem, and language, destined to launch an extensive debate on conscience and acting against it in twelfth- and thirteenth-century scholasticism. In his exegesis of Ezekiel, following Origen, Jerome equates the ox, lion, and man in the prophet's vision with passion, spirit, and intellect. The fourth creature, the eagle, he calls *synderesis* and conscience, two mental functions that he conflates. Jerome offers no Latin translation of synderesis. He then propounds a contradiction. Synderesis/conscience is the *scintilla rationis* not extinguished even in Cain. But unlike the Cain of Genesis, Jerome's Cain has no remorse for his sin. And, Jerome observes, we encounter people every day who seem to have no sense of right and wrong, and no compunction whatever for their sins.[20]

Bernard of Clairvaux offers another approach. Central to the argument of his *Liber de gratia et libero arbitrio* (ca. 1128) is the utter freedom of the will, a "self-determining habit of the soul."[21] If subjected to external necessity or constraint of any kind, acts of the will are morally null. Nor do acts stemming from unwilled states such as inattention, faulty memory, and the like entail moral guilt or innocence. Acts must be fully willed to be on Bernard's moral map. Will acts with "reason always as its companion and, in a way, its handmaiden . . . but . . . many things may be done by it [will] against it [reason], . . . against its counsel and judgment." When this disconnect occurs, reason at

---

Augustine the Theologian (New York, 1970), 196–97; for its illustration in art, see P. Courcelle, *Les Confessions de Saint Augustine dans la tradition littéraire: Antécédents et postérité* (Paris, 1963), 679–80 and plate 47. On Hercules elsewhere in Augustine, see S. MacCormack, *The Shadows of Poetry: Vergil in the Mind of Augustine* (Berkeley, 1998), 119, 137, 214–15. On the theme of ordering charity, fine introductions remain J. Burnaby, *Amor Dei: A Study of the Religion of St. Augustine* (London, 1938), and J. Rief, *Der Ordobegriff des jungen Augustinus* (Paderborn, 1962). Although Augustine's presentation of memory, intellect, and will in his *De trinitate* 8–14, ed. W. J. Mountain and F. Glorie, CCSL 16 (Turnhout, 1968), as an analogy of the Trinity would appear to make these mental faculties coequal, debate continues on whether he regards intellect or will as primary. Accenting intellect and giving the palm to Stoic influence is S. Byers, "Augustine on the 'Divided Self': Platonist or Stoic?" *Augustinian Studies* 38 (2007): 105–18, reprising the position of J. Lössl, "Intellect with a (Divine) Purpose: Augustine on the Will," in *The Will and Human Action from Antiquity to the Present*, ed. T. Pink and M. W. F. Stone (London, 2004), 53–77. Current advocates of Augustinian voluntarism include R. Sorabji, "The Concept of Will from Plato to Maximus the Confessor," in ibid., 6–28; J. Wetzel, "Body Double: Saint Augustine and the Sexualized Will," in Hoffmann, *Weakness of Will* (above, n. 3), 58–81.

20 Jerome, *Commentariorum in Hezekielem libri XIV* 1.1.6–8a, ed. F. Glorie, CCSL 75 (Turnhout, 1964). On Origen as Jerome's source, see G. Madec, *Ambroise et la philosophie* (Paris, 1974), 125–27, and D. Kries, "Origen, Plato, and Conscience (*Synderesis*) in Jerome's Ezekiel Commentary," *Traditio* 57 (2002): 67–83. As is noted by R. Mellinkoff, *The Mark of Cain* (Berkeley, 1981), 1–21, 29–31, 40–50, Jewish exegetes sometimes treat Cain as repentant and sometimes not. The Church Fathers and early medieval Christian authors except Jerome (although she does not reference his Ezekiel commentary) mostly view Cain as repentant, although 12th-century scholastics such as Hugh of Saint Victor and Peter Comestor consider him an excommunicate condemned to eternal punishment.

21 Bernard of Clairvaux, *Liber de gratia et libero arbitrio* 1.2, in *Opere di San Bernardo*, ed. F. Gastaldelli, 6 vols. (Milan, 1984–2008), 1:360; repeated at 2.3, 1:364; trans. D. O'Donovan in Bernard of Clairvaux, *On Grace and Free Will*, Cistercian Fathers Series 19 (Kalamazoo, 1977), 55, 57.

once tells us that we have sinned and that the punishment we incur is just, because our moral choice was freely willed.[22]

For Bernard, judgment is the locus of our ethical first principles, and counsel applies these principles. Just as the will can reject good principles and good counsel, so counsel is also fallible. It can move us to act inspired by pleasure or expediency. The rectitude of our judgment is no guarantee of the rectitude of our counsel in planning its implementation. Bernard cites the example of Saint Peter's threefold denial of Christ. Peter knew exactly what he was doing and that it was wrong, but he let his self-love and desire for self-preservation outweigh his love of truth and love for Christ. Still, Peter repented at once, was forgiven by Christ, and remained his chief disciple. As this analysis suggests, Bernard's larger goal is to accentuate the positive. Even serious sinners against conscience can repent and be redeemed.[23] Bernard's *Liber de gratia et libero arbitrio* won the respect of the scholastics.[24] Dantists should follow their lead.[25]

22 Bernard, *Liber de gratia* 2.3–5 (Gastaldelli ed. 1:362–66). The quotation is at 2.3 (1:362–64): "rationem semper comitem et quodammodo pedissequam: ... sed ... multa faciat per ipsam contra ipsam, ... contra eius consilium sive iudicium."

23 Bernard, *Liber de gratia* 4.11–12, 5.15, 7.21, 12.38–40 (1:372–74, 378, 386, 404–8). For an alternative reading that places this passage in the context of modern discussions of akrasia, see C. Trottmann, "Bernard de Clairvaux sur la faiblesse de la volonté et la duperie de soi," in Hoffmann et al., *Das Problem der Willensschwäche* (above, n. 3), 147–72.

24 On scholastic appropriations of this work, see U. Faust, "Bernhards 'Liber de gratia et libero arbitrio': Bedeutung, Quellen und Einfluss," *Analecta monastica* 6 (1952): 35–51; J. Châtillon, "L'Influence de S. Bernard sur la pensée scolastique du XIIe et du XIIIe siècle," in *Saint Bernard théologien*, Actes du congrès de Dijon, 15–19 septembre 1953 (Rome, 1953), 268–88; noting in detail its particular appeal to Franciscans is J. G. Bougerol, "Saint Bonaventure et Saint Bernard," *Antonianum* 46 (1971): 5, 22–24, 30–31, 53–60, 79. On its use by Aquinas, see M. B. Pennington, "The Influence of Bernard of Clairvaux on Thomas Aquinas," *Studia Monastica* 16 (1974): 281–91; M. D. Jordan, "Thomas Aquinas and the Life of Contemplation," in *Bernardus Magister*, ed. J. R. Sommerfeldt, Cistercian Studies Series 135 (Spencer, MA, 1992), 449–60; Kent, *Virtues of the Will* (above, n. 4), 112–13, 118. It is striking that P. Delhaye, "La conscience morale dans la doctrine de S. Bernard," in *Saint Bernard théologian* (above), 209–22, can discuss this topic without ever referencing Bernard's treatise on grace and free will. One may ignore M. Corbin, *La grace et la liberté chez Saint Bernard de Clairvaux* (Paris, 2002), an exercise in the author's personal theology.

25 The standard approach, ignoring this text altogether, is found in *Enciclopedia Dantesca*, s.v. "Bernardo di Chiaravelle." Dantists who address other aspects of Bernard's work but not his treatise on grace and free will include R. D. Di Lorenzo, "Dante's Saint Bernard and the Theology of Liberty in the *Commedia*," in Sommerfeldt, *Bernardus Magister*, 497–515; S. Botterill, *Dante and the Mystical Tradition: Saint Bernard of Clairvaux in the Commedia* (Cambridge, 1994); idem, "The Figure of St. Bernard in Dante's *Commedia*," in *Seminario dantesco internazionale* 1, Atti del primo convegno tenutosi al Chauncey Conference Center, Princeton, 21–23 ottobre 1994, ed. Z. G. Barański (Florence, 1997), 149–70; F. Mazzoni, "San Bernardo e la visione poetica della *Divina Commedia*," in ibid., 171–241; F. Drago Rivera, *S. Bernardo e l'ascesa del Paradiso*, Società Dante Alighieri Quaderni 12 (Milan, 1995). R. Kay, "Dante in Ecstasy: *Paradiso* 33 and Bernard of Clairvaux," *Mediaeval Studies* 66 (2004): 183–212, mentions the anthropology in this treatise but only as a curtain-raiser for his discussion of Bernard's mystical doctrine. The only Dantist to date to suggest the possible influence of Bernard on Dante's view of free will is F. Mazzoni, *Con Francesco Mazzoni: Chiose inedite a 'Paradiso' I–XI*, Atti della giornata di studio, Firenze, 14 novembre 2007 (Florence, 2008), 127.

But it was to Jerome that scholastics turned their attention in their earliest works, owing to the fact that Peter Lombard cites Jerome on the scintilla rationis not extinguished in Cain, with his approval. While the Lombard does not mention synderesis, commentators on his *Sentences* in the next century and a half do, debating the issue repeatedly.[26] By the mid-thirteenth century, they had agreed on some points: synderesis and conscience are different mental functions. Ethical decisions occur in the practical not the theoretical intellect. The scintilla rationis is inextinguishable. While synderesis or conscience tells us how to apply our ethical first principles to concrete cases, the will may or may not choose to follow its advice.

More detailed surveys of these debates are provided elsewhere, but brief mention of four leading solutions is useful here. Bonaventure thinks that our knowledge of first principles requires the *lux naturalis*, a subdivision of the divine illumination needed in all modes of human cognition. He locates both the general principles and the judgment of how to apply them in the conscience. Synderesis is the efficient cause of the will. But while synderesis cannot be extinguished, it can be impeded by voluntary opposition as well as by our passions and intellectual obtuseness. Conscience can also make mistakes and violate its own norms in applying those norms.[27]

In Albert the Great's account, synderesis is the locus of the inerrant and unexcogitated ethical principles that inform the conscience. Synderesis acts as the formal cause of our moral actions and conscience as their material cause. Albert models this process as a deductive syllogism. Synderesis supplies the major premise. Practical reason supplies the minor premise. Conscience draws the conclusion. Will then commits us to act or avoid action. The final decision lies with the will.[28]

26 Peter Lombard, *Sententiae in IV libris distinctae* 2. d. 39. c. 33, ed. I. C. Brady, 3rd ed., 2 vols. (Grottaferrata, 1971–81), 1:556. Cf. Saarinen, *Weakness of the Will* (above, n. 4), 65, 67–68, who thinks it was the Lombard's disciple Peter of Poitiers who first put Jerome into play. For the most recent overview of this topic from Peter Lombard through John Duns Scotus, with literature to date and *loci* in the texts, see M. L. Colish, "*Synderesis* and Conscience: Stoicism and Its Medieval Transformations," in *From Knowledge to Beatitude: St. Victor, Twelfth-Century Scholars, and Beyond; Essays in Honor of Grover A. Zinn, Jr.*, ed. E. A. Matter and L. Smith (Notre Dame, IN, 2013), 229–46.

27 Bonaventure, *Comm. In II Sent.* d. 39. a. 1. q. 1–3, a. 2. q. 1–3, in *Opera omnia*, ed. Collegium S. Bonaventurae, 11 vols. in 10 (Quaracchi, 1882–1902), 2:897–917. On Bonaventure's pan-illuminist epistemology, see S. P. Marrone, *In the Light of Thy Countenance: Science and the Knowledge of God in the Thirteenth Century*, 2 vols. (Leiden, 2001), 1:28–108, 122–88, 201–50. A brief but accurate account (although see Dougherty, Harsting, and Friedman, "40 Cases of Plagiarism" [above, n. 4], 369) is provided by M. W. F. Stone, "Moral Psychology before 1277: The Will, *liberum arbitrium*, and Rectitude in Bonaventure," in Pink and Stone, *Will and Human Action* (above, n. 19), 99–126.

28 Albert the Great, *Comm. In II Sent.* d. 5. a. 6 ad 6–7, d. 24. a. 14, d. 39. a. 2; *Summa de creaturis* pars 2; *De homine* q. 71–72, in *Opera omnia*, ed. S. C. A. Borgnet, 38 vols. (Paris, 1890–95), 27:121, 412–14, 621–22; 35:590–602. On Albert's position, see C. T. Dijon, "La syndérèse selon Albert le Grand," in *Albertus Magnus: Zum Gedanken nach 800 Jahren; Neue Zugänge, Aspekte und Perspektiven*, ed. W. Senner et al. (Berlin, 2001), 255–75; M. Perkams, "Gewissenirrtum und Gewissensfreiheit," *Philosophisches Jahrbuch* 112 (2005): 35, 36, 49; J. Müller, "*Agere contra conscientiam*: The Relationship between Weakness of Will and Conscience in Albert the Great," in *Intellect et imagination dans la philosophie médiévale*, Actes du XIe congrès international de philosophie

Thomas Aquinas breaks ranks along with Alexander of Hales by holding that synderesis, the spark of reason, is indeed extinguished in some people, namely, the mentally defective and congenitally insane. Otherwise, he agrees that the scintilla rationis is retained even in the worst of sinners, including the damned. Aquinas adds that in ethics pertaining to supernature, faith must join synderesis for its principles to be correct. But where natural law and natural reason suffice, synderesis governs alone. He adopts Albert's syllogism model. Everything up through the judgment of conscience remains in the realm of knowledge. In order to move from knowledge to act, free will must operate. Just as conscience can err in making specific applications of the norms retained by synderesis, so also the will can choose not to carry out the directives of conscience, whether or not they are correct. Error and sin can occur both ways.[29]

John Duns Scotus, the last scholastic whose work Dante could have known, offers an elegant analysis with notable parallels to that of Bernard. For Duns Scotus, the general principles we cognize require no Bonaventuran illumination; they are located in the synderesis. Conscience applies these principles to concrete cases. Both synderesis and conscience inform the will when it chooses the good out of love for justice. But neither synderesis nor conscience binds the will; they are only partial causes of the will's action. For the will can move itself. Thus, it can act against conscience purely on its own initiative. Even when it acts in harmony with conscience, the will may be drawn by advantage rather than by justice. Duns Scotus aligns himself with Seneca and the Christian tradition by judging moral acts in light of their intentions. With Bernard he stresses the radical freedom of the will, agreeing that reason, however labeled, makes recommendations that the will can reject. Further, when acting against conscience, the will may suborn reason to invent justifications for its evil choices.[30]

---

médiévale, Porto, 26–31 août 2002, ed. M. C. Pacheco and J. F. Meirinhos, 4 vols. (Turnhout, 2006), 3:1303–15. One may ignore S. B. Cunningham, *Reclaiming Moral Agency: The Moral Philosophy of Albert the Great* (Washington, DC, 2008), 119–24, 125, who considers the morality of external acts in Albert but not their psychogenesis or inner intentions.

29 Thomas Aquinas, *Comm. In II Sent.* d. 7. q. 1 ad 2, d. 24. q. 2. a. 3–4, d. 39. q. 3. a. 1–3; *In III Sent.* d. 33. q. 2. a. 4. sol. 4, ed. P. Mandonnet and M. F. Moos, 4 vols. (Paris, 1929), 2:182–86, 609–15, 995–1005; 3:1066–67; *Quaestiones disputatae de veritate* q. 16. a. 1–q. 17. a. 1–4, ed. R. Spiazzi, 9th rev. ed., 2 vols. (Turin, 1953), 1:320–25; *Summa theologiae* Ia q. 79. a. 12–13, IaIIae q. 19. a. 5–6, Blackfriars ed. and trans., 61 vols. (New York, 1964–76), 11:187–95, 18:61–67. For a recent and judicious study balancing will and intellect in Aquinas, see M. S. Sherwin, *By Knowledge and Love: Charity and Knowledge in the Moral Theology of St. Thomas* (Washington, DC, 2005), 1–62. On the scintilla rationis in Alexander of Hales, see H. P. Weber, "The *Glossa in IV Sententiarum* by Alexander of Hales," in *Mediaeval Commentaries on the Sentences of Peter Lombard*, ed. P. W. Rosemann (Leiden, 2010), 2:105–7.

30 John Duns Scotus, *Ordinatio* 2. d. 39, in *The Philosophical Theology of John Duns Scotus*, trans. A. B. Wolter, ed. M. M. Adams (Ithaca, 1990), 45–46, 162–66. On Duns Scotus, see M. E. Ingham, "Practical Wisdom: Scotus' Presentation of Prudence," in *Duns Scotus: Metaphysics and Ethics*, ed. L. Honnefelder et al. (Leiden, 1996), 568–71; eadem, *La vie de la sagesse: Stoïcisme du moyen âge* (Fribourg, 2007), with a fine discussion of Duns Scotus's synthesis of Franciscan and Dominican teachings on this issue at 69–99, 103–8, and 113–28. For a useful recent survey of Duns Scotus and his scholastic predecessors on intellectualism and voluntarism in ethics, acknowledging their differences but accenting the point that they all see these faculties as functional correlatives, see T. Hoffmann,

As we see, it was possible for medieval theologians to offer robust analyses of the problem of acting against conscience without invoking Aristotle, even after the *Nicomachean Ethics* became available to them. Another medieval tradition relevant to this subject is canon law. Canonists in the twelfth and thirteenth centuries do not cite Aristotle, but they have much to say on the culpability of unwilled actions, whether occasioned by force or fear. They distinguish among various kinds of threat, and between *coactio absoluta* and *coactio conditionaliter*. They use the idea of the constant man, as found in Roman law, as a criterion in judging degrees of coercion and the culpability they entail. Whether expressing the equanimity of the Stoic sage or the courage and steadfastness of the ideal Roman patrician, the constant man holds fast to his values in the face of pressure. Some popes appealed to this norm in judging actual cases of forced marriage, and it found its way into the canonical literature, although without producing clear agreement on how to define its limits. Some canonists are lenient on this and other issues, arguing that it is possible to retain a pure and upright intention, guiltless in God's sight, even if one is constrained to act in contravention of one's moral principles. Other canonists take a harder line. Arguing that it is better to suffer evil than to commit it, they see as culpable to some degree any departure from one's moral commitments. These canonical positions have been known and richly documented for some time, although they are rarely noted in Dante scholarship.[31]

Neither the arguments of the canonists nor the theological discussions which do not cite Aristotle are acknowledged by the Dante scholars who focus attention on the medieval fortunes of book 7 of the *Nicomachean Ethics*. To be sure, Bernard wrote before the translation of the *Nicomachean Ethics*. The scholastic arguments noted above all occur in commentaries on the *Sentences*, the work of fledgling theologians. They may or may not recur in the authors' later works, if there are later works. This includes Albert and Aquinas, who also commented on the *Nicomachean Ethics*. As a genre, *Sentences* commentaries do not get the attention they deserve in research on Dante's possible sources, despite the fact that most students of theology in his century were taught at the mendicant *studia*, where theological education began—and often ended—with Peter Lombard's *Sentences*, amplified, if at all, by the *Sentences* commentaries of Bonaventure or Aquinas, or their abbreviations. The curricula and libraries of Santa Maria Novella and Santa Croce, well known to Dante, attest to that fact.[32]

"Intellectualism and Voluntarism," in *The Cambridge History of Medieval Philosophy*, ed. R. Pasnau and C. van Dyke, 2 vols. (Cambridge, 2010), 1:414–27, with literature on this debate cited at 1:417 n. 7.

31 S. Kuttner, *Kanonistische Schuldlehre von Gratian bis auf die Dekretalen Gregors IX*, ST 64 (Vatican City, 1935), 299–330. On the theme of the constant man, see also J. A. Brundage, *Medieval Canon Law* (London, 1995), 166–68, who regards him as a mythical or fictitious figure and who agrees that papal and canonical applications of this norm led to variegated conclusions in the 12th and 13th centuries.

32 For Dante's access to the lectures and the libraries of Santa Maria Novella and Santa Croce, see C. T. Davis, "Education in Dante's Florence," in *Dante's Italy and Other Essays* (Philadelphia, 1984), 146–47; idem, "The Florentine *Studia* and Dante's 'Library'," in *The Divine Comedy and the Encyclopedia of the Arts and Sciences*, ed. G. Di Scipio and A. Scaglione (Amsterdam, 1988), 338–66. Our knowledge of education in the mendicant *studia* has been much enriched by M. M. Mulchahey,

In any case, Aristotle's akrasia proves to be less relevant to Dante than many of the available positions just discussed. For the Latin Aristotle, incontinentia stemming from spirit is less culpable, because it is more rational, than incontinentia stemming from passion. Dante disagrees. While Virgil cites the *Nicomachean Ethics* as his authority in describing sins as motivated by "incontinence, malice, and mad brutishness" (*incontinenza, malizia, e matta bestialitade*; *Inf.* 11.79–84; quotation at 11.82–83), the least serious sins for Dante are those of the flesh, and the worst sins are the most, not the least, intellectual. Aquinas also treats sins stemming from the passions as the least serious because he regards emotional states as more transitory than mental dispositions and as relinquished sooner.[33] Dante ignores that explanation as well. While the sins of Dante's incontinent may be swift to arrive, they are no swifter to depart than any other kind of sin. Nor does akrasia as weakness of will describe any of the damned.[34] All who cross the Acheron embrace their sins with full commitment. Dante does not admit any mitigating factors in lessening his sinners' guilt. The damned were all healthy adults in command of their faculties. They may have fallen only once. But if they died impenitent, their fall is conclusive and their eternal punishment is just.

Do Dante's sinners retain a grasp of moral first principles? Is the scintilla rationis unextinguished in the damned, as Aquinas and most of his predecessors say? Are they flagellated by their conscience, as are Seneca's sinners?[35] In Dante's lexicon, the assaults sin makes on conscience include obscuring or soiling (*Purg.* 13.88–89; *Par.* 17.124) or more usually biting or gnawing (*Inf.* 11.52, 19.119; *Purg.* 3.6–9, 33.93). But, with a few exceptions, the souls able to register these assaults are portrayed as alive, or as operating in time for the duration of the poem, starting with the pilgrim himself.

Dante presents the pilgrim both as acting against conscience and as acting in good conscience. In *Inferno* 1 and 2, he is awakened morally and realizes that he has gone

---

First the Bow Is Bent in Study: Dominican Education before 1350 (Toronto, 1998), 134–41, 215, 553, and B. Roest, *A History of Franciscan Education (ca. 1210–1517)* (Leiden, 2000), 7, 9–11, 43, 65–97, 114–15, 123, 127–34. See also W. J. Courtenay, "Programs of Study in the Fourteenth Century," in *Manuels, programmes de cours et techniques d'enseignement dans les universités médiévales*, ed. J. Hamesse (Louvain-la-Neuve, 1994), 346–49.

33 See, for instance, Thomas Aquinas, *ST* IaIIae q. 78. a. 4 ad 2–3, 25:200–202.

34 Scholars wanting to read Dante as an Aristotelian or Thomist have wrestled with these discrepancies, from W. H. V. Reade, *The Moral System of Dante's Inferno* (Oxford, 1909; repr. Port Washington, NY, 1969), 11–13, 16, 66, 183–87, 214–22, 356, 382–430, to T. K. Swing, *The Fragile Leaves of the Sybil: Dante's Master Plan* (Westminster, MD, 1962), 59–60, 137, 154–56, 159–60, 164, to T. G. Bergin, *Dante* (New York, 1965), 269–71, and D. Davidson, "How Is Weakness of Will Possible?" in *Essays and Events* (Oxford, 2001), 24–25. Unhappy efforts to explain sloth, in particular, in terms of weakness of will have been made from P. H. Wicksteed, *Dante and Aquinas* (London, 1913), 164–65, to J. Freccero, *Dante and the Poetics of Conversion*, ed. R. Jacoff (Cambridge, MA, 1986), 85, and M. Migiel, "Canto XVIII: Love, Free Will, and Sloth," in *Purgatorio*, California Lectura Dantis, ed. A. Mandelbaum et al. (Berkeley, 2008), 194–98.

35 See the extremely scanty treatment, merely listing *loci* in Dante's works, ignoring the issue of acting against conscience, and citing as his only possible source Aquinas, *De veritate* 17.1, in *Enciclopedia Dantesca*, s.v. "Coscienza."

astray. He is blocked by the vices, traditionally identified as lust, pride, and avarice, signified by the three beasts he meets in the dark wood. To the morally oblivious, these vices may seem unexceptional or even attractive. But the pilgrim now sees them as wrong and dangerous. He is beset by conflict. This is not a Pauline tension between flesh and spirit or an Augustinian tension between two loves, but a conflict between two modes of fear.[36] He fears the vicious beasts. Reason tells him to flee. But he also fears the trip to do just that which Virgil proposes. Seneca would judge this latter fear to be an irrational passion, although it is allayed when the pilgrim learns of the trip's heavenly warrants. But the pilgrim's initial fear, *pace* Seneca, is salubrious, a first step toward the fear of the Lord that is the beginning of wisdom.

The pilgrim does show recovery of his moral bearings during the trip. Having heard Brunetto Latini's prophecy of his future, the pilgrim avers that conscience will fortify him against the blows of fortune: "as long as conscience does not chide, / I am prepared for Fortune as she wills" (*pur che mia coscïenza non mi garra, / ch'a la Fortuna, come vuol, son presto*; *Inf.* 15.92–93). Good conscience also steels him to do his duty to the reader, overcoming his fear of reporting the horrible punishment of Bertran de Born: "[I] saw a thing I would be loath / to mention without further proof, / were I not comforted by conscience" (*e vidi cosa ch'io avrei paura, / sanza più prova, di contarla solo; / se non che coscïenza m'assicura*; *Inf.* 28.113–15). Yet, despite the progressive strengthening of his faculties, the pilgrim still balks at entering the refining fire that purges lust—"against my will, I stood stock still" (*E io pur fermo e contra coscïenza*; *Purg.* 27.33)—although he knows it is right and necessary for him to do so. It is only after he has risen from Lethe that he can leave behind a conscience able to accuse him of sin against it: "nor does my conscience prick me for it" (*né honne coscïenza che rimorda*; *Purg.* 33.93). Short of heaven's gate, anyone, at any time—even Virgil (*Purg.* 3.6–9)—can commit acts against conscience, in matters large and small, but also regret and correct them.

These references to conscience are straightforward. There is also one passage in the *Commedia* in which Dante presents conscience ironically. The simoniac Pope Nicholas III reacts violently after the pilgrim upbraids him: "whether gnawed by anger or by conscience, / he kicked hard with both his feet" (*o ira o coscïenza che 'l mordasse, / forte spingeva con ambo le piote*; *Inf.* 19.119–20). This either/or construction does not fool the reader. *Pace* the theologians from Jerome to Aquinas, the denizens of Dante's *Inferno* have lost the scintilla rationis. But Dante's Cain, like the Cain of Genesis but unlike Jerome's Cain, is able, by means of it, to feel remorse. He is not unrepentant among the damned but has won a place in *Purgatorio* (*Purg.* 14.133), on the path to eventual salvation. While the souls in *Inferno* have lost "the good of the intellect" (*il ben de l'intelletto*;

36 On this point, cf. Freccero, *Dante and the Poetics of Conversion*, 1–10, 18–20, 24, 29–54, seconded by G. Mazzotta, "Dante: Healing the Wounded Will," in Hoffmann, *Weakness of Will* (above, n. 3), 139, 144–46.

Inf. 3.18), they do not lack intelligence. Some can predict the future.[37] As Duns Scotus would recognize, many of them are quite capable of confecting elaborate speeches rationalizing their sins and shifting the responsibility for them.[38] They reflect the reprehensible applications made by the willful misuse of reason. They may complain about their punishments and seek to elicit the pilgrim's sympathy, but none of the damned manifests remorse for the sins themselves or the self-flagellation seen by Seneca as attaching to conscious wrongdoing.

There is but one sinner in *Inferno* presented by Dante as having acted against conscience: the ex-*condottiere* Guido da Montefeltro (*Inf.* 27.58–120). The career he gave up relied less on force than fraud, as he confesses: "my deeds were not / a lion's but the actions of a fox" (*l'opere mei / non furon leonine, ma di volpe*; *Inf.* 27.74–75). Guido became a Franciscan friar but then terminally trashed his repentance. Acceding to the request of Pope Boniface VIII, who promised him absolution before the fact, Guido abetted him in an unjust war, advising him on how to recruit allies and then defraud them. The facts of this case were well known to Dante's readers. Despite the spin Guido puts on the tale, the offer of absolution reflects the awareness on both sides that Guido's immoral advice, and his giving of political advice at all, was sinful and a contravention of his religious calling. When he died unrepentant, not even an advocate with the charisma of Francis of Assisi could save him from the demon who claimed his soul. The demon points out, quite rightly, that prophylactic absolution is a logical and theological impossibility. The fraudster is himself defrauded; but it was all Boniface's fault, says Guido. Some Dantists see Guido's account as itself fraudulent. Guido's Franciscan conversion was a sham. It was the old Guido who advised the pope, with his eyes wide open.[39] Others think Guido's conversion was honest, whether or not he was utterly victimized by Boniface. A Guido who was a false friar would have been as lacking in verisimilitude

37 Thus, Francesca da Rimini (*Inf.* 5.105), Farinata (*Inf.* 10.97–108), Brunetto Latini (*Inf.* 14.61–78), Nicholas III (*Inf.* 19.76–87), Vanni Fucci (*Inf.* 24.143–51), and Pier da Medicina, Ingioletto di Carignana, and Camiscione de' Pazzi (*Inf.* 28.75–93), although their forecasts are all negative, focusing on the crimes and punishments of other sinners, Dante's future misfortunes, and unhappy events to come in Italian politics.

38 Thus, Francesca blames "Love," the book that she and Paolo were reading, and God's withdrawal of his friendship (*Inf.* 5.97–138); Ciacco blames the envy of the Florentines (*Inf.* 6.49–90) and Pier delle Vigne that of his fellow counselors (*Inf.* 13.33–78); Jacopo Rusticucci blames his wife (*Inf.* 16.43–45); Venedico Caccianemico blames the socialization of his native Bologna (*Inf.* 18.63); Guido da Montefeltro blames Pope Boniface VIII (*Inf.* 27.26–117); Master Adam blames the noble family that hired him to counterfeit the coinage (*Inf.* 30.88–90); Ugolino della Gherardesca blames Archbishop Ruggieri (*Inf.* 33.13–90).

39 See, for example, A. Hatcher, "Dante's Ulysses and Guido da Montefeltro," *Dante Studies* 88 (1970): 109–17; J. G. Truscott, "Ulysses and Guido," *Dante Studies* 91 (1973): 58–62, 69; J. Petrie, "Canto XXVII: False Counselors; Guido da Montrefeltro," in *Inferno*, California Lectura Dantis, ed. A. Mandelbaum et al. (Berkeley, 1998), 357–67, with a review of the controversial literature to date; Dante Alighieri, *The Divine Comedy*, trans. and comm. M. Musa, 3 vols. in 6 (Bloomington, 1996–2004), 1.2:357, 359–67, 368, 369; J. A. Scott, *Understanding Dante* (Notre Dame, IN, 2003), 381 n. 9.

as a Boniface who was not a corrupt pope.[40] If we take Guido's Franciscan conversion seriously, then he did act against conscience. He weighed the alternatives and choose to let sinful considerations override his religious commitments.

Dante clearly sets up Guido's case for comparison with Buonconte da Montefeltro, his kinsman and fellow *condottiere*, whose last-minute "little tear" (*lagrimetta*; *Purg.* 5.107) gave the angel victory over the devil competing for his moribund soul and won him a place in *Purgatorio*. Rational calculation plays no role in that account; Dante presents Buonconte as a man of action, not a man of thought. But a suggestive, if less obvious, comparison is with Piccarda Donati and Constance of Sicily (*Par.* 3.103–20). They, too, forswore monastic vows, in their case in order to marry. Guido and Piccarda both describe these events with verbs in the passive voice. As they tell their tales, they did not act but were acted upon. Guido says that it was the pope "who drew me back to my old ways" (*mi rimise ne le prime colpe*; *Inf.* 27.7). In her own case, not naming Corso, the brother who had her abducted from the convent and forced into an unwanted marriage, Piccarda cites only the generic agency of malicious men: "Then men more used to evil than to good / carried me off, away from the sweet cloister" (*Uomini poi, a mal più ch'a ben usi / fuor mi rapiron de la dolce chiostra*; *Par.* 3.106–7). She mentions no agent at all in Constance's case: "She was a sister and, like me, she had the shadow / of the holy veil torn from her head. / But, even after she was cast into the world / against her will and against proper custom, / the veil was never loosened from her heart" (*sorella fu, e così le fu tolta / di capo l'ombra de le sacre bende. / Ma poi che pur al mondo fu rivolta / contra suo grado e contra buona usanza / non fu dal vel del cor già mai disciolta*; *Par.* 3.113–17). Reflecting her own humility, Piccarda presents Constance as the more stalwart, in some way preserving her monastic commitment when thrust back into secular life. As Piccarda explains, as ex-nuns their neglect of their vows makes them the least of the saints; they fitly dwell in the lowest celestial sphere: "and this our lot, which seems so very low, / is given us because of vows neglected / and, in part, no longer valid" (*E questa sorte che par giù cotanto, / però n'è data, perchè fuor negletti / li nostri voti, e vòti in alcun canto*; *Par.* 3.55–57). Beatrice confirms that the heaven of the moon suits

40 See, for example, A. Chiari, "Il canto di Guido da Mantefeltro," in *Lettere dantesche* (Bergamo, 1973), 83–110; Dante Alighieri, *The Divine Comedy*, trans. and comm. C. S. Singleton, Bollingen Series 80, 3 vols. in 6 (Princeton, NJ, 1977), 1.2:490; C. J. Ryan, "Free Will in Theory and Practice," in *Dante Soundings: Eight Literary and Historical Essays*, ed. D. Nolan (Dublin, 1981), 101–11; Alfredo Cottignoli, "La prospettiva dell'eterno (Inf. XXVII)," in *Le metafore della ragione: Dante, Manzoni, Tenca* (Pisa, 1988), 36–51; G. Muresu, "La 'rancura' di Guido da Montefeltro (Inferno XXVII)," *Studi danteschi* 70 (2005): 62–86. Accenting Dante's critique of leaders from the Romagna is A. Battistini, "Miti, leggende e personaggi di Romagna nei primi commentatori del *Commedia*," in *Dante e la fabbrica della Commedia*, ed. A. Cottignoli, D. Donini, and G. Grappioni (Ravenna, 2008), 295–98; placing full blame on Boniface, as well as emphasizing that the incident as reported is historically accurate, is M. Seriacopi, *Bonifacio VIII nella storia e nell'opera di Dante* (Florence, 2003), 206–13. The view of J. Markalin, "Dante's Guido da Montefeltro: A Reconsideration," *Dante Studies* 100 (1982): 25–40, treating Guido's speech as merely about rhetoric, pure and simple, has found no critical support.

the souls housed there: "assigned to this place for failing in their vows" (*qui relegate per manco di voto*; *Par.* 3.30).

The situation of Piccarda and Constance remains troubling to the pilgrim, as it has been to a number of Dantists. The stories of Piccarda and Constance are not fully parallel. While Piccarda's marriage may have advanced her brother's family strategy, she played no public role. But Constance inherited a throne. She needed to make a marriage alliance and produce a legitimate heir. In royal families, good and proper custom meant setting aside one's private desires and accepting one's political obligations. While, like all rulers, she had advisers, it is scarcely conceivable that Constance exercised no personal agency and invoked no rational calculation in her marital decision. Once married, Piccarda and Constance stayed married. Piccarda does not mention widowhood in her own case. But Constance was widowed. At that point, in theory, she could have returned to the convent. But, instead, she continued to fulfill her political duties, governing her kingdom as regent for her infant son. Along with the lack of symmetry between Piccarda and Constance, and setting aside their location in the lowest celestial sphere, that of the inconstant moon, there remains the issue of their degree of culpability for leaving their monastic calling.

The pilgrim is understandably confused as to why Piccarda and Constance are among the saints. In *Paradiso* 4 and 5, Beatrice offers an elaborate and controversial argument, in three parts. The one to which she devotes the most attention is the refutation of astral determinism. She capitalizes on earlier speeches given on this subject by Marco Lombardo and Virgil. Marco likewise condemns astral determinism (*Purg.* 16.65–129). Without invoking the language of synderesis and conscience, or the Stoics' *passio*, *propassio*, and *consensus* reprised by the Church Fathers and scholastics,[41] Virgil explains that counsel puts our reactions and inclinations to the test of our moral principles, and that free will then makes its choice (*Purg.* 18.16–75). His account of the psychodynamics of decision-making is compatible with the analyses of Bernard and the scholastic *Sentences* commentators. Beatrice agrees that we have free will and offers no dissent from Virgil's description of its exercise, although she is not interested in reprising the intramental operations he describes. Her second point is more problematic. Beatrice states that the greatest sacrifice of free will we can make to God is a monastic vow. Any fit recompense for abandoning such a vow must be a still greater sacrifice. But what can be greater than the greatest sacrifice we can give? Beatrice does not propose an answer. She mentions, in passing, that ecclesiastical dispensation is a legitimate way of terminating a vow (*Par.* 5.55–57), but she does not present ecclesiastical dispensation as an ethical solution to the dilemma faced by her ex-nuns.

41 The leading ancient Latin source, Aulus Gellius, *Noctes atticae* 12.5, 19.1, was reprised by Jerome and Augustine as a standard explanation of the psychogenesis of ethical decision-making, serving as a template for the discussion of the extent to which this process applies to the human Christ. Peter Lombard expressly cites Jerome, *Commentariorum in Matheum* 1.5.28, ed. D. Hurst and M. Andraien, CCSL 77 (Turnhout, 1977), on the point in *Sent.* 3. d. 15. c. 2.1–3, 2:98–99; see, on this topic Colish, *Stoic Tradition* (above, n. 16), 1:337–38; 2:179, 208, 223–24; eadem, *Peter Lombard*, 2 vols. (Leiden, 1994), 1:444, 447; 2:492.

Finally, Beatrice distinguishes between absolute and relative will. As she sees it, compulsion represses our free will. But, she adds, if we fail to resist force, or fail to counteract it when we can, we become complicit in the deeds to which we are compelled. This judgment of guilt is one she applies to Piccarda and Constance. Their circumstances do not excuse them completely:

> Even if violence is done when the one who bears it / in no way consents to the one who deals it out, / these souls were not excused on that account. / For the will, except by its own willing, is not spent, / but does as by its nature fire does in flame, / though violence may force it down one thousand times. / Thus, if it stays bent, whether much or little, / it then accepts the force, as indeed did these, / since they could have returned to the holy place.
>
> *Se vïolenza è quando quel che pate / nïente conferisce a quel che sforza, / non fuor quest' alme per essa scusate: / ché volontà, se non vuol, non s'ammorza, / ma fa come natura face in foco, / se mille volte vïolenza il torza. / Per che, s'ella si piega assai o poco, / segue la forza; e così questo fero / possendo rifuggir nel santo loco.* (*Par.* 4.73–81)

Beatrice maintains that Piccarda and Constance failed to resist removal from the convent, and that they could have returned to monastic life after having been married but failed to do so. They are not exculpated by their acquiescence in the duties of marriage and, for Constance, those of rulership, motherhood, and regency, as well. Their will was a relative one. What truly obliges is absolute will, which requires adherence to the highest good and to our primary commitments, come what may. Beatrice's *exempla virtutis* in making this point are Saint Lawrence, martyred for the Christian faith (*Par.* 4.83); the patriot Mucius Scaevola, dismembered for his refusal to aid his country's enemy (*Par.* 4.84); and Alcmaeon, who accepted death because he could not act with filial piety toward one parent without betraying it toward the other (*Par.* 4.103–5).

Despite the fact that, on Beatrice's account, Piccarda and Constance exercised relative not absolute will and thus incurred some degree of guilt by marrying and staying married, they have attained sanctity. She does not really explain this happy outcome. Beatrice does not agree with Bernard's teaching that an unwilled act of any kind is morally null, hence utterly free from guilt. Nor does she invoke Bernard's example of Peter, rejecting Christ and then repenting, being forgiven, and advancing to sanctity. When Saint Peter makes his appearance in the *Commedia,* his assignment is simply to examine the pilgrim on faith. He makes no allusion to his own fall and repentance (*Par.* 24.34–111). Nor is martyrdom a moral category in its own right for Dante, as he places martyred souls in various heavens depending on why they died. While elsewhere, in the speech of the poet Folco, Dante laments the attention given to the study of the Decretals (*Par.* 9.134–35), Beatrice invokes neither the lenient nor the rigorist canonists in assessing the guilt entailed by her ex-nuns' change of calling. To be sure, the pilgrim encounters other saints who effected major changes in their lives. In the heaven of Venus, he meets Cunizza da Romano and Rahab (*Par.* 9.32–36, 9.115–26). Each of these souls canceled a meretricious past, Cunizza by her charity and Rahab by facilitating Joshua's victory in the Battle of Jericho. These saints overcame a previous state of serious sin by acts of great virtue. But they offer no guidance to the sanctification of Piccarda and Constance, who moved from monasticism to a sacramental, if less exalted, state by submitting to marriage. Nor does Beatrice explain their situation in terms of the fall-back position to which she appeals elsewhere, namely, the mystery of divine grace and predestination (*Par.* 9.105, 20.52–53, 20.75, 20.130–32).

For some Dantists, Beatrice's treatment of Piccarda and Constance remains a mystery. They do not see her argument as having any support in the previous intellectual tradition. One notable hypothesis advanced is that these ex-nuns were granted dispensations from their monastic vows, which would have been necessary since prior vows are a marital impediment. They did, indeed, abandon the cloister under pressure, replacing the monastic vows from which they were released with the marriage vows that they did not want. They can be seen as culpable to some degree. But, so the hypothesis continues, they repented, underwent purgation—and a rather speedy one at that—and have graduated to sainthood.[42] This scenario, plausible though it may be, is another possibility that Beatrice does not air. Nor does she mention akrasia as weakness of will in *Paradiso* 4 and 5. Her teaching has been seen by some Dantists as extremely harsh. Although they rarely consider the options offered by Bernard and the canonists as roads not taken, they regard Beatrice's argument as far outstripping contemporary theology and canon law, which they see as more flexible and realistic on vows, dispensations, and ethical decision-making in general. While Dante may have wished to condemn prelates who cheapened dispensations, his severity on this issue has impressed these Dantists as an instance in which he leaves his possible sources behind and marches to his own drummer, raising the bar even vis-à-vis the teachings of Aristotle and Aquinas, the Dantists' favorite default positions.[43] Even if we leave Bernard and the canonists out of the reckoning, is Beatrice's doctrine a Dantean innovation, or does it have a basis in either Aristotle or Aquinas?

While some Dantists have sought a solution to the problem of acting against conscience in Aquinas on book 3 of the *Nicomachean Ethics*, the Angelic Doctor actually departs from Aristotle both in his commentary on that text and in his *Summa theologiae*. In *Nicomachean Ethics* 3.1, Aristotle distinguishes between compulsion and partly

42 This scenario is proposed by Singleton, *Divine Comedy* (above, n. 40), 3.3:103.

43 See, for instance, A. Sacchetto, "Dottrina e poesia nel cielo della Luna (IV del *Paradiso*)," in *Dieci letture dantesche* (Florence, 1960), 209–11; S. Pasquali, "Canto V," in *Paradiso*, Lectura Dantis Scaligera (Florence, 1968), 150–58; G. di Pino, "Canto IV," in ibid., 110–14; idem, "Quel che Timeo dell'anime argomenta," in *Temi di critica dantesca* (Bari, 1973), 184–86; G. Vagranini, "Il Canto IV del 'Paradiso'," in *Nuove letture dantesche* (Florence, 1972), 5:317–39; M. Pastore Stocchi, "Il canto V del 'Paradiso'," in ibid., 5:341–74; G. Angiolillo, "Canto IV," in *Paradiso*, Lectura Dantis Napolitana, ed. P. Giannantonio (Naples, 2000), 68–72; G. Oliva, "Canto V," in ibid., 73–87; *Divine Comedy*, trans. Musa (above, n. 39), 3.2:34, 43–48; R. Hollander, comm. on Dante, *Paradiso*, trans. R. Hollander and J. Hollander (New York, 2007), 102–3.

voluntary action. In the case of compulsion, "the agent or the person acted upon contributes nothing," as with a captain whose ship is blown off course by a storm. Exemplifying partly voluntary action is a captain who jettisons cargo when his ship is beset by a storm. As Aristotle observes, "No one jettisons cargo voluntarily; but for his own safety and that of others, any sensible person will do it."[44] The second captain's situation illustrates the fact that we can choose to do something that we do not want to do. Both of Aristotle's captains are faced with forces of nature beyond their control. Both outcomes affect what is done or suffered physically. For Aristotle, as one commentator observes, "voluntariness is a property of actions, not motivations."[45]

But for Dante and Aquinas, free will or its nullification also applies to purely mental states, and motivations assuredly count. Aquinas agrees with Aristotle that what we do under compulsion is not voluntary and is, hence, morally irrelevant. But what we do when we are afraid we do of our own free will, and for such actions we are morally responsible. The same exercise of our intellectual and affective faculties occurs in the state of fear as is operative in our other acts of moral choice. Ignoring the fact that both Aristotle's captains are confronted by natural forces beyond their control, Aquinas argues that compulsion alone is the consequence of an involuntary external force. The decision of someone who acts in response to fear is a consequence of a voluntary internal force. He wills to make a frightening choice, one he judges to be deeply flawed, to avoid what he fears even more. As Aquinas sees it, the fearful moral agent has the power to achieve his own attitude adjustment—to valorize one fear over another. On this analysis, as with the captain who jettisons cargo, the decision of a person motivated by fear is quite simply voluntary (*simpliciter voluntaria est*)[46]—not partly voluntary, as Aristotle has it, but fully voluntary. Aquinas's second captain subjects his decision to a rational calculus of greater and lesser goods and evils. He chooses to abandon a lesser good, the safety of his cargo, for a greater good, the safety of those on board. One might also decide to abandon what one holds to be a greater good for a lesser good, as do Piccarda and Constance. It is worth stressing that the issue of interest for Aquinas, in the passage of the *Summa theologiae* where he makes this point, is not the merits of particular moral choices but rather the intramental process by which we make them. Where Aristotle would grant Piccarda and Constance more latitude as having made a partly voluntary choice in light of the external pressures imposed upon them, Aquinas would judge the complicity that Beatrice attributes to their exercise of relative will to be fully voluntary. If Aquinas makes a better case for their culpability than Aristotle, Aristotle, *mutatis mutandis*, makes a better case than Aquinas for their only partial guilt and comparatively rapid moral rehabilitation.

44 Aristotle, *NE* 3.1 (37).

45 S. S. Meyer, "Aristotle on the Voluntary," in *The Blackwell Guide to Aristotle's Nicomachean Ethics* (above, n. 3), 150. This feature of Aristotle's argument has not been noted by Dantists who cite *NE* 3 here as a source. See, for example, Singleton, *Divine Comedy*, 3.3:85–86, 89, 90–92.

46 Thomas Aquinas, *ST* IIaIIae q. 6. a. 6, 17:24; see also idem, *Sententia libri Ethicorum* 3.1, in *Opera omnia*, Leonine ed., 48 vols. (Rome, 1882–1985), 47.1: 117–20.

There is another a passage in *Nicomachean Ethics* 3.1—one that has escaped most commentators on *Paradiso* 4 and 5—that lends support to the rigorous side of the alternatives posed by Beatrice. The example of Saint Lawrence was well known in Dante's day and certainly available to anyone conversant with the *Golden Legend*. Both Seneca (*De beneficiis* 4.27.2 and 7.15.2) and Augustine (*De civitate dei* 4.20 and 5.18) recycle Livy (*Ab urbe condita* 2.12–13) on the subject of Mucius Scaevola. But while Ovid (*Metamorphoses* 9.406–15) and Statius (*Thebaid* 2.265–305) report the story of Alcmaeon as told by Euripides, the Latin Aristotle also presents an ethical analysis and recommendation in his case. In *Nicomachean Ethics* 3.1, Aristotle asserts that death can be an acceptable way to resolve irreconcilable moral obligations. Such was Alcmaeon's dilemma when faced with the paternal demand that he commit matricide to avenge his father's death. As Aristotle remarks, this is a hard saying: "But some things perhaps we cannot be compelled to do, and rather than do them, we ought to die after the most terrible suffering."[47] Beatrice's rigor may find a rationale in this passage. She may also find support for the normative value of absolute will in Aquinas's substitution, for Aristotle's partly voluntary choices in the face of forces beyond our control, of the fully voluntary choices that, he maintains, derive from the management of fear that is within our control.

To conclude, there is both less, and different, Aristotle at issue here than has typically been noticed by Dante scholars, and a richer trove of authorities who could provide the poet with alternative approaches to acting against conscience. Seneca offers an acute diagnosis of the self-inflicted ills of those who do so, even though Stoic *apatheia* fails to go the distance for Dante, fear of the Lord is a praiseworthy move toward virtue, and the damned do not experience the Senecan self-flagellation of conscience. Unlike Dante, Seneca disdains righteous indignation as a vice, a form of anger to which no sage succumbs, but both authors agree that writing well is the best revenge. The account of moral decision-making offered by Bernard of Clairvaux, his exemption of all unwilled actions from moral guilt, and his stress on divine mercy and forgiveness of even the most serious sins constitute a viable option for explaining the condition of the souls who act against conscience and yet are placed in the heaven of the moon. This option was available but not chosen by Dante's Beatrice. The substance, if not the terminology, of Virgil's description of the psychogenesis of moral decision-making is compatible with Bernard's account and that of the main scholastic *Sentences* commentators alike. For all these authorities, the bottom line is the freedom of the will. Beatrice is given the last word. She is less interested than Bernard, the scholastics, or Virgil in the intramental processes involved in moral decisions. Grounds for both the inculpation and the exculpation of persons forced or frightened into contravening their moral principles were widely available in the canonical literature, a resource not exploited by any of the pilgrim's guides. Once Dante's classical and medieval sources on acting against conscience are considered in their full breadth, his own intellectual choices are both

47 Aristotle, *NE* 3.1 (38). According to Singleton, *Divine Comedy*, 3.3:93, Aquinas regards this reference to Alcmaeon as satirical.

clarified and problematized. Whether framed in terms of synderesis and conscience, conscience and fear, judgment or counsel and will, or will as constrained absolutely or conditionally, these positions receive Dante's support at some points in the *Commedia* but not at others. While Aristotle's akrasia does not provide a cogent template for Dante on acting against conscience, other features of Aristotle's doctrine in the *Nicomachean Ethics*, both in their own right or as ignored and reinscribed by Aquinas, may help to frame, if not resolve, the problems embedded in Beatrice's teaching on the moral status of souls in the heaven of the moon, a passage that remains, for many Dantists, a crux in the *Commedia*.

From Anna Komnene to Dante

The Byzantine Roots of Western Debates on Aristotle's Nicomachean Ethics

MICHELE TRIZIO

THANKS TO ROBERT GROSSETESTE'S Latin translation, the corpus of Greek-Byzantine commentaries on Aristotle's *Nicomachean Ethics*, probably assembled between the eleventh and twelfth centuries, became the most popular and consequential Byzantine philosophical work in the Latin West.[1] Little is known of the circumstances surrounding its composition, which gathers together ancient and Byzantine commentaries on this Aristotelian work.[2] As a Byzantinist who is currently producing

1 The first modern (partial) edition of Grosseteste's Latin translation of this corpus was made by W. Stinissen, *Aristoteles over de vriendschap: Boeken VIII en IX van de Nicomachische Ethiek met de commentaren van Aspasius en Michaël in de Latijnse vertaling van Grosseteste* (Brussels, 1963). The standard edition used nowadays is H. P. F. Mercken, *The Greek Commentaries on the Nicomachean Ethics in the Latin Translation of Robert Grosseteste, Bishop of Lincoln (†1253): Eustratius on Book I and the Anonymous Scholia on Books II, III, and IV*, CLCAG 6.1 (Leiden, 1973); idem, *The Greek Commentaries on the Nicomachean Ethics in the Latin Translation of Robert Grosseteste Bishop of Lincoln (†1253): The Anonymous Commentator on Book VII, Aspasius on Book VIII, Michael of Ephesus on Books IX and X*, CLCAG 6.3 (Leuven, 1991). I am preparing the critical edition of Michael of Ephesus's and Anonymous's commentaries on book 5 of the *Nicomachean Ethics*, along with the as-yet-unedited commentary on book 6 by Eustratios of Nicaea. On Grosseteste's translation, see R. A. Gauthier, *Ethica Nicomachea*, Aristoteles Latinus, 26.1–3, fasciculus primus, Corpus Philosophorum Medii Aevi (Leiden and Brussels, 1974), clii–cclii. Unless otherwise specified, my citations from Byzantine commentators on the *Nicomachean Ethics* come from the CLCAG volumes above.

2 On the composition of this corpus, see H. P. F. Mercken, "The Greek Commentators on Aristotle's Ethics," in *Aristotle Transformed: The Ancient Commentators and Their Influence*, ed. R. Sorabji (Ithaca, NY, 1990), 407–44, esp. 407–10. The Greek text is edited in *Eustratii et Michaelis et Anonyma in Ethica Nicomachea Commentaria*, ed. G. Heylbut, CAG 20 (Berlin, 1892). As a result of several misreadings, Heylbut's edition, which ignores several manuscripts that may have improved the text, is regrettably poor, as was shown almost a hundred years ago by G. Mercati, "Fra i commentatori greci di Aristotele," *Mélanges d'Archéologie et d'Histoire* 35 (1915): 191–219, repr. in G. Mercati, *Opere Minori 2*, ST 78 (Vatican City, 1937), 458–80. The corpus edited by Heylbut on the basis of Paris, Bib. Nat MS Coisl. gr. 161 (14th century) differs from that translated by Grosseteste in the latter's inclusion of a second commentary on book 5 of the *Nicomachean Ethics* by Michael of Ephesus

a critical edition of Grosseteste's Latin translation, I can think of no other Byzantine work, except the *Corpus Dionysiacum*, which was more widely read in the West than these commentaries. Nor is this an irrelevant point when one considers that Aristotle's *Ethics* is one of the few Aristotelian works that was transmitted directly through Greek-Latin interaction avoiding the Arabic mediation so common in the thirteenth century.[3]

These commentaries had great influence on the teaching of Aristotle's *Nicomachean Ethics* in medieval and Renaissance universities, and it would be impossible to account for all the topics discussed by medieval masters and later humanists whom it influenced. So, in this article, I will investigate a topic as dealt with by commentators whose influence on Latin readers is relatively evident, Eustratios of Nicaea (ca. 1050–ca. 1120) and Michael of Ephesus (ca. 11th–12th centuries).[4] The topic will be the so-called Averroist theories that spread in thirteenth-century Western universities. As I will demonstrate, such views gave shape to the intellectual background of even Dante himself, conveying Arabic theories on happiness and intellection with an emphasis on the intellectual life as a path to assimilation or conjunction with the first cause, as is present in the Byzantine commentaries on the *Nicomachean Ethics,* in particular those of Eustratios. I will therefore investigate Eustratios's and Michael's impact on certain influential *Ethics* commentaries by medieval masters in the arts faculties of the late thirteenth century.

From Constantinople to Florence: Manuscripts, Places, and Interpreters

Little is known about the composition of the corpus of Greek-Byzantine commentaries on the *Ethics*, including Byzantine commentaries by Eustratios (books 1 and 6) and Michael of Ephesus (books 5, 9–10),[5] third-century anonymous scholia (on books 2–5),[6] a commentary by the second-century Peripatetic Aspasius (on book 8),[7] and an anonymous

---

(11th–12th centuries). This latter commentary is edited in *Michaelis Ephesii in librum quintum Ethicorum Nicomachorum commentarium*, ed. M. Hayduck, CAG 22.3 (Berlin, 1901).

3 For an overview of the transmission of Aristotle's work in the West, see the informative J. Brams, *La riscoperta di Aristotele in Occidente* (Milan, 2003).

4 On Eustratios, see M. Cacouros, *"Eustrate de Nicée,"* in *Dictionnaire de Philosophes Antiques,* ed. R. Goulet (Paris, 2000), 3:378–88; on Michael, see Mercken, "Greek Commentators," 429–36.

5 On Michael's work and mysterious biography, see Mercken, *Greek Commentaries*, CLCAG 6.3, 13*–21.*

6 On these scholia, depending partly on Adrastus of Aphrodisias (2nd century), see P. Moraux, *Der Aristotelismus bei den Griechen von Andronikos bis Alexander von Aphrodisias,* vol. 2, *Der Aristotelismus im I. und II. Jh. n. Chr.*, Peripatoi 6 (Berlin and New York, 1984), 323–30; Mercken, "The Greek Commentators," 421–29.

7 On Aspasius, see F. Becchi, *Aspasio commentatore di Aristotele*, in *Aufstieg und Niedergang der römischen Welt*, vol. 36.7, ed. W. Haase (Berlin and New York, 1994), 5365–96; Mercken, "The Greek Commentators," 438–41; J. Barnes, "An Introduction to Aspasius," in *Aspasius: The Earliest Extant Commentary on Aristotle's Ethics*, ed. A. Albert and R. W. Sharples, Peripatoi 17 (Berlin and New York, 1999), 1–50, repr. in idem, *Method and Metaphysics: Essays in Ancient Philosophy,* vol. 1 (Oxford, 2011).

(maybe thirteenth-century) Byzantine commentator (on book 7).[8] Since Robert Browning's scholarship on George Tornikes' funeral oration for Anna Komnene, it has been commonly accepted that the original compilation dates to early twelfth-century Constantinople and was compiled at Anna's behest.[9] Today, however, scholars tend to dismiss Browning's hypothesis of a philosophical circle surrounding Anna, on the grounds that neither literary nor paleographic evidence actually suggests the existence of collaboration between intellectuals around one and the same project.[10] By the same token, there is no need to take literally, as Browning did,[11] Tornikes' reference to the death of Anna's father Emperor Alexios I in 1118 as the beginning of Anna's interests in moral philosophy.[12] This is nothing more than the stereotypical topos on the death of a loved one as the beginning of a philosophical life.[13] There is nothing to prevent us from supposing that Eustratios's and Michael of Ephesus's scholarship on Aristotle may also have commenced before this date. More important, before becoming acquainted with Anna Komnene, Eustratios had been in contact with Mary of Alania (d. after 1103), to whom he had dedicated his meteorological treatises. This suggests that Eustratios's scholarly activity may have been supported by different patrons at different times.[14]

Constantinople

The manuscript tradition of these commentaries still awaits a thorough reconstruction to account for both the tradition of the text and the individual readers, and apparently the Commentaria in Aristotelem Graeca et Byzantina project at the Aristoteles-Archiv in Berlin will cast light on this in coming years. Nevertheless, all the available evidence suggests that this set of commentaries was regarded as an essential tool for understanding

8 On this commentary, see E. Fisher, "The Anonymous Commentary on Nicomachean Ethics VII," in *Medieval Greek Commentaries on the Nicomachean Ethics*, ed. C. Barber and D. Jenkins, Studien und Texte zur Geistesgeschichte des Mittelalters 101 (Leiden and Boston, 2009), 45–62. On the composition of the corpus and its variants as witnessed by the manuscript tradition, see Mercken, *Greek Commentaries*, CLCAG 6.1, *5.

9 Cf. R. Browning, "An Unpublished Funeral Oration on Anna Comnena," *Proceedings of the Cambridge Philological Society* 188, n.s. 8 (1962): 1–12, repr. in idem, *Studies on History, Literature and Education* (London, 1977), and in Sorabji, *Aristotle Transformed*, 393–407.

10 See, e.g., M. Mullet, "Aristocracy and Patronage in the Literary Circles of Comnenian Constantinople," in *The Byzantine Aristocracy, XI to XIII Centuries*, ed. M. Angold, BAR International Series 221 (Oxford, 1984), 173–201, 178. On the intellectual climate around Anna, see P. Frankopan, "The Literary, Cultural and Political Context for the Twelfth-Century Commentary on the Nicomachean Ethics," in *Medieval Greek Commentaries*, ed. Barber and Jenkins, 45–62.

11 Cf. Browning, "Unpublished Funeral Oration," 6–7.

12 See Georgios Tornikes, *Orationes*, 14, in *Georges et Démétrios Tornikès, Lettres et Discours*, ed. J. Darrouzès, Le monde byzantine (Paris, 1970), 270.18–21.

13 Browning's reconstruction has also been criticized by T. M. Conley, "The Alleged Synopsis of Aristotle's Rhetoric by John Italos and Its Place in the Byzantine Reception of Aristotle," in *La Rhétorique d'Aristote: Traditions et commentaires de l'Antiquité au XVIIe siècle*, ed. G. Dahan and I. Rosier-Catach (Paris, 1998), 49–64, 59–60.

14 P. Polesso Schiavon, "Un trattato inedito di meteorologia di Eustrazio di Nicea," *Rivista di Studi Bizantini e Neoellenici* 12–13 (1965–66): 285–304.

Aristotle's *Nicomachean Ethics*. In fact, it is preserved in the most important manuscripts containing the *corpus Aristotelicum*, or parts of it, and the ancient and late antique commentaries on it.[15] Of these, Paris, Bib. Nat. MS Coisl. 161 is worthy of mention. It contains the *Magna Moralia* (fols. 1r–16v); the *Nicomachean Ethics*, together with the Greek-Byzantine commentaries (fols.16v–165v); the *Politics* (fols. 168r–219v); the *Economics* (fols. 220r–225r); an anonymous prologue to the *Metaphysics* (fol. 226rv); the *Metaphysics* (fols. 228–405v), together with Alexander of Aphrodisias's commentary on books A–Δ, Michael of Ephesus's commentaries on books Z–N,[16] and Syrianus's own commentaries on this work (on book Γ, fols. 266r–286v; on book B, fols. 410r–421r; books M–N, fols. 421r–447v); as well as Pseudo-Alexander of Aphrodisias's *Quaestiones* (1.25) (fols. 447v–448r).[17] There is no need to stress the value of this manuscript as a witness to the *corpus Aristotelicum* and its commentaries;[18] it was copied by one of the fourteenth-century's most important scribes, famed for his commitment to copying Aristotelian works, namely, the so-called Anonymous Aristotelicus,[19] identified by Brigitte Mondrain as a certain monk Malachias.[20]

Eustratios's work, in particular, seems to have been quite consequential for later generations of Byzantine intellectuals. For example, George Pachymeres' unedited commentary on the *Nicomachean Ethics*—to be distinguished from the paraphrase contained in his *Philosophia* (book 11)—commences with the very words Eustratios used in the introduction to his commentary on book 1 of this work, and thorough study may reveal even greater dependence on Eustratios's commentaries.[21] Furthermore, Barlaam of Calabria (d. ca. 1348), one of the most controversial figures in fourteenth-century Byzantium,

15 See B. Mondrain, "La constitution du corpus d'Aristote et de ses commentateurs aux XIIIe–XIVe siècles," *Codices Manuscripti* 29 (2000): 19–21.

16 On the ascription to Michael of this commentary, see C. Luna, *Trois études sur la tradition du commentaires anciens à la Metaphysique d'Aristote*, Philosophia Antiqua 88 (Leiden, Boston, and Cologne, 2001), 53–71.

17 On this manuscript, see R. Devresse, *Bibliothèque National, Département de manuscrits: Catalogue des manuscrits grecs*, vol. 2, *Le fond Coislin* (Paris, 1945), 145–46.

18 See, for instance, Concetta Luna's investigation on the importance of this manuscript for the textual tradition of Syrianus's commentary on the *Metaphysics*: C. Luna, "Mise en page et transmission textuelle du commentaire de Syrianus sur la Métaphysique," in *The Libraries of the Neoplatonists*, ed. C. D'ancona Costa, Philosophia Antiqua 107 (Leiden and Boston, 2007), 121–33.

19 On this scribe, see D. Harlfinger, *Die Textgeschichte der pseudo-aristotelischen Schrift "Peri atomôn grammôn": Ein kodikologisch-kulturgeschichtlicher Beitrag zur Klärung der Überlieferungsverhältnisse im Corpus Aristotelicum* (Amsterdam, 1971), 55–57. See also M. Rashed, *Die Überlieferungsgeschichte der aristotelischen Schrift De Generatione et Corruptione*, Serta Graeca 17 (Wiesbaden, 2001), 230.

20 Cf. B. Mondrain, "L'ancien empereur Jean VI Cantacuzène et ses copistes," in *Gregorio Palamas e oltre: Studi e documenti sulle controversie teologiche del XIV secolo bizantino*, ed. A. Rigo, Orientalia Venetiana 16 (Florence, 2004), 249–96.

21 The existence of this commentary has been noticed by P. Golitsis, "George Pachymère come didascale: Essai pour une reconstitution de sa carrière et de son enseignement philosophique," *JÖB* 58 (2008): 56, 67–68 (incipit of the work). The incipit of the work as reported by Golitsis is an abridged version of Eustratius Graecus, *In I EN* 1.3–9 and *In I EN* 4.14–21.

quotes from Eustratios in his *Letters* to Palamas,[22] while Nikephoros Gregoras incorporates Eustratios's intellectualistic interpretation of Adam's Fall to support his views on the irrational animal's superiority over human beings.[23] Another witness is the paraphrase of the *Nicomachean Ethics* published in the Commentaria in Aristotelem Graeca series as Heliodorus of Prusa's and wrongly attributed to Andronicus of Rhodes, Olympiodorus, or the fourteenth-century emperor John VI Kantakouzenos. In fact, this paraphrase is nothing other than an abridged version of Aristotle's own text incorporating several notes, scholia, and comments from Greek-Byzantine commentaries on the *Ethics* and must, therefore, be considered a product of late Byzantium.[24] The same Kantakouzenos knew *Eustratius cum aliis* well enough to use Eustratios's comment on Aristotle's bizarre etymology of the word σωφροσύνη ("that which saves prudence")[25] that the virtues are connected like sisters in his writings against the Byzantine Thomist Prochoros Kydones, as John compares the connection between the virtues with that between the divine names.[26] Finally, even the *Protheorumena* to the *Nicomachean Ethics* by the well-known George Gennadios Scholarios, preserved in three fifteenth-century manuscripts, seem to incorporate a vast amount of material from Eustratios of Nicaea and the other Greek-Byzantine commentators on the *Nicomachean Ethics*.[27]

22 Compare Barlaam Calabrius, *Epistulae*, 1, *Dalla controversia palamitica alla polemica esicastica*, ed. A. Fyrigos (Rome, 2005), 242.588–92 and 246.633–37, with Eustratius Graecus, *In VI EN* 317.21–23, and *In VI EN* 379.27–30.

23 Compare Nikephoros Gregoras, *Solutiones Quaestionum*, vol. 1, ed. P. L. M. Leone, "Nicephori Gregorae Antilogia et Solutiones Quaestionum," *Byzantion* 40 (1970): 471–516.493, 178–494.191, with Eustratius Graecus, *In I EN* 297.16–31.

24 On this paraphrase and its dependence on the Greek-Byzantine commentaries on the *Nicomachean Ethics* as published in CAG 20, see M. Trizio, "Eliodoro di Prusa fra i commentatori greci di Aristotele," in *Atti del VII Congresso Nazionale della Associazione Italiana di Studi Bizantini, Venezia, 25–28 novembre 2009* (Bari, 2013), 803–30.

25 Aristotles, *Ethica Nicomachea*, 6.5.1140b11–13.

26 Joannes Kantakouzenos, 1.38, "Refutationes duae Prochori Cydonii," in *Iohannis Cantacuzeni Refutationes Duae Prochori Cydonii et Disputatio cum Paulo Patriarcha Latino Epistulis Septem Tradita*, ed. F. Tinnefeld and E. Voordeckers, CCSG 16 (Turnhout, 1987), 54.9–55.19:

> Εἰ γὰρ ἐπ' ἀνθρώπου, εἴ τις ἐρεῖ τινα μίαν τῶν τεσσάρων γενικῶν ἀρετῶν, ἔστω δὲ φρόνησιν, μίαν μὲν εἴρηκε τῷ λόγῳ, ἀδύνατον δὲ ἐκείνῃ μὴ συνθεωρεῖσθαι καὶ τὰς λοιπάς, ἀνδρίαν φημὶ καὶ δικαιοσύνην καὶ σωφροσύνην, ἔτι τε εἰ ἀνδρίαν εἴποι, συμπεριλαμβάνεσθαι ὡσαύτως ἀνάγκη καὶ τὰς λοιπάς, φρόνησίν φημι καὶ δικαιοσύνην καὶ σωφροσύνην, καὶ περὶ τῶν λοιπῶν δύο ὡσαύτως—ἀλλήλαις γάρ εἰσιν ἀνακεκραμμέναι καὶ οὐ διατοῦτο συμπεφυρμέναι, ἀλλ' ἑκάστη τὸ ἴδιον πάλιν ἔχει σημαινόμενον—, πολλῷ γε μᾶλλον ἐπὶ τῶν ὀνομάτων τοῦ ἁπλουστάτου θεοῦ. = Eustratios, *In VI EN* 309.36–310.1: λέγω δὴ ἀνδρεία, δικαιοσύνη καὶ σωφροσύνη. τί δὴ πρὸς ταῦτά φαμεν; πρῶτα μέν, ὅτι ἀδελφαὶ ἀλλήλων αἱ ἀρεταὶ καὶ πολλὴν φέρουσαι πρὸς ἀλλήλας τὴν ὁμοιότητα, ὥστε καὶ ἀλλήλαις συνεισφέρεσθαι ὡμολόγηνται· καὶ οὐδὲν θαυμαστόν, εἰ ὁ περὶ μιᾶς αὐτῶν λόγος παρεισάγει καὶ τὰς λοιπάς.

27 On these *Protheorumena*, see Harlfinger's note in P. Moraux, *Aristoteles Graecus*, vol. 1 (Alexandria and London), Peripatoi 8 (Berlin and New York, 1976), 4–5. See also T. Dorandi, "Préliminaires de Georges Scholarios à L'Éthique à Nicomaque d'Aristote et aux Entretiens d'Épictète," in *Rhetorica Philosophans: Mélanges offerts à Michel Patillon*, ed. L. Brisson and P. Chiron, Textes et Tradition 20 (Paris, 2010), 297–309.

Florence

As stated in the introduction, Robert Grosseteste's mid-thirteenth century translation and the later translation by Bernardus Felicianus[28] made the *corpus* of Greek-Byzantine Commentaries on the *Nicomachean Ethics* an essential tool for medieval university masters, Renaissance authors, and early modern humanists seeking to understand the Aristotelian text. In his letter to Malatesta in 1400 (*Ep.* 3.391), Coluccio Salutati stated that he possessed (and annotated) a full version of Eustratios of Nicaea's commentary on Aristotle's *Ethics*.[29] This thirteenth-century manuscript (Florence, Biblioteca Nazionale Centrale, MS. Conv. Soppr. I.5.21),[30] of English provenance, is the same one that was owned and annotated by Leonardo Bruni. In one of his letters, Bruni writes: "Eustratius enim natione graecus est et inter doctissimos apud graecos habetur. Liber certe *Ethicorum* in lingua sic perite commentatus est, ut solus commentator illorum meruerit appellari."[31] Unsurprisingly then, Bernardo Segni's vernacular translation of the *Nicomachean Ethics* names Eustratios as first among the commentators, beside Thomas Aquinas, Walter Burley, and Donato Acciaiuoli,[32] the latter pair known to be faithful Eustratios readers.[33]

Before Segni, it is again Salutati who provides insight into the availability of the commentaries on *Nicomachean Ethics* by the Byzantine commentators and the Latin commentaries heavily influenced by the Byzantine ones. In his letter to master Francesco di Bartolomeo Casini, on 6 October 1404, Salutati praises an essay by Francesco on the *Nicomachean Ethics* as better than the commentaries by Eustratios, Michael of Ephesus, Albert the Great, Albert of Saxony, Gerald Odo, Walter Burley, John Buridan, and Henry of Freimar.[34] Salutati clearly exaggerates, but his praise makes it clear that by the time of this letter—and doubtless even before—these Latin commentaries, full of quotes from

28 See the reprint in Eustratius, Aspasius, Michael Ephesius, et al., *Aristotelis Stagiritae Moralia Nicomachia*, trans. J. B. Felicianus, CAG 11.1–2 (Stuttgart, 2006).

29 Coluccio Salutati, *Ep.* 16, ed. F. Novati, *Epistolario di Coluccio Salutati*, vol. 3 (Rome, 1896), 391.5–7. But see also *Ep.* 3.31.4–9.

30 On this manuscript, see S. H. Thomson, *The Writings of Robert Grosseteste, Bishop of Lincoln (1235–1253)* (Cambridge, 1940), 69; G. Lacombe et al., *Aristoteles Latinus: Codices, pars posterior, supplementa indicesque* (Leiden, 1955) (hereafter *AL*), 965, no. 1408; B. L. Ulmann and P. Stadter, *The Public Library of Renaissance Florence: Niccolò Niccoli, Cosimo de' Medici and the Library of San Marco*, Medioevo e Umanesimo 10 (Padua, 1972), 312, 315; J. Hankins, *Humanism and Platonism in the Italian Renaissance*, vol. 1, Storia e Letteratura 215 (Rome, 2004), 232–34 (app. 5), 235–39 (app. 6).

31 Leonardo Bruni, *Ep.* 5.1, ed. F. P. Luiso, *Studi sull'epistolario di Leonardo Bruni*, Studi Storici 37 (Rome, 1980), 106; *Ep.* 7.4.128.

32 *L'Ethica d'Aristotile tradotta in lingua volgare fiorentina et commentata per Bernardo Segni* (Florence, 1550), 7.

33 For a statistical study on Eustratios quotations in Burley's commentary on the *Nicomachean Ethics*, see J. J. Walsh, "Some Relationships Between Gerald Odo's and John Buridan's Commentaries on Aristotle's *Ethics*," *Franciscan Studies* 35 (1975): 258, n. 17. On Acciaiuoli reader of Eustratios, see L. Bianchi, "Un commento 'umanistico' ad Aristotele: L' Expositio super libros Ethicorum di Donato Acciaiuoli," *Rinascimento* 2nd ser., 30 (1990): 29–55.

34 Coluccio Salutati, *Ep. 8*, ed. F. Novati, *Epistolario di Coluccio Salutati*, vol. 4 (Rome, 1905), 37.16–38.3.

Eustratius cum aliis, were known and available to thirteenth- and fourteenth-century Florentine readers. This is important, for in considering Dante's association with Eustratios of Nicaea and the other Greek-Byzantine commentators on the *Ethics*, it means that these works were not only directly available but, through such authors as Albert the Great, Thomas Aquinas, and all the others mentioned above, who were well-known to Dante and many other authors of the time, were indirectly almost unavoidable. That no proof exists of Dante's direct acquaintance with Eustratios and the other Greek-Byzantine commentators on the *Ethics* should not disappoint, because evidence shows him to have been well acquainted with some of these eminent readers of Eustratios.[35]

In fact, in Dante's time, the libraries of the monastic orders in Florence already owned a considerable number of books on Aristotelian moral philosophy, in addition to scholastic commentaries on these works, as Dante himself mentions in *Convivio* 2.2.17.[36] The library of the Franciscan convent of Santa Croce shows entries dating back to 1319 or earlier for Aristotle's *Nicomachean Ethics*, *Politics*, and *Magna Moralia* (now Florence, Bibl. Laur., MS Plut. XIII sin. 6),[37] while a copy of Thomas Aquinas's commentary on the *Nicomachean Ethics* (Florence, Bibl. Laur., MS Plut. XXIX dext. 10, fols. 1r–93r) was present by the end of thirteenth century.[38] That library also kept the thirteenth-century

35 No direct influence of Eustratios of Nicaea upon Dante has so been far detected. The excellent S. Gentili, *L'uomo aristotelico alle origini della letteratura italiana* (Rome, 2005), often refers to Eustratios and Michael of Ephesus, but never as the direct source of a passage in Dante. On Dante's acquaintance with Albert the Great's work, see C. Vasoli, "Dante, Alberto Magno e la scienza dei 'Peripatetici'," in *Dante e la scienza*, ed. P. Boyde and V. Russo, Interventi Classensi 16 (Ravenna, 1995), 55–70; G. Fioravanti, "Dante e Alberto Magno," in *Il pensiero filosofico e teologico di Dante Alighieri*, ed. A. Ghisalberti (Milan, 2001), 93–102, where the reader can also find a reassessment of other scholarly views. However, it should be noted that whether or not Dante actually read Albert's commentaries on the *Nicomachean Ethics* is still a matter of debate (see, e.g., ibid., 93–96).

36 On schools and intellectual trends in Dante's Florence, see C. T. Davis, "Education in Dante's Florence," *Speculum* 40 (1965): 415–31, repr. in idem, *Dante's Italy and Other Essays* (Philadelphia, 1984), 137–65; idem, "The Florentine Studia and Dante's Library," in *The "Divine Comedy" and the Encyclopedia of Arts and Sciences*, ed. G. Di Scipio and A. Scaglione (Amsterdam and Philadelphia, 1988), 339–66.

37 Cf. idem, "The Early Collection of S. Croce in Florence," *Proceedings of the American Philosophical Society* 107, no. 5 (1963): 401, n. 8 and 410. See *AL* 939, no. 1367. The *Magna Moralia* were also copied in MS Florence, Bibl. Laur., MS Plut. XXVII dext. 9, fols. 176r–188v (*AL* 948, no. 1379). On the medieval library of Santa Croce, see also G. Brunetti and S. Gentili, "Una biblioteca nella Firenze di Dante: I manoscritti di S. Croce," *Studi (e testi) italiani: Semestrale del Dipartimento di italianistica e spettacolo dell'Università di Roma "La Sapienza"* 6 (2000): 21–55. To these manuscripts, one should also add the manuscripts Florence, Bibl. Laur., MS Plut. VIII dext. 6, fols. 325r–337r = *AL* 931, no. 1353, containing the *Ethica Vetus*—see C. Marchesi, *L'Etica Nicomachea nella tradizione latina Medievale (documenti e appunti)* (Messina, 1904), 29—Florence, Bibl. Laur., MS Plut. XII sin. 9, fols. 4r–71r = *AL* 936, no. 1364, containing the *Liber Ethicorum*, that is, Grossateste's translation (see Marchesi, *L'Etica*, 39–40), Florence, Bibl. Laur., MS Plut. XIII sin. 11, fols. 105r–180v = *AL* 943, no. 1372, containing the *Liber Ethicorum* (see Marchesi, *L'Etica*, 38), and Florence, Bibl. Laur., MS Plut. XXVII dext. 9, fols. 176r–188v = *AL* 948, no. 1379, containing the *Magna Moralia*.

38 Cf. Davis, "The Early Collection," 407, n. 40. For a description of this manuscript, see Thomas Aquinas, *Sententia libri Ethicorum*, Opera Omnia 47.1 (Rome, 1969), 4*, n. 23. This work is also

manuscript Florence, Bibl. Laur., MS Plut. XV, sin. 9 (fols. 15r–16r),[39] which contained the *Liber de bona fortuna*, a Latin translation of two fragments from the *Magna Moralia* (2.8.206b30–1207b19), and the *Eudemian Ethics* (7.14.b37–1248b11), with which Dante was well acquainted.[40] The Badia Fiorentina has the manuscript Florence, Bibl. Naz., MS Conv. Soppr. A 5 2769, the first part of which dates to the thirteenth century and contains the *Liber Ethicorum,* with marginalia from the commentaries by Eustratios and Albert the Great (fols. 1r–47r).[41] The thirteenth-century manuscript Florence, Bibl. Laur., MS Gadd. Plut. LXXXIX inf. 41 (fols.134r–144r) contains the *Summa Alexandrinorum*,[42] Herman the German's Latin translation of an Arabic compendium of a lost Greek epitome of Aristotle's *Nicomachean Ethics*, a work so well known to Dante that he criticized Taddeo Alderotti's translation of it (*Conv.* 1.10.10).[43] Thomas Aquinas's commentary on the *Nicomachean Ethics* was probably also available through the thirteenth-century manuscript Florence, Bibl. Laur., MS Gadd. Plut., LXXXIX sup. 44 and present in the Dominican convent of San Marco as a fifteenth-century gift from Cosimo de' Medici.[44] Finally, the library of Santissima Annunziata in Florence probably owned Florence, Bibl. Naz., MS Conv. Soppr. G. V. 1290 (fols. 1r–73v) in the mid-fourteenth century; that manuscript contained the *Liber Ethicorum* with glosses from Thomas Aquinas's commentary as well as the *Magna Moralia* (74r–101v).[45]

---

present in Florence, Bibl. Laur., MS Conv. Soppr. 95, fols. 203r–204r (= *AL* 921, no. 1334). On this latter manuscript, see R. Blum, *La biblioteca della Badia Fiorentina e i codici di Antonio Corbinelli*, ST 155 (Vatican City, 1951), 185ff.

39 See *AL* 947, no. 1377.

40 See V. Cordonier, "Bona natiuitas, Nobility, and the Reception of Aristotle's Liber de bona fortuna from Thomas Aquinas to Dante Alighieri (c. 1260–1310)," in *The Question of Nobility: Aspects of the Medieval and Renaissance Conceptualization of Man,* ed. A. A. Robiglio, Studies on the Interaction of Art, Thought, and Power 5 (Leiden and New York, 2013).

41 *AL* 958, no. 1397.

42 *AL* 923, no. 1338; Marchesi, *L'Etica*, 105.

43 In Marchesi, *L'Etica*, xli–lxxxvi, on the basis of MS Florence, Laur., Gadd. Plut. LXXXIX inf. 41. On this work, see D. M. Dunlop, "Observations on the Medieval Arabic Version of Aristotle's Nicomachean Ethics," in *Oriente e Occidente nel Medioevo: Filosofia e scienze*, Accademia Nazionale dei Lincei, Atti dei Convegni 13 (Rome, 1971), 229–50; idem, "The Arabic Tradition of the Summa Alexandrinorum," *Archives d'Histoire Doctrinale et Littéraire du Moyen Âge* 49 (1982): 253–63; idem, "Introduction," in *The Arabic Version of the Nicomachean Ethics,* ed. A. A. Akasoy and A. Fidora, Aristoteles Semitico-Latinus 17 (Leiden and Boston, 2005), 1–109. On the Latin tradition of the text, see M.-T. D'Alverny, "Remarques sur la tradition manuscrite de la Summa Alexandrinorum," *Archives d'Histoire Doctrinale et Littéraire du Moyen Âge* 49 (1982): 265–72; A.A. Akasoy and A. Fidora, "Hermannus Alemannus und die alia translatio der Nikomachischen Ethik," *Bulletin de Philosophie Médiévale* 44 (2002): 79–93; M. Ullmann, *Die Nikomachische Ethik des Aristoteles in Arabischer Übersetzung*, pt. 2 (Wiesbaden, 2012), 67–122. On Alderotti and the *Summa Alexandrinorum*, see Gentili, *L'uomo aristotelico* (above, n. 35), 27–55.

44 *AL* 923, no. 1339; Marchesi, *L'Etica*, 38. See also M. Braccini, *Mostra di codici ed edizioni dantesche: 20 aprile–31 ottobre 1965*, Comitato nazionale per le celebrazioni del VII centenario della nascita di Dante (Florence, 1965), 11; Thomas Aquinas, *Sententia* 4* (it is not clear whether or not this MS, copied in southern France, was available to Florentine readers before the 15th century).

45 *AL* 960, no. 1402.

According to Tommaso Sardi's famous library catalogue of the Dominican monastery of Santa Maria Novella, composed in 1489, at least one copy of *Eustratius cum aliis* in Latin translation was there,[46] known today as Florence, Bibl. Laur., MS Plut. add. LXXIX 13,[47] and used by Vettori for his 1585 edition of Aristotle's *Ethics*.[48] This catalogue also mentions other material of interest to us, such as two copies of Aquinas's commentary on the *Ethics*,[49] now lost; Albert the Great's *Super ethica*, likely lost as well;[50] Buridan's commentary on the same work;[51] and additional copies of the *Ethics*,[52] including a translation by Bruni.[53] This confirms, once again, that scholastic commentaries and works related to Aristotle's *Ethics*, such as those by Albert of Saxony, Burley, Giles of Rome, Gerald of Odo, and Buridan, were known to Salutati and Bruni's generation of Florentine humanists, as well as to earlier ones.[54]

How many of these thirteenth- to early fourteenth-century manuscripts, including *Eustratius cum aliis,* which contained the commentaries by Albert and Thomas on the *Ethics*, were in Florentine libraries in Dante's time is unknown. There is, however, little doubt that at the start of fourteenth century, Aristotle's moral philosophy and related medieval Latin works were readily available to Florentine readers. Hence, the Greek-Byzantine compilation of commentaries on the *Ethics* must have been available both directly and indirectly, through such thirteenth-century interpreters as Albert the Great. In the end, Bruni celebrates Eustratios as singly deserving of the title "commentator," as thirteenth-century scholastic authors regarded Eustratios as *the* "commentator"

46 Thomas de Sardis, "Inventarium omnium librorum conventus Sancte Marie Novelle de Florentia ordinis predicatorum," in *La biblioteca di S. Maria Novella in Firenze, dal sec. XIV al sec. XIX*, ed. S. Orlandi (Florence, 1952), 42, no. 331. According to Sardi, the entry no. 324 contains *Eustathij super libros ethicorum*. Since often in the 13th and 14th centuries Eustratios's name is misspelled as Eusthatius, I doubt that this is "Eustachio d'Arras," as suggested by Orlandi, and am more inclined to identify this MS as a lost copy of the commentaries by *Eustratius cum aliis*. In this I follow C. H. Lohr, "Medieval Latin Aristotle Commentaries (A–F)," *Traditio* 23 (1967): 313–414, 406. An attempt to identify the MSS mentioned by Sardi in present-day Florentine libraries has been made by G. Pomaro, "Santa Maria Novella: Un convento nella città," *Memorie Domenicane* 11 (1980), 325–470, which is nevertheless largely inapplicable to the scope of this paper.

47 *AL* 912, no. 1318; Marchesi, *L'Etica*, 38–39.

48 See B. G. Biagiarelli, *La biblioteca Medicea-Laurenziana nell'anno della sua apertura al pubblico (11 giugno 1571)* (Florence, 1971), 71.

49 Orlandi, *La biblioteca* (n. 46 above), 42, no. 315, 316. See also Thomas Aquinas, *Sententia*, 32*.

50 Orlandi, *La biblioteca*, 42, no. 318.

51 Ibid., 42, no. 319.

52 Ibid., 42, no. 314.

53 Ibid., 42, no. 317.

54 For more information on the place of the *Nicomachean Ethics* in the curricula of Italian universities and the circulation of commentaries on it, see J. Kraye, "Renaissance Commentaries on the *Nicomachean Ethics*," in *The Vocabulary of Teaching and Research between Middle Ages and Renaissance*, ed. O. Weijers, *Proceedings of the Colloquium: London, Warburg Institute, 11–12 March 1994*, CIVICIMA: Études sur le vocabulaire du moyen âge 8 (Turnhout, 1995) 96–117, and D. A. Lines, *Aristotle's Ethics in the Italian Renaissance (ca. 1300–1650): The Universities and the Problem of Moral Education*, Education and Society in the Middle Ages and Renaissance 13 (Leiden, 2002), 80–108, 167–220.

on Aristotle, a title he shared with Averroes. And it may be true, then, that the humanists' agenda aimed at bypassing scholasticism and its alleged misinterpretations of the classics in order to restore an interpretation of the text as close as possible to that of the authentic Greek work.[55] But despite this rejection of the scholastic heritage, for the early generations of Italian humanists the main source for understanding Aristotle's *Nicomachean Ethics—Eustratius cum aliis*—remained the same as in the thirteenth and fourteenth centuries, together with the most relevant scholastic commentaries on this Aristotelian work.

As a matter of fact, the fifteenth-century catalogue of the library of the Augustinian monastery of Santo Spirito also shows entries for Aristotle's *Ethics* and the Greek-Byzantine commentaries in medieval and early Renaissance Florence. Again, it is difficult to discern which of these manuscripts were incorporated early enough to be available to Dante. Yet this catalogue shows entries for Heustachij (Eustratios) on the *Ethics,*[56] Albert the Great's *Super ethica,*[57] and Aquinas's commentary on this Aristotelian work.[58] Aristotle's *Ethics* was, unsurprisingly, present, as was his *Politics.*[59] Burley's commentary on the *Ethics* was present, though it entered the library quite late, in the fifteenth century, together with other manuscripts donated by Guglielmo Becchi, prior of the Augustinians.[60] Robert Kilwardby's *De ortu scientiarum*, which contains several quotes from Eustratios's commentaries on books 1 and 6 of the *Ethics,* is likewise listed in this catalogue.[61]

Oxford

The reception and teaching of Aristotle's moral philosophy in England is still "an underground history."[62] The first statutory evidences for the teaching of the *Nicomachean*

55 On this, see S. Ebbersmeyer, *Homo agens: Studien zur Genese und Struktur frühhumanistischer Moralphilosophie*, Quelle und Studien zur Philosophie 95 (Berlin and New York, 2010), 10–16.

56 See *Inventarium librarie conventus Sancti Spiritus de Florentia*, ed. D. Gutiérrez, "La biblioteca di S. Spirito in Firenze nella seconda metà del secolo XV," *Analecta Augustiniana* 25 (1962); 5–88, esp. 28, no. 25, though apparently this manuscript entered the library of Santo Spirito in 15th century as a gift from Guglielmo Becchi. Like Orlandi (above, n. 46), Gutiérrez also takes Heustachij as referring to Eustachius of Arras. But the incipit of the work mentioned in the entry at stake ("Philosophia in duas partes est divisa") doubtless belongs to Eustratios of Nicaea's commentary on book 1 of the *Nicomachean Ethics* (see Eustratius Latinus, *In I EN* 1.3).

57 Gutiérrez, "La biblioteca," 28, no. 32.

58 Ibid., 65, no. 385; 407, no. 405.

59 Ibid., 74, no. 475.

60 Ibid., 28, no. 33.

61 Ibid., 31, no. 59.

62 See C. F. Briggs, "Moral Philosophy in England After Grosseteste: An 'Underground' History," in *The Study of Medieval Manuscripts of England: Festschrift in Honor of Richard W. Pfaff*, Medieval and Renaissance Texts and Studies, ed. H. H. Brown and L. Ersham Voigts (Tempe, AZ, 2010), 357–86. On manuscript evidence for the reception of Aristotle's moral philosophy in the English Middle Ages, see also C. Lohr, "Aristotelica Britannica," *Theologie und Philosophie* 58 (1978): 81–85, 87–88, 90, 92, 94–96, 98. See also, more in general, D. R. Leader, *A History of the University of Cambridge*, vol. 1, *The University to 1546*, ed. C. Brooke (Cambridge, 1988), 163–67; D. Luscombe, "The Ethics

Ethics in Oxford and Cambridge date, respectively, from the beginning of the fourteenth century and 1390.[63] Yet, the existence of a thirteenth- and fourteenth-century English commentary tradition on the *Nicomachean Ethics* shows that the tradition of this Aristotelian work and *Eustratius cum aliis* in England, as witnessed by medieval English scholars such as Kilwardby, Burley, and the like, is of just as much interest.[64]

Neither the autograph version of Grosseteste's Latin translation of the *Nicomachean Ethics* and its commentaries nor its Greek model has survived,[65] but two fifteenth-century Greek manuscripts copied in Reading in 1495 and 1497 by the Greek émigré John Servopoulos are likely based upon the Greek manuscript owned by Grosseteste.[66] The latter must surely have owned a Greek manuscript of the *Nicomachean Ethics* and its Greek-Byzantine commentaries at the time of his translation of the *Corpus Dionysiacum*, in about 1239–40.[67] His translation of the so-called *Corpus Ethicum*—including the

---

and the Politics in Britain in the Middle Ages," in *Aristotle in Britain During the Middle Ages: Proceedings of the International Conference at Cambridge 8–11 April 1994*, ed. J. Marenbon, Société Internationale pour l'Étude de la Philosophie Médiévale, Rencontres de Philosophie Médiévale 5 (Turnhout, 1996), 337–49, and Lines, *Aristotle's Ethics* (above, n. 54), 69–70, n. 22.

63 For Oxford, see *Statuta antiqua universitatis oxonenisis*, ed. S. Gibson (Oxford, 1931), 33–34; for Cambridge, see M. B. Hackett, *The Original Statutes of Cambridge University: The Text and Its History* (Cambridge, 1979), 277; see also Lines, *Aristotle's Ethics,* 69.

64 For manuscript evidence on the English circulation of Aristotle's work on moral philosophy and the related commentaries, including the *Nicomachean Ethics* and the Greek-Byzantine commentaries translated by Grosseteste, see Briggs, "Moral Philosophy," 375–88.

65 The manuscript tradition of Grosseteste's translation has been convincingly reconstructed by Gauthier, *Ethica Nicomachea* (above, n. 1), clxxiv–clxxxvi.

66 These manuscripts are Oxford, Corpus Christi College 106, and Oxford, New College 240/241. On the importance of these manuscripts, see A. C. Dionisotti, "On the Greek Studies of Robert Grosseteste," in *The Use of Greek and Latin*, ed. A. C. Dionisotti, A. Grafton, and J. Kraye, Warburg Institute Surveys and Texts 16 (London, 1988), 38. See also Gauthier, *Ethica Nicomachea*, cxcv–cxcix. On Servopoulos, see P. Canart, "Scribes grecs de la Renaissance," *Scriptorium* 16, no. 1 (1963), 56–82, esp. 68; R. Weiss, *Humanism in England During the Fifteenth Century* (Oxford, 1941), 147–48; Harlfinger, *Die Textgeschichte* (above, n. 19), 416; R. W. Hunt, *The Survival of Ancient Literature: Catalogue of an Exhibition of Greek and Latin Classical Manuscripts Mainly from Oxford Libraries Displayed on the Occasion of the Triennial Meeting of the Hellenic and Roman Societies 28 July–2 August 1975* (Oxford, 1975), t. 52; I. Hutter, *Corpus der byzantinischen Miniaturenhandschriften: Oxford Bodleian Library* (Stuttgart, 1982), 3:155; J. Harris, *Greek Emigres in the West, 1400–1520* (Camberley, 1995), 148; idem, "Greek Scribes in England: The Evidence of Episcopal Registers," in *Through the Looking Glass: Byzantium through British Eyes; Papers from the Twenty-Ninth Spring Symposium of Byzantine Studies, King's College, London, March 1995*, ed. R. Cormack and E. Jeffreys, Publication of the Society for the Promotion of Byzantine Studies 7 (Oxford, 2000), 121–26.

67 See Mercken, *The Greek Commentaries,* CLCAG 6.1, *40–*42. For the dating of Grosseteste's scholarship on the *Corpus Dionysiacum* and the *Nicomachean Ethics,* I rely on D. A. Callus, "The Date of Grosseteste's *Translations* and Commentaries of Pseudo-Dionysius and the Nicomachean Ethics," *Recherches de théologie ancienne et médiévale* 14 (1947): 186–209. See also J. Dunbabin, "Robert Grosseteste as Translator, Transmitter and Commentator: The *Nicomachean Ethics,*" *Traditio* 28 (1972): 460–77. For a summary of the debate on the date of Grosseteste's translation of the *Nicomachean Ethics* and the commentaries, see Mercken, *The Greek Commentaries*, CLCAG 6.1, *39. On the general issue of the chronology of Grosseteste's work, see J. McEvoy, *The Philosophy of Robert Grosseteste* (Oxford,

translation of the *Ethics* and commentaries; the *Summa ethicorum,* that is, a summary of the *Ethics* by Grosseteste himself; the Pseudo-Aristotelian *De virtute;* and Pseudo-Andronicus's *De passionibus*—must have been a huge task, and it was not accomplished until approximately 1246.[68] Unsurprisingly, then, some of the most important extant thirteenth-century manuscripts containing Grosseteste's translation and the Greek-Byzantine commentaries originated in England or were copied by English scribes. These are Cambridge, Peterhouse MS 116;[69] the aforementioned Florence, Bibl. Naz., MS Conv. Soppr. I.5.21;[70] Vatican, Biblioteca Apostolica Vaticana, MS Vat. Lat. 2171;[71] Eton College 122;[72] Florence, Bibl. Laur., MS Plut. LXXIX 13;[73] and Oxford, All Souls College MS 84.[74] Apparently the first three, including the one owned by Salutati and Bruni, are closely related and originated from the same English scriptorium.[75]

In fact, medieval English scholars started using Grosseteste's translation of the *Ethics* and commentaries as soon as it was finished. Kilwardby's *De ortu scientiarum,* written between 1247 and 1250, is the first non-Grosseteste work to explicitly reference Eustratios's commentaries.[76] But this work includes unreferenced quotes from Eustratios as well, which have, to my knowledge, gone unnoticed until now. The most striking case is Kilwardby's statement that both Christian and ancient philosophers regarded beatitude ("beatitudo") as man's spiritual good ("bonum hominis spirituale"), but while the first called it beatitude, the latter called it happiness ("felicitas"). Despite a reference to Augustine's *De trinitate,* this distinction, including Kilwardby's remark that Christian beatitude cannot be achieved in this life, while philosophical happiness entails man's virtuous life in the present condition, is entirely borrowed from Eustratios's commentary on book 1 of the *Nicomachean Ethics.*[77] By the same token, the *Sapientiale,* written prior to 1256 by the Franciscan and former pupil of Grosseteste Thomas of York

1982), 453–519; idem, "Questions of Authenticity and Chronology Concerning Works Attributed to Robert Grosseteste and Edited 1940–1980," *Bulletin de philosophie médiévale* 23 (1981): 64–90; 24 (1982): 69–89. On the broader issue of Grosseteste's Greek scholarship, see R. W. Southern, *Robert Grosseteste: The Growth of an English Mind in Medieval Europe* (Oxford, 1986), 181–86; J. McEvoy, *Robert Grosseteste* (Oxford, 2000), 113–21. On Grosseteste's motivation in translating the *Nicomachean Ethics* and the commentaries, see Mercken, *The Greek Commentaries,* CLCAG 6.3, *40–*45.

68 On this work and their manuscript tradition, see Thomson, *Writings* (above, n. 30), 65–66, 68–70, 85–86, 88, 233–34.

69 *AL* 355, no. 252.

70 *AL* 355, nos. 965, 1408.

71 *AL* 1226, no. 1859.

72 *AL* 370, no. 281.

73 *AL* 912, no. 1318; Marchesi, *L'Etica* (above, n. 37), 38–39.

74 *AL* 415, no. 374.

75 See Gauthier, *Ethica Nicomachea* (above, n. 1), clxxiv–clxxvi.

76 This was first noticed by A. Pelzer, "Les versions latines des ouvrages de morale conservés sous le nom d'Aristote en usage au XIIIe siècle," *Revue néo-scholastique de philosophie* 23 (1921): 316–41, 378–412, at 404.

77 Compare Robertus de Kylewardeby, *De ortu scientiarum* 36, ed. A. G. Judy (O.P.), *Robert Kilwardby, O.P., De ortu scientiarum,* Auctores britannici medii aevi 4 (London and Toronto, 1976), 124.16–27:

(d. before 1269), contains several quotes from Eustratios on crucial points, such as the commentator's counter-critique of Aristotle's criticism of the Platonic ideal good and the disagreement between the Platonists and Aristotle on the status of later concepts abstracted from the sensible particulars, which Eustratios had formulated by cribbing from Proclus's commentary on the *Parmenides*.[78]

The case of Thomas of York shows that when it comes to medieval English philosophical literature, reconstructing the fortune of Grosseteste's translation of the *Nicomachean Ethics* requires us to extend the inquiry to works other than the commentaries on this Aristotelian work, especially if one considers that many such commentaries by medieval English scholars are now lost.[79] For example, the *Communiloquium* by the Franciscan John of Wales, lector in Oxford from about 1258 to 1262, and later regent master of theology in Paris, ascribes an example of *concordia* before enemies to a *Commentator in ethicis* who can hardly be identified with Grosseteste. In fact, contrary to what has been stated,[80] here John refers to Michael of Ephesus's commentary on

---

> *Bonum hominis spirituale tam secundum catholicos quam secundum antiquos philosophos beatitudo est, quam philosophi plurimum vocant felicitatem, sed catholici potius beatitudinem. Haec secundum veritatem catholicam non potest plene haberi in hac vita mortali, ut ostendit Augustinus libro XIII De Trinitate. Tamen secundum opinionem philosophicam antiquam multorum aeternam et beatam vitam Dei visionis ignorantium videbatur aliquando plene posse acquiri et haberi in hac vita, de quibus videtur Aristoteles fuisse, qui posuit quod felicitas est actus perfectus secundum virtutem, quem, ni fallar, posuit hominem habere in hac vita, si sic perseveraverit, agens scilicet secundum virtutem ut ei possibile*

with Eustratius Latinus, *In I EN* 6.33–40:

> *In primo autem libro huius negotii de fine quaerit ad quem virtutes ducunt directae, qui felicitas apud antiquos sapientes nominatur. Hic autem finis est finis humanae vitae, cuius gratia homo in praesenti mundo conversatur. Est autem hic finis a principio quidem moderativus passionum, quod agreste et immoderatum coniugatarum nobis irrationabilium passionum constringens et ut duce ratione et duci et ferri suadens, ad ultimum pertingere ad impassibilitatem, qui finis beatitudo apud nos dicitur.*

For an analysis of this important passage and its historic importance, with no reference however to its source, see A. J. Celano, "The Understanding of the Concept of Felicitas in the pre-1250 Commentaries on the Ethica Nicomachea," *Medioevo* 12 (1986): 45–46; I. Zavattero, "Felicitas-beatitudo," in *Mots médiévaux offerts à Ruedi Imbach*, ed. I. Atucha (Porto, 2011), 291–302.

78 Thomas of York's *Sapientiale* is still unedited, but the sections of this work containing these Eustratios references have been edited in F. Retucci, "Tommaso di York, Eustrazio e la dottrina delle idee di Platone," in *Per perscrutationem philosophicam: Neue Perspektiven der mittelalterlichen Forschung; Zum 60. Geburstag Loris Sturlese gewidmet*, ed. A. Beccarisi, R. Imbach, and P. Porro, Corpus Philosophorum Teutonicorum Medii Aevi (Hamburg, 2008), 77–108, esp. 101.21–20 (Eustratius Latinus, *In I EN* 69.89–95); 105.144–106.160 (Eustratius Latinus, *In VI EN*, MS Eton College 122, 112va). The latter Eustratian passage concerns the disagreement between the Platonists and Aristotle on the value of later-born concepts abstracted from the individuals, and relies on Proclus, "In Parmenidem," in *Procli in Platonis Parmenidem Commentaria*, vol. 2, ed. C. Steel, Oxford Classical Texts (Oxford, 2008), 980.10–13.

79 Cf. above, n. 62.

80 See J. Swanson, *John of Wales: A Study of the Works and Ideas of a Thirteenth-Century Friar*, Cambridge Studies in Medieval Life and Thought, 4th series, 10 (Cambridge, 1989), 69. Swanson,

book 9 of the *Nicomachean Ethics*, where he recalls the case of the concordia among the Greeks in front of Xerxes and the Persian threat.[81]

The Augustinian friar John Wilton (d. 1310) wrote a commentary, now lost, on the *Nicomachean Ethics*.[82] Yet it is probable that John's lost commentary on the *Ethics* included numerous references to the Greek-Byzantine commentators translated by Grosseteste. Several years later, in his *Quaestio de anima intellectiva*, Thomas Wilton (d. 1322) attributes the view that the intellectual virtues first require the moral ones to the commentator on book 9 of the *Nicomachean Ethics,* in this case, Michael of Ephesus rather than Averroes.[83] Meanwhile, the commentary on the *Sentences* written in about 1320 by the Franciscan John of Reading refers to Eustratios's and Grosseteste's *notulae* on the *Ethics* concerning the subalternation of all the sciences to theology.[84] Further evidence suggesting a consistent influence of these commentaries on the medieval English scholars includes a vast number of references to Eustratios's imagery of the moral virtues as sisters, which, as shown above, also attracted the attention of Byzantine authors such as John VI Kantakouzenos, shaping the medieval theory of the relationship between the cardinal virtues. For example,

---

the high quality of her work notwithstanding, often unconvincingly identifies John's references to the *commentatores in Ethicis* to Grosseteste himself (e.g., at 46, 62, 105, 121–23, 140, 199). Yet almost all of these are references to *Eustratius cum aliis* translated by Grosseteste, as already cautiously suggested by Luscombe, "Ethics" (above, n. 62), 340. Furthermore, scholars regard it highly improbable that Grosseteste himself wrote a commentary on the *Ethics*. On this, see Mercken, *The Greek Commentaries*, CLCAG 6.1, *54–*58.

81 Johannes Gallensis, *Communiloquium sive Summa Collationum* 1.1.5, Venetiis 1497, fol. 7ra: "Unde commentator ix ethi.: concordia magnorum gratia (*ex* grata *corr.*) toti civitati et totis grecis" = Michael Ephesius, *In IX EN*, 250.77–78.

82 See C. H. Lohr, "Medieval Latin Aristotle Commentaries," *Traditio* 27 (1971): 303. Other lost commentaries on the *Nicomachean Ethics* by medieval English scholars include that by Robert Crowche, lecturer in Oxford between 1278 and 1279 (cf. C. H. Lohr, "Medieval Latin Aristotle Commentaries," *Traditio* 29 [1973]: 99–100); John Baconthorpe (d. ca. 1348) (see Lohr, "Medieval Latin" [1970]: 154–55); Roger Swyneshead (d. 1365), a Benedictine who taught in Oxford in about 1330 (cf. Lohr, "Medieval Latin" [1973]: 122); the Carmelite Richard of Lavenham (fl. ca. 1399–1403), who taught at Oxford (cf. C. H. Lohr, "Medieval Latin Aristotle Commentaries," *Traditio* 28 [1972]: 393–94); and the Carmelite Thomas Netter of Walden (ca. 1375–1430), who studied at Oxford in the late 14th century (cf. Lohr, "Medieval Latin" [1973]: 184). Extant but still unedited are the *quaestiones* on ethics by John Tytynsale (d. 1289), master of arts at Merton College, Oxford (cf. Lohr, "Medieval Latin" [1973]: 99–100); Richard Kilvington (ca. 1302–1361) (cf. Lohr, "Medieval Latin" [1972]: 392–93, and E. Jung, "Works by Richard Kilvington," *Archives d'histoire doctrinale et littéraire du Moyen Âge* 67 [2000]: 182–223); and Anonymous, *Conclusiones libri ethicorum* (cf. Lohr, "Medieval Latin" [1973]: 146). For an overview on later commentaries on the *Nicomachean Ethics*, see Luscombe, "Ethics," 343.

83 Thomas de Wylton, *Questio de anima intellectiva* 60, in *Thomas Wilton: On the Intellectual Soul*, ed. L.O. Nielsen-C. Trifogli, Auctores Britannici Medii Aevi 19 (Oxford, 2010), 36.11–13. The reference goes to Michael Ephesius, *In X EN* 408.63–65, 409.78–80, as pointed out by G. Guldentops, "Review of *Thomas de Wylton, Questio de anima intellectiva*, ed. L.O. Nielsen-C. Trifogli, *Thomas Wilton: On the Intellectual Soul*, Auctores Britannici Medii Aevi 19 (Oxford, 2010)," *Recherches de Théologie et Philosophie Médiévales* 78, no. 2 (2011): 533.

84 See S. J. Livesey, *Theology and Science in the Fourteenth Century: Three Questions on the Unity and Subalternation of the Sciences from John of Reading's Commentary on the Sentences*, Studien und Texte zur Geistesgeschichte des Mittelalters 25 (Leiden, 1989), 102.27–30, 129.7–9.

the famed John Duns Scotus (ca. 1265/66–1308), who studied in Oxford and lectured on Peter Lombard's *Sentences* in Paris at the beginning of fourteenth century, endorses this Eustratian imagery against Henry of Ghent's use of the same analogy.[85]

To return to the commentary literature on the *Nicomachean Ethics* in the fourteenth century, Burley's commentary on the *Ethics* famously relied on the Greek-Byzantine commentaries translated by Grosseteste and his *notulae*, that is, Grosseteste's marginal notes.[86] A statistical study of the occurrences of these commentaries in Burley's own commentary counts about 265 explicit quotes from Eustratios alone and 105 explicit quotes from Grosseteste's work, including the *notulae*. The Arabic authors definitively played a minor role: Averroes is quoted explicitly only five times and Avicenna only twice.[87] Burley belongs to a later generation of commentators. In fact, he quotes from earlier medieval Latin commentaries such as that of Albert the Great on the *Nicomachean Ethics* (eighteen times), which means that he could rely on a consistent commentary tradition that had developed earlier in Paris and, more importantly, Cologne.

Paris

It may be true that medieval English scholarship on Aristotle's moral philosophy is less consistent than continental works,[88] but, in its way, the early Parisian reception of *Eustratius cum aliis* is no less a *terra incognita*. In 1255, almost ten years after Grosseteste translated the *Ethics* and its commentaries, and a few years after Albert the Great's commentary on the *Ethics* based upon this translation, the Paris university still prescribed twelve weeks of lectures on the *Ethica nova* and *vetus*, the twelfth-century translation by Burgundio of Pisa, which was known in the thirteenth century only in fragmentary form, and another work, or six weeks of lectures on this Aristotelian work alone.[89]

85 Johannes Duns Scotus, *Ordinatio* 3.d.36, *Opera Omnia* 10 (Grottaferrata, 2007), 227.112–16, 238.291–95, against Henricus de Gandavo, *Quodlibeta V*, q. 19 in corp., Paris 1518 (fol. 189Y).

86 Gualterus Burlaeus, *Expositio super decem libros ethicorum*, Venetiis 1481. On Grosseteste's *notulae*, see S. Harrison Thomson, "The 'Notulae' of Grosseteste on the Nicomachean Ethics," *Proceedings of the British Academy* 19 (1933): 195–218; Mercken, *The Greek Commentaries*, CLCAG 6.1, *48–*54.

87 Cf. Walsh, "Some Relationships" (above, n. 33).

88 See Briggs, "Moral Philosophy" (above, n. 62), 360–61.

89 See *Carthularium universitatis Parisiensis*, ed. H. Denifle and E. Chatelain (Paris, 1889), 1: n. 20, 78: "Ethicas quantum ad quatuor libros in xij septimanis, si cum alio legantur; si per se non cum alio, in medietate temporis." I take this as a reference to the three books of the *Ethica nova* and *vetus* which, due to a different division of the text, were considered by 13th-century commentators to be four. I rely on Anonymus, *Lectura in ethicam veterem*, Paris, Bibl., Nat., MS lat. 3804A, fol. 153va:

> *In tribus libris istius uoluminis et in libro precedente istum librum, seu in primo Ethice, determinat Aristoteles de uirtute in genere. In quarto autem istius libri et in aliis libris quos non habemus determinat Aristoteles de speciebus uirtutis et de earum differentiis. In quarto enim determinat de fortitudine; in quinto de castitate et illum quintum non habemus. . . . Et sic patet ordo quattuor librorum priorum ad quintum et ceteros quos non habemus.*

on which see I. Zavattero, "Le prologue de la *Lectura in Ethicam ueterem* du 'Commentaire de Paris' (1235–1240): Introduction et texte critique," *Recherches de Théologie et Philosophie Médiévales* 77, no. 1 (2010): 1–33. But see the caveat by R. A. Gauthier, *L'Éthique à Nicomaque*, vol. 1 (Louvain-la-Neuve,

In his prologue to his *Sentences* commentary, written in about 1250–52, Bonaventure still quotes the *Ethica vetus*.[90] Between 1260 and 1270, a revised version of Grosseteste's translation of the *Ethics* without the commentaries—accomplished by a scholar tentatively but not definitively identified as the well-known thirteenth-century translator William of Moerbeke—circulated in Paris[91] and is mentioned in the price list of the *stationarium* of the University of Paris on 25 February 1304.[92]

Only three manuscripts containing the *Nicomachean Ethics* and its Greek-Byzantine commentaries appear to have been copied from a thirteenth-century Parisian exemplar divided into *peciae* and therefore liable to have been circulated within the University of Paris.[93] Apparently even Aquinas, considered the one to have collected Albert's lectures on the *Nicomachean Ethics* in Cologne, was not a regular Eustratios reader. In fact, in quoting from the Greek-Byzantine commentaries translated by Grosseteste, Aquinas relies heavily on Albert the Great's own commentary on the *Ethics*.[94] However, a close look at the number of quotations from *Eustratius cum aliis* among late thirteenth-century Parisian masters suggests a wider circulation of the Greek-Byzantine commentaries than we can infer today on the basis of manuscript evidence, in particular among arts masters. This is exemplified by the two anonymous commentaries *per quaestiones* written in about 1280 and preserved in Paris, Bibl. Nat., MS lat. 14698, and Erlangen, Universitätsbibl. MS 213 (Irm. 485), fols. 47ra–80vb—more on this later—or Peter of Auvergne's *quaestiones* on books 1 and 2 of the *Nicomachean Ethics*, which were probably also written in about 1280, when Peter was rector of the Paris arts faculty.[95] Some years later, between 1289 and 1299, Radulphus Brito, another arts master, wrote his *quaestiones* on the *Nicomachean Ethics*,[96] and between the end of thirteenth and the beginning of fourteenth century, two other commentaries *per modum quaestionis* were written by two *artistae*: one of them has yet

2002), 113, n. 92. On the text tradition of the Latin translation of the *Nicomachean Ethics* before Grosseteste, see Gauthier, *Ethica Nicomachea* (above, n. 1), xvi–cli.

90 Bonaventura, *In I Sent., proem.*, q. 2, arg. 5, *Opera Omnia* 1 (Grottaferrata, 1883), 10.

91 On this issue and the different positions, see Gauthier's observation in Thomas Aquinas, *Sententia* 232*–235*. See also Gauthier, *L'Éthique*, 125–31; idem, *Ethica Nicomachea*, ccxi–ccxlvii, esp. ccxxxix–ccxlvii. For a *nihil obstat* argument in favor of Moerbeke, see Jozef Brams, "The Revised Version of Grosseteste's Translation of the *Nicomachean Ethics*," *Bulletin de philosophie médiévale* 36 (1994): 45–55.

92 See *Carthularium Universitatis Parisiensis*, 2: n. 642, 107.

93 The manuscripts are Paris, Bibl. Nat., MS Lat. 17832 (*AL* 584, no. 714), Reims, Bibl. Munic., MS 876 (*AL* 597, no. 741), Wien, Nationalbibl., MS 2327 (*AL* 287, no. 108). See Gauthier, *Ethica Nicomachea,* clxxvi–clxxix.

94 See Gauthier's remarks in Thomas Aquinas, *Sententia* 246*–256*.

95 Text edited in A. Celano, "Peter of Auvergne's Quaestiones on Books I and II of the *Ethica Nicomachea*: A Study and Critical Edition," *Medieval Studies* 48 (1986): 1–110. On Peter, see O. Weijers, *Le travail intellectuel à la Faculté des arts de Paris: Textes et maîtres (ca. 1200–1500)*, vol. 7, Répertoire des noms commençant par P. Studia Artistarum, Etudes sur la Faculté des arts dans les Universités médiévales 15 (Turnhout, 2007), 95–127.

96 Text edited in I. Costa, *Le quaestiones di Radulfo Brito sull' "Etica Nicomachea": Introduzione e testo critico*, Studia Artistarum 17 (Turnhout, 2008).

to be identified. His commentary is known as the Anonymous of Erfurt and preserved in Erfurt, Amplon., MS F. 13, fols. 84ra–117va; the other has been attributed to Gilles of Orleans and is preserved in Paris, BnF MS lat. 16089, fols. 195ra–233va.[97] All these commentaries are influenced by *Eustratius cum aliis* and its early interpreters, such as Albert the Great.

Cologne

Albert's scholarship on *Eustratius cum aliis* is a trademark of the Western reception of these commentaries to such an extent that not only Thomas, but also the thirteenth-century Parisian *artistae,* echoed Albert's fondness for these texts. In general, scholars of Dante's time and afterward could scarcely have ignored the existence and importance of this Byzantine commentator. Several facts show that Italian libraries held many manuscripts containing Eustratios's commentary, though, unfortunately, these manuscripts are lost,[98] and the basis for Bruni's and the other humanists' admiration for Eustratios as a commentator on Aristotle's *Ethics* was laid by early scholasticism. Albert the Great, one of the first in the West to have used Grosseteste's translation of the *Ethics* and the Greek-Byzantine commentaries, mentions Eustratios as "commentator." His *Super ethica*, composed between 1248 and 1252 in Cologne in the recently founded *Studium Generale* of the Dominican order, counts more than three hundred explicit quotes from Grosseteste's translation of the aforementioned commentaries.[99]

Albert, who had surely owned a copy of *Eustratius cum aliis* since at least 1249, when he was composing book 4 of his commentary on Peter Lombard's *Sentences*,[100] wrote another commentary on the *Ethics* some twenty years after the first, probably between 1267 and 1270.[101] There, and in many other commentaries on Aristotle, Albert keeps referring to Eustratios as an authoritative commentator, even when dealing with Eustratios's disagreement with Aristotle. It is worth mentioning that Albert's first commentary emphasizes Eustratios's famous defense of the Platonic ideal good against Aristotle's criticism of it in book 1 of the *Ethics,* in a way that, years later, will be repeated by the Franciscan Bonaventure, in a harsher reappraisal of Eustratios's anti-Aristotelian arguments.[102] In fact, while plagiarizing the passage from Albert's commentary, Bonaventure's

97 On these commentaries, see idem, "Autour de deux commentaires inédits sur *l'Étique à Nicomaque*," in *Christian Readings of Aristotle from the Middle Ages to the Renaissance*, ed. L. Bianchi, Studia Artistarum 29 (Turnhout, 2011), 211–72.

98 Cf. Lines, *Aristotle's Ethics* (above, n. 54) 163.

99 Albertus Magnus, *Super Ethica Commentum et Quaestiones*, ed. W. Kübel, *Opera Omnia* 14.1–2 (Münster, 1968–70, 1987).

100 Cf. F. Pelster, *Kritische Studien zum Leben und zu Schriften Alberts des Grossen* (Freiburg, 1920), 123.

101 Albertus Magnus, *Ethica*, ed. A. Borgnet, *Opera Omnia* 7 (Paris, 1891).

102 Aristoteles, *Ethica Nicomachea* 1.6.1096a11–1097a14; Eustratius Graecus, *In I EN* 39.25–58.13. On this text, see K. Giocarinis, "Eustratios of Nicaea's Defense of the Doctrine of the Ideas," *Franciscan Studies* 24 (1964): 159–204; C. Steel, "Neoplatonic Sources in the Commentaries on the Nicomachean Ethics by Eustratius and Michael of Ephesus," *Bulletin de Philosophie Médiévale* 44 (2002): 51–57.

Collationes in hexaemeron relies on Eustratios, mentioned as *commentator*, in order to reject Aristotle's criticism of the supreme good as an idea. Like Albert, he claims that Eustratios's counter-critique demolished Aristotle's arguments: "his arguments have no force, and have been solved by the Commentator" (*et nihil valent rationes suae, et Commentator solvit eas*).[103]

After Albert, Eustratios became the commentator who, in the guise of defending the Platonic ideas, saved divine exemplarism from Aristotle's attack. Unsurprisingly, then, due to the Neoplatonism evident in his commentaries on the *Ethics* and Albert's authoritative reappraisal of it, Eustratios gained the status of reference author for later generations of the German Dominican tradition. In his commentary on Proclus's *Elements of Theology*, for example, the Dominican Berthold of Mogsburg quotes Eustratios's claim that according to the Platonists, the first good must be the transcendent cause of all other goods. "Si enim omnia illud appetunt," writes Berthold, quoting from Eustratios, "super omnia ex necessitate est."[104] In doing so, Berthold must have noticed that this statement by Eustratios is a quote from proposition 8 of Proclus's *Elements of Theology*, the very text upon which Berthold was commenting.[105]

Reassessing Averroism: The "Eustratian" Roots of so-called Latin Averroism

While reconstructing the medieval fortune of *Eustratius cum aliis,* I also tried to account for the variety of topics that were influenced by Grosseteste's translation of the Greek-Byzantine commentaries on the *Nicomachean Ethics*. The existence and status of the highest good, the unity of the virtues, the disagreement between Plato and Aristotle, and the notion of concordia are just some of the many issues that medieval masters discussed through the lens of the Greek-Byzantine commentators. Other topics include the status of prudence, or practical wisdom, as intermediate between the moral and the intellectual virtues, which, for example, Giles of Rome's *De regimine principum*, composed between 1277 and 1281, explicitly ascribes to Eustratios of Nicaea.[106]

103 Albertus Magnus, *Super Ethica* 1.6.27.40–45; Bonaventura, *Collationes in hexaemeron* 6.2, Opera Omnia 5 (Grottaferrata, 1891), 360–61. On Albert's reading of Eustratios's anti-Aristotelian arguments, see I. Costa, "Il problema dell'omonimia del bene in alcuni commenti scolastici all'Ethica Nicomachea," *Documenti e Studi sulla Tradizione Filosofica Medievale* 17 (2006): 157–230.
104 Bertholdus de Mosburch, *Expositio Super Elementationem Theologicam Procli, 1–13*, ed. L. Sturlese and M.R. Pagnoni-Sturlese, Corpus Philosophorum Teutonicorum Medii Aevi 6.1 (Hamburg, 1984), 187.73–74 = Eustratius Latinus, *In I EN* 77.16–17.
105 Proclus, *Elementatio theologica*, 8, in *The Elements of Theology: A Revised Text with Translation, Introduction, and Commentary,* ed. E. R. Dodds, 2nd ed. (Oxford, 1963), 8.31–32 = Proclus, *Elementatio theologica a Guillelmo de Morbecca translata* 8, ed. H. Boese, Ancient and Mediaeval Philosophy, De Wulf-Mansion Centrum, series 1, 5 (Leuven, 1987), 7.3–4: "si enim omnia entia bonum appetunt, palam quia quod prime bonum ultra entia est."
106 On this, see R. Lambertini, "Tra etica e politica: La prudentia del principe nel De regimine di Egidio Romano," *Documenti e Studi sulla tradizione filosofica medievale* 3 (1992): 92–95.

Giles is a paradigmatic case study of the reception of *Eustratius cum aliis*. While it is clear that he utilizes this corpus of commentaries, at the same time it appears that Giles's reading of Eustratios, Michael of Ephesus, and the others cannot be separated from the interpretation of these Greek-Byzantine commentators by scholars such as Albert the Great and Aquinas.[107] This goes to what has been said before: in dealing with the medieval Latin fortune of Grosseteste's translation of these commentaries, one has to consider the indirect tradition as well. But Giles's *De regimine* is important for another reason. As convincingly demonstrated by Concetta Luna, this work, which was vastly present in Italian libraries, especially in monasteries, was regarded right from the beginning not only as belonging to the genre of the Mirror of Princes, but also as a sort of commentary on the *Nicomachean Ethics*,[108] a work of moral and political philosophy written for a layman (King Philip IV of France) that eventually leads us directly to the same discussion and framework as Dante.[109] Yet reconstructing such a bridge would far exceed the scope of the present essay, and I will therefore confine myself to the investigation of the medieval debate of another sensitive topic for medieval masters and Dante himself, which was influenced by the Greek-Byzantine commentators on the *Nicomachean Ethics*: the discussions on the role of philosophy in human happiness and the natural desire for knowing the separate substances as elaborated by those medieval masters commonly labeled "Latin Averroists."

When discussing the label "Latin Averroism," especially in connection with Dante, one must refer to Maria Corti's consequential notion of "felicità mentale," that is, the idea that somehow Dante's "amoroso uso di sapienza" (*Conv.* 3.12.11–12) relates to the intellectual trends that arose in the Paris arts faculty of the late thirteenth century. There, masters such as Boethius of Dacia thought that philosophy could lead to happiness in this life, an idea that later influenced the intellectual milieu in Bologna and Florence.[110] Obviously, one cannot dismiss Bruno Nardi's scholarship on this subject,[111]

107 On this, see idem, "Il filosofo, il principe e la virtù: Note sulla ricezione e l'uso dell'Etica Nicomachea nel De regimine principum di Egidio Romano," *Documenti e studi sulla tradizione filosofica medievale* 2 (1991): 254–55.

108 See C. Luna, *Introduzione*, *Opera Omnia* 1.1.11 (Prolegomena: Catalogo dei Manoscritti [1001–1075] De regimine principum), ed. F. Del Punta and C. Luna, Corpus Philosophorum Medii Aevi: Testi e Studi 12 (Florence, 1993), ix–xxxiii. On the medieval circulation of this work, especially in England, see also C. F. Briggs, *Giles of Rome's* De regimine principum*: Reading and Writing Politics at Court and University, c. 1275–1525* (Cambridge, 1999), 91–106, 152–70.

109 On this, see R. Imbach, *Dante, la philosophie et les laïcs*, Initiations à la philosophie médiévale 1 (Fribourg and Paris, 1996), 49–86, 173–96.

110 See O. Kristeller, "A Philosophical Treatise from Bologna Dedicated to Guido Cavalcanti: Magister Jacobus de Pistorio and His 'Quaestio de Felicitate'," in *Medioevo e Rinascimento: Studi in onore di Bruno Nardi* (Florence, 1955), 427–63, repr. in idem, *Studies in Renaissance Thought and Letters*, Storia e Letteratura: Raccolta di Studi e Testi 178 (Rome, 1993), 509–37; M. Corti, *La felicità mentale: Nuove prospettive per Cavalcanti e Dante* (Turin, 1983).

111 See, e.g., B. Nardi, *Sigieri di Brabante nel pensiero del rinascimento italiano* (Rome, 1945); idem, "Note per una storia dell'averrosimo latino, I: Controversie sigeriane," *Rivista di Storia della Filosofia* 1 (1947): 19–25; idem, "L'averroismo bolognese nel secolo XIII e Taddeo Alderotto," *Rivista di Storia della Filosofia* 4 (1949): 11–22; idem, *Saggi sull'aristotelismo padovano dal secolo XIV al secolo XVI*

but Corti's notion of "felicità mentale" clearly provided the basis for most of the present reconstructions of Averroist tendencies in the Middle Ages.[112] Nevertheless, in tackling this topic, one may fruitfully wonder, what are the basic tenets of Latin Averroism? Scholars tend to agree that Corti's "felicità mentale" applies best to a certain number of medieval masters at the Paris arts faculty who more or less shared the aforementioned view that happiness can be reached in this life by exercising man's noblest faculty: the intellect. More important, it has recently been suggested that this standpoint not only stems from Arabic source material available in the West, as the very notion of Latin Averroism implies, but precisely from the Byzantine commentaries on the *Ethics*, particularly those of Eustratios on books 1 and 6.[113]

The reader may be surprised that I have not yet mentioned the well-known concept of "copulatio," and even the well-known theory of the unity of the intellect, among the basic tenets of so-called Latin Averroism.[114] In fact, it may be true that, taking a cue from a famous passage of Albert the Great, many medieval masters referred to this notion in describing perfection as the intellectual conjunction or *copulatio* with the separate substances.[115] But this notion is not mentioned by either Boethius of Dacia's *De*

(Florence, 1958). See also M. Grabmann, "L'aristotelismo italiano al tempo di Dante con particolare riguardo all'Università di Bologna," *Rivista di Filosofia Neoscolastica* 38 (1946): 260–77.

112 For a reconstruction of the state of affairs on this topic, with emphasis on the role of Maria Corti's scholarship, see G. Fioravanti, "La felicità intellettuale: Storiografia e precisazioni," in *Le felicità nel medioevo: Atti del convegno della Società Italiana per lo Studio del Pensiero Medievale (S.I.S.P.M.), Milano 12–13 settembre 2003*, ed. M. Bettetini and F. Paparella (Louvain-La-Neuve, 2005), 1–12.

113 See L. Bianchi, "La felicità intellettuale come professione nella Parigi del Duecento," *Rivista di Filosofia* 78 (1987): 181–99; idem, *Il vescovo e i filosofi: La condanna parigina del 1277 e l'evoluzione dell'aristotelismo scolastico* (Bergamo, 1990), 149–95; idem, "Felicità terrena e beatitudine ultraterrena: Boezio di Dacia e l'articolo 157 censurato da Tempier," in *Chemins de la pensée médiévale*, ed. P. J. J. M. Bakker (Turnhout, 2002), 193–214; idem, "Felicità intellettuale, 'ascetismo' e 'arabismo'," in Bettetini and Paparella, *Le felicità nel medioevo*, 13–34, esp. 32–34; A. J. Celano, "Boethius of Dacia: 'On the Highest Good'," *Traditio* 43 (1987): 199–214, 207–8; A. De Libera, *Raison et foi: Archéologie d'une crise d'Albert le Grand à Jean Paul II* (Paris, 2003), 322.

114 Obviously, "copulation" here does not refer to Averroes' explanation (*Commentarium Magnum in Aristotelis De Anima Libros*, ed. F. S. Crawford, The Mediaeval Academy of America, Publications 59, Corpus Philosophorum Medii Aevi, Corpus Commentariorum Averrois in Aristotelem, Versionum Latinarum 6.1 [Cambridge, 1957], 3.20) of the way individual *phantasmata* relate to the separate, unique potential intellect, but—according to a broader meaning of the word—to the philosopher's conjunction with the separate substances, which is unanimously regarded as one of the major tenets of the so-called Latin Averroists.

115 Cf., e.g., Albertus Magnus, *De anima*, lib. 3, tract. 3, cap. 11, ed. C. Stroick, *Opera Omnia* 7.1 (Münster, 1968), 221.6–223.38. On Albert's influence on the "Latin Averroists," see R. A. Gauthier, "Trois commentaires 'averroïstes' sur l'Éthique à Nicomaque," *Archives d'Histoire doctrinale et littéraire du Moyen Age* 16 (1948): 280; E. P. Mahoney, "Albert the Great and the Studio Patavino in the Late Fifteenth Century and Early Sixteenth Centuries," in *Albertus Magnus and the Sciences: Commemorative Essays*, ed. J. Weisheipl, Studies and Texts 49 (Toronto, 1980), 537–563, esp. 552–54; L. Bianchi, "Filosofi, uomini e bruti: Note per la storia di un'antropologia 'averroista'," *Rinascimento*, 2nd ser., 32 (1992): 185–201; A. De Libera, "Averroïsme étique et philosophie mystique: De la félicité intellectuelle à la vie bienheureuse," in *Filosofia e Teologia nel Trecento: Studi in onore di Eugenio Randi*, ed. L. Bianchi, Textes et Etudes du Moyen Âge 1 (Louvain-la-Neuve, 1994), 33–56; idem, "Albert le

summo bono,[116] regarded as the manifesto of the late thirteenth-century Parisian Latin Averroists, or James of Pistoia's *Quaestio de felicitate*, dedicated to Guido Cavalcanti and deemed by Oscar Kristeller and Maria Corti to be the link between the idea of intellectual eudaimonism supported by the Parisian *artistae* and the intellectual milieu in Bologna and Florence.[117] Furthermore, Averroes is quoted explicitly only once in his *De summo bono*, so Boethius's speculation on the highest good and the related theory of happiness can hardly be labeled "Averroist," if by this label one means a direct influence of Averroes' work.[118] As for James of Pistoia, his claim that happiness consists in knowledge of the separate substances and God bears no trace of any reference to the notion of "copulation";[119] on the contrary, by adding the clause "sicut possibile est homini," James echoes the late antique definition of philosophy attributed to Plato (*Theaetetus* 172b9), which was accessible to medieval Latin readers via many sources,[120] including Michael of Ephesus's commentary on book 10 of the *Ethics*, which famously discusses happiness and contemplative life in a way that resembles the argument in James's *Quaestio de felicitate*.[121] In fact, Michael refers to the "incorporales quaedam substantiae separatae

---

Grand et la mystique allemande," in *Philosophy and Learning: University in the Middle Ages*, ed. J. F. M. Hoenen, J. H. Josef Schneider, and G. Wieland, Education and Society in the Middle Ages and Renaissance 6 (Leiden, New York, and Cologne, 1995), 29–42; C. Steel, "Medieval Philosophy: An Impossible Project? Thomas Aquinas and the 'Averroist' Ideal of Happiness," in *Was ist Philosophie im Mittelalter: Akten des X. Internationalen Kongresses für Mittelalterliche Philosophie der Société Internationale pour l'Étude de la Philosophie Médiévale, 25. bis 30. August 1997 in Erfurt*, ed. J. A. Aertsen and A. Speer, Miscellanea Mediaevalia 24 (Berlin, 1998), 152–74.

116 I will refer here to the standard edition of this text as published in *Boethii Daci Opera*, Corpus Philosophorum Danicorum Medii Aevi 6.2 (Copenhagen, 1976), 369–77.

117 Cf. above, n. 110. A new edition of James's *Quaestio de Felicitate* appeared in I. Zavattero, *La "Quaestio de Felicitate" di Giacomo da Pistoia: Un tentativo di interpretazione alla luce di una nuova edizione critica del testo*, in Bettetini and Paparella, *Le Felicità nel medioevo*, 355–409. The absence of the notion of "copulatio" in James of Pistoia has been noted by Fioravanti, "La felicità intellettuale," 11–12.

118 Moreover, it is probably a secondhand quote. Cf. Bianchi, "Felicità intellettuale," 24–25.

119 James of Pistoia, *Quaestio de felicitate* 452.227–229: "relinquitur quod felicitas nihil aliud est quam continue sicut possibile est homini intelligere substantias separatas et precipue ipsum Deum" (= ed. Zavattero, 401.184–187). On the difference between Boethius of Dacia's and James of Pistoia's approaches, see Zavattero, *La "Quaestio de Felicitate,"* 362–65.

120 E.g., Arnulfus Provincialis, *Divisio scientiarum*, ed. C. Lafleur, *Quatre introductions à la philosophie au XIIIe siècle: Textes critiques et étude historique*, Université de Montréal. Publications de l'Institut d'études médiévales (Montreal and Paris, 1988), 310, 144–46.

121 Michael Ephesius, *In X EN*, 409.81–84: "Dicit autem ipse (scil. Aristoteles) quoniam, quia est felicitas animae operatio, rationabile ipsam maxime dicere secundum extremam animae operationem. Extrema autem ipsius operatio est unitio ad meliora et assimulatio Deo secundum possibile, ut ait Plato, homini"; 409.3–410.11:

> *Sive utique intellectus ipsum oportet vocare, ut ego ipsum nomino, sive vitam rationalem, ut Plato, quod utique optimum, ut dicebam, aptum natum est principari, et cum hoc intelligentiam habere et comprehensionem quod sunt bona, et horum quidem vere bona, haec autem apparenter, et quoniam sunt incorporales quaedam substantiae separatae a corporibus et secundum se ipsas stantes, et ante has quidem, causa quaesdam omnium substantia ens, omnimode perfecta operatio, continens et gubernans Omnia.*

a corporibus" as the object of the intellect, a statement that may well have pleased Michael's Latin readers.

Whether James had direct access to Eustratios's or Michael's commentaries is unknown, but the similarities between his reference to happiness as knowledge of the separate substances, endorsed by others before him, and Michael's statement that happiness consists in having intellection of the separate substances, described in Platonic terms as purely good and self-identical realities, is striking. It demonstrates that the copyright of intellectual eudaimonism endorsed by several thirteenth-century medieval masters was not simply Arabic. In fact, looking at the late thirteenth- to early fourteenth-century Averroist commentaries on the *Ethics* studied by Gauthier,[122] one will notice that most references to the idea of happiness as consisting in intellectual connection with the separate substances are supported, even when they rely on the notion of *copulatio* or conjunction, by quotes from Eustratios. For example, Gilles of Orleans's *Quaestiones supra decem libros Ethicorum*, transmitted through Paris, Bib. Nat., MS Lat. 16089 (fols. 195ra–233va), states that "modo dico quod finis extrinsecus hominis ultimus consistit in bono separato, finis autem intrinsecus eius ultimus non, sed magis consistit in operatione propria contemplativa secundum sapientiam; unde Eustratius dicit quod hac operatione *copulamur* causae increatae."[123] Likewise, the anonymous *Quaestiones in ethicam*, transmitted through Erfurt, MS Amplon. F. 13 (fols. 87ra–117va), states that "unde dicit Eustratius quod si nobis cura est *copulari* causae incausatae, oportet nos intendere et subicere ad apprehensionem proprii boni quod est nobis respectu illius communis boni."[124]

Taking their cue from Eustratios's defense of the Platonic ideal good against Aristotle's criticism, these passages absorb the *copulatio* theory through the prism of this Byzantine commentator's Neoplatonic interpretation of the Christian view of man's creation in the image of God and the need to join the uncaused cause through purification and mortification of the passions.[125] This passage must have impressed medieval Latin readers, for another so-called Averroist commentator on the *Ethics*, whose *Quaestiones super libro ethicorum* is transmitted in Erlangen, MS Universitätsbibl. 213

122 Cf. Gauthier, "Trois commentaires," 187–336. For a discussion of the chronology of these commentaries, see R. Hissette, "La date de quelques commentaires à l'Ethique," *Bulletin de Philosophie Médiévale* 18 (1976): 79–83.

123 I report the text as published in Costa, "Il problema dell'omonimia del bene," 207.77–80 (above, n. 103). Parts of Gilles's *Quaestiones* are edited in E. Canavesio, "Las 'Quaestiones supra decem libros ethicorum' de Gilles d'Orléans (libro primero)" (Ph.D. diss., Catholic University of Louvain, 1973), unavailable to me.

124 Text published in Costa, "Il problema dell'omonimia del bene," 215.87–89.

125 The reference goes to Eustratius Latinus, *In I EN* 9.7–13:

> *Ad imaginem enim Dei plasmati sumus et similitudinem, et necesse est nosmet abdolare ad archetipum (id est principalem formam vel principale exemplar), omne quod praeter naturam est repurificantes et materialem irrationabiltatem excutientes et eam quae ad mortale corpus habitudinem persequentes et propriam nobis ipsis bonam vitam coinducentes,* ***siquidem cura est nobis incausatae causae copulari.***

(fols. 47ra–80vb),[126] quotes it, without reference to the theory of *copulatio*, as an example of the striving for the highest good requiring abstinence from pleasures and vice: "sic enim voluit Eustracius, qui dixit quod qui vult promoveri ad summum bonum hominis debet studere omnia ad mortificacionem passionum."[127]

In general, other arguments by Eustratios clearly correspond to doctrines endorsed by these arts masters, for example: "qui autem ab ipsius perturbatione liberatus est intellectus desideranter ad primam pulchritudinem *copulatur* et prima bonitate potiri festinate."[128] Here, Eustratios once again suggests that copulation with the first beauty, evidently to be equated with God, requires the intellect's purification from passions and external hindrances. By the same token, he makes it clear elsewhere that the most divine among men are those who break all relationships with matter and have their intellect united with God: "isti autem sunt quotquot a materiis omnino secundum habitudinem recedentes extra carnem et mundum effecti vivunt super omnia visibilia et intellectum habent divinis *counitum*."[129] Doubtless, the masters at the Parisian arts faculty who supported intellectual eudaimonism must have found these Eustratian statements attractive, as is illustrated by the cases of Gilles of Orleans and the anonymous *Quaestiones in ethicam*.

Yet more striking are the similarities a medieval master might have detected between Grosseteste's Latin rendering of certain Eustratios passages and the Latin translations of texts from the Arabic tradition, such as the Pseudo-Aristotelian *Liber de causis*. This is evident in the commentary *per quaestiones* on the *Ethics* recently ascribed to Radulphus Brito and written after 1289.[130] There the thirteenth-century arts master elaborates on an argument favoring the view that happiness consists in joining the separate highest good: "felicitas humana et perfectio consistit ex unione ipsius ad suam primam causam, sicut vult commentator Libri de Causis."[131] The commentator on the *Liber de causis* at issue

126 On this text, see K. Giocarinis, "An Unpublished Late-Thirteenth-Century Commentary on the Nicomachean Ethics of Aristotle," *Traditio* 15 (1959): 299–326. For remarks and criticism to Giocarinis's study on this text, see R.-A. Gauthier, "Review of: K. Giocarinis, An Unpublished Late-Thirteenth-Century Commentary on the Nicomachean Ethics of Aristotle," *Bulletin Thomiste* 10, no. 3 (1959): 875–76.

127 Anonymus, *Quaestiones super libro Ethicorum*, MS Erlangen Universitätsbibl. 213 (fols. 47ra–80vb), q. 67, fol. 59vb9–11. I am grateful to Iacopo Costa for providing me with a full transcription of this text.

128 Eustratius Latinus, *In I EN* 100.64–66.

129 Ibid. 171.1–172.4. On this and other similar occurrences of the term "copulatio" in Eustratios, see Bianchi, *Felicità intellettuale* (above, n. 113), 31, n. 48.

130 The attribution to Brito, first suggested by R.-A. Gauthier, "Review of O. Lottin, Psychologie et Morale aux XIIe et XIIIe siècles," *Bulletin thomiste* 8, no. 8 (1947–53): 82–85, has been convincingly demonstrated by I. Costa, *Le Quaestiones di Radulfo Brito sull' "Etica Nicomachea": Introduzione e testo critico*, Studia Artistarum: Études sur la Faculté des arts dans les Universités médiévales 17 (Turnhout, 2008), 99–137 (on the authorship), 139–55 (on the chronology of this work). On Brito, see S. Ebbesen, "Radulphus Brito: The Last of the Great Arts Masters; Or: Philosophy and Freedom," in *Geistesleben im 13. Jahrhundert*, ed. J. Aertsen and A. Speer, Miscelanea Mediaevalia 27 (Berlin and New York, 1999), 231–51.

131 Radulphus Brito, *Quaestiones super libro ethicorum*, q. 20, 219.28–29.

is none other than Aquinas,[132] whose text as quoted by Brito is nearly identical to that quoted from Eustratios by Gilles of Orleans and the anonymous author of *Quaestiones super ethicam* transmitted in MS Erfurt, Amplon. F. 13 (fols. 87ra–117va). This demonstrates, once again, that Latin readers of *Eustratius cum aliis* saw their commentaries as an opportunity to endorse a form of intellectual eudaimonism identical to that which resulted from Latin interpretations of the Arabic source material available in the West.

More important, in Brito's view, is that the only way to retain the idea that happiness consists in joining the first cause and highest good is by supporting Eustratios's defense of the Platonic separate ideal good, at least in regard to what Brito and others call "finis extrinsecus."[133] He refers to Eustratios's defense of the Platonic separate ideal good explicitly when he writes: "et Eustratius multum reprehendit Aristotelem eo quod istud Platoni imposuit, cum Plato sic non intellexit sicut Aristoteles sibi imposuit."[134] Following this assumption, he then writes: "Tamen in bono separato quod est prima causa aliqualiter consistit humana felicitas,"[135] and "et est intelligendum quod ista speculatio vel coniunctio per cognitionem intellectus nostri ad primam causam secundum quod est possibile in hac vita est quodammodo possessio humana, et acquiritur in homine per studium et exercitium."[136]

The latter passage, so similar to that of James of Pistoia,[137] adds some interesting elements that can be traced back to Albert the Great, such as the emphasis on the notion of "studium," that is, learning as that which allows human conjunction with the agent intellect and the separate substances.[138] The other so-called Averroist commentaries on the *Ethics* adopt the same strategy as Brito. For example, the one transmitted by MS Erlangen, Universitätsbibl. 213 incorporates Eustratios's distinction between a supreme, highest good, and all secondary goods that participate in it.[139] But all these statements

132 Thomas Aquinas, *Super librum de causis expositio*, ed. H. D. Saffrey, Textus Philosophici Friburgenses 4–5 (Fribourg, 1954), prol., 1.4–6.

133 Radulphus Brit., *Quaestiones*, q. 20, 221.103–112.

134 Ibid., 220.61–63.

135 Ibid., 220.79,80.

136 Ibid., 221.92–95.

137 Cf. above, n. 119.

138 On this point, see L. Sturlese, *Vernunft und Glück: Die Lehre vom "intellectus adeptus" und die mentale Glückseligkeit bei Albert dem Großen*, Lectio Albertina 7 (Münster, 2005).

139 Anonymus, *Quaestiones super libro Ethicorum*, MS Erlangen Universitätsbibl. 213 (fols. 47ra–80vb), q. 9, f. 49rb:

> *Intelligendum est, sicut dicit Eustrachius, quod quoddam est bonum commune omnium, quod est causa omnium bonorum et summum et maximum, et illud est primum principium in tota natura; aliud est bonum proprium uniscuiusque quod est sibi intrinsecum, et hoc est perfectio uniuscuiusque, et hoc est bonum in quo immediate fertur omnium appetitus. Ideo bonum proprium uniuscuiusque non est unum, et sic non omnia appetunt bonum unum proprium. Sed quia bonum proprium uniuscuiusque dicitur bonum per participationem primi boni, etiam istud in quolibet invenitur, ideo appetendo proprium bonum, unumquodque appetit bonum summum, quod est unum; et sic omnia appetunt unum bonum commune.*

are shaded by Albert's influence. Take Brito's claim that "et Eustratius multum reprehendit Aristotelem eo quod istud Platoni imposuit, cum Plato sic non intellexit sicut Aristoteles sibi imposuit." This can easily be traced back to Albert the Great's first commentary on the *Ethics*, where he writes: "dicendum secundum commentatorem, quod hoc falso imponit aristoteles Platoni."[140]

From Albert the Great onward, Eustratios's commentaries on the *Ethics* became an essential part of medieval debates on happiness as the knowledge of or conjunction with God, the highest good, and the separate substances. This, as I have said, was likely due to Eustratios's Neoplatonic approach to Aristotle's anti-Platonic arguments in book 1 of the *Ethics*. The commentator defends the idea that the good, the object of everything we desire and strive for, must be the transcendent cause of all things. It is unsurprising, then, that Eustratios starts from Aristotle's definition of the good as that which everything desires, present at the beginning of the *Ethics*,[141] and discusses (*In I EN* 45.25–30) the way in which Platonists interpret the word τἀγαθόν referred to by Aristotle. Who are the Platonists that discuss Aristotle's definition of the good? All evidence suggests that Eustratios is referring here to proposition 8 of Proclus's *Elements of Theology*, where Proclus accepts the Aristotelian definition of the good only insofar as it is regarded as the primal good existing beyond all things.[142]

So, the foundation for Eustratios's fortune in the West lies in this Byzantine commentator's provision of another channel for the transmission of Proclus and Neoplatonism as an alternative to Pseudo-Dionysius the Areopagite and the Pseudo-Aristotelian *Liber de causis*. Intriguingly, Eustratios also appears to have been influential to those medieval Latin masters endorsing a view of happiness as knowledge of the separate substances and God without referring to the notion of "copulation." This is the case, as suggested by Luca Bianchi, in Boethius of Dacia's *Summo bono*, regarded as the manifesto of so-called Latin Averroism,[143] and often invoked to explain certain passages of Dante's *Convivio*.[144] In fact, in the final part of this short work, Boethius accepts the identification of the first principle and cause with the highest good in a way that is strongly reminiscent of Eustratios's Neoplatonic defense of the good as a separate and transcendent cause of all

140 Albertus Magnus, *Super ethica*, 1.6.25.1–2.

141 Aristoteles, *Ethica Nicomachea*, 1.1.1094a2–3: διὸ καλῶς ἀπεφήναντο τἀγαθόν, οὗ πάντ' ἐφίεται.

142 Cf. above, n. 105. A comparison between the two texts leaves no doubt on Eustratios's dependence upon Proclus. See Proclus, *El. Theol.* 8.8.31–31: εἰ γὰρ πάντα τὰ ὄντα τοῦ ἀγαθοῦ ἐφίεται, δῆλον ὅτι τὸ πρώτως ἀγαθὸν ἐπέκεινά ἐστι τῶν ὄντων = Eustratius Graecus, *In VI EN* 45.30–31: *εἰ γὰρ πάντα ἐκείνου ἐφίεται*, ὑπὲρ τὰ πάντα ἐξ ἀνάγκης ἐστί.

143 See Bianchi, "Felicità intellettuale" (above, n. 113), 28–29.

144 See, e.g., P. Falzone, *Desiderio della scienza e desiderio di Dio nel Convivio di Dante*, Pubblicazioni dell'Istituto italiano per gli studi storici (Bologna, 2010), 103, n. 4; 163; 168; 207, n. 187; 227, n. 221; 269, n. 33.

particular goods.[145] Furthermore, Boethius's description of the anagogic ascent of the philosopher, who by investigating effects works his way back to the higher causes and ultimately to the first cause, is nearly identical to that in Eustratios's commentary on book 6 of the *Ethics*.[146] This is not even to mention Boethius's references to irrational and sensitive hindrances as that which prevents men from reaching the goal of their

145 Compare Boethius de Dacia, *De summo bono* 376.209–377.225:

> *Considerans etiam quod sicut omnia sunt ex hac prima causa, sic omnia ad ipsam ordinantur; nam ens illud in quo principium, a quo omnia, coniungitur fini, ad quem omnia, hoc est ens primum secundum philosophos et secundum sanctos deus benedictus. In hoc tamen ordine latitudo est, et entia, quae in hoc ordine primo principio magis sunt propinqua, sunt entia nobiliora et magis perfecta. Quae autem sunt in hoc ordine magis remota a primo principio, illa sunt entia magis deminuta et minus perfecta. . . . Et sicut exercitus est unus ab unitate ducis, et bonum exercitus per se est in duce, in aliis autem est secundum ordinem quem habent ad ducem, sic ex unitate huius primi prinicipii est unitas huius mundi, et bonum huius mundi secundum participationem ab hoc primo principio et ordinem ad ipsum, ut nullum sit bonum in aliquo ente mundi, nisi sit ab hoc primo principio participatum.*

with Eustratius Latinus, *In I EN* 78.54–79.74:

> *Quoniam enim omnia illud bonificans est et omne illud bonificans est et omne secundum uniuscuiusque analogiam participans illo bonum dicitur, nullus intellectum habens dubitabit. Quid enim si hoc quidem magis bonum, hoc autem minus vel hoc quidem ipsi propinquius, illud autem remotius vel hoc quidem bonum secundum se ipsum, ut sanitas corporis et animae virtus, hoc autem ad horum aliquid conferens, ut diaeta et exercitium et pharmacum aliquod et medicamentum vel ut mala dispositio et durities corporis, ut animae constans et impassibile adveniat? Ordo enim omnibus est ut hoc quidem honorabilius in ipsis sit, hoc autem in honorabilitate secundum, hoc autem secundum ipsius ordinem. . . . Vel expetat quis unius ordinis omnia esse et unius speciei et unius naturae et differentiam auferat entium omnium existentiae et ordinis neque ornatum esse neque harmoniam aliquam in ipsis, sed inaniter confundi omnia, vel si ornatus et ordo et omnia quidem ex uno, tamen non secundum speciem neque secundum genus, sed est differentia multa in ipsis, ut haec quidem infima sint, haec autem suprema, erunt et haec quidem meliora, haec autem peiora, et haec quidem propinquiora remotiore, haec autem remotiora.*

146 Compare Boethius de Dacia, *De summo bono*, 375.176–83:

> *Ideo philosophus speculando entia causata, quae sunt in mundo, et naturas eorum et ordinem eorum ad invicem indicitur in cognitionem altissimarum causarum rerum, quia cognitio effectuum est quadam manuductio in cognitionem suae causae, et cognoscens causas superiores et naturas earum esse tales, quod necesse est eas habere aliam causam, inducitur in cognitionem primae causae.*

with Eustratius Latinus, *In VI EN*, MS Eton College 122, 121va:

> *Haec autem in corporibus speculata, quae sunt sensibilia et singularia, quibus apponentes et horum varietatem et constitutionem et continuitatem et deductionem stupefacti (et admirantes), semper ad proximam per rationalem et intellectualem speculationem recurrimus causam, usquequo per media disposita ad primum et unum principium obviemus.*

On the Neoplatonic source of this passage, see Trizio, *Neoplatonic Source-Material in Eustratios of Nicaea's Commentary on Book VI of the* Nicomachean Ethics, in *Medieval Greek Commentaries* (above, n. 8), 71–109, here at 86–88.

natural desire for knowledge,[147] which echoes Eustratios and Michael of Ephesus on the purification from passions, false opinions, and sense perception.[148] Ultimately, even Boethius's standard description of the first cause as unmoved and unchangeable can be traced back to Eustratios's commentary on book 6 of the *Ethics*.[149]

As for Michael of Ephesus, some of his comments on book 10 of the *Ethics* must have attracted the attention of medieval Latin readers as well. His claim, for example, that "extrema et perfecta felicitas est secundum intellectum vita et cognitio divinorum et contactus" perfectly corresponds to intellectual eudaimonism and the idea of happiness as the intellectual conjunction with the separate substances endorsed by late thirteenth-century Parisian arts masters.[150] Think once more of Boethius and his commentary on Aristotle's *Topics*, where he writes: "Ideo optima vita, quae est in homine possibilis, est vita intellectualis."[151] In discussing this statement, we may consider the several occurrences of the notion of "intellectualis vita" in Michael of Ephesus,[152] which he, in turn, borrowed from Proclus.[153]

One may object that some of these positions may have traveled on other currents, such as Arabic sources or the work of Albert the Great, Aquinas, or both, like the distinction

147 Boethius de Dacia, *De summo bono*, 373.106–120.

148 Cf. above, n. 125 See also Eustratius Latinus, *In VI EN*, MS Eton College 122, 102vb:

> *Non enim secundum eo quod est de practicis virtutibus dicere hoc scilicet et de intellectualibus convenientia pertransire, si non et magis hoc primum et principalius. Propter intellectualia enim indigemus practicis ut, utique non a passionibus perturbati et obtenebrati impedimentum ipsa speculari volentes veritatem habeamus.*

and Michael Ephesius, *In X EN* 451.98–107:

> *Diligit autem cognatum Dei intellectum qui totam virtutem amplexatur fugiens multiformes appetitus et connutritos sensus ut mentem decipientes, et phantasias ut formativas et ut partitivas et ut variam impossibilitatem quantacumque inducentes, avertensque opiniones ut varias et ipsas et ad exteriora ferentes et sensui et phantasiae commixtas—omnis enim opinio cum sensu irrationabili et phantasia operatur—, recurrensque ad scientiam et intellectum, post hanc autem ad intellectualem vitam et ad simolices appositiones, in quo factus, eas quae illinc refulgentias suscipit et luce immaculata repletur.*

This latter passage is a quote from Proclus's commentary on the *Alcibiades*, as shown by Steel, "Neoplatonic Sources" (above, n. 102), 55.

149 Compare Boethius de Dacia, *De summo bono*, 376.196–98: "Et causa etiam est incommutabilis semper uno modo se habens, quia transmutatio non est possibilis nisi in rebus imperfectis," with Eustratius Latinus, *In VI EN*, MS Eton College 122, 107rb: "Omnes autem opinamur non sola esse ingenita, sed haec quidem neque proprie entia, semper autem fientia et deficientia, vere autem neque aliquando entia secundum circa Platonem *Timaeum*, esse autem proprie entia semper secundum eadem et similiter habentia, quia et primum principium immobile omnino et intransmutabile."

150 Michael Ephesius, *In X EN* 421.15–16. See Bianchi, "Felicità intellettuale" (above, n. 113), 30, n. 47.

151 Boethius de Dacia, *Topica*, in *Boethii Daci Opera*, Corpus Philosophorum Danicorum Medii Aevi 6.1 (Copenhagen, 1976), 237.17–18. This passage has been already noticed by Bianchi, "Felicità intellettuale," 30, n. 45.

152 For a list of these occurrences see ibid., 29, n.44.

153 Cf. Steel, "Neoplatonic Sources," 35.

between the absolute good and the good insofar as it is attainable by men.[154] Dante (*Conv.* 15.3.2–5) finds his own way of dealing with this issue by supporting Severinus Boethius's definition of the good as presented in his *De consolatione philosophiae*.[155] But given that the arts masters' dependence on Eustratios is evident, the fact that Eustratios and Michael of Ephesus's arguments were, to some extent, available through other sources only supports a view of their commentaries on the *Ethics* as very consequential. Medieval Latin readers could have easily detected the very same Neoplatonic flavor in these works as in the Arabic source material of the time, such as the *Liber de causis,* but in the end, it was Albert the Great, the first and most consequential medieval reader of *Eustratius cum aliis*, who wrote in his *De anima* that, on the conjunction with the separate substances as the goal of human existence, Eustratios and Michael hold the same view as the Arabic philosophers.[156] Given the enduring influence of Albert's writings on the so-called Latin Averroists,[157] it would not be improper to state that the reception of *Eustratius cum aliis* in the West was characterized from the start by the attempt, rightly or wrongly, to see these works as another source for the complex of doctrines in the Greek-Arabic Peripatetic tradition.

A case study for this would be Albert's interpretation of Eustratios's distinction between the different modes of being and acting in the separate intelligence and the particular soul: the latter, Eustratios claims, possesses all forms present in the intelligence in a secondary manner. In his *De causis et processu universitatis a prima causa*, a commentary on the *Liber de causis*, Albert refers this distinction to the text of proposition 10 of *Liber de causis*: "Omnis intelligentia plena est formis; verumtamen ex intelligentiis sunt quae continent formas minus universales et ex eis sunt quae continent formas plus universals."[158] In so doing, Albert must have noticed the Neoplatonic flavor common to *Liber de causis* and Eustratios: both crib from proposition 177 of Proclus's *Elements of Theology*.[159] It is, in the end, the very idea in Dante's *Convivio* (4.26.5), in regard to the human soul; he writes: "La quale, incontanente produtta, riceve da la vertù del motore del cielo lo intelletto possibile; lo quale potenzialmente in sé adduce tutte le forme universali, secondo che sono nel suo produttore, e tanto meno quanto più dilungato da la prima Intelligenza è."[160]

154 See Bianchi, "Felicità intellettuale," 28, n. 39.

155 Boethius, *De consolatione philosophiae*, 3.2.2–3, ed. C. Moreschini, *Bibliotheca scriptorum Graecorum et Romanorum Teubneriana* (Leipzig, 2000), 60.6–11.

156 Albertus Magnus, *De anima*, lib. 3, tr. 3, cap. 11, 221.69–222.14. On this passage, see M. Trizio, "'Qui fere in hoc sensu exponunt Aristotelem': Notes on the Byzantine Sources of the Albertinian Notion of 'Intellectus Possessus'," in *Via Alberti: Texte-Quellen-Interpretationen*, ed. L. Honnefelder, H. Möhle, and S. Bullido-Del Barrio, Subsidia Albertina 2 (Münster, 2009), 79–110.

157 After Gauthier, "Review of Giocarinis" (above, n. 126), 875–76, Albert's influence on the so-called "averroist" commentaries on the *Nicomachean Ethics* is nowadays widely accepted.

158 Pseudo-Aristoteles, *Liber de Causis*, prop. 10, ed. A. Pattin, "Le Liber de Causis: édition établie à l'aide de 90 manuscrits," *Tijdschrift voor filosofie* 28 (1966): 90–203, 70.8–11; Albertus Magnus, *De causis et processu universitatis a prima causa*, lib. 2, tr. 2, cap. 20, ed. W. Fauser, *Opera Omnia* 17.2 (Münster, 1993), 114.82–115.4. See Trizio, "'Qui fere'," 95–97.

159 Proclus, *Elementatio Theologica*, prop. 177, 156.1–4.

160 For a recent discussion of this passage, sources, and interpretations, see Falzone, *Desiderio* (above, n. 144), 69–80.

Dante's Averroism?

What has been vaguely defined as Latin Averroism is nothing other than a series of philosophical tenets derived from several sources: not only Arabic, but also Byzantine commentaries on the *Nicomachean Ethics*, probably mediated through the interpretation by Albert the Great. The idea endorsed by several late thirteenth-century arts faculty masters that since every man naturally desires to know (as Aristotle himself states at the beginning of the *Metaphysics*),[161] happiness and the fulfilment of this desire can be achieved in this life through contemplation of the separate substances and God (and, in some cases, through a *copulatio* with them), can be traced back to these Byzantine commentators.

Investigating the role of Averroism in Dante's work would go far beyond the scope of this study. Yet, starting from this reassessment of the so-called Latin Averroism among late thirteenth-century Parisian arts masters, we will discuss Dante's position on some of the philosophical tenets, such as the natural desire to know the separate substances. This topic, well known to Dante specialists, is discussed in *Convivio* 3.15.7–10. Such an investigation becomes pressing when one considers that these passages have been linked to so-called Latin Averroism and the Parisian *artistae*.[162] Here are Dante's words:

> *Veramente può qui alcuno forte dubitare come ciò sia, che la sapienza possa fare l'uomo beato, non potendo a lui perfettamente certe cose mostrare; con ciò sia cosa che 'l naturale desiderio sia a l'uomo di sapere, e sanza compiere lo desiderio beato essere non possa.* ***8.*** *A ciò si può chiaramente rispondere che lo desiderio naturale in ciascuna cosa è misurato secondo la possibilitade de la cosa desiderante: altrimenti andrebbe in contrario di se medesimo, che impossibile è; e la Natura l'avrebbe fatto indarno, che è anche impossibile.* ***9.*** *In contrario andrebbe: chè, desiderando la sua perfezione, desiderrebbe la sua imperfezione; imperò che desiderrebbe sè sempre desiderare e non compiere mai suo desiderio (e in questo errore cade l'avaro maladetto, e non s'accorge che desidera sè sempre desiderare, andando dietro al numero impossibile a giungere). Avrebbelo anco la Natura fatto indarno, però che non sarebbe ad alcuno fine ordinato. E però l'umano desiderio è misurato in questa vita a quella scienza che qui avere si può, e quello punto non passa se non per errore, lo quale è di fuori di naturale intenzione.* ***10.*** *E così è misurato ne la natura angelica, e terminato in quanto [a] quella sapienza che la natura di ciascuno può apprendere. E questa è la ragione per che li Santi non hanno tra loro invidia, però che ciascuno aggiugne lo fine del suo desiderio, lo quale desiderio è con la bontà de la natura misurato. Onde, con ciò sia cosa che conoscere di Dio e di certe altre cose quello esse sono non sia possibile a la nostra natura, quello da noi naturalmente non è desiderato di sapere. E per questo è la dubitazione soluta.*

Let me compare Dante's position in this passage with the philosophical tenets that characterize the doctrines of the so-called Latin Averroists, namely, the idea that happiness

161 Aristoteles, *Metaphysica*, 1.1.980a21.
162 See, e.g., B. Nardi, *Nel Mondo di Dante*, Storia e Letteratura 5 (Rome, 1944), 225–26.

can be achieved in this life intellectually, and that a natural desire to know the separate substances exists. Here Dante famously poses his "forte dubitare," admitting, on the one hand, the existence of a natural desire for knowledge but suggesting, on the other, that this desire cannot be fulfilled, as human beings cannot grasp the noblest and most divine things. He then attempts to solve this aporia by elaborating on the notion of natural desire. In this respect, Dante supports the Neoplatonic view, present in the *Liber de causis*, that each thing's natural desire relates to its capacity and rank. The alternative, Dante says, if a thing could not achieve its desire, is that nature would have made something in vain ("indarno").[163] More important, this desire, argues Dante, would be in vain if unrelated to an achievable object or goal. Thus, he concludes, the desire for knowledge is not in vain insofar as it does not exceed the limit of the human condition. As men cannot grasp the divine essence and divine things, it follows that there is no natural desire to know the separate and noblest realities.

Contrary to what he suggests in *Convivio* 4.13.5–7, where he allows science to reach its goal and perfection, Dante is clearly denying the existence of a natural desire for knowledge of the separate substances. Indeed, one may contend that in *Convivio* 4.13.5–7 he is dealing with science, not with the natural desire to know the separate substances. Yet, as is well known, Dante commences the *Convivio* (1.1.1) with a quote from the beginning of Aristotle's *Metaphysics* ("all men naturally desire to know") and the assumption that science provides human beings with happiness upon reaching its goal. This passage is key for the Parisian arts masters and their views on happiness as something achievable in this life, either by joining or simply contemplating the separate substances and God. But even though both Dante and the *artistae* start from the same assumption, that is, man's natural desire for knowledge, they diverge in regard to the goal of this desire. Dante could not have been more resolute in denying the existence of a natural desire for the separate substances and God. In so doing, Dante distances himself from Latin Averroism as well as Aquinas, deemed by Giovanni Busnelli and Giuseppe Vandelli as an alternative source for Dante's argument in *Convivio* 3.15.7–10.[164] On the contrary, he seems to stand with those theologians who opposed the allegedly heretical views spread at the University of Paris following their 1277 condemnation by the bishop of Paris, Étienne Tempier. Strikingly, one of the 219 views condemned in the syllabus produced by Tempier's episcopal commission reads "quod non est excellentior status quam vacare philosophiae" and targets precisely the view present in Boethius's *De summo bono*.[165]

163 This argument reflects the motto "natura nihil facit frustra," which is widely used in the works of 13th-century medieval masters and can be traced back, among the many other Aristotelian passages, to Aristoteles, *De anima*, 3.9.432b20–21.

164 See P. Porro, "Tra il 'Convivio' e la 'Commedia': Dante e il 'forte dubitare' intorno al desiderio naturale di conoscere le sostanze separate," in *1308: Eine Topographie historischer Gleichzeitigkeit*, ed. A. Speer and D. Wirmer, Miscellanea Mediaevalia 35 (Berlin and New York, 2010), 631–59, 639–46.

165 See D. Piché, *La condemnation Parisienne de 1277* (Paris, 1999), 92; see also R. Hisette, *Enquête sur le 219 articles condamnés à Paris le 7 Mars 1277*, Philosophe Médiévaux 22 (Louvain, 1977), 15–18.

So, while denying the existence of a natural desire for the separate substances and God, Dante redefines the limits and scope of philosophical inquiry in a way that reflects the intellectual climate following Tempier's condemnation of this view. Unsurprisingly, then, the previously mentioned passage in the *Convivio* shows remarkable similarities with arguments elaborated by one of the most famous post-1277 theologians, Geoffrey of Fontaines, as Pasquale Porro has first suggested few years ago. In his *Quodlibet 8*, Geoffrey espouses an argument that looks almost identical to that on which Dante would later elaborate. Geoffrey starts from the assumption, attributed to Averroes' commentary on the *Metaphysics*, that our intellect can actually grasp the separate substances, as otherwise nature would have acted "otiosely."[166] Yet, according to Geoffrey, the same argument can be reversed: is this by nature a thing which someone can perform or achieve? The answer is a negative one: since no one has ever achieved any knowledge of the separate substances, at least in this lifetime, it is clear that such knowledge is, by nature, impossible.[167]

Whether Dante had access to Geoffrey's *Quodlibeta* is not known, but the similarities between his *Convivio* 3.15.7–10 and Geoffrey's *Quodlibet 8* are remarkable: both texts simply overturn the argument ascribed to Averroes that, since nature does not act in vain, a natural desire to know the separate substances exists, and precisely because nature does not act in vain, such a desire must not exist.[168]

166 The reference goes to Averroes, *In Aristotelis librum II Metaphysicorum commentarius*, in *Die lateinische Übersetzung des Mittelalters auf handschriftlicher Grundlage mit Einleitung und problemgeschichtlicher Studie*, ed. G. Darms, Thomistiche Studien 11 (Fribourg, 1966), 53–54.

167 Godefridus de Fontibus, *Quodlibet 8*, ed. J. Hoffmans, *Le huitième Quodlibet de Godefroid de Fontaines (texte inédit)*, Les philosophes belges, Textes et Études 4.1 (Louvain, 1924), 72:

> *Et potest poni exemplum ad reprobandum dictum istorum, sicut etiam reprobatur ratio Commentatoris ponentis quod substantiae separatae secundum se ipsas possunt apprehendi ab intellectu nostro. Arguit enim in principio secundi Metaphysicae, quod sic, quia si impossibile esset nobis illas substantias intelligere, natura egisset otiose, quia fecit illud quod est in se naturaliter intellectum aliis non esse intellectum ab aliquo sicut si fecisset solem non comprehensum ab aliquo visu. Sed eodem modo potest argui contra. Cum natura ab eo quod est possibile non deficit in omnibus generaliter in quibus est operatio ad consequendum ea quae sunt naturaliter possibilia, sed potius in paucioribus, praecipue quantum ad tales; ergo non debet dici aliquid esse hominibus possibile naturaliter nisi ab aliquibus attingatur. Sed quantumcumque perfecti viatores non pervenerunt ad hoc quod substantias separatas sic secundum se intelligerent; ergo otiose natura egisset talem possibilitatem quae numquam reduceretur ad actum. Ergo cum non sunt inventi qui de talibus talem habuerunt intellectum, supponendum est ex hoc quod hoc non est possibile secundum naturam; sed bene est possibile alio modo; et ideo natura non egit otiose; et cetera.*

The parallel between *Conv.* 3.15.7–10 and this passage by Geoffrey was first suggested by Porro, "Tra il 'Convivio'," 654–56. For other possibile parallels with late-13th century medieval scholars and a discussion of modern scholars' interpretations of *Conv.* 3.15.7–10, see Falzone, *Desiderio* (above, n. 144), 169–248.

168 In so doing, I believe, Dante distances himself from Peter of Auvergne, arts master in about 1275 in Paris, who has been suggested as a source for *Conv.* 3.15.7–10 by Falzone, *Desiderio*, 164–69, on the basis of some similarities between this Dante passage and Peter's *Questions* on books 1 and 2 of the *Nicomachean Ethics.* Falzone thinks of Petrus de Alvernia, *Quaestiones supra librum*

Conclusions

Reassessing Dante's Averroism goes far beyond the scope of this chapter. Yet I would note that the overtones of *Convivio* 3.15.7–10 appear to be radically anti-Averroist, as in this passage Dante tackles and rejects the most important standpoint endorsed by the thirteenth-century Parisian arts masters: the existence of a natural desire for knowledge of the separate substances and God. Ultimately, this will imply a reassessment of the traditional understanding of the passage "dal *Convivio* alla *Commedia*," to paraphrase the title of a famous article by Bruno Nardi,[169] as in the *Convivio* one can already find a theological concern that paves the way for Dante's solution in the *Commedia*. So, for example, in *Purgatorio* 21.1–3, Dante writes: "La sete natural che mai non sazia se non con l'acqua onde la femminetta samaritana domandò la grazia," that is to say, the thirst for knowledge can be appeased only through grace, an external source.

This theological concern in *Convivio* 3.15.7–10, evident in Dante's attempt at defining the limits proper to philosophical inquiry, ends up admitting the existence of a supernatural beatitude, as in *Convivio* 3.15.2:

> *E qui si conviene sapere che li occhi de la Sapienza sono le sue demonstrazioni, con le quali si vede la veritade certissimamente; e lo suo riso sono le sue persuasioni, ne le quali si dimostra la luce interiore de la Sapienza sotto alcuno velamento: e in queste due cose si sente quel piacere altissimo di beatitudine, lo quale è massimo bene in Paradiso.*[170]

---

ethicorum, 2, q. 49, ed. A. C. Celano, "Peter of Auvergne's Questions on the Books I and II of the Ethica Nicomachea," *Mediaeval Studies* 48 (1986): 1–110, 80–81:

> *Dicendum quod homo potest esse felix in hac vita felicitate que est perfectio hominis. Et huius racio est quia natura nichil facit frustra, nec deficit in necessariis. Appetitus autem naturaliter inest homini, et maxime appetitus est respectu primi scibilis. Et ideo non potest ille appetitus esse frustra, quia frustra dicitur illud quod natum est finem includere et non includit. Igitur in unione respectu primi scibilis cum consistat felicitas, manifestum quod possibile est hominem felicitari in hac vita. . . . Ad tercium argumentum est dicendum quod maior vera est; est enim felicitas illud ultimum, quo adeptu, nichil amplius desiderari potest. Et tamen assumitur in minorem quod, cognitis substanciis separatis, adhuc remanet desiderium. Dico quod non remanet cum racione; racio enim non dicit illud esse desiderandum quod impossibile est haberi, licet appetitus possit hoc appetere.*

I am not a Dante specialist, but, despite the evident linguistic similarities, it seems to me that Peter's argument differs considerably from *Conv.* 3.15.7–10. In fact, Peter states here that one, there actually exists in all men a natural desire for the first cause, the noblest object of knowledge, and two, this desire is appeased once and for all when it reaches its goal. That is to say, there is no *regressus ad infinitum*. Contrariwise, in *Conv.* 3.15.7–10, Dante denies the existence in men of a desire for something they cannot attain, otherwise—and here Peter of Auvergne's argument is reversed—nature would have acted "indarno."

169 B. Nardi, "Dal Convivio alla Commedia," in idem, *Dal Convivio alla Commedia: Sei saggi danteschi, con premessa alla ristampa di O. Capitani*, Istituto Storico Italiano per il Medio Evo, Nuovi Studi Storici 18 (Rome, 1992). For a discussion of Nardi's view, see Porro, "Tra il 'Convivio'," 632–34, esp. 634, n. 11, where the reader can find a discussion of other scholars' views on this subject.

170 Further theological passages in the Convivio are listed in Porro, "Tra il 'Convivio'," 658, n. 59.

Here we see that despite the originality of some of Dante's arguments, some orthodoxy remains, namely, a theological concern that can be traced back to certain articles condemned by Bishop Tempier in 1277 and the generations of theologians belonging to the post-1277 Parisian intellectual milieu. Against the so-called Latin Averroists, Tempier condemned the view (art. 157) "quod homo ordinatus quantum ad intellectum et affectum, sicut potest sufficienter esse per virtutes intellectuales et alias morales de quibus loquitur philosophus in ethicis, est sufficienter dispositus ad felicitatem aeternam."[171] That is to say, happiness cannot be achieved solely through man's natural faculties and dispositions.

And there is another possible reference to a late thirteenth-century scholar that clarifies the framework of Dante's denial of a natural desire for knowing divine things: in his *Summa*, written in 1276, one year before Tempier's intervention with the aid of the same Henry, the secular Master Henry of Ghent discussed the *quaestio* "utrum homo appetat scire ea quae notitiam naturalis rationis excedunt," and attributes it to the *philosophi*, probably a reference to the "Averroist" Parisian masters, the very view rejected by Dante.[172] Henry states that the *philosophi* allow the end of human existence to be reached naturally in this life, as humanly possible, in terms of knowledge of the first principles. Not according to the *quidditas* of these principles, but only insofar as their *quia* is concerned. Thus, according to Henry's account of the position of the *philosophi*, these deny the natural desire of knowing those noble objects, for their *quidditates* cannot be grasped; otherwise, nature would have created desire in vain.[173] Intriguingly, Henry concedes to the "Averroists" that there is actual desire for knowing the separate substances, though this desire cannot be achieved naturally by the inquiry of the created effects but only *per gratiam*; and not in this life, unless one is a theologian, but in the future one.[174] More

171 Piché, *La condemnation Parisienne de 1277* (above, n. 165), 126.

172 The importance of Henry's *quaestio* has been rightly pointed out by Falzone, *Desiderio* (above, n. 144), 169–248.

173 Henricus de Gandavo, *Summa (Quaestiones ordinariae)*, art. 4, q. 5, ed. G. A. Wilson, *Opera Omnia* 21 (Leuven, 2005) 290.57–64:

> *Philosophi vero ponentes finem humanae cognitionis ex puris naturalibus haberi et in vita ista ex cognitione scientiarum speculativarum et primorum principiorum quantum homini possibile est, et quod in modica cognitione divinorum consistit eius summa perfectio et delectatio, licet non possit attingere ad quidditates substantiarum separatorum et eorum quae apud illas sunt, dicerent quod homo nulla appetitum haberet sciendi illa, ex quo ex suis naturalibus ad ea pervenire non possem, ne illa appetitus esset frustra.*

174 Henricus de Gandavo, *Summa*, art. 4, q. 5, 294, ed. Wilson, 135–148:

> *Revera magna est confusio philosophorum, qui haec omnia videre poterant, immo quia necessario viderunt et in se ipsis experimentati sunt, et tamen in infimis perfectionem humanae notitiae posuerunt. Unde et multi eorum ex desiderio quod perceperunt hominem habere ad illa cognoscenda, bene perceperunt quod notitia illarum non esset homini impossibilis, quoniam desiderium naturale non potest esse frustra neque otiosum, ut manifeste concludit Averroes super Iium Metaphysicae. Et ideo multis et variis modis, sed erroneis conati sunt ostendere quomodo homo ad perfectam notitiam illorum posset in vita ista pervenire. Viderunt enim bene, ut dicit Augustinus*

important, Henry's more nuanced discussion of the natural desire for that which goes beyond reason seems to treat as wrong the same position, here ascribed to the *philosophi*, probably the Latin Averroists, as later endorsed by Dante, the argument that, since there cannot be any quidditative knowledge of the separate substances, there is no such desire. And yet, Henry's argument not only calls into question once again Dante's alignment with the thirteenth-century "Averroistic" tendencies at Paris, but also puts to question the Eustratian legacy of these tendencies. While rejecting the view that knowledge of the separate substances is possible only according to the *quia* by means of the natural inquiry of the created effects and their natural order,[175] Henry targets the very same view that Boethius of Dacia had defended, probably by borrowing from Eustratios.[176]

But I shall leave the task of investigating and discussing these issues to Dante specialists. The aim of this essay was to demonstrate that a set of philosophical tenets commonly regarded as the cornerstone of Latin Averroism, the same tenets condemned in 1277 by Tempier and rejected by Dante (*Conv.* 3.15.7–10), do not have a purely Greek-Arabic copyright, so to speak, but also hark from Byzantium. After Albert the Great, the Byzantine commentators Eustratios of Nicaea and Michael of Ephesus are consistently invoked by thirteenth-century Parisian arts masters to endorse their views on happiness as the contemplation of, and in certain cases conjunction with, the first and highest good.

Certainly, in interpreting Eustratios and Michael of Ephesus, Albert the Great considered these Byzantine scholars members of the Peripatetic tradition, which, according to Albert, also includes the Arabic philosophers. This link is obvious if one considers the strong Neoplatonic flavor pervading Byzantine commentaries on the *Ethics*. It is the same flavor that emanated from the Pseudo-Aristotelian *Liber de causis*, which shares the source with Eustratios and Michael of Ephesus: the Neoplatonist *Proclus*. The familiarity that thirteenth-century medieval masters already had with Neoplatonic vocabulary made it easier for them to appropriate these Byzantine commentaries and use them as an essential tool for constructing the theory of earthly happiness as contemplation of the separate substances and God. This view, which many scholars labeled as "Averroist," and which medieval masters ascribed to Eustratios, formed the background for the

---

> *Super Iovianum, quo oportebat tendere, sed viam ignoraverunt, quae est via fidei, qua oportet prius oculum mentis purgari, ut tandem ad illorum notitiam homo mereatur pervenire, non per naturam, sed per gratiam nec in in hac vita nisi forte ex privilegio speciali, sed in futura.*

On Henry's view on this subject and the related bibliography, see M. Leone, "Metaphysics, Theology and the Natural Desire to Know Separate Substances in Henry of Ghent," *Quaestio* 5 (2005), 513–26.

175 Henry's position is well summarized in Henricus de Gandavo, *Summa*, art. IV, q. 5, 294, ed. Wilson, 148–54:

> *Errabant ergo dicentes separata quoad essentias et quidditates suas cognosci posse ex puris naturalibus, plus dando naturae quam habuerit. Errabant etiam dicentes quod quidditates illae clare ab homine cognosci non possent, quia ex naturalibus ad illas non posset attingere, denegando naturae quod habuit, scilicet potentiam receptivam illius ex dono alterius. Medio est ergo tenendum, scilicet ut notiam illorum recipere poterit, sed quod propria actione ad illam attingere non poterit.*

176 Cf. above, n. 146.

doctrine rejected by Dante in the *Convivio* concerning the existence of a natural desire for knowledge of separate and divine things.

These observations suggest the potential fruitfulness of a thorough study on the influence of these Byzantine commentators in the West. Commenting on Anna Komnene's philosophical interest and patronage, her biographer wrote: "for books are an inviolable storehouse of words, and writing is an indestructible memorial of thought, while the ear is often violated by oblivion as by robbers." There could not be any better formula to summarize the fate of these Aristotle commentators, Eustratios and Michael, who ended their lives in the disgraced circle of the ostracized, the former after a condemnation for heterodoxy in 1117, the latter probably suffering the same fate as his probable patron, Anna Komnene, who was forced to retire from public life after the death of her father.[177] And yet, as shown in this study, the afterlife of these Byzantine scholars was characterized by the fame and prestige that their books gained when translated and read, far from Byzantium, thanks to what we may call the Komnenian heritage in Western debates on the *Nicomachean Ethics*.

177 On Eustratios's condemnation, see V. Grumel and J. Darrouzès, *Les regestes des Actes du patriarcat de Constantinople,* vol. 1, *Les Actes des Patriarches*, pts. 2–3, *Les Regestes de 715 à 1206,* Le patriarcat Byzantin, Série 1, 2nd ed. (Paris, 1989), 460–61, 1003. On Michael's misfortune, I rely on the scholia to the *Politics* published by Immish in the appendix to his edition of this Aristotelian work. See Aristoteles, *Politica*, post fr. Susemihlium recognovit O. Immish (Lepizig, 1909), 295–329. These witnesses are translated and discussed by E. Barker, *Social and Political Thought in Byzantium: From Justinian I to the Last Paleologue* (Oxford, 1957), 136–41.

Reading One's Way to Happiness

Dante, Cicero, and the Promise of the Greeks

FILIPPO NAITANA

Sì come dice lo Filosofo nel principio de la Prima Filosofia, tutti li uomini naturalmente desiderano di sapere. La ragione di che puote essere ed è che ciascuna cosa, da providenza di prima natura impinta, è inclinabile a la sua propria perfezione; onde, acciò che la scienza è ultima perfezione de la nostra anima, ne la quale sta la nostra ultima felicitade, tutti naturalmente al suo desiderio semo subietti.[1]

As the Philosopher says at the beginning of the *First Philosophy*, all men by nature desire to know. The reason for this can be and is that each thing, impelled by a force provided by its own nature, inclines towards its own perfection. Since knowledge is the ultimate perfection of our soul, in which resides our ultimate happiness, we are all therefore by nature subject to a desire for it.

IN THE *CONVIVIO*, A SINGLE WORD from the vast lexicon of Greek thought, infused into Christian culture, seems to carry the entire weight of Dante's architecture of knowledge: *eudaimonia*, or "happiness." In fact, the very premise of Dante's ambitious project is Aristotle's claim that happiness and human desire for knowledge are indissolubly linked. Since many obstacles exist between his readers and the "abito di scienza" needed to pursue happiness, Dante invites them to a fourteen-course banquet of knowledge that will grant them the chance to achieve their "nobilissima perfezione." He envisions each course as consisting of a song (the food) and a commentary (the bread). The latter was to illustrate the meaning of the former and allow his readers to appreciate not only the beauty of the songs but also their "sottile ammaestramento." Among the subjects to be discussed, two were to receive special importance:

1 Dante, *Convivio*, ed. C. Vasoli and D. De Robertis, 5 vols. (Milan, 1988), 1.1.1–2. Unless otherwise noted, all English translations are from *Dante's Il Convivio (The Banquet)*, trans. R. H. Lansing (New York and London, 1990); my occasional emendations are indicated by brackets. The "Prima Filosofia" refers to Aristotle's *Metaphysics* (1.1). On Dante's notion of "scienza" as "ultima perfezione," see *Conv.* 1.13.5, 2.13.6, 3.11.14, 3.15.4, 4.13.9.

virtue and love, that is, the love of wisdom (*Conv.* 1.1.2–14, 1.2.17). As is often the case with Dante, he will do less than promised and at the same time much more: less because he interrupted the *Convivio* after writing the commentary to the third song, leaving it unfinished; more because, within the first four books, he not only investigates moral philosophy but also embarks on a veritable tour de force of linguistics, poetics, cosmology, and, of course, politics. Moreover, by linking his role as master of ceremonies in the banquet of knowledge to Aristotle's eudaimonism, the poet connects his claim for the dignity of the Italian vernacular to the vast body of literature on the meaning and pursuit of happiness, a "genre" that was the *ortus conclusus* of philosophers and theologians and one of the most powerful embodiments of "high culture." Indeed, few other matters unleashed the Western imagination as did happiness. From Plato to Aristotle, from Albert the Great and Thomas Aquinas, to Kant, Hegel, and Nietzsche, some of the greatest thinkers of all time took on the challenge of exploring the significance of happiness and its attainment. How does one discern happiness? Does the path to happiness ever coincide with the path to power, wealth, pleasure, or love? Are virtue and faith necessary to achieve happiness? Is there a conflict between individual fulfillment and the pursuit of the common good? Such questions have shaped Western culture for more than two thousand years, breaking the boundaries of, and establishing unsuspected links between, poetry, moral philosophy, theology, and political doctrine. These are also some of the very questions that the *Convivio* brings into focus and that energize the arc of Dante's intellectual trajectory.

Traditionally, scholars have framed Dante's discourse on *felicitade* in the *Convivio* within the classical academic debate on the poet's philosophical affiliation, that is to say, primarily to support either an Averroistic or a Thomistic reading of his work.[2] Corti's influential book *La felicità mentale: Nuove prospettive per Cavalcanti e Dante*, despite its use of language and concepts from structuralism and semiotics, represents a "dynamic variation" of just such a model. In this reading, the discussion on Dante's conception of happiness advances the overarching thesis that his philosophical trajectory starts under the spell of the Latin Averroists (or radical Aristotelians) and, by the time of the *Commedia,* embraces theological orthodoxy in the form of Thomism.[3] Yet, ultimately,

2 The *Convivio* is the focus of this article, but the poet's discourse on happiness in the *Commedia* is very much in need of readdressing as well. For an insightful discussion of the body of work on the poet's intellectual formation, see Z. Baranski, *Dante e i segni: Saggi per una storia intellettuale di Dante Alighieri* (Naples, 2000), 9–39. On Dante and the question of happiness, see, at minimum, these essentials: É. Gilson, *Dante the Philosopher*, trans. D. Moore (New York, 1949), 130–42, 91–201; B. Nardi, *Nel mondo di Dante* (Rome, 1944), 209–45; idem, *Dal "Convivio" alla "Commedia": Sei saggi danteschi,* Nuovi studi storici 18 (Rome, 1960; repr. ed., 1992), 285–313; M. Corti, *La felicità mentale: Nuove prospettive per Cavalcanti e Dante* (Turin, 1983), 53–61, 127–29, republished within the posthumous volume M. Corti, *Scritti su Cavalcanti e Dante* (Turin, 2003), 9–175; P. Dronke, *Dante's Second Love: The Originality and the Contexts of the Convivio* (Leeds, 1997), 40–71.

3 Corti builds on Nardi's studies, in which the *Commedia* would also follow an Averroistic phase represented by the *Convivio*; in Nardi's case, such reading relies heavily on an Averroistic

what these studies have in common is a reliance on a cause and effect between the late medieval "rediscovery" of Aristotle and Dante's own discovery of philosophy as a path to happiness, a feature all the more surprising when one considers the absolute centrality of the eudaimonistic problem within *the entirety* of the Western tradition. The burden of this essay is twofold: to better explain the modes and nature of Dante's engagement in the *Convivio* with medieval Aristotelianism on this defining question, and to show the pivotal, and as yet neglected, role played by Cicero in such engagement.

There were, indeed, compelling reasons for discussing Dante's conception of *felicitade* in the light of the intellectual disputes of the thirteenth century. When he wrote the *Convivio,* the Church condemnations that had led to the expulsion of Siger of Brabant from the University of Paris were still a vivid memory, and some of them concerned both the "when" and "how" happiness can be achieved.[4] Boethius of Dacia—who, together with Siger, led the party of the radical Aristotelians at the Paris athenaeum—had devoted an entire work, *De summo bono,* to this very subject, and James of Pistoia, *magister* at the University of Bologna, had dedicated his *Quaestio de felicitate,* a work very much in line with the Parisian masters, to none other than Guido Cavalcanti.[5] Moreover, between 1263 and 1266—that is to say, at the height of the academic careers of both Siger and Boethius—Brunetto Latini was in political exile in Paris attending to both the *Rettorica* and his *Trésor.* Without bringing into play Dante's alleged stay in Paris—which speaks more to scholars' desire for an all-knowing Dante, always in the thick of the essential debates of his time—these indications suggest that he was likely acquainted with

interpretation of Albert the Great's philosophical eclecticism. B. Nardi, *Saggi di filosofia dantesca* (Florence, 1930; repr., 1967), 255–75, 297–302; Nardi, *Nel mondo di Dante,* 237–45; Nardi, *Dal "Convivio,"* 6–150.

4 In the year 1277, Bishop of Paris Étienne Tempier—having been solicited by Pope John XXII to look into the "mistakes" disseminated at the University of Paris—officially condemned 219 theses. These writings, which included works by members of the faculty of arts, were found to contain both philosophical and theological "errors"; the punishment was excommunication for not only those who taught them but also for those who simply listened. Some of the theses regarded the nature of human happiness and the means to achieve it. The 172nd thesis, for instance, stated that man can indeed reach happiness "in ista vita, et non in alia"; Corti, *La felicità mentale,* 58, and R. Hissette, *Enquête sur les 219 articles condamnés à Paris le 7 mars 1277* (Louvain, 1977) 266–68. What follows is a selection of the ponderous bibliography on the intellectual disputes of the 13th century: F. Van Steenberghen, *Aristotle en Occident: Les origines de l'aristotélisme parisien* (Louvain, 1946); É. Gilson, "Boèce de Dacie et la double verité," *Archives d'histoire doctrinale et littéraire du moyen âge* 22 (1955), 81–99; M. D. Chenu, *La Théologie comme science au XIII*[e] *siècle,* 3rd ed. (Paris, 1957); G. R. Evans, *Old Arts and New Theology: The Beginnings of Theology as an Academic Discipline* (Oxford, 1980); J. M. M. H. Thijssen, *Censure and Heresy at the University of Paris, 1200–1400* (Philadelphia, 1998); D. Piché, *Problème des universaux à la faculté des arts de Paris entre 1230 et 1260: Édition critique sélective, traduction française, analyses structurelle et formelle et étude historico-philosophique* (Paris, 2005).

5 P. O. Kristeller, "A Philosophical Treatise from Bologna Dedicated to Guido Cavalcanti: Magister Jacobus de Pistorio and his 'Questio de Felicitate'," *Medioevo e Rinascimento* 1 (1955): 425–63 (Latin text, 442–63). Corti, *La felicità mentale,* 5–7. Both Kristeller and Corti saw in this treatise's dedication proof of both the long-debated connection between the poets of the *dolce stil novo* and the academic circles in Bologna, as well as the circulation of radical Aristotelianism in that athenaeum.

not only the recently "canonized" Aristotle,[6] but also the more subversive and, therefore, possibly more attractive one that came to life in the university lessons and writings of the Latin Averroists. To be sure, Dante's provocative choice to place Siger in the *Paradiso* among the twelve theologians in the sky of the sun (*Par.* 10.133–38) shows that he gave the matter more than a passing thought. With pleasing symmetry, Thomas Aquinas—acting as a guide in that very heaven, in addition to commenting on the *Nicomachean Ethics*—had devoted a substantial part of both his *Summa theologiae* (1a–2ae, 1–5) and *Summa contra gentiles* (3.24–63) to the discussion of happiness. Yet, as we shall see, in negotiating Aristotle's eudaimonism, Dante finds a path that is definitely his own: autonomous, that is, from the Philosopher's late medieval commentators and followers, heterodox and orthodox alike. But what truly sets the poet's meditation on the pursuit of happiness apart is that, while freely helping himself to both the words and the intelligence of philosophers and theologians, he incorporates a series of concerns to which those who were seated "a quella mensa dove lo pane de li angeli si manuca" (at the table where the bread of the angels is eaten; *Conv.* 1.1.7) were irreparably deaf.

To begin, a few words should be said about the triangulation of knowledge, virtue, and happiness as it was originally formulated by Aristotle in the *Nicomachean Ethics*, as the conception of eudaimonia contained therein represents, in Dante's view, the apex of the ancient inquiry into "questo nostro fine, che ciascuno disia naturalmente" (this end of ours, which everyone by nature desires). Indeed, he crowns its author "maestro e duca de la ragione umana, in quanto intende a la sua finale operazione" (master and leader of human reason, insofar as it is directed to man's final activity; *Conv.* 4.6.8). "Fine" (end) and "operazione" (operation, activity) are both strategic terms within the Philosopher's lexicon on happiness. The first represents continuity between the *Ethics* and previous inquiries on the nature of happiness, the second a departure. Aristotle accepts the notion prominent in classical ethics that happiness is the "supreme good," the "ultimate end" to which every human action tends, but suggests that without clearly defining what such an end is and how to achieve it, the notion is nothing more than a truism. In other words, granted the premise that everything has a "purpose" or "end" (*telos*) and that there is a hierarchy among various ends—that is, that we pursue some ends in the light of other, more important ones—and that happiness is at the very top of such a hierarchy (that ultimately everything we do, we do in the attempt to be happy), we need not only understand why that is so, but also make sure that our claims have some basis in reality. It is not a coincidence, in fact, that the Philosopher opens his discussion on eudaimonia by attacking Plato's formulation of happiness as something quintessentially transcendent, to which one needs to aspire.[7] Those who want to teach about the "supreme good" should

6 As is well known, not long after the Church condemnations of 1210–15, Aristotle's "fortune" in the Western world had a surprising epilogue; thanks primarily to the titanic work of mediation done by Albert the Great and Thomas Aquinas, he became an *auctoritas* and his opus acquired an almost sacred value.

7 Aristotle, *The Nicomachean Ethics* (hereafter referred to as NE), trans. H. Rackham (Cambridge, 2003), 1096a11–1097a14.

concern themselves with what is within men's powers rather than what lies beyond them. Such is the declared goal of Aristotle's inquiry: not simply to study and know, but to teach how to act on knowledge. Having a clear understanding of what the "ultimate end" is enables humans to direct their energies toward what is conducive to happiness, just like archers are given a target at which to aim (*NE* 1094a.18–25). What Aristotle understands as the "ultimate good" exemplifies how truly misleading lexical continuity can be. While the etymology of eudaimonia emphasizes the idea that human happiness is something bestowed from a benevolent, external source,[8] in the *Ethics* it becomes something earned through a series of well-considered choices. In Aristotle's model, happiness depends on exercising the one quality unique to man: rational thought. Reason is what ultimately renders us unique; it raises us above the level of vegetative and animal life. Hence, happiness is not a state but "an activity according to virtue."[9] In its utmost form, it consists in intellectual contemplation as the one activity that actualizes the highest kind of human potential, namely, the capacity for applying our distinctive gift to things that are sublime and eternal. Such activity, in fact, not only expresses in its purest form man's "function," but it is also the most self-sufficient, the one accompanied by the worthiest form of pleasure. The life of moral virtue—identified at its noblest with a political and military career—is the second best end that one can follow, because it harbors some important limitations: it is spent in the pursuit of honor (and, therefore, is not the ultimate end) and is less self-sufficient (as honor is not something personal and inalienable but bestowed by others, and because moral actions rely more heavily on goods, such as wealth and power, that are subject to fortune). Both forms of happiness build on something to which human beings are naturally drawn: knowledge. In the case of the intellectual virtues, knowledge is acquired through a theoretical process; in that of the moral ones, it is gained through the repetition of virtuous acts (a sort of "interiorization").[10]

8 The word *eudaimonia* is part of a lexicon rooted in the poetry of Greece's archaic period. *Makaria*, one translation of happiness, derives from the root *megas*, meaning wide or ample. *Makaria* usually referred to the perfect state of beatitude enjoyed by the gods, a plenitude that can only be experienced for a few fleeting moments in life. Given the innate instability of the human condition, these moments are transient; after they vanish, life resumes its usual oscillation between pleasure and pain. Man's incapacity to turn these epiphanies into a stable form of well-being accounts for the most commonly used words for happiness: *eudaimonia*, which stresses how the good life is ultimately a gift granted by a benevolent *daemon*, and *eutichia*, which refers to those among human beings who are blessed with a favorable fate. For more, see C. de Heer, *Makar, Eudaimon, Olbios, Eutyches: A Study of the Semantic Field Denoting Happiness in Ancient Greek to the End of the 5th Century B.C.* (Amsterdam, 1968).

9 Crucial to Aristotle's understanding of the virtues is the distinction between *phronesis*, or what we might call practical wisdom, and *sophia*. While the former has as its object what is contingent and mutable, *sophia*—the highest form of wisdom—investigates those realities that are eternal. Phronesis—while not one of the moral virtues—is "liminal" to them, so to speak, and consists in that kind of knowledge that translates into good and useful decisions. *Sophia* is intelligence applied to the most sublime objects and is therefore completely free from any utilitarian logic (and, technically speaking, its highest form is identified with metaphysics).

10 *NE* 1176b1–1179a33. For more on Aristotle's conception of happiness, see A. J. P. Kenny, *Aristotle on the Perfect Life* (Oxford, 1992); R. Kraut, *Aristotle on the Human Good* (Princeton, NJ,

Despite branding Plato's transcendent good as a utopia, Aristotle's theory of happiness retains a strong element of that intellectualism permeating the history of classical Greek philosophy.[11] The supreme form of happiness achievable on this earth is identified with an activity of the intellect that surpasses in its intrinsic worth any good to which human beings could possibly aspire. On the other hand, after exposing the limitations of the active life, the Stagirite acknowledges that the kind of happiness one finds in philosophical speculation is, in practice, too divine for most. This last point is crucial to appreciating how truly problematic it is to read Dante's appropriation of Aristotle's eudaimonia in light of Latin Averroism. The idea of an intellectual bridge between history and transcendence, the hinge on which the Averroistic interpretations of eudaimonism rest, is completely absent from the *Convivio*. The radical Aristotelians do not shy away from declaring that the path to human happiness passes through a progressive assimilation of everything that is knowable, and that the final destination of such an intellectual ascent is the knowledge of not only the "separate intelligences" (or, theologically speaking, the angels) but even the uncaused cause, that is to say, God. Dante, instead, conforms to the clear distinction that Aristotle makes between ethics and metaphysics. Moreover, the acknowledgment of a hierarchy between the moral and speculative virtues (and, thus, of a hierarchy between the happiness of the active life and that of the contemplative life) never undermines the purely moral dimension. This is true not only in the first three books[12] but also the fourth, in which the ship of Dante's *ingegno* is about to abandon the *mare nostrum* of philosophical discourse and venture into the mighty ocean of poetic theology: "Veramente l'uso del nostro animo è doppio, cioè pratico e speculativo (pratico è tanto quanto operativo), l'uno e l'altro dilettosissimo, avegna che quello del contemplare sia più, sì come di sopra è narrato.... E in questo [come in] quell'altro è nostra beatitudine e somma felicitade." (In point of fact the use of our mind is twofold, namely, practical and speculative ["practical" signifying "operative"], each of which is most delightful, although that of contemplation is more so, as has been explained above.... This [as well as] the other constitutes our blessedness and supreme happiness; *Conv.* 4.22.10–11). Like Aristotle, the poet links virtue with pleasure. The latter is, indeed, a feature of happiness, both in the case of the active life and in the contemplative one. Even though contemplation is more perfect than action, they are both "dilettosissimi."[13] This is, however, by no means the pleasure of the

1989); G. R. Lear, *Happy Lives and the Highest Good: An Essay on Aristotle's "Nicomachean Ethics"* (Princeton, NJ, 2004).

11 For Plato and Aristotle's "convergence" on fundamental philosophical matters, see L. Gerson, *Aristotle and Other Platonists* (Ithaca, NY, 2005).

12 "Quella che è qui l'umana natura non pur una beatitudine abbia, ma due, sì com'è quella de la vita civile, e quella de la contemplativa...." (human nature as it exists here has not only one blessedness but two, namely, that of the civil life and that of the contemplative life; *Conv.* 2. 4.10).

13 Dante uses the terms *felicitade* and *beatitudine* interchangeably, as he does with the Latin *felicitas* and *beatitudo* in *De monarchia* (1.16.2, 3.15.7–11). While today's reader might associate *beatitudo* specifically with the theologically charged meaning of "beatitude," this is typically not the case in late medieval philosophical and theological treatises written in Latin. This is true even of Thomas

Epicureans. For the poet, not only is learning about and meditating on sublime things a source of great pleasure, but so is behaving virtuously. Indeed, moral actions grant a pleasure far more fulfilling than mere sensual delight. It is clear that for Dante—as well as for Aristotle—despite the hierarchy between the two kinds of virtues, the happiness achievable through the moral ones has its own kind of perfection that cannot (and should not) be understood as a function of the intellectual ones. Here, on the contrary, is how the question is framed by Boethius of Dacia in his *De summo bono*:

> the operations of all man's lower powers are for the sake of the operations of his highest power, the intellect. And if, among the operations of the intellective power, there is one which is best and most perfect, all others naturally exist for its sake. When a man performs such an operation, he enjoys the highest state possible for man. Such men are the philosophers, who spend their lives in the pursuit of wisdom. Wherefore, all powers found in the philosopher operate according to the natural order, the prior for the sake of the posterior, the lower for the sake of the higher and more perfect. But all other men, who live according to lower powers and choose their operations and the pleasures found in such operations, are not ordered in accord with nature. They sin against the natural order.[14]

For the Parisian master, the happy few who pursue the delights of reason and intellectual desire (that is to say, the philosophers) not only deserve to be praised and highly esteemed, they are, in fact, the *only* ones who live according to the natural order. Dante, on the other hand, disavows the Latin Averroists' claim that philosophical speculation can indeed bridge the gap between humanity and divinity. With Aristotle, he emphasizes the legitimacy of focusing on the virtues that are within man's reach, that is to say, the moral ones. Thus, the poet takes a path that is indeed *opposite* from that of the radical Aristotelians. His interpretation acknowledges the superiority of the intellectual

---

Aquinas, who in his treatment of the *summum bonum* creates a very clear hierarchy between the perfect happiness of the Christian afterlife and anything that can be pursued in this life. In fact, in the *Summa contra gentiles,* he makes no distinction between the two terms, so much so that at the end of the discussion he calls the perfect happiness of the direct vision of God "summa et perfecta felicitas" (3.26.2). Similarly, in the *Summa theologiae,* where he renders the ultimate vision with the word *beatitudo* rather than *felicitas,* he also employs *beatitudo* in reference to the happiness *huius vitae*, associated with moral and intellectual life (1a–2ae, 4.5).

14 *operationes omnium virtutum inferiorum quae sunt in homine sunt propter operationes virtutis supremae, quae est intellectus. Et inter operationes virtutis intellectivae, si aliqua est optima et perfectissima, omnes naturaliter sunt || propter illam. Et cum homo est in illa operatione, est in optimo statu qui est homini possibilis. Et isti sunt philosophi, qui ponunt vitam suam in studio sapientiae. Unde omnes virtutes quae sunt in philosopho operantur secundum ordinem naturalem: prior propter posteriorem et inferior propter superiorem et perfectiorem. Omnes autem alii homines qui vivunt secundum virtutes inferiores eligentes operationes enim et delectationes, quae sunt in illis operibus, innaturaliter ordinati sunt et peccant contra ordinem naturalem.*

Boethius of Dacia, *On the Supreme Good*, ed. J. F. Wippel (Toronto, 1987), 31–32.

virtues but expands on the more utilitarian side of Aristotle's eudaimonism; in so doing, he reveals the true spirit of the *Ethics*, as when he informs the reader that,

> *propiissimi nostri frutti sono le morali vertudi, però che da ogni canto sono in nostra podestade.... E queste sono quelle che fanno l'uomo beato, o vero felice, ne la loro operazione, sì come dice lo Filosofo nel primo de l'Etica quando diffinisce la Felicitade, dicendo che "Felicitade è operazione secondo virtude in vita perfetta."* (*Conv.* 4.17.2–3, 8)
>
> the moral virtues are the fruits most proper to us, since they lie in every respect within our own power.... It is through the exercise of these virtues that a man is made content or happy, as the Philosopher says in the first book of the *Ethics* where he defines Happiness by saying that "Happiness is activity in accordance with virtue in a perfect life."

Like the Philosopher, Dante balances his eulogy of the intellectual virtues with a robust dose of pragmatism. In a manner consistent with the dictates of philosophical discussion, the poet presents a counterargument to his claim that moral virtues are "propiissimi nostri frutti": since the kind of happiness man finds in philosophical contemplation is superior to that of the active life, one might ask why the focus should be on the intellectual virtues rather than the moral ones. To a possible objector, he responds that in every doctrine one must consider the faculties of the learner and help him or her by following the most fruitful path. As moral virtues appear to be more common (with respect to the intellectual ones), it is much more profitable for the reader to pursue that path over the other (*Conv.* 4.17.11–12).[15]

In this respect, if Dante is not a follower of the Latin Averroists in their radicalization of Aristotle's intellectualism neither is he a rigorous Thomist, as he has often been portrayed. In the fourth book, for instance, after offering a catalogue of the moral virtues, Dante returns to the locus now familiar to the reader of the two paths to happiness: the active life and the contemplative one. This time, he places the authority of the Gospel on par with that of the Philosopher:

> *Veramente è da sapere che noi potemo avere in questa vita due felicitadi, secondo due diversi cammini, buono e ottimo, che a ciò ne menano: l'una è la vita attiva, e l'altra la contemplativa; la quale, avvegna che per l'attiva si pervegna, come detto è, a buona felicitade, ne mena ad ottima felicitade e beatitudine, secondo che pruova*

15 In fact, in book two of the *Convivio*, he goes so far as to claim that, "cessando la Morale Filosofia, l'altre scienze sarebbero celate alcuno tempo, e non sarebbe generazione né vita di felicitade, e indarno sarebbero scritte e per antico trovate" (if Moral Philosophy ceased to exist, the other sciences would be hidden for some time, and there would be no generation or happiness in life, and in vain would these bodies of knowledge have been discovered and written down long ago; *Conv.* 2.14.18). On the place of ethics in Dante's classification of the sciences in the *Convivio*, see Gilson, *Dante the Philosopher* (above, n. 2), 99–112.

lo Filosofo nel decimo de l'Etica. E Cristo l'afferma con la sua bocca, nel Vangelio di Luca, parlando a Marta, e rispondendo a quella: "Marta, Marta, sollicita se' e turbiti intorno a molte cose: certamente una cosa è necessaria," cioè "quello che fai." E soggiugne: "Maria ottima parte ha eletta, la quale non le sarà tolta." E Maria, secondo che dinanzi è scritto a queste parole del Vangelio, a' piedi di Cristo sedendo, nulla cura del ministerio de la casa mostrava; ma solamente le parole del Salvatore ascoltava. Che se moralemente ciò volemo esponere, volse lo nostro Segnore in ciò mostrare che la contemplativa vita fosse ottima, tutto che buona fosse l'attiva: ciò è manifesto a chi ben vuole porre mente a le evangeliche parole. (*Conv.* 4.17.9–11)

We must know, however, that we may have two kinds of happiness in this life, according to two different paths, one good and the other best, which lead us there. One is the active life, the other the contemplative life; and although by the active, as has been said, we may arrive at a happiness that is good, the other leads us to the best happiness and state of bliss, as the Philosopher proves in the tenth book of the *Ethics*. Christ affirms this with words from his own lips in the Gospel of Luke, when speaking to Martha and replying to her: "Martha, Martha, you are distressed and trouble yourself about many things; truly one thing alone is necessary," namely, what you are doing. He adds: "Mary has chosen the best part, which shall not be taken from her." As made clear in the verses just preceding these words of the Gospel, Mary, who was sitting at the feet of Christ, showed no concern for domestic affairs, but simply listened to the words of the Savior. The moral sense of these words is that our Savior sought thereby to show that the contemplative life was the best, even though the active life was good. This is evident to anyone who considers well these words of the evangelist.

This passage has been offered by Corti as proof of a turning point in Dante's discourse on happiness and a caesura in his network of sources, most notably marked by an increased number of quotations from Scriptures.[16] In this view, Dante would be moving from a phase of theological transgression under the aegis of the radical Aristotelians to a more orthodox theology. Yet Dante is not quoting Luke, as Corti argues. Instead, he is rewriting a passage from Aquinas's *Summa contra gentiles*:

Now, there is nothing in this life so like this ultimate and perfect felicity as the life of those who contemplate truth, to the extent that it is possible in this life. And so, the philosophers who were not able to get full knowledge of this ultimate happiness identified man's ultimate happiness with the contemplation which is possible in this life. On this account, too, of all other lives the contemplative is more approved in divine Scripture, when our Lord says: "Mary hath chosen the better part," namely, the contemplation of truth, "which shall not be taken from her" (Luke 10:42). In fact, the contemplation of truth begins in this

16 Corti, *La felicità mentale* (above, n. 2), 59–60; 123–45.

life, but it reaches its climax in the future; whereas the active and civic life does not go beyond the limits of this life."[17]

What is particularly interesting for our purposes is not so much that Dante appropriates from the text in question without acknowledging it, but that he suppresses Aquinas's own emphasis on the fact that the philosophers *mistook* contemplation for beatitude, and that the latter pertains not to this life but the next one and is to be identified with the direct vision of God (*Contra gentiles* 3.60.2). Indeed, here the poet applies a lesson that he had learned in the very works of the Angelic Doctor, who in his *summae* and philosophical commentaries, when it serves his purpose, paints a seductive image of harmony between words, authors, and works that—upon closer reading—reveal instead a profound irreconcilability. Similarly, Dante avails himself of just enough to advance his own hypotheses yet avoids "burdening" the reader with more information on their context. In fact, the great Dominican sees both the active life and that of philosophical contemplation as functions of Christian beatitude; while Dante, though he acknowledges that such perfect happiness exists, insists throughout the *Convivio* that each and every path should be understood on its own terms, rather than in terms of a hierarchy.[18] It should also be

17 Thomas Aquinas, *Summa contra gentiles*, ed. C. Pera (Turin, 1946), 3.63.7.

> *Huius autem ultimae et perfectae felicitatis in hac vita nihil est adeo simile sicut vita contemplantium veritatem, secundum quod est possibile in hac vita. Et ideo philosophi, qui de illa felicitate ultima plenam notitiam habere non potuerunt, in contemplatione quae est possibilis in hac vita, ultimam felicitatem hominis posuerunt. Propter hoc etiam, inter alias vitas, in Scriptura divina magis contemplativa commendatur, dicente domino, Lucae 10–42:* Maria optimam partem elegit, scilicet contemplationem veritatis, quae non auferetur ab ea. *Incipit enim contemplatio veritatis in hac vita, sed in futura consummatur: activa vero et civilis vita huius vitae terminos non transcendit.*

Thomas Aquinas, *Summa contra gentiles*, book 3, *Providence*, pt. 1, trans. V. J. Bourke (South Bend, IN, 1975), 209.

18 Dante, in other words, is still being consistent with what he had clearly stated in book three:

> *Veramente può qui alcuno forte dubitare come ciò sia, che la sapienza possa fare l'uomo beato, non potendo a lui perfettamente certe cose mostrare; con ciò sia cosa che 'l naturale desiderio sia a l'uomo di sapere, e sanza compiere lo desiderio beato essere non possa. A ciò si può chiaramente rispondere che lo desiderio naturale in ciascuna cosa è misurato secondo la possibilitade della cosa desiderante: altrimenti andrebbe in contrario di sé medesimo, che impossibile è; e la Natura l'avrebbe fatto indarno, che è anche impossibile. In contrario andrebbe: ché, desiderando la sua perfezione, desiderrebbe la sua imperfezione; imperò che desiderrebbe sé sempre desiderare e non compiere mai suo desiderio (e in questo errore cade l'avaro maladetto, e non s'accorge che desidera sé sempre desiderare, andando dietro al numero impossibile a giugnere). Avrebbelo anco la Natura fatto indarno, però che non sarebbe ad alcuno fine ordinato. E però l'umano desiderio è misurato in questa vita a quella scienza che qui avere si può, e quello punto non passa se non per errore, lo quale è di fuori di naturale intenzione.* (*Conv.* 3.15.7–10)

> Nevertheless, some might have serious doubts here about how it can be that wisdom is able to make a man happy without its being able to reveal certain things to him perfectly, given that man has a natural desire to know, without fulfillment of which he cannot be blessed. To this we may simply reply that the natural desire within all things is proportionate to the capacity

noted that neither the reading of Aristotle through a refashioning of Aquinas—which is prominent throughout the *Convivio* as is the "voice" of Albert the Great—nor the pairing of the authority of the Scriptures with that of the Philosopher is a novelty introduced in the fourth book.[19] In short, rather than advancing Corti's theory that book four of the *Convivio* marks, "l'intervento di un punto di vista piu' cristianamente etico e di un punto di vista teologico a fianco di quello filosofico" (the intervention of a more markedly Christian ethical point of view and a theological point of view alongside the philosophical one) and acts as prelude to the poet's shift in the *Commedia,* "dal sicuro influsso dell'aristotelismo radicale . . . al fascino della grandiosa e armonica costruzione tomistica" (from the certain influence of radical Aristotelianism . . . to a fascination for the grandiose and harmonic construction of Thomism),[20] this passage is an eloquent example of what the poet has being doing throughout the *Convivio,* that is, putting "vocabuli d'autori, e di scienze e di libri" (*Conv.* 2.12.5) at the service of his own authorial intent.[21]

I would argue that in order to better appreciate such intent we should refamiliarize ourselves with Dante as a reader of philosophy and take more seriously his self-portrait as someone who inhabits and writes from a liminal space within the vast landscape of knowledge. "[F]uggito de la pastura del vulgo" (having fled the pasture of the common herd; *Conv.* 1.1.10), he does not belong to the small group who sits at the "beata mensa" where the bread of wisdom is served; yet *because* he is not too far removed from those who are starved for *scienza,* he is more inclined to share what he is able to gather for himself. Too often we tend to forget that Dante's interest in philosophy is not that of a scholar and is, thus, profoundly different from that of Siger and Boethius of Dacia,

within that thing which has desire; otherwise desire would run counter to itself, which is impossible, and nature would have created it in vain, which is likewise impossible. It would run counter to itself because by desiring its perfection it would desire its imperfection, since it would always desire to continue desiring and would never fulfill its desire (and it is into this error that the accursed miser falls, by failing to perceive that he desires to continue desiring by seeking to realize an infinite gain). Nature would also have created it in vain because it would not have been directed to any specific end. Therefore human desire within this life is proportionate to the wisdom which can be acquired here, and this limit is not transgressed except through an error which lies outside of Nature's intention.

19 In book two, for instance, in discussing the immortality of the soul, he first refers to Aristotle's *De anima* and then concludes, "Ancora, n'accerta la dottrina veracissima di Cristo, la quale è via, verità e luce: via, perché per essa sanza impedimento andiamo a la felicitade di quella immortalitade" (Moreover, we are made certain of this by the most truthful teaching of Christ, which is the way, the truth, and the light: the way, because by it we proceed without impediment to the happiness of this immortality; *Conv.* 2.8.14).

20 M. Corti, *Dante a un nuovo crocevia* (Florence, 1982), 79; Corti, *La felicità mentale* (above, n. 2), 60.

21 My discussion of the passage in question (*Conv.* 4.17.9–11) is meant to draw attention to the level of ideological autonomy that Dante's intertextual practices reveal, not to enter the scholarly debate on the "shipwreck" of the *Convivio*; I will therefore simply state here that, while I agree that book four represents an important transition in the poet's intellectual and creative trajectory, such transition should not be reduced to a generic transcending of a philosophical experience in favor of theological orthodoxy in the form of Thomism.

as well as that of Aquinas. Quite different is also the depth of Dante's knowledge of philosophy, as becomes evident once we get past the aura of omniscience that his work projects on the reader, even—or particularly, in fact—the scholarly ones.[22] A poignant example of the fact that Dante's enthusiasm for philosophy often prevails over profound knowledge can be found in book two of the *Convivio*; there, the poet refers to Boethius's *De consolatione philosophiae*—one of the works most widely read and commented on throughout the Middle Ages[23]—as "non conosciuto da molti" (not known to many; *Conv.* 2.12.2). Such a statement casts an unsettling light on many scholarly speculations about the genealogies of Dante's discourse on ethics. Yet Dante understood even too well that what was really at stake beneath the surface of the battle between philosophers and theologians was nothing less than the defining principle of culture as it was known. In the case of the Averroistic interpretations of Aristotle's eudaimonism condemned by Étienne Tempier, as it had been with Aristotle's newly translated works half a century earlier, there is never one single doctrine at stake. Rather, it is the idea of knowledge being advanced and how such knowledge frames the question of man's place in history and his relationship with eternity. *This* is the subtext of academic disputes such as that on the nature of human happiness as much as that surrounding the eternity of the world or the so-called separate intelligences. If Dante's *Convivio* shares anything of significance with the Latin Averroists, it is a vertiginous sense of euphoria for the new possibilities opened by the "rediscovery" of Aristotle. What the *Nicomachean Ethics* had in common with the *Physics* and *Politics* is this sense of empowerment, for lack of a better word; in the same way the world of nature is knowable through proper dedication to study, so happiness is within reach for those who cultivate virtue and knowledge, and political order can indeed be achieved. Yet what the poet aims to accomplish in the *Convivio,* building on Aristotle's eudaimonism, is something radically different from the hyper-intellectualized treatises of the radical Aristotelians and ultimately more ambitious than even the cultural mediation pursued by Albert the Great and Thomas Aquinas: to rework classical ethical theory in order to respond to the questions of his age.

The poet's discourse on happiness in the *Convivio* is an integral part of his reflection on the diffusion of philosophy and its profoundly political significance, and his

22 To acknowledge such idiosyncrasies in the poet's relationship with his sources means to confront our own idiosyncratic relationship with Dante as a cultural monument, a theme to which, albeit from very different perspectives, both Baranski and Barolini have poignantly drawn attention. It is, indeed, crucial to appreciating the poet's achievements—in the case of Dante's discourse on happiness as well as for his work at large—to get past the aura of omniscience and authority that emanate from the *Commedia* throughout the entirety of his opus. Baranski, *Dante* (above, n. 2); T. Barolini, *The Undivine Comedy: Detheologizing Dante* (Princeton, NJ, 1992) 3–20.

23 On the fortune of the *De consolatione philosophiae* in the Middle Ages, see P. Courcelle, "Étude critique sur les commentaires de la Consolation de Boèce (XIe–XVe siècles)," *Archives d'histoire doctrinale et littéraire du Moyen Âge* 12 (1939): 5–140; P. Courcelle, *La Consolation de Philosophie dans la tradition littéraire: Antécédents et postérité de Boèce* (Florence, 1967); L. Nauta, "The Consolation: The Latin Commentary Tradition, 800–1700," in The Cambridge Companion to Boethius, ed. J. Marenbon (Cambridge, 2009), 255–78.

appropriation of the Latinized Aristotle is one that anchors philosophical speculation in history. In Dante's vision, not only are happiness and knowledge connected, but the question of who has access to this knowledge is absolutely central. At the heart of the *Convivio* is the ambition to open *scienza* to a readership far more vast than the intellectual elite to which both Aquinas and the Parisian masters belonged (and for whom they wrote). This crucial point brings us to one of the most striking lacunas in the body of scholarship on Dante and the question of happiness, that of the pivotal role played by the Roman tradition, starting with one of the two authors who, by Dante's own account, sparked in him a desire for the study of philosophy and motivated him to attend "le scuole de li religiosi e a le disputazioni de li filosofanti": Cicero (*Conv.* 2.12.1–7).

In book one of the *Convivio*, while passionately attacking those who "commendano lo volgare altrui e lo loro proprio dispregiano" (praise the vernacular of others and disparage their own; *Conv.* 1.11.1), Dante reminds us that, "[c]ontra questi cotali grida Tullio nel principio d'un suo libro, che si chiama Libro di Fine de' Beni, però che al suo tempo biasimavano lo latino romano e commendavano la gramatica greca, per simiglianti cagioni che questi fanno vile lo parlare italico e prezioso quello di Provenza" (against men of this sort Tully cries out at the beginning of one of his books called *The Book on the End of Goods*, because in his time they found fault with Roman Latin and praised the Greek language for reasons similar to those for which these men judge the Italian language vile and Provençal precious; *Conv.* 1.11.14). The true significance of Dante's choice to model his response to disparagers of the Italian *volgare* after that of Cicero to detractors of Latin emerges when one considers the particular matter at hand in Cicero's book. *De finibus bonorum et malorum* is, in fact, a treatment of ethics that discusses happiness in relationship to the three most important philosophical systems of his time: Epicureanism, Stoicism, and Peripateticism, the very same schools of philosophy Dante explicitly acknowledges. The title, which translates (in the plural) the juxtaposition *télos agaton / télos kakon*, openly refers to the previously discussed notion of happiness as "the supreme good," the one good atop a hierarchy of ends. The aim is declaredly pragmatic: to make accessible to readers of Latin a part of Greek thought he considered most useful. "For what problem does life offer," wonders the Great Orator, "so important as all the topics of philosophy, and especially the question raised in these volumes—What is the End, the final and ultimate aim, which gives the standard for all principles of well-being and of right conduct? What does Nature pursue as the thing supremely desirable, what does she avoid as the ultimate evil?"[24]

Crucial for our purposes is that in book one—a substantial part of which is occupied by the author's declaration of intent—Cicero makes an explicit connection between

24 "Quid est enim in vita tanto opere quaerendum quam cum omnia in philosophia, tum id quod his libris quaeritur, qui sit finis, quid extremum, quid ultimum quo sint omnia bene vivendi recteque faciendi consilia referenda; quid sequatur natura ut summum ex rebus expetendis, quid fugiat ut extremum malorum?" Cicero, *De finibus bonorum et malorum* 1.4.11–12, trans. H. Rackham (Cambridge, MA, 1914, repr. 1983), 12, 14.

the pursuit of happiness and the popularization of philosophy. At least four categories of people, he informs the reader, are going to criticize his attempt "to present in a Latin dress subjects that philosophers of consummate ability and profound learning have already handled in Greek":[25] one, those who disapprove of philosophy altogether; two, those who do not strongly oppose the study of philosophy, provided that it is not taken too seriously; three, those who make a point of despising Latin because they know Greek (and claim to prefer to read everything in the original); and four, those who think that such writing is beneath his status as a leading politician and that he should devote himself to worthier "fields of authorship." After referring to his now-lost *Hortensius* as a response to the first class of critics, Cicero moves on to answer the other potential objections, and in so doing spares no sarcasm. Not only is the kind of restraint that the second class of critics preaches hard to practice, it is utterly foolish. The study of wisdom, once taken up, is not something that easily tolerates boundaries or restrictions; therefore, setting limits to something that is by nature unlimited is even more unreasonable than rejecting it altogether. More difficult, in Cicero's view, is to respond to those who demonstrate contempt for their mother tongue; difficult, that is, since their attitude is astonishing and even grotesque. Why should the very same people who find it perfectly normal to read, in Latin, plays translated word for word from the Greek refuse to read, in the same language, works of profound learning and great importance, such as those by Plato on morality and happiness? Cicero claims to have no argument with those who know Greek well enough to read in the original rather than Latin translations or popularizations such as his own, yet one has to be careful not to push refinement of taste to the point of caprice. Finally, he implies that some of those who claim to be so concerned with the primacy of the originals for their higher level of sophistication pretend to read Greek rather than actually do so, because they consider it fashionable. To the snobbery of the poseurs, Cicero contrasts his understanding of popularizing philosophy as part and parcel of his civic duties, a feature of his political activity rather than something beneath the status of those who play a prominent role in public life. In fact, he declares that at the service of such a task he will exert exactly the same "zeal, enthusiasm, and energy" that he devoted to politics when appointed by the Roman people (*De finibus* 1.4.10).

Far from being just reference material, book one of *De finibus* very much resembles a blueprint of Dante's "cultural program" as it emerges in the *Convivio*. All key elements of Cicero's discourse are present in the banquet of knowledge: the claim that to recognize the centrality of the eudaimonistic problem (for both the realization of the individual and the advancement of civil society) necessarily entails a responsibility to treat the subject in a language accessible to a wide rather than an elite audience; the defense of the expressive power of the mother tongue and the ambition to expand its domain to subjects that are traditionally off limits to it; the denunciation of intellectual pretense and fashions; the firm belief in the necessity of an alliance between philosophical wisdom

25 "... cum quae summis ingeniis exquisitaque doctrina philosophi Graeco sermone tractavissent ea Latinis litteris mandaremus"; *De finibus* 1.1.1. For what follows, see *De finibus* 1.1.1–1.4.12.

and political leadership; and the popularization of philosophy as ultimately another way of being politically active, to turn knowledge into action.

The strategic role played by *De finibus* in Dante's renegotiation of Aristotle's eudaimonism becomes even more evident when we take a closer look at the ways Cicero applied his notion of *utilitas* to Greek thought. It is important to emphasize that in making the case that his native language was able to treat subjects that were traditionally the prerogative of the Greeks (such as the nature of happiness), Cicero poses a question that will play a crucial role in late medieval culture and is, indeed, vital to the author of the *Convivio*: that of the respective merits of the translation of philosophy versus its popularization. Direct translation from the Greek, he maintains, if done properly, is a patriotic service and a worthwhile enterprise. Yet his way of mediating between the philosophers and readers of Latin is of a different nature entirely: though relying on a reconfiguration of the writings of others, it nevertheless involves authorial intent.

> And supposing that for our part we do not fill the office of a mere translator, but, while preserving the doctrines of our chosen authorities, add thereto our own criticism and our own arrangement: what ground have those objectors for ranking the writing of Greece above compositions that are at once brilliant in style and not mere translations from Greek originals? . . . Yet even supposing I gave a direct translation of Plato or Aristotle, exactly as our poets have done with the plays, would it not, pray, be a patriotic service to introduce those transcendent intellects to the acquaintance of my fellow countrymen? As a matter of fact, however, this has not been my procedure hitherto, though I do not feel I am debarred from adopting it. Indeed I expressly reserve the right of borrowing certain passages, if I think fit, and particularly from the philosophers just mentioned, when an appropriate occasion offers for so doing; just as Ennius regularly borrows from Homer, and Afranius from Menander.[26]

He is borrowing, rearranging, quoting, but also exercising critical capacity, inquiring while offering a picture as exhaustive as possible of the debate on the *summum bonum* (*De finibus* 1.4.12). Unlike Cicero, Dante had no ambition in the *Convivio* to provide the reader with such an exhaustive treatment, but what is described here uncannily resembles the "texture" of his own philosophical prose. Moreover, in both authors the questions of cultural mediation and the dignity of the native language are closely intertwined. In the passage quoted above, Cicero rehearses an argument in the positive

26 *Quid si nos non interpretum fungimur munere, sed tuemur ea quae dicta sunt ab iis quos probamus, eisque nostrum iudicium et nostrum scribendi ordinem adiungimus? Quid habent cur Graeca anteponant iis quae et splendide dicta sint neque sint conversa de Graecis?. . . Quanquam si plane sic verterem Platonem aut Aristotelem ut verterunt nostri poetae fabulas, male, credo, mererer de meis civibus si ad eorum cognitionem divina illa ingenia transferrem. Sed id neque feci adhuc nec mihi tamen ne faciam interdictum puto. Locos quidem quosdam, si videbitur, transferam, et maxime ab iis quos modo nominavi, cum inciderit ut id apte fieri possit; ut ab Homero Ennius, Afranius a Menandro solet.* (*De finibus* 1.2.6, 1.3.7)

that he later presents in the negative: cultural mediation without craftsmanship and discernment does not simply translate into poor appreciation of what is being mediated, but it reflects negatively on the medium itself. While even an adequate translation is nothing short of a patriotic service, pedestrian translations of works that were mediocre to begin with are one of the reasons why Romans not only turn from philosophy but also have such a low opinion of their native language (*De finibus* 1.3.8). "But given a noble theme, and a refined, dignified and graceful style," he asks, "who would not read a Latin book?"[27] In book one of the *Convivio,* Dante also insists on the question of craftsmanship and brings the issue of translation into his defense of the vernacular:

> *Onde pensando che lo desiderio d'intendere queste canzoni, a alcuno illitterato avrebbe fatto lo comento latino transmutare in volgare, e temendo che 'l volgare non fosse stato posto per alcuno che l'avesse laido fatto parere, come fece quelli che transmutò lo latino de l'Etica—ciò fu Taddeo ipocratista—providi a ponere lui, fidandomi di me più che d'un altro. . . . Molti sono che amano più d'essere tenuti maestri che d'essere, e per fuggir lo contrario, cioè di non essere tenuti, sempre danno colpa a la materia de l'arte apparecchiata, o vero a lo strumento: sì come lo mal fabbro biasima lo ferro appresentato a lui, e lo malo citarista biasima la cetera, credendo dare la colpa del mal coltello e del mal sonare al ferro ed alla cetera, e levarla a sé. Così sono alquanti, e non pochi, che vogliono che l'uomo li tegna dicitori; e per scusarsi dal non dire o dal dire male accusano ed incolpano la materia, cioè lo volgare proprio, e commendano l'altro lo quale non è loro richesto di fabbricare. E chi vuole vedere come questo ferro è da biasimare, guardi che opere ne fanno li buoni artefici, e conoscerà la malizia di costoro che, biasimando lui, si credono scusare.* (*Conv.* 1.10.10–11, 1.11.11–13)

> Thinking, therefore, that the desire to understand these *canzoni* would have induced some unlearned person to have the Latin commentary translated into the vernacular, and fearing that the vernacular might have been set down by someone who would have made it seem offensive, as did the one who translated the *Ethics* from Latin—and that was Thaddeus the Hippocratist—I arranged to set it down, trusting in myself more than in another. . . . There are many who love to be considered masters rather than to be such, and to avoid the opposite, that is, not being so considered, they always lay the blame on the material furnished for their craft, or on their tools. For example, a bad smith blames the iron supplied to him, and the bad lute player blames the lute, thinking to throw the fault of the bad knife or the bad music on the iron or the lute, and to remove it from himself. In the same way there are some, and not a few, who wish to be considered writers; and to excuse themselves from not writing or from writing badly, they accuse and blame their material, that is, their own vernacular, and praise another which they have not been required to work with. Whoever

27 "Res vero bonas verbis electis graviter ornateque dictas quis non legat?"; *De finibus* 1.3.8.

wishes to see in what way this iron is deserving of blame should look at the works which good craftsmen make with it and he will recognize the disingenuousness of those who think to excuse themselves by blaming it.

In Dante's case, the question of language as craft and that of translation is framed within an argument that is more complex and ambiguous, conditioned as it is by the poet's effort to contain the centripetal force of his own authorial ambitions; he is, simultaneously, troubled by an "anxious sense of poetry as a problematic discourse," determined to assert control over the significance of his *canzoni,* and intent on acquiring not only legitimacy but *auctoritas.*[28] While Cicero argues that Latin is ready to accommodate not only Greek poetry but the much more precious wealth of Greek philosophy—and elsewhere in the text remarks on the inferior status of poetry vis-à-vis philosophy (*De finibus* 5.3.3)—Dante's philosophical prose in the *Convivio* is allegedly at the service of his *canzoni.* Cicero, far from following Lucretius in his complaint regarding the poverty of Latin (*De rerum natura* 1.136–46; 3.258–62), dismisses such a notion as a fashionable cliché and proudly affirms that Latin has an even richer vocabulary than Greek.[29] Dante launches into a lengthy explanation as to why a commentary in Latin would have been out of place—one reason being the unpleasant possibility that the Latin commentaries were to be as poorly translated as Aristotle's *Ethics*[30]—and concedes the

28 See A. R. Ascoli, *Dante and the Making of a Modern Author* (Cambridge, 2008), 159, 67–174. Ascoli's in-depth study has helped us to better appreciate both the true magnitude of Dante's authorial ambitions in the *Convivio,* as well as the complex strategies through which they are pursued and how they relate to the arc of the poet's intellectual and creative trajectory.

29 "But for my part I can never cease wondering what can be the origin of the exaggerated contempt for home products that is now fashionable. It would of course be out of place to attempt to prove it here, but in my opinion, as I have often argued, the Latin language, so far from having a poor vocabulary, as is commonly supposed, is actually richer than the Greek." (*Ego autem mirari satis non queo, unde hoc sit tam insolens domesticarum rerum fastidium. Non est omnino hic docendi locus, sed ita sentio et saepe disserui, Latinam linguam non modo non inopem, ut vulgo putarent, sed locupletiorem etiam esse quam Graecam; De finibus* 1.3.10) Cicero is as assertive about his role as cultural mediator as he is regarding his native language's worth, as in chapter four, where he claims that no one had done more to make Greek philosophy available to the readers of Latin than he (*De finibus* 1.4.11). As a matter of fact, Cicero's unapologetic self-awareness is matched only by the actual impact of his "cultural entrepreneurship." He is without question—as Augustine understood—the single most important mediator between the philosophical tradition of classical antiquity and Roman culture. An essential part of this cultural mediation consisted in the craft of words. In fact, Cicero is responsible for a substantial part of Latin philosophical lexicon (a fact that implicitly proves Lucretius's point rather than his own), including the word *beatitudo,* which together with *felicitas* would become the standard for "happiness." On Cicero and Greek philosophy, see J. C. Davies, "The Originality of Cicero's Philosophical Works," *Latomus* 30 (1971): 105–19; P. Boyancé, *Études sur l'humanisme cicéronien* (Brussels, 1970); J. Glucker, "Cicero's Philosophical Affiliations," in *The Question of Eclecticism: Studies in Later Greek Philosophy,* ed. J. M. Dillon and A. A. Long (Berkeley, 1988), 34–69; *Cicero the Philosopher,* ed. J. G. F. Powell (Oxford, 1995).

30 Cornish's recent study on vernacular translation sheds new light on Dante's polemical engagement with the practice of *volgarizzamento.* A. Cornish, *Vernacular Translation in Dante's Italy: Illiterate Literature* (Cambridge, 2011), 126–56.

superiority of Latin over the vernacular. Yet, despite this last homage to the language of the *litterati*, it is "lo naturale amore de la propria loquela" (*Conv.* 1.10.5) that permeates virtually every word of the *Convivio*; indeed, it should come as only a partial surprise that in *De vulgari eloquentia* (1.1.2–5), the poet reverses the hierarchy between Latin and his native language. Ultimately, in laying the claim for their native languages to take on the question of happiness, both authors openly confront a complex of cultural inferiority: in the case of Cicero, that of the Romans toward Greek culture (which manifested itself either through total rejection or in the "desire to be Greek out and out," ridiculed in book one); in Dante's case, that of the Italians toward Latin as well as the more established vernaculars, such as Provençal. In fact, in both *De finibus* and the *Convivio*, from the very first the reader is thrust onto the scene of a cultural battle and carried along by the author's impatience with intellectual pretension and fads. Among Dante's targets are not only his fellow Italians who hide their lack of facility with the mother tongue behind the celebration or even the adoption of the "lingua strana" and those who snub their language for lack of discernment, sheer cowardice, or vainglory (*Conv.* 1.11.1–21), but also the literati who are perpetrators of a commercialization of knowledge (*Conv.* 1.9.2–5). It is against such a cultural landscape that the poet contrasts his desire to "dare a molti . . . dare utili cose . . . sanza essere domandato lo dono" ([give] to many . . . [give] useful things . . . [give] a gift without its being asked; *Conv.* 1.8.2–3).

While Cicero is more daring than Dante in discussing his native language in relation to what was, at the time, *the* language of ideas, the poet articulates more fully—and in some respects more radically—the question of readership in terms of access to *scienza*. The *Convivio* begins with a discussion of the many obstacles that prevent countless people from acquiring the precious knowledge granted by philosophy. Once again, such discussion draws the reader "out of the classroom," so to speak, and into the very center of the contradictions of history. For instance, in the catalogue of impediments that stand between the multitudes who are starved for knowledge and the food that they naturally crave, we find "lo difetto del luogo dove persona è nata e nutrita, che tal ora sarà da ogni studio non solamente privato, ma da gente studiosa lontano" (the handicap that derives from the place where a person is born and bred, which at times will not only lack a university but be far removed from the company of educated persons; *Conv.* 1.1.4). Ignorance is not always a matter of choice and can, indeed, be the result of a lack of opportunity or the logistics of life. Quite strikingly, in the poet's view, these logistics encompass the matter of gender. In fact, in his sanguine attack on the literati—the ones entrusted by a corrupt society with the very treasures of wisdom that the poet wishes to give freely instead of trading them for money or privilege—Dante submits that waiting for the "servigio" that the *Convivio* intends to provide are not only men but also women; they hold the qualities necessary to appreciate such wisdom, although they do not as yet possess "litteratura":

> *Ché la bontà de l'animo, la quale questo servigio attende, è in coloro che per malvagia disusanza del mondo hanno lasciata la litteratura a coloro che l'hanno fatta di donna meretrice; e questi nobili sono principi, baroni, cavalieri, e molt'altra nobile*

gente, non solamente maschi ma femmine, che sono molti e molte in questa lingua, volgari, e non litterati. (*Conv.* 1.9.5)

> For goodness of mind, which this service attends to, is found in those who because of the world's wicked neglect of good have left literature to those who have changed it from a lady into a whore; and these noble persons comprise princes, barons, knights, and many other noble people, not only men but women, of which there are many in this language who know only the vernacular and are not learned.

In their apparent simplicity, these few lines have monumental implications. If philosophy is instrumental to the attainment of happiness, Dante, by granting women access to a readership from which they had been previously barred, elects them active partners in the most vital and defining of human pursuits. While Aristotle considered women deficient in reason and therefore crippled in their capacity for virtue, both moral and intellectual (*Politics* 1254b13–1260a32), Dante sketches a portrait of women craving for and equipped to have not only "intelletto d'amore" but of ethics, politics, physics, and more.[31] As he will make abundantly clear in book four, the kind of nobility to which the poet refers in the passage above is not something guaranteed by family lineage (whether combined with wealth or not); it is, instead, "a seed of happiness" that one chooses either to cultivate or neglect each day. In Dante's view, in order for this choice to be more than just an academic conceit, one needs at least the minimum set of intellectual coordinates (such as, for instance, an understanding of the nature of virtue and the strategic role it plays in the pursuit of *felicitade*). In the *Convivio,* Dante claims to provide just such indispensable equipment. In point of fact, what he offers his readers is much more: it is a space for critical thought. By following the poet along the many stations, stops, and departures that constitute the journey of the *Convivio,* and becoming acquainted with such *auctoritates* as Aristotle and Aquinas, they have the opportunity to become—even more than acute readers of poetry—better readers of the world around them. In fact, while often uneven as self-commentary, conditioned as it is by his desire to prove that "non passione ma vertù sia stata la movente cagione" of the *canzoni*,[32] Dante's philosophical prose is most persuasive and thought-provoking when it leans toward sociopolitical commentary. This is the case with the connections he establishes between issues of nobility, gender, and the empowerment that comes with knowledge. For instance, after formally paying homage to tradition and proclaiming Latin superior to the vernacular

31 Essential for the question of gender in Dante and late medieval Italian literature is T. Barolini, *Dante and the Origins of Italian Literary Culture* (New York, 2006), 11–13, 281–378.

32 "Temo la infamia di tanta passione avere seguita, quanta concepe chi legge le sopra nominate canzoni in me avere segnoreggiata: la quale infamia si cessa, per lo presente di me parlare, interamente, lo quale mostra che non passione ma vertù sia stata la movente cagione." (I fear the infamy of having yielded myself to the great passion that anyone who reads the *canzoni* mentioned above must realize once ruled me. This infamy will altogether cease as I speak now about myself and show that my motivation was not passion but virtue; *Conv.* 1.2.16).

"e per la [sua] nobiltà e per vertù e per bellezza" (because of its nobility, its virtue, and its beauty; *Conv.* 1.5.7), Dante thunders his distaste for what is the *reality* of "litteratura," which very much resembles a world upside down: that is, those who are endowed with true nobility are exiled from the wisdom that "litteratura" safeguards, while others who are far from noble have free access to such precious knowledge and "acquistano la lettera" not for its proper use but out of greed (*Conv.* 1.9.3). Similarly, in book four, Dante engages with the tradition of philosophical debate on nobility while also presenting *nobilitade* as the scandal of fourteenth-century politics:

> *Sì che non dica quelli de li Uberti di Fiorenza, né quelli de li Visconti da Melano: "Perch'io sono di cotale schiatta, io sono nobile"; ché 'l divino seme non cade in ischiatta, cioè in istirpe, ma cade ne le singulari persone, e, sì come di sotto si proverà, la stirpe non fa le singulari persone nobili, ma le singulari persone fanno nobile la stirpe.* (*Conv.* 4.20.5)
>
> So let none of the Uberti of Florence or the Visconti of Milan say "Because I am of such a race I am noble," for the divine seed does not fall upon a race [that is, family stock] but on individuals; and as will be proved below, family stock does not make individuals noble, although individuals make family stock noble.

In his discussion of *nobilitade,* the poet connects a traditional question of ethics—that purely theoretical relationship between happiness and virtue—with a new one: the meaning of nobility at a time of rapid social change and utmost political instability. What is more, in attacking the definition of nobility as "antica ricchezza e belli costumi" (ancestral wealth and fine manners; *Conv.* 4.3.6)—which Dante attributes to Frederick II but is, in fact, largely Aristotelian—he skillfully tests the boundaries of both the authority of the emperor and the Philosopher.[33] In short, to sit at Dante's table might not carry the same prestige as being a guest at the "beata mensa," but it could very well prove an even more exhilarating experience.

To conclude, the poet's *innamoramento* with philosophy recounted in the *Convivio* meant embracing the belief—deeply engrained in the history of ancient thought—that ethics is first and foremost the science of happiness. Dante employs Aristotelian philosophy as a theoretical platform for his banquet of knowledge and embraces a seemingly reverential attitude toward the "maestro e duca della ragione."[34] Yet he shows remarkable freedom in appropriating Aristotle's eudaimonism and weaves a discourse on the ultimate human desire, the implications of which were neither in the *Nicomachean Ethics,* which he relentlessly cites, nor in the late medieval commentaries and treatises engaged with eudaimonia, from which he more discreetly "borrows." Indeed, Aristotelianism—though essential—is not enough to explain Dante's *felicitade* as it emerges in the

33 *Conv.* 4.19.4–5; 4.20.5, 9–10*;* 4.22.11–12. Ascoli, *Dante and the Making of a Modern Author* (above, n. 28), 87–108.

34 See, for instance, *Conv.* 3.5.7, 4.6.8, 4.8.15.

Convivio. In order to best appreciate the scope of the poet's discourse on happiness, we have to consider not only the contingency of the philosophical debate in all its contemporary urgency but also its "longue durée." Crucial to this appreciation is understanding the use to which Dante puts the various doctrinal elements that he reconfigures rather than simply interrogating the text in terms of philosophical affiliations or doctrinal originality. As I have shown, Cicero's *De finibus* is key to better comprehending how Dante engages with the tradition of Greek eudaimonism and frames Aristotle's conception of happiness as self-fashioning within a discourse on what might be best characterized as the "cultural politics" of his day. In fact, it is Cicero's particular brand of *utilitas* applied to Greek thought, as well as his understanding of writing as social commitment, that helps Dante bring into sharp focus the question of readership and its relationship to the empowerment that Aristotelian philosophy promises. Ultimately, at the crossroads between virtue, knowledge, and happiness, the poet, like Cicero, is hard at work bridging the gap between the great tradition of philosophy and the world of history.

Aristotle's *Mezzo*, Courtly *Misura*, and Dante's Canzone *Le dolci rime*

Humanism, Ethics, and Social Anxiety

TEODOLINDA BAROLINI

THIS ESSAY EXPLORES THE INTERNALIZATION of Aristotle into vernacular culture, indeed, into that hyper-vernacular outpost of medieval culture that is the high lyric tradition. As my title indicates, I will be looking at Dante's unique mix of Aristotelian learning and vernacular traditions: the ways in which Dante blends classical learning with the courtly roots of his poetic culture to form an ethics that incorporates both frames of reference. As I have done before, but from a somewhat different vantage, I will press the idea of Dante's remarkably hybrid and culturally enriched formulations, showing first the mature expression of these ideas in the *Commedia* and then highlighting the earlier lyric phase in which these ideas are incubated, in particular in the Aristotelian lyric—the label itself is indicative of Dante's pioneering genius—*Le dolci rime*.[1] Finally, I will illuminate the ways in which Dante's hybrid, ethical formulations are enmeshed in social realities, as demonstrated in the canzone on courtliness, *Poscia ch'Amor*. Given that the mean between avarice and prodigality is located by Aristotle in the virtue of liberality, a virtue of enormous resonance for the ethos of knighthood and *cortesia*, the Aristotelian template allows for an easy pivot on Dante's part from ethics in the moral and philosophical sphere to ethics in the social and historical sphere. In the concluding section, I will tease out the social anxiety that can be glimpsed behind the poet's cultural positioning.

1 See, for instance, T. Barolini, "Medieval Multiculturalism and Dante's Theology of Hell," *Italiana* 9 (2000): 82–102, repr. in *Dante and the Origins of Italian Literary Culture* (New York, 2006), 103–21. On bringing Aristotle into Italian literary contexts, see S. Gentili, *L'uomo aristotelico alle origini della letteratura italiana* (Rome, 2005), further discussed in note 8, below. J. Rosenfeld, *Ethics and Enjoyment in Late Medieval Poetry: Love after Aristotle* (Cambridge, 2011), deals with French and English material.

Merging the Aristotelian Mean and Lyric *Misura* in the Ethical Framework of the *Commedia*

We begin with the ethics of the courtly lyric and how it informs the Aristotelian framework of the *Commedia*. The philosophy of desire that underwrites the courtly lyric can view passion as invincible, not susceptible to the moderating influences of any other force, and in this sense can be understood as a vernacularization of Virgil's "Omnia vincit amor; et nos cedamus amori" (Love conquers all, so let us yield to love; *Eclogues* 10.69). But it can also subscribe to the idea that reason is the force that can and should moderate desire. For Occitan poets, this idea of moderation is embedded in the concept *mezura*, which comes into the Italian lyric tradition as *misura*. By the time we reach Dante, we are dealing with an amateur philosopher who recognizes and utilizes the overlap between Occitan *mezura* and Aristotelian incontinence. I argue that Dante's deliberate merging of Aristotelian ethics with the vernacular ethical tradition is a form of early humanism.

This imbrication is on display in the fifth canto of the *Inferno*, which is devoted to the circle of lust. Here the *contrapasso* is based on the idea of an infernal wind that buffets the "carnal sinners" as, in life, they were buffeted by sexual passion. The metaphor of the "bufera infernal" (*Inf.* 5.31) is a rich, cultural mosaic of Augustine's analysis of desire, with the human *cor inquietum* struggling toward the divine *quies*, and the Bible; the commentator Guido da Pisa suggested as intertext for Dante's *bufera* Isaiah's "Cor impii quasi mare fervens quod quiescere non potest" (The heart of the wicked man is like a troubled sea that cannot rest; Isa. 57:20).[2] Interestingly, and to my knowledge not previously noted by the commentary tradition, Dante's metaphor of an infernal wind that endlessly compels the souls in its grip—"La bufera infernal, che mai non resta, / mena li spirti con la sua rapina; / voltando e percotendo li molesta" (The hellish wind that never rests sweeps the spirits with its force; hurling and battering it molests them; *Inf.* 5.31–33)[3]—also draws on Aristotle's discussion of compulsion in *Nicomachean Ethics*. In book 3 of that work, Aristotle illustrates compulsion with the example of a person being carried by a wind: "Those things, then, are thought involuntary, which take place by force or owing to ignorance; and that is compulsory of which the moving principle is outside, being a principle in which nothing is contributed by the person who acts—or, rather, is acted upon, e.g., *if he were to be carried somewhere by a wind, or by men who had him in their power*" (*NE* 3.1; italics mine).[4] I believe that Aristotle's example contributes to Dante's construction of the *contrapasso* in *Inferno* 5. Moreover, I suggest that this

2 Guido da Pisa, *Expositiones et Glose super "Comediam" Dantis or Commentary on Dante's "Inferno,"* ed. V. Cioffari (Albany, 1974), 101.

3 The text is from *La "Commedia" secondo l'antica vulgata*, ed. G. Petrocchi, 4 vols. (Milan, 1966–67). Translations are my own unless otherwise noted.

4 I first published this Aristotelian intertext for the *bufera* in "Dante and Cavalcanti (On Making Distinctions in Matters of Love): *Inferno* 5 in Its Lyric and Autobiographical Context," *Dante Studies* 116 (1998): 31–63, repr. in Barolini, *Dante and the Origins of Italian Literary Culture*, 70–101, citation p. 74. The citation is from *The Nichomachean Ethics*, trans. D. Ross (1925; rev. Oxford, 1990), 48.

passage offers Dante not only imagery that is suitable for Francesca in *Inferno* 5 but also for Piccarda in *Paradiso* 3. While Francesca is analogous to one who is "carried somewhere by a wind," Piccarda is analogous to a person who is carried somewhere "by men who had [her] in their power." Francesca, who is now carried by a wind, speaks of her past actions as involuntary and of herself as having been acted upon rather than acting; she is the perfect embodiment of Aristotle's example of compulsion transplanted to the Christian afterlife.

I raise this Aristotelian intertext to foreground Dante's use of classical material in his Christian underworld and signal his productive contamination of vastly different cultural systems.[5] Among the other cultural strands that feed into canto 5, the most important is the early Italian courtly lyric. The ideology and metaphorics of the *bufera infernal* draw on lyric language for tempestuous passion that goes back to Giacomo da Lentini and Guido delle Colonne at the beginning of the Italian tradition. Guido delle Colonne's canzone *Amor, che lungiamente m'hai menato*, for instance, which I have called "a lyric version of *Inferno* 5 without the eschatological context,"[6] is shaped by the dialectic between *menare* and *posare* (the very verbs used in *Inferno* 5). The *canzone*'s conclusion compares the wind to the force of love, stating that as the wind beats the waves into a frenzy, so love agitates the lover, giving him no peace: "c'Amor mi sbatte e smena, che no abento, / sì come vento smena nave in onda" (for Love shakes me and drives me, so that I have no peace, as the wind drives a ship in the waves; *Amor, che lungiamente*, 63–64).[7]

The ethical scaffolding behind this imagery is spelled out by Dante in verse 39 of *Inferno* 5, where carnal sinners are defined as those "who subordinate reason to desire" ("che la ragion sommettono al talento"). This same ethical scaffolding, whereby desire must be subordinated to reason in order for the human soul to be in alignment and function virtuously, is also present in early Italian lyrics. In other words, Dante was by no means the first poet to conceive of love as potentially "tempered" by reason.[8] Guido delle Colonne explicitly theorizes that reason, "senno," is the counterweight to passion:

5 For the classical material as Dante's signature innovation to the visionary tradition, see A. Morgan, *Dante and the Medieval Other World* (Cambridge, 1990), who notes Dante's originality in including classical figures, "totally unrepresented in the earlier medieval texts" (p. 57); and Barolini, "Medieval Multiculturalism" (above, n. 1).

6 Barolini, "Dante and Cavalcanti," 75.

7 Italian lyric poets other than Guittone d'Arezzo, Guido Cavalcanti, and Dante Alighieri are cited from the edition of G. Contini, *Poeti del Duecento*, 2 vols. (Milan and Naples, 1960).

8 This is a common misunderstanding, recently reprised in Gentili, *L'uomo aristotelico* (above, n. 1). Gentili does not recognize *misura* as a lyric value prior to Dante's adoption of the "dottrina aristotelica della temperanza" (Aristotelian doctrine of temperance; p. 187). Hence, she does not discuss it in the context of earlier love poetry, although she does note the connection between *misura* and Aristotle's doctrine of the mean in the *Novellino*: "Federico risponde correttamente 'misura,' ossia identifica il bene supremo nel giusto mezzo virtuoso" (Frederick correctly replies "misura," in other words he identifies the supreme good in the just and virtuous mean; p. 177). Her discussion of *ragione* versus *senso* in the lyric tradition pits Dante and the "dottrina aristotelica della temperanza" against Cavalcanti, and posits Dante as the first love poet whose concept of love is informed by the doctrine of temperance, being "di estrazione teologica e di matrice tomasiana, per cui l'amore sensuale può

Forza di ***senno*** *è quella che soverchia*
ardir di core, asconde ed incoverchia.
Ben è gran ***senno,*** *chi lo pote fare,*
saver celare—ed essere signore
de lo suo core quand'este 'n errore.
(*Amor, che lungiamente m'hai menato*, 48–52; boldface mine)

Force of reason is that which overcomes boldness of heart, hides and covers it. It is great wisdom, for the one who can do it, to know how to hide [love] and to be lord of his heart when it is in error.

Elaborating the troubadour topos of *fol'amor*, Guido delle Colonne writes that love causes even the wisest to stray, and that he who loves most has least judgment—"misura"—and is most "folle": "Amor fa disvïare li più saggi: /e chi più ama men' ha in sé misura, / più folle è quello che più s'innamora" (Love makes the wisest go off the path: he who loves most has least measure in himself; most mad is the one who is most in love; *Amor, che lungiamente,* 53–55]). These verses feature the moderating force of *senno* and *misura*, terms that carry the ideological valence of the Occitan *sen* and *mezura* from which they derive.

Of troubadour *mezura*, Topsfield writes that "*Mesura* is the rational control by which a man can choose to think and act in the way that will bring him happiness," and that it is "the quality of the man who controls his thoughts in order to be wise and courtly in word and deed."[9] Cherchi shows that the *mezura* of the troubadours coincides with the virtue known to classical antiquity as temperance, a virtue whose cultural prominence in medieval France he links to the widespread circulation of Ciceronian ethical values through works like the twelfth-century adaptation of Cicero's *De officiis* attributed to William of Conches, *Moralium dogma philosophorum*.[10] In that work, Ciceronian *temperantia* is defined as "dominium rationis in libidinem et alios motus importunos" (the absolute rule of reason over passions and any other unfit impulses). As proof of the correspondence between *mezura* and *temperantia*, Cherchi offers the *ensenhamen* on the four cardinal virtues written by the thirteenth-century troubadour Daude de Pradas (1214–1282), in particular the passage on temperance, in which Daude presents the terms "mesura, / Contenenza o atempranza" (*mezura*, continence, or temperance) as synonyms.

Dante does not use *contenenza* or *incontenenza*, or even *misura* or *dismisura*, in *Inferno* 5. Rather, he defines lust as a "subordination of reason to desire," and thus as a

---

essere 'temperato' dall'anima razionale in modo da condurre all'amore spirituale, cioè a Dio" (of theological extraction and a Thomistic matrix, so that sensual love can be "tempered" by the rational soul in such a way as to lead to spirtual love, i.e. to God; p. 187). Gentili does not discuss *Le dolci rime* or any of Dante's moral canzoni.

9 L. T. Topsfield, *Troubadours and Love* (Cambridge, 1975), 83 and 87.

10 See P. Cherchi, *Andreas and the Ambiguity of Courtly Love* (Toronto, 1994), the chapter "Mezura." For the treatise attributed to William of Conches, see pp. 44–47; the definition of *temperantia* from the *Moralium* is on 47. The passage from Daude de Pradas is on 48.

failure to exercise rational control over desire. Lust is a lack of restraint or *misura*; it is therefore excess, incontinence. This is an Aristotelian view, which sees lust as excess; it is not a condemnation of all desire, but a condemnation only and specifically of excess desire. This Aristotelian understanding coincides with the particular vernacular viewpoint whose exponents I have been citing. If, on the one hand, it is not surprising that the definition of lust in canto 5 can be retrofitted to fit under the rubric of incontinence—after all, in *Inferno* 11 Dante will announce that the moral structure of hell derives from Aristotle's *Ethics*—it is, on the other hand, a definition that Dante criticism knows and acknowledges in taxonomic terms but frequently loses track of in philosophical terms. The taxonomy is clear: in *Inferno* 11 Dante explicitly places circles 2 to 5 (lust, gluttony, avarice/prodigality, and anger) under the Aristotelian rubric of incontinence. The philosophy is less clear: the philosophical implications of defining desire in terms of incontinence are frequently overlooked in a critical tradition that has insisted for centuries on the binary of secular versus divine love. Defining desire in terms of incontinence means that it is not defined dualistically, for the Aristotelian system of virtue as a mean between two sinful extremes is a unitary system, based on a spectrum of behaviors, not a dualistic one.

As part of his dramatic announcement that hell is morally structured according to Aristotle's *Ethics*, Dante, in *Inferno* 11, twice uses the technical term "incontenenza" in a paired usage that constitutes its only appearance in the *Commedia*:

> *Non ti rimembra di quelle parole*
> *con le quai la tua Etica pertratta*
> *le tre disposizion che 'l ciel non vole,*
> ***incontenenza**, malizia e la matta*
> *bestialitade? e come **incontenenza***
> *men Dio offende e men biasimo accatta?* (*Inf.* 11.79–84; boldface mine)
>
> Don't you remember those words with which your *Ethics* treats the three dispositions that heaven does not want: incontinence, malice, and mad bestiality? And how incontinence offends God less and procures less blame?

The Aristotelian term "incontenenza" is featured in a high-profile moment that sends the reader directly back to the *Ethics*, and it does not occur again. How can the condition of incontinence embrace circles 2 to 5 of hell and yet receive so little verbal recognition? The answer is that the concept of incontinence is embedded in glosses, like the definition of lust as the subordination of reason to desire, and it is present in the invocation of the vernacular equivalent of *incontenenza*, namely, *misura*. Dante's use of the lyric term *misura*, on the one hand, and the philosophical term *incontenenza*, on the other, is a way of demonstrating the convergence of two cultural strands into the same conceptual node.

Thus, if we attend to the presentation of the sins of incontinence as it unfolds, rather than read retrospectively from the didactic explanation of *Inferno* 11, we note that we meet the word *misura* long before we meet the word *incontenenza*, with the result that we can observe a program of cultural integration as it occurs. This program of mixing the classical and the vernacular is betokened, for instance, by the verse that tells us that the misers and the prodigals are equally without *misura* in their approach to material wealth: "che con misura nullo spendio ferci" (they did no spending with *misura*; *Inf.* 7.42). The Bosco-Reggio commentary offers this cogent gloss: "che non fecero nessuna spesa (*spendio*) con misura, cioè non seppero rimanere nel giusto mezzo tra avarizia e prodigalità" (they undertook no spending with *misura*, in other words they did not remain at the just mean between avarice and prodigality).[11] By making explicit that the failure to spend in a measured fashion is synonymous with the inability to remain at the virtuous mean between avarice and prodigality, the Bosco-Reggio commentary effectively lays bare the Aristotelian framework that governs this part of Dante's hell.

Dante, however, has not yet been so explicit; in *Inferno* 7 he uses language not to declare his reliance on Aristotle, which he will do only in *Inferno* 11, but rather to suggest the synchrony that he sees between the ethics of desire embedded in the vernacular culture of the courtly lyric and that espoused by the Greek *maestro di color che sanno.* Moreover, if we bear in mind that the mean between avarice and prodigality is located by Aristotle in the virtue of liberality, a virtue of enormous resonance for the ethos of knighthood and for Dante's own theory of what constitutes "true" nobility (whose definition is expounded by him in the canzone *Le dolci rime* and then massively elaborated in book 4 of the *Convivio*), then we can see how the Aristotelian template allows for an easy pivot on Dante's part from ethics in the moral and philosophical sphere to ethics in the social and historical sphere.

While the commentaries draw attention to the Aristotelian mean when glossing the specific verse "che con misura nullo spendio ferci" (*Inf.* 7.42), there is a critical blind spot vis-à-vis the larger manifestations of Aristotle's presence in *Inferno* 7: for instance, why are the prodigals here with the misers? Only Aristotle and an ethical system based on a spectrum in which sin is the extreme—in this case avarice is one extreme and prodigality the other—and virtue is the mean can account for the provocative and rarely discussed pairing of prodigals and misers in the fourth circle of Dante's hell. As Dante says, these souls are gripped by opposing sins, which force them constantly to move "da ogne mano a l'opposito punto" (from each side toward the opposite point; *Inf.* 7.32); they are divided by sins that are contrary to each other: "colpa contraria li dispaia" (contrary sin divides them; *Inf.* 7.45). From the moment that we are shown two groups of opposed sinners in the fourth circle, prodigals as well as misers, we need to be aware that we are not operating in a univocally Christian ethical framework. We should already be able to infer, long before reaching *Inferno* 11, that these first circles of hell are not simply governed, as their order might have induced us to believe, by the system of the seven capital vices, for that system does not include prodigality.

11 *Inferno*, ed. U. Bosco and G. Reggio (Florence, 1979), 109.

We are in a hybrid moral universe, therefore, and more work needs to be done on the implications and expressions of this hybridity. For instance, Aristotle claims that avarice is a greater evil than prodigality, and Dante places the misers on the left-hand side, thus following Aristotle, but at the same time he gives a peculiarly Christian twist to his treatment, pointing out the tonsured heads of his misers, and asking "se tutti fuor cherci" (if all were clerics; *Inf.* 7.38). Virgil's reply is a marvel of condensed cultural *contaminatio* in its juxtaposition of the highest ranks of the Catholic hierarchy with the Aristotelian idea of excess (embedded in the word "soperchio"): "Questi fur cherci, che non han coperchio / piloso al capo, e papi e cardinali, / in cui usa avarizia il suo soperchio" (These were clerics, who do not have a hairy cover to their heads, and popes and cardinals, in whom avarice plies its excess; *Inf.* 7.46–48).

Dante's hybridity continues to be visible in purgatory. Given that the seven terraces of purgatory are governed by the Christian system of the seven capital vices, the classical/Christian contamination that is Dante's unique hallmark as an author in the visionary tradition seems at first to have disappeared, but it has not: the treatment of the fifth terrace is problematic, precisely because of the renewed coupling of avarice with its Aristotelian counterpart, prodigality. Why is an Aristotelian formulation of this particular sin so important to Dante that he reiterates it in purgatory? The answer lies, *in malo*, in the importance of *concupiscentia* for Dante's political thought and, *in bono*, in the importance of liberality—the Aristotelian mean between avarice and prodigality—for aspects of Dante's culture as disparate as *cortesia* and Franciscanism. The language used by Stazio regarding vices that are related to each other as opposites, "per dritta opposizione," echoes "a l'opposito punto" and "contraria colpa" used for avarice and prodigality in *Inferno* 7, and inserts into *Purgatorio* the Aristotelian ethical scheme of opposing vices that flank a virtuous mean: "E sappie che la colpa che rimbecca / per dritta opposizione alcun peccato, / con esso insieme qui suo verde secca" (And know that the fault that counters any sin as its opposite with it here finds its sap dried out; *Purg.* 22.49–51). It is as though Stazio were saying that the Aristotelian doctrine of the mean continues to inform Dante's thinking, even when it is no longer as visible as it was in hell.

And maybe one reason that Aristotle's doctrine can continue to inform Dante's thinking in the realm of the seven capital vices is that it informed the thinking of Occitan and Italian poets who did not know the *Nicomachean Ethics* but who knew the idea of *mezura*; in other words, it informed the courtly culture from which Dante drank in great gulps as a young poet. Stazio, in describing his prodigality, references the idea of the mean with great precision, saying that he was excessively distant from avarice, but yet he does not describe himself as afflicted by *incontenenza*. Instead, Stazio uses the word *dismisura*, beloved of Occitan and later moralists, including Dante himself in the canzone *Doglia mi reca* (a canzone that is effectively an indictment of *dismisura* and an encomium to *misura*).[12] There Dante uses it precisely in the context of avarice:

12 The only use of *misura* in Dante's lyrics is also from *Doglia mi reca*, in praise of virtue: "O cara ancella e pura, / colt'ha' nel ciel misura: / tu sola fai signore, e questo prova / che tu sè possession che

"Come con dismisura si rauna, / così con dismisura si ristrigne" (Just as they gather immoderately, so they hoard immoderately; *Doglia mi reca*, 85–86).[13] Stazio sends us back not to the Aristotelian language of *Inferno* 11 but to the Occitan-inflected language of *Inferno* 7: "Or sappi ch'avarizia fu partita / troppo da me, e questa dismisura / migliaia di lunari hanno punita" (Know now that avarice was much too far removed from me, and this lack of *misura* has been punished by thousands of lunar months; *Purg.* 22.34–36).[14]

Moreover, all the sins labeled forms of *incontenenza* in hell still reverberate to the idea of incontinence in purgatory. Anger is formulated according to the doctrine of the mean, in other words, according to the idea of a righteous and a nonrighteous wrath, in Giudice Nin's "dritto zelo / che misuratamente in core avvampa" (righteous anger that burns with *misura* in the heart; *Purg.* 8.83–84) and again in the beatitude that marks the departure from the terrace of wrath: "*Beati / pacifici*, che son sanz' ira mala!" (*Beati pacifici*, who are without sinful wrath; *Purg.* 17.68–69). As with *Inferno* 7's "Mal dar e mal tener lo mondo pulcro / ha tolto lor" (Sinful giving and sinful holding have taken the beautiful world from them; *Inf.* 7.58–59), where "mal dar" and "mal tener" refer to the Aristotelian extremes and invoke an implicit and contrasting "buon dar" and "buon tener," "ira mala" rewrites the beatitude to align with the idea of sinful wrath versus righteous wrath, as previously encountered in Giudice Nin's "dritto zelo." The vernacular formulation of incontinence may be found, too, on the terrace of gluttony, where the gluttonous are blamed for having "pursued their appetite beyond *misura*" (per seguitar la gola oltra misura; *Purg.* 23.65). Finally, Dante's purgatorial treatment of lust also lends itself to an Aristotelian template, in the reclassification of same-sex love so that it is no longer a form of violence against nature but rather a passion susceptible to incontinence, just like heterosexuality, and in the articulation of a spectrum with respect to chastity that puts marriage at the mean, with the extremes held by absolute chastity on one end and bestial excess on the other.[15] We could add that the exempla in *Purgatorio*, which represent not just the sin being punished but the virtue that is its opposite, lead us to think ethically in terms of extremes and means—in an Aristotelian way.

---

sempre giova" (O precious and pure handmaid, it was in heaven that you found your standard: you alone confer lordship, and this proves you to be a possession that can never fail; *Doglia mi reca*, 39–42).

13 Dante's lyric poems are cited in the one-volume edition with commentary of D. De Robertis, *Rime* (Florence, 2005). Translations of Dante's poems are those of K. Foster and P. Boyde, *Dante's Lyric Poetry*, 2 vols. (Oxford, 1967).

14 The only other presence of *dismisura* in the *Commedia* also belongs to the context of "wealth management": "La gente nuova e i sùbiti guadagni / orgoglio e dismisura han generata, / Fiorenza, in te, sì che tu già ten piagni" (The new folk and their sudden gains have generated in you, Florence, such arrogance and *dismisura* that you already weep of it; *Inf.* 16.73–75).

15 On the spectrum with marriage as the mean, see T. Barolini, "'Only Historicize': History, Material Culture (Food, Clothes, Books) and the Future of Dante Studies," *Dante Studies* 127 (2009): 37–54, esp. 51–53; on Dante and sexuality more broadly, see eadem, "Dante's Sympathy for the Other, or the Non-Stereotyping Imagination: Sexual and Racialized Others in the *Commedia*," *Critica del Testo* 14, no. 1 (2011): 177–204.

We are observing Dante's early humanism, his work of cultural commingling. This work causes fascinating slippages, like the Aristotelian coupling of *ira* and *accedia* in hell followed by their Christian uncoupling in purgatory: in hell righteous anger is the mean flanked by the extremes of the pullulating *tristi* and the rabid *iracondi* (*Inferno* 8); these two extremes disaggregate in purgatory to become two of the seven vices, *ira* and *acedia*. The inverse occurs in the case of lust: purgatory combines on the terrace of lust both the normative and same-sex excess desire that had been deeply sundered in hell (*Inferno* 5 for the lustful and *Inferno* 15 for sodomy, viewed not as a form of excess desire but as violence against nature). We are witnessing Dante weave in and out of different cultural value systems. This work is exemplified by the bricolage of the *bufera*, with its overlapping lyric/courtly, biblical, Augustinian, and Aristotelian resonances. An intellectual who is proud of his ability to get his understanding of *contenenza* directly from Aristotle (and from Aristotle in Latin, without the mediation of a bad translator, as he calls Taddeo Alderotti in the *Convivio*), Dante's use of the terms *misura* and *dismisura* in the *Commedia,* in effect, reconnect vernacular courtly poets to the *ur*-source of their ethics, an Aristotle they did not know.

The Aristotelian *Mezzo* Translated and Cited in a Lyric Poem: *Le dolci rime*

The work of mixing the lyric tradition with Aristotle begins very early for Dante. A sonnet to Dante da Maiano from the early 1280s, *Savere e cortesia*, already conjoins courtly values—*cortesia*—to *savere*, and the *savere* in question is Aristotelian scholasticism, as we see from the verse "vertute naturale od accidente" (inborn or accidental virtue; 10). Of the "sphere that turns most widely" in the incipit of the sonnet *Oltra la spera che più larga gira* (a sonnet that exists in a redaction that predates the *Vita Nuova*), De Robertis writes: "È questa la prima definizione 'fisica,' in poesia, del Paradiso" (This is the first "physical" description, in poetry, of paradise).[16] In the *Vita Nuova*'s prose gloss to this sonnet, Dante cites Aristotle's *Metaphysics*, writing "e ciò dice lo Filosofo nel secondo de la Metafisica" (and this is what the Philosopher says in the second book of the *Metaphysics*; *VN* XLI.6 [30.6]).[17]

Most important for the development we are tracing is the canzone *Le dolci rime*, where Dante does something that I believe is unprecendented: he cites—indeed translates—the *Nicomachean Ethics* in a lyric poem. Prior to Dante, Guittone d'Arezzo names Aristotle in his poetry, in this respect, as in so many others, showing himself to be in the cultural vanguard; we cannot discount the importance of Guittone's contribution in a discussion of the vernacular roots of humanism. In the canzone *Vergogna ho,*

16 The quote is from the commentary of Domenico De Robertis to his edition of the *Vita Nuova* (Milan, 1980), 245. In citing the *Vita Nuova,* I use the traditional (Barbian) chapter divisions adopted by De Robertis; these are in Roman numerals and are followed by Gorni's chapter divisions in Arabic numerals in parentheses. See *Vita Nova*, ed. G. Gorni (Turin, 1996).

17 This is the second reference to the Philosopher in the pages of the *libello*; the first is at *Vita Nuova* XXV.2 (16.2).

lasso, ed ho me stesso ad ira,[18] Guittone acknowledges the high ethical standards of pagan philosophers, citing the *onestas* that will eventually be the currency of Dante's limbo ("onesta vita / fu lor gaudio e lor vita"):

> *Già filosofi, Dio non conoscendo,*
> *né poi morte sperando guiderdone,*
> *ischifar vizi aver tutta stagione,*
> *seguendo sì vertù, ch'onesta vita*
> *fu lor gaudio e lor vita*. (*Vergogna ho, lasso*, 43–47)

> The philosophers of old, who did not know God, nor hoped for any reward from death, had such contempt for vice at all times, and so followed virtue, for a righteous life was their delight and their commitment.

In the canzone *Degno è che che dice omo el defenda*, Guittone argues that virtue is found not just in fellow Christians but also "in others" (in altroi), and offers as examples of the virtuous others the "filosofi orrati" (honored philosophers) of old, who did not pursue enjoyment of the senses but life of the intellect:

> *E se dicem, Dio ciò fece nei soi,*
> *troviall'anche in altroi,*
> *in filosofi orrati e magni manti;*
> *ch'è ben razional seguir ragione*
> *e non sensi gauder, ma intelletto*. (*Degno è*, 46–50)

> And if we say, God made it so in his followers, we find it also in others, in honored philosophers and in many great men; for it is indeed reasonable to follow reason and not to pursue enjoyment for the senses, but for the intellect.

Guittone goes on to cite "'l saggio Aristotel" on what makes man happy: "segondo che 'l saggio Aristotel dice / e mostra omo felice / vertù ovrando" (according to what the sage Aristotle says when he shows that man is happy in the operation of virtue; *Degno è*, 54–56). His Aristotelian definition of happiness will be echoed by Dante in *Le dolci rime*: "vertute, dico, che fa l'uom felice / in sua operazione" (meaning by virtue that which makes a man happy in his actions; *Le dolci rime*, 83–84). *Misura* is important to

18 This canzone deploys, in discussing vice and virtue, the *servo/signore* metaphor that Dante adopts in *Doglia mi reca*, and also mentions the need to keep reason "on top" in language very similar to *Inferno* 5.39 ("sommette" and "sotto ragione"): "Come poi donque lo minore e 'l maggio / sommette a vizio corpo ed alma e core? / Ed è servaggio alcun, lasso, peggiore, / od è mai segnoria perfetta alcona, / che sua propia persona / tenere l'omo ben sotto ragione?" (How therefore can a lesser or a greater man submit to vice his body, soul, and heart? And is there a worse servitude, alas, or is there a more perfect lordship, than for a man to keep his body well under the control of reason?; *Vergogna ho, lasso*, 25–30). Guittone d'Arezzo is cited from *Le Rime di Guittone d'Arezzo*, ed. F. Egidi (Bari, 1940).

Guittone, as well, his teaching epitomized by these verses: "Donque misura ci convene avere / in tutte cose ch'ave l'omo a fare, / ché tuttor noce fare oltra misura" (Therefore we should have *misura* in all the things that we do, since it is always harmful to act beyond *misura*; *Qual omo si diletta in troppo dire*, 9–11).[19]

While I do not believe that Guittone reaches Dante's understanding of *misura* as the vernacular equivalent to Aristotle's doctrine of the mean, he certainly offers a new benchmark: he writes lyric poetry that, on the one hand, synthesizes Aristotle's description of the virtuous life and, on the other, considers *misura* a key component of such a life, a privileged synonym of *ragione* and *senno*.[20] Guittone links these two ethical projects—not actively as Dante does, but rather by featuring both in his verse.

The fifth stanza of *Le dolci rime* begins with Aristotle's definition of happiness, already seen in Guittone's *Degno è*, and moves on to a translation of the *Ethics*, a work that is explicitly named in the poem ("secondo che l'Etica dice"):

> *Dico ch'ogni vertù principalmente*
> *vien da una radice,*
> *vertute, dico, che fa l'uom felice*
> *in sua operazione.*
> *Quest'è, secondo che l'Etica dice,*
> *un abito eligente*
> *lo qual dimora in mezzo solamente,*
> *e tai parole pone.* (*Le dolci rime*, 81–88)

> I affirm that every virtue stems ultimately from one root, meaning by virtue that which makes a man happy in his actions. This is, as the Ethics states, a "habit of choosing which keeps steadily to the mean"—those are the very words. (trans. Foster and Boyde)

De Robertis points out the significance of Dante's expression "e tai parole pone"; Dante is saying that these are the very words of the Aristotelian text. He glosses as follows: "Traduce letteralmente (onde 'e tai parole pone,' ossia: queste testuali parole) 'Est . . . habitus electivus in medietate existens'" (He translates literally [hence "e tai parole pone," or rather: these literal words] "Est . . . habitus electivus in medietate existens").[21]

19 Interestingly, this sonnet begins by indicting excess speech. Excess spending is indicted in the sonnet on gluttony, one of the cycle of sonnets on the vices: "ispendi oltra misura" (*Vizio di gola*, 4). We are reminded of Dante's *tenzone* with Forese Donati, in which gluttony is connected to poverty and thievery, and of the gluttonous excess of the *brigata spendereccia* of *Inferno* 29.

20 For example: "e perché non misura hai, né ragione" from *O tu, de nome Amor, guerra de fatto*, 27; and "In ogni cosa vol senno e misura" (this is the incipit of the sonnet).

21 See De Robertis commentary (above, n. 13), 69. Barbi-Pernicone gloss as follows: "Dante sottolinea che la definizione data nei versi precedenti risponde esattamente al testo dell'*Etica*" (Dante underlines that the definition given in the preceding verses corresponds exactly to the text of the *Ethics*); see *Rime della maturità e dell'esilio*, ed. M. Barbi and V. Pernicone (Florence, 1969), 427.

Le dolci rime was written in the mid-1290s.[22] De Robertis places the canzone "probabilmente non a gran distanza della *Vita Nova*" (probably not at great distance from the *Vita Nuova*; 53). Years later, Dante again wrote the title "Etica" into his poetry, in the previously cited passage in *Inferno* 11 in which Virgil directs Dante to his *Ethics*: "Non ti rimembra di quelle parole / con le quai la tua Etica pertratta" (Don't you remember those words with which your *Ethics* treats; *Inf.* 11.79–80). These verses feature a similar nod to the "parole" of the original Aristotelian text: "quelle parole / con le quai la tua Etica pertratta," recalls "e tai parole pone" from *Le dolci rime*. In the *Inferno*, the directive to remember Aristotle's "parole" is shortly followed by an even more precisely material reference to the physical "carte" in which Dante read the *Physics*: "se tu ben la tua Fisica note, / tu troverai, non dopo molte carte" (if you study well in your *Physics*, you will find, after not too many pages; *Inf.* 11.101–2). Dante first began to construct himself as an addressee worthy of the phrases "la tua Etica" and "la tua Fisica" in *Le dolci rime*, where he tackles the topic of true nobility and the virtues that derive from it in Aristotelian terms that explicitly include the doctrine of the mean, the "mezzo": "un abito eligente / lo qual dimora in mezzo solamente" (a habit of choosing which keeps steadily to the mean; *Le dolci rime*, 87–88).

Le dolci rime is the only one of Dante's canzoni to be philosophical in the technical sense, adopting the language and syllogistic method of the scholastic *quaestio* to a stanza and rhyme scheme of Guittonian complexity and achieving a unique result, both as a long and difficult text of 146 verses and at the level of its reception: *Le dolci rime* is unique among Dante's canzoni in occasioning a Latin commentary, the 1355 commentary of the jurist Bartolo da Sassoferrato.[23] At this point of our discussion, we must acknowledge the other contemporary philosophical canzone to receive a Latin commentary, namely, Cavalcanti's *Donna me prega*, the technical diction and rigorous structure of which may have inspired *Le dolci rime*. *Donna me prega* is still more famous than *Le dolci rime*, partly because of its dark allure as the theoretical exposition of Guido's turn from light and love, and partly because Dante subsequently placed his canzone in the *Convivio*, where he submerged it in a vast ocean of prose that has drawn attention not to the poem it purportedly glosses but away from it.

Donna me prega contains lots of Aristotle, although not an ostentatious citation of the "Etica" by name. Among his nods to the vernacular tradition, Cavalcanti uses the by this time classic term *misura*, defining love as excess, "oltra misura": "L'essere è quando—lo voler è tanto / ch'oltra misura—di natura—torna" (Love's mode of being

22 De Robertis notes in his commentary: "siamo ancora nell'àmbito delle 'nòve rime'; e l'inclusa polemica antiimperiale è della stagione communale di Dante" (we are still in the environment of the "nòve rime"; and the anti-imperial polemic included in the canzone dates from the period of Dante's life in the Florentine commune; p. 52).

23 See De Robertis's commentary: "La canzone, in grazia dell'argomento, ha avuto il privilegio dell'abbastanza precoce (1355), e unico, commento latino del famoso giurista Bartolo da Sassoferrato" (Thanks to its subject matter, the canzone had the privilege of the precocious [1355] and unique Latin commentary of the famous jurist Bartolo da Sassoferrato; p. 54).

is such that desire goes beyond the *misura* of nature; *Donna me prega*, 43–44).[24] Clearly there is no doctrine of temperance, whether Aristotelian or vernacular, preached in *Donna me prega*, which famously holds that love pertains to the senses rather than the intellect. Thus, in *Donna me prega* we find the common phrase "oltra misura" deployed in an uncommon way: rather than apply "oltra misura" to the reckless behavior of a particular lover, as had been done by his Occitan and Italian predecessors, Cavalcanti considers *oltra misura* to be the essence of love itself. He thus breaks with the old courtly ethics that, by exhorting the lover to the practice of *misura*, indicates a belief in the redeeming power of intellect and in the possibility of controlling passion with reason. If love is *oltra misura* in its essence, then human efforts to control it are in vain.

In the first decade of the fourteenth century, most likely in the second half of the decade, circa 1306–8, Dante wrote the unfinished philosophical treatise *Convivio*, and he placed *Le dolci rime* at the opening of its fourth book, an elaborate and magnificently digressive investigation of the core questions posed by the canzone (in imitation of the questions in *Donna me prega*):[25] "che cosa è gentilezza, e da che vene, / e dirò i segni che 'l gentil uom tene" (I will say what it is, whence it comes, and the distinctive features that a noble person possesses; *Le dolci rime*, 79–80). Undoubtedly, the prose treatise allows Dante to demonstrate a much greater knowledge of Aristotle than he had thus far been able to demonstrate in lyric form.[26] We should not forget, however, that it is in the substantially earlier canzone that Dante first writes philosophy and first really engages Aristotle. Indeed, the germ for the idea of the *Convivio*—a text devoted to the popularizing of philosophy, much of it Aristotelian—comes from the canzone *Le dolci rime*, in which Dante first popularized Aristotelian philosophy by incorporating it in a vernacular lyric poem.

From *Le dolci rime* to *Poscia ch'Amor*, from Philosophy to Social History

Written a decade or so earlier than the treatise, in the mid-1290s, circa 1294–96, *Le dolci rime* belongs to the period of great ferment after the composition of the *Vita Nuova*. During this time, Dante wrote poems as disparate as the love poems that chronicle a love other than Beatrice (poems that the *Convivio* claims are for Lady Philosophy), the *tenzone* with Forese Donati, and the *rime petrose*. He also wrote a moral canzone on courtly virtue, *Poscia ch'Amor*, which unpacks the definition of nobility from *Le dolci*

24 Cavalcanti is cited from the edition of D. De Robertis, *Guido Cavalcanti, Rime, con le rime di Iacopo Cavalcanti* (Turin, 1986).

25 As De Robertis notes in his commentary: "Tre questioni, sullo schema di quelle enunciate nei vv. 10–14 di *Donna me prega*" (Three questions, following the scheme of the questions pronounced in verses 10–14 of *Donna me prega*; p. 67).

26 On the other hand, even in the treatise Dante was still learning: Dante seems not to have known the *Politics* in *Convivio* 4, citing as Frederick's a definition of nobility that is in fact Aristotle's and that he will cite as Aristotle's in the *Monarchia*. A. R. Ascoli, however, thinks he is feigning not to know Aristotle's definition in *Convivio*; see A. R. Ascoli, *Dante and the Making of a Modern Author* (Cambridge, 2008), 105.

rime in ways that move us away from the realm of philosophy and toward the domain of social history. In other words, in the dynamic between *Le dolci rime,* on the one hand, and *Poscia ch'Amor,* on the other, we can see the ways in which, as I noted earlier, the Aristotelian template allows for an easy turn on Dante's part from ethics in the moral and philosophical sphere to ethics in the social and historical sphere.

Devoting three stanzas to refutation of previous faulty definitions of nobility and three stanzas to the construction of a positive definition, *Le dolci rime* follows a tight, logic-driven—indeed, syllogistic—path, leavened by occasional flashes of passion and sarcasm that do not, however, alter the logical course of the argument. By contrast, *Poscia ch'Amor* is, as Foster and Boyde note, "more rhetorical, less logical than *Le dolci rime* . . . the weapon is the rhetorical question, not the syllogism."[27] The change in linguistic and rhetorical texture reflects the move from the stoa of the philosophers to the great hall of the *palazzo*: if *Le dolci rime* is theory of nobility, *Poscia ch'Amor* is praxis, picking up on the practical aspects that are left hanging by the high theoretical discourse of *Le dolci rime.* In other words, to be clear, the questions *Poscia ch'Amor* seeks to answer include what, exactly, are the "reggimenti belli" (good manners) referred to in *Le dolci rime*, verse 24. In other words, how much should a nobleman spend, and how should he dress and speak? *Le dolci rime* posits the existence of outward signs that demonstrate inner nobility—"e dirò i segni che 'l gentil uom tene" (*Le dolci rime*, 80)—but its discussion of these "segni" remains genteel (pun intended) and abstract: a catalogue of the virtues that are appropriate to the noble man or woman at different stages of life. *Poscia ch'Amor,* instead, jumps immediately into the fray, taking us into a world of social anxiety and social one-upmanship.

Social anxiety courses through Dante's poetry from the earliest forays of his correspondence sonnets with Dante da Maiano, which are laced with aggression and barely masked rivalry. The sonnets perform a ritual testing of male *valore* in the poetic agora.[28] Susan Noakes has carefully set out the context for the social anxiety that percolates through the *tenzone* with Forese Donati, and Albert Ascoli has illuminated the process whereby Dante, in book 1 of *Convivio,* forges authority by confronting his anxiety about his reputation.[29] *Poscia ch'Amor*'s vituperation of those who throw away their wealth, feigning liberality and nobility of character when in actuality they are not liberal but prodigal, is both profoundly Aristotelian (liberality as the virtuous mean between prodigality and avarice) and brimming with social anxiety: we can feel Dante's frustration that these sham nobles can still be thought of as do-gooders by their fellow citizens (similarly, in *Inferno* 6, the great Florentines known for good works turn out to be "among the darkest souls"; 85).[30]

27 See Foster and Boyde, *Dante's Lyric Poetry* (above, n. 13), 228–29.

28 See my commentary to the sonnets exchanged between Dante Alighieri and Dante da Maiano in *Rime giovanili e della "Vita Nuova,"* ed. T. Barolini, with notes by M. Gragnolati (Milan, 2009).

29 S. Noakes, "Virility, Nobility, and Banking: The Crossing of Discourses in the *Tenzone* with Forese," in *Dante for the New Millennium*, ed. T. Barolini and H. W. Storey (New York, 2003), 241–58; A. R. Ascoli, *Dante and the Making of a Modern Author*, chap. 2.

30 There is a deep connection between *Poscia ch'Amor* and *Inferno* 6: in *Poscia ch'Amor* Dante did a trial run for the indictment of Florentine high society that he later crystallizes in *Inferno* 6's lapidary

The *Inferno*'s meditations on unethical wealth management indicate the continuing depth of Dante's frustration: the prodigals who do not spend their wealth appropriately, in *Inferno* 7; the wastrels who dissipate their wealth, most likely on gaming and whoring, in *Inferno* 13; the "gente nuova" whose sudden wealth is responsible for Florentine "orgoglio e dismisura," in *Inferno* 16.73–74; and the sarcastic reference to the "temperate spese" (*Inf.* 29.126) of the Sienese gilded youth known as the *brigata spendereccia,* in *Inferno* 29.[31]

While no mechanism may exist that can fully allay Dante's frustration at watching the non-noble *vili* of his city manage to pass themselves off as *gentili* by virtue of their wealth, in *Poscia ch'Amor* he turns to the one mechanism that he has at hand, namely, Aristotle's doctrine of the mean. Not in the clean crisp language of *Le dolci rime*, but in a convoluted expression of his disgust, Dante describes those who throw away their material possessions in the belief that they will automatically be enrolled among the virtuous as a result: "Sono che per gittar via loro avere / credon potere / capere—là dove li boni stanno / che dopo morte fanno / riparo nella mente / a quei cotanti c'hanno conoscenza" (There are those who think that to dissipate their wealth is the way to win a place with the worthy who after death continue to dwell in the minds of such as are wise; *Poscia ch'Amor*, 20–25). Such people may as well keep their money: "Ma lor messione a' bon' non può piacere, / perché tenere / savere—fôra" (But their extravagance cannot meet with good men's approval; so that they would be wiser to keep their cash; *Poscia ch'Amor*, 26–28). In other words, the Aristotelian mean cannot be achieved by cheating: liberality is not the same as prodigality. To be liberal rather than prodigal requires that real virtue be deployed in the giving, not mere reckless abandon.

In the language of *Poscia ch'Amor* on dissipation ("gittar via loro avere"), language that finds its way into the "Mal dar e mal tener" of *Inferno* 7, we see the Aristotelian doctrine of the mean, a paradigm that held a constant place in Dante's thinking from at least the time of *Le dolci rime* in the mid-1290s. After *Poscia ch'Amor*, the paradigm was picked up and revernacularized in the post-exilic canzone *Doglia mi reca,* which resonates with the lyric *misura/dismisura* rather than the Aristotelian *mezzo* of *Le dolci rime*: "Come con dismisura si rauna, / così con dismisura si ristrigne" (*Doglia mi reca*, 85–86). The language of *Doglia mi reca* is subsequently picked up and echoed in the prose of *Convivio* 4.

In 1293, the Florentine *Ordinamenti di Giustizia* were passed, which prohibited certain magnate families of great wealth and power, including the Cavalcanti and Donati, from participation in Florentine government. Dante's writings from this period, the *tenzone* with Forese, for instance, show how far from immune he was from worry about his own lower status as a scion of a poor family of minor nobility, a worry that must

"Giusti son due, e non vi sono intesi" (Two men are just, and are not understood there; *Inf.* 6.73). Indeed, *Poscia ch'Amor* concludes with a similarly terse indictment: "Color che vivon fanno tutti contra" (The present generation, without exception, does just the reverse).

31 On the issues around wealth management and masculinity, see my "Sociology of the *Brigata*: Gendered Groups in Dante, Forese, Folgore, Boccaccio—From 'Guido, i' vorrei' to Griselda," *Italian Studies* 67, no. 1 (2012): 4–22.

have been aggravated by his sense of overwhelming intellectual superiority and authentic friendship with men who belonged to the magnate class.[32] I believe that the anxiety expressed by the *tenzone* with Forese is contemporaneously expressed, albeit in very different form, by *Le dolci rime*, which is a principled but also anxiety-driven resistance to the definition of nobility as "antica possession d'avere / con reggimenti belli" (long-standing possession of wealth together with pleasing manners; *Le dolci rime*, 23–24). In *Le dolci rime,* Dante deconstructs "antica possession d'avere"; in *Poscia ch'Amor* he tackles "con reggimenti belli": in both canzoni he uses Aristotelian ethics as a bulwark against the social posturing of men with requisite lineage and wealth but inferior virtue, and as a way to leverage the social position of a man like himself—a superior man with insufficient wealth if not lineage.

The doctrine whereby virtue is "a 'habit of choosing which keeps steadily to the mean'"—"un abito eligente / lo qual dimora in mezzo solamente" (*Le dolci rime*, 86–87)—like the doctrine of *misura* that precedes it, was never just about theory: as we can see in the Occitan context, as well, it was always connected to the behavior of real people wielding real power, and hence to issues of social status and positioning. Within the Florentine context, the *Ordinamenti di Giustizia* levied real consequences on real families of power and wealth for their nonvirtuous behavior. Dante was consumed with his social standing, as the *tenzone* with Forese shows us; that he aimed to excel in all things cultural goes without saying. The philosophical canzone *Le dolci rime* combines both obsessions. Dante addresses the question of his precarious social standing directly, by destroying the conventional definition of nobility, replacing it with the Aristotelian definition of virtue and then positing that nobility exists wherever virtue is present: "È gentilezza dovunqu'è vertute" (Nobility is wherever virtue is; *Le dolci rime*, 101). He addresses it indirectly, that is culturally, by showing that he can bring Aristotle into the prestigious lyric tradition better than Guittone.

But can Dante bring Aristotle into the lyric tradition better than Cavalcanti, the dear friend who wrote the Aristotelian, perhaps even Averroist, *Donna me prega* and who, as a magnate, needed no social empowering? The many purposes of *Le dolci rime* come more clearly into focus, its work of social self-promotion in tandem with its authentic concern for the larger social good, when we recall that sometime in this same period, perhaps to shake Dante from depression after the death of Beatrice, Cavalcanti sent his friend the following sonnet:

I' vegno 'l giorno a·tte 'nfinite volte
e trovoti pensar troppo vilmente:
molto mi dol della gentil tua mente
e d'assai tue vertù che·tti son tolte.
Solevanti spiacer persone molte,

32 It is worth noting that both the Cavalcanti and Donati lineages are classified by Carol Lansing in *The Florentine Magnates* (Princeton, 1991) as "older houses of the traditional aristocracy" (183).

tuttor fuggivi la noiosa gente;
di me parlavi sì coralemente
che·ttutte le tue rime avìe ricolte.
Or non ardisco, per la vil tua vita,
far mostramento che·ttu' dir mi piaccia,
né 'n guisa vegno a·tte che·ttu mi veggi.
Se 'l presente sonetto spesso leggi,
lo spirito noioso che·tti caccia
si partirà dall'anima invilita.

I visit you a thousand times a day
and find you steeped too much in shameful thoughts.
It pains me deeply that your noble mind
and many virtues have been stripped away.
You once would treat crowds with contempt
and always fled from those who are mundane;
of me you used to speak so cordially
that I collected every poem you sent.
I now dare not, since you've demeaned yourself,
acknowledge that I like your poetry,
nor will you see me if I visit you.
If you reread this sonnet several times,
the loathsome spirit persecuting you
will be dispelled from your degraded soul.[33]

Even if considered a salutary intervention, the fact remains that the magnate Cavalcanti indicts his friend for the slide of his "gentil tua mente" into "la vil tua vita," tarring him repeatedly with a word, *vile*, which in *Convivio* is defined as the opposite of *nobile.* However many times a day Guido drops in on Dante, he finds him thinking "troppo vilmente" (2); he used to collect his friend's poetry, but now does not dare, on account of Dante's base life, "per la vil tua vita" (9), to make a show of liking Dante's verse. He concludes by saying that Dante's soul has become "invilita"—made *vile.*

For Dante, whose social position was less secure than Cavalcanti's, and whose status was profoundly enmeshed with his sense of his virtue, this violent demotion, whereby his virtues are literally stripped away from him—"assai tue vertù che·tti son tolte" (4)— cannot have been easy to countenance. Perhaps a need to reclaim his personal *gentilezza* after his friend's indictment feeds into the passion that pulses through the reasoned syllogisms of *Le dolci rime*. If so, the private motivation in no way limits the reach of a canzone that uses Aristotelian ethics as a lever of social change.

33 The translation is Richard Lansing's, composed for *Dante's Lyric Poetry: Poems of Youth and of the "Vita Nuova,"* commentary by T. Barolini with a new verse translation by R. Lansing (Toronto, 2014).

Pseudo-Dionysius and the Representation of Light in Dante's *Paradiso*

DIEGO SBACCHI

IN MY STUDY I WILL TRY TO ANALYZE the presence of light[1] in Dante's *Paradiso*,[2] arguing that the influence of Pseudo-Dionysius is crucial to understanding this element, which is widespread throughout the final stretch of Dante's journey in the otherworld. The relevant aspects on which I will focus include the very presence of light, the components of the *Paradiso* that become light, the progression of illumination, the process of simplification and union due to light, the unity of light, and the "separate union" produced by light. I will also argue that Dante's *Paradiso* shares some features with Byzantine icons, as both Dante's final vision and these paintings are inspired and molded by the same source, that is, Pseudo-Dionysius.

The possible sources for Dante's *Commedia* treat light in different ways. Reading the *Aeneid*, we see that Elysium is just a *locus amoenus* blessed by a never-ending spring: light is present, but it is part of a human landscape that reminds us of an earthly paradise (6.637–41).[3] The Bible has no detailed description of God's abode, and it mentions only the brightness of the blessed souls, who will be dressed in white and as radiant

1 Light is understood in each of its possible manifestations: plain light or fire, sun, rays of light, shining objects, and so on. On this topic, see also G. Di Pino, *La figurazione della luce nella Divina Commedia* (Messina, 1962); E. Guidubaldi, *Dante Europeo*, vols. 1–3 (Florence, 1965–68); D. Ottaviani, *La philosophie de la lumière chez Dante: Du Convivio à la Divine comédie* (Paris, 2004); S. Longuet, *Couleurs, foudre et lumière chez Dante* (Paris, 2009).

2 Quotations from the *Commedia* are from Dante Alighieri, *La Commedia secondo l'antica vulgata*, ed. G. Petrocchi, 4 vols. (Milan, 1966–67). The English translation used is Dante Alighieri, *Paradiso*, trans. R. Hollander and J. Hollander (New York, 2007).

3 Virgil, *Eclogues, Georgics, Aeneid 1–6*, with an English translation by H. Rushton Fairclough and revised by G. P. Goold (Cambridge, MA, 1999): "His demum exactis, perfecto munere divae, / devenere locos laetos et amoena virecta / Fortunatorum Nemorum sedesque beatas. / Largior hic campos aether et lumine vestit / purpureo, solemque suum, sua siderea norunt." (This at length performed and the task of the goddess fulfilled, they came to a land of joy, the pleasant lawns and happy seats of the Blissful Groves. Here an ampler ether clothes the meads with roseate light, and they know their own sun, and stars of their own.)

as the stars or the sun. This holds true for the Old and New Testaments: the prophet Daniel, speaking of the end of the world, says that "the wise shall shine brightly like the splendor of the firmament, and those who lead the many to justice shall be like the stars forever" (Dan. 12:3).[4] According to the evangelist Matthew, Jesus preaches that after the Judgment, "the righteous will shine like the sun in the kingdom of their Father" (Matt. 13:43).[5] John, in the Apocalypse, predicts that "night will be no more, nor they will need light from lamp or sun, for the Lord God shall give them light, and they shall reign forever and ever" (Apoc. 22:5).[6] These representations are quite predictable if we consider that God is often represented as light and, therefore, those close to him reflect his brightness.[7] To some extent, this is what we find in Dante's poem, but he takes a number of independent thoughts and organizes them into a philosophically systematic whole.

In visions derived from the Scriptures or popular belief, light is not always an essential element; sometimes, it is not even present. From those of late antiquity and medieval times, I have selected visions that represent paradise as an ascent through the heavens, as in Dante's work.[8] There is no light in the *Apocalypse of Baruch* (also known as *III Baruch*), the vision of Furseus recounted by Bede in the *Historia ecclesiastica gentis anglorum*, or the *Vision of the Monk Alberic*. Light is mentioned in the *Pharsalia*,[9] the *Reichenau Apocryphon*[10] (also known as *Apocalypse of the Seven Heavens*), the *Revelation of Moses*,[11] the *Ascensio Isaiae*,[12] and the *Visio beati Esdrae*.[13] In addition, the vision of Salvius, in the seventh book of Gregory of Tours's *Historia Francorum*, makes it clear that there is also

4 "Qui autem docti fuerint, fulgebunt quasi splendor firmamenti; et qui, ad iustitiam erudierint multos, quasi stellae in perpetuas aeternitates." The Bible is quoted from *Nova Vulgata Bibliorum Sacrorum editio* (Vatican City, 1986).

5 "Iusti fulgebunt sicut sol in regno Patris eorum."

6 "Nox ultra non erit, et non egent lumine lucernae neque lumine solis, quoniam Dominus Deus illuminabit super illos, et regnabunt in saecula seculorum."

7 See, e.g., the book of Exodus (Exod. 19:18), the Gospel of John (John 1:4–9 or 8:12), or the Letter of James (James 1:17).

8 Overviews of these visions are in E. Gardiner, *Visions of Heaven and Hell before Dante* (New York, 1989); eadem, *Medieval Visions of Heaven and Hell: A Sourcebook* (New York, 1993); and A. Morgan, *Dante and the Medieval Other World* (Cambridge, 1990).

9 Lucan, *The Civil War*, trans. J. D. Duff (Cambridge, MA, 1969): "Illic postquam se lumine vero / implevit" (9.11–12) (When he had steeped himself in the true light of that region).

10 R. Bauckham, "*The Apocalypse of the Seven Heavens*," *Apocrypha* 4 (1993): 141–75. "Ubi dominus habitat super lapidem preciosum, unde venit lux et ignis de lapide" (p. 153) (where God lives on a precious stone from which stone light and fire come).

11 M. Gaster, "Hebrew Visions of Hell and Paradise," *Journal of the Royal Asiatic Society* 25, no. 3 (1893): 571–611. Here, Moses's body is changed from flesh to fire, and the angels he meets in every heaven have different colors of fire.

12 C. Leonardi, "Il testo dell'*Ascensio Isaiae* nel Vat. Lat. 5750," *Cristianesimo nella storia* 1 (1980): 59–74. "Uidi angelus gloriosum . . . sed claritatem magnam et sanctam habentem" (p. 73) (I saw a glorious angel . . . but having a great and holy brightness).

13 O. O. Wahl, *Apocalypsis Esdrae, Apocalypsis Sedrach, Visio Beati Esdrae* (Leiden, 1977): "Ibi lux et gaudium et laetitia et salutatio; . . . posuerunt me in nubem flammeam" (59–60) (There were light, joy, happiness and saluting; . . . they put me in a burning cloud).

a progressive increase in brightness,[14] and in the case of the *Vision of a Woman* recorded by Lull, bishop of Mentz,[15] as in all the others, light is mentioned but not given a key role in the narrative or in the theological questions. References to light in other visions are more than passing remarks: in Cicero's *Somnium Scipionis,* we are told that the characters of the dialogue, Scipio Aemilianus and Scipio Africanus, look at things "from a lofty place which was bathed in clear starlight"; moreover, we are taught that man "has been given a soul out of those eternal fires which you call stars and planets,"[16] and that after death, the righteous ones dwell in a place that "was the circle of light which blazed most brightly among the other fires."[17] In the *Book of the Secrets of Enoch* (also known as *II Enoch*), those who take Enoch up to heaven, the angels, the Lord's face as Enoch sees it on the tenth heaven, and the Lord's ointment are all bright; in addition, the righteous are described as being covered in shining light. In the *Vision of Adamnán,* the land of the saints, their clothing, and the mighty Lord are bright, much like in *Visio Godeschalci* and *Visio monachi de Eynsham,* where an increasing light appears to the pilgrim and his guide, along with a pleasant smell, the white garments of the blessed, and joy.[18] Light is also used very often in the *Liber de scalis.* That work describes the prophet Muhammad's

14 Gregory of Tours, *Storia dei franchi: I dieci libri delle storie,* ed. M. Oldoni (Naples, 2001): "Deinde per portam luce ista clariorem introductus sum in illud habitaculum, in quo omne pavimentum erat quasi aurum argentumque renitens, lux ineffabilis, amplitudo inenarrabilis . . . in quo superpendebat nube omne luce lucidior, in quo non sol, non luna, non astrum cerni poterat, sed super his omnibus naturali luce splendidius effulgebat" (7.1). The English translation can be found in Gregory, Bishop of Tours, *History of the Franks,* ed. E. Brehaut (New York, 1969): "Then I was taken through a door brighter than this light into that dwelling in which all the pavement was like shining gold and silver, a brightness and spaciousness beyond description . . . a cloud hung over it brighter than any light, in which no sun or moon or star could be seen, but excelling all these it gleamed more brightly than the light of nature."

15 E. Duemmler, *Epistolae merowingici et karolini aevi, Monumenta Germaniae Historica* (Berlin, 1895), *ep.* 115, p. 403: "alias claritate solis, alias lunae, alias stellarum radiis proprie communiterque fulsisse cognovit" ([She] understood that [the souls] were shining on their own and along with others, some because of the brightness of the sun, some of the moon, some of the rays of the stars).

16 A similar situation with souls coming out of stars can be found in Plutarch, *Moralia,* ed. P. H. De Lacy and B. Einarson (London and Cambridge, MA, 1959), 7:591, p. 471. In the essay known as *De genio Socratis,* we read that Timarchus, in his vision, is taught that

> in the stars that are apparently extinguished, you must understand that you see the souls that sink entirely into the body; in the stars that are lighted again, as it were, and reappear from below, you must understand that you see souls that float back from the body after death, shaking off a sort of dimness and darkness as one might shake off mud; while the stars that move about on high are the daemons of men said to "possess understanding."

This is, of course, a typically Platonic topic, as Dante himself tells us in *Par.* 4.22–24.

17 Cicero, *De re publica; De legibus,* trans. C. W. Keyes (London, 1961). The following quotations are presented according to their order in the text: "de excelso et pleno stellarum inlustri et claro quodam loco" (6.11); "animus datus est ex illis sempiternis ignibus, quae sidera et stellae vocatis" (6.15); "splendidissimo candore inter flammas circus elucens" (6.16).

18 H. Thurston, "Visio monachi de Eynsham," *AB* 22 (1903): 225–319. "Maior semper et lucis claritas et odoris suavitas et ibidem degentium candor et iocunditas arridebat" (p. 312) (An ever-increasing brightness of light and sweetness of smell and whiteness of the people dwelling there and joy were delightful).

ascent to God through eight heavens, where he meets angels and men from the Old and New Testament; all wear shining garments or crowns, or have luminous faces and hair. A progression of light is also present, and this is especially evident in the passage from one heaven to the next, as the substance of each heaven is increasingly brighter: from the iron of the first to the copper of the second, the silver of the third, and so forth. One does not find the processes of simplification and union produced by light and its quality of unity; in this vision, we do not see just one light but many lights that are unrelated to each other.

This brief overview is useful because it helps us contextualize Dante's choices for the last *cantica*. It makes the differences between his vision and the others more evident, while also clarifying that the way he treats light is also very different as it becomes the very expression of a philosophical school. Light in Dante is a pillar in the structure of his paradise, because every main character is assimilated to light, namely, the blessed souls, angels, planets (or heavens or stars), and God (or Christ or the Virgin). The poet calls these characters "candori" (white splendors), "face" (torch), "facella" (torch), "favilla" / "faville" (spark / sparks), "fiamma" / "fiamme" (flame / flames), "fiammelle" (flickering flames), "foco" (fire), "folgor" (lights), "fuochi" (flames), "gemma" / "gemme" (jewel / jewels), "incendio" / "incendi" (fire / fiery lights), "lampa" (light), "luce" / "luci" (radiance, light / lights), "lucerna" / "lucerne" (light / lights, lamps), "lume" / "lumi" (light / lights), "lumera" (radiance), "scintilla" (spark), "sol" (sun), "sole" / "soli" (sun / suns), "splendor" (splendor), "splendore" / "splendori" (splendor / splendors), and "stelle" (stars, i.e., the Scriptures). An analysis of the relevant concordances shows how consistent Dante is in his use of these terms, which gives rise to a vivid perception that we are being plunged into a sea of light.[19] We must also consider this imagery in view of the fact that light is reflected by mirrors: in a previous study, I proved that this metaphor is Neoplatonic and, in particular, Pseudo-Dionysian. "Mirror" is another way in which Dante defines the blessed, angels, planets, and God, echoing and giving poetic form to what he read in *De caelesti hierarchia* by Pseudo-Dionysius.[20] These are also vibrating and living lights, as we understand by recalling the countless times they grow brighter when pleased to answer Dante's questions and resolve his doubts, and by recalling that they emanate rays of splendor. The image of Christ as one who with his rays brightens the blessed, who, in turn, are compared to a garden nourished by his light, is very suggestive (*Par.* 23.70–72, 79–84):

Perché la faccia mia sì t'innamora,
che tu non ti rivolgi al bel giardino
che sotto i raggi di Cristo s'infiora?
. . . .

19 *Concordanza della Commedia di Dante Alighieri*, ed. L. Lovera (Turin, 1975).

20 See D. Sbacchi, *La presenza di Dionigi Areopagita nel* Paradiso *di Dante* (Florence, 2006), 93–113.

Come a raggio di sol, che puro mei
per fratta nube, già prato di fiori
vider, coverti d'ombra, li occhi miei;
vid'io così più turbe di splendori,
folgorate di sù da raggi ardenti,
sanza veder principio di folgóri.[21]

This kind of illumination applies to the blessed souls, as we read when Beatrice suggests that Dante turn around to see other blessed souls and he observes many lit by each other's rays: "Come a lei piacque, li occhi ritornai, / e vidi cento sperule che 'nsieme / più s'abbellivan con mutüi rai" (*Par.* 22.22–24).[22] Note, we do not drown in this sea of light, as if puzzled and bewildered by its amazing and changing presence. On the contrary, Dante's ascent to God is steady, and the question is, why does he not lose his way to him, given the surrounding landscape?

In the biblical tradition, God is often associated with light, and those close to him—angels and blessed souls—share his brightness. Of the latter, Dante says that they are literally wrapped in light; in *Paradiso* 8.52–54, Charles Martel tells Dante that "La mia letizia mi ti tien celato / che mi raggia dintorno e mi nasconde / quasi animal di sua seta fasciato."[23] This image may have been influenced by Martianus Capella, who describes Astronomia as having the very same appearance.[24] Finally, we have also read that Cicero, in the *Somnium Scipionis,* calls the stars "ignes" (fires). I believe that all these references are justified and useful, but they still do not explain why Dante made his choices or the framework into which we should set them for interpretation.

The key is Pseudo-Dionysius. He considers light the very essence of the presence and the action of God, who is the first light according to both Dionysius (*De caelesti hierarchia* 3.2) and Dante (*Par.* 29.136). God, then, is the first in a chain that extends to the

21 Why does my face arouse you so to love / you do not turn to see the lovely garden / now blossoming beneath the rays of Christ? . . . As, lit by the sun's rays streaming through broken clouds, / my eyes, sheltered by the shade, / once saw a field of flowers, / so now I saw a many-splendored throng / illuminated from above by blazing rays, / but could not see the source of all that brightness.

22 "I turned my eyes as she had urged and saw / one hundred little globes that made each other brighter / in the glittering reflections of one another's rays."

23 "It is my happiness that hides me from you, / as it enfolds and hides me in its shining rays, / like the creature that is sheathed in its own silk."

24 M. Capella, *Le nozze di Filologia e Mercurio*, ed. I. Ramelli (Milan, 2001), 578: "Et ecce globus quidam lucis aetheriae et concava perspicui ignis aggestio, ut apparebat intra se quandam virginem claudens, miti vertigine sensim volutus inlabitur" (8.810). W. H. Stahl, *Martianus Capella and the Seven Liberal Arts: The Marriage of Philology and Mercury* (New York, 1977): "Before their eyes a vision appeared, a hollow ball of heavenly light, filled with transparent fire, gently rotating, and enclosing a maiden within" (2:317). The importance of the body in the otherworld along with its transformations, alterations, and improvement is the topic of M. Gragnolati, *Experiencing the Afterlife: Soul and Body in Dante and Medieval Culture* (Notre Dame, IN, 2005), esp. 82–87.

bottom of the universe—a chain that Dante climbs. What the Greek thinker writes in *De caelesti hierarchia* 1.1–2 is significant:

> Every good endowment and every perfect gift is from above, coming down from the Father of lights. But there is something more. Inspired by the Father, each procession of the Light spreads itself generously toward us, and, in its power to unify, it stirs us by lifting us up. It returns us back to the oneness and deifying simplicity of the Father who gathers us in. For, as the sacred Word says, "from him and to him are all things." Let us, then, call upon Jesus, the Light of the Father, the "true light enlightening every man coming into the world," "through whom we have obtained access" to the Father, the light which is the source of all light. To the best of our abilities, we should raise our eyes to the paternally transmitted enlightenment coming from sacred scripture and, as far as we can, we should behold the intelligent hierarchies of heaven and we should do so in accordance with what scripture has revealed to us in symbolic and uplifting fashion. We must lift up the immaterial and steady eyes of our minds to that outpouring of Light which is so primal, indeed much more so, and which comes from that source of divinity, I mean the Father. This is the Light which, by way of representative symbols, makes known to us the most blessed hierarchies among the angels. But we need to rise from this outpouring of illumination so as to come to the simple ray of Light itself. Of course this ray never abandons its own proper nature, or its own interior unity. Even though it works itself outward to multiplicity and proceeds outside of itself as befits its generosity, doing so to lift upward and to unify those beings for which it has a providential responsibility, nevertheless it remains inherently stable and it is forever one with its own unchanging identity. And it grants to creatures the power to rise up, so far as they may, toward itself and it unifies them by way of its own simplified unity.[25]

25 Pseudo-Dionysius, *The Complete Works*, trans. C. Luibheid (New York, 1987), 145–46. The Latin text is in Pseudo-Dionysius, *Dionysiaca*, ed. P. Chevallier (Paris and Bruges, 1937–50), 2:723–33:

> *Omne datum bonum et omne donum perfectum desursum est descendens a Patre luminum; sed et cunctus a Patre motae luminis apparitionis processus ad nos bonitatis dono veniens, rursus sicut unum faciens virtus suscitative nos adimplet et convertit ad congregantis Patris unitatem et deificam simplicitatem. Etenim ex ipso omnia et ad ipsum sicut sanctus dixit sermo. Igitur Jesum invocantes, qui est paternum lumen, quod est quod verum est quod illuminat omnem hominem venientem in hunc mundum, per quem ad principem luminis Patrem adductionem habuimus, ad sanctissimorum eloquiorum a patribus traditas illuminationes (sicut est possibile) respiciamus; et ab ipsis significative nobis et sursumactive manifestas caelestium mentium hierarchias (sicut potentes sumus) inspiciamus. Et principalem et superprincipalem thearchici Patris luminis donationem, quae angelorum nobis in formativis signis manifestat beatissimas hierarchias immaterialibus et non-trementibus mentis oculis intus suscipientes, rursus ex ipsa ad simplicem ipsius suscitemur radium. Etenim neque ipsa aliquando a propria singulari unitate relinquitur. Sed ad sursumactionem et unificam provisorum coniuctionem ut decet bonam multiplicata et procedens manet intra se ipsam fixe in immobili identitate singulariter fixa. Et ad ipsam (sicut est fas) respicientes iuxta proportionem suam extendit et unum facit secundum simplificativam ipsius unitionem.*

The gist of the *Paradiso* is in what we have just read: every display of light coming from God brings us up to him,[26] to union with him, and to his simplicity; because of this illumination, we can look at the heavenly angelic hierarchies, and through them look at the illumination itself, that is, God. It is a peculiar illumination insofar as it does not lose its own unity and identity even though it gets multiplied; on the contrary, it shares its unity and simplicity with others. Simplicity means that knowing God is a process toward simplification, ending in unity. God is simple because he takes up the complexity of reality; he sums up everything else and remains the only self-sufficient being. By ascending from one illumination to the next, we are left with sheer light. Representing God, then, is as simple as drawing a geometric figure, a point of light surrounded by nine circles, and in that light Dante sees "un semplice sembiante . . . che tal è sempre qual s'era davante" (*Par.* 33.109, 111).[27] God's unity and simplicity are eternal and unchangeable; he always shows "una sola parvenza" (*Par.* 33.113),[28] and it is Dante's sight that grows stronger and becomes capable of seeing the complexity within God, for instance, the mystery of the Trinity and the Incarnation. The light of God is also unity as it is theologically explained to Dante by Saint Thomas (*Par.* 13.52–63):

> *Ciò che non more e ciò che può morire*
> *non è se non splendor di quella idea*
> *che partorisce, amando, il nostro Sire;*
> *ché quella viva luce che sì mea*
> *dal suo lucente, che non si disuna*
> *da lui né da l'amor ch'a lor s'intrea,*
> *per sua bontate il suo raggiare aduna,*
> *quasi specchiato, in nove sussistenze,*
> *etternalmente rimanendosi una.*
> *Quindi discende a l'ultime potenze*
> *giù d'atto in atto, tanto divenendo,*
> *che più non fa che brevi contingenze.*[29]

Pseudo-Dionysius's works are quoted according to the translation by John the Saracen, because it is one of the closest to Dante's time; it was finished before 1167. On this choice and on the various translations with or without the translation by Anastasius the Librarian of the scholia by Maximus the Confessor, see Sbacchi, *La presenza di Dionigi Areopagita* (above, n. 20), xiii–xviii.

26 See the very beginning of Dante's ascent to God: "S'i' era sol di me quel che creasti / novellamente, amor che 'l ciel governi, / tu 'l sai, / che col tuo lume mi levasti" (Whether I was there in that part only which you / created last is known to you alone, O Love who rule / the heavens and drew me up there with your light; *Par.* 1.73–75).

27 "A single aspect / for It is always what It was before."

28 "Sole semblance."

29 That which does not die and that which must / are nothing but a bright reflection of that Idea / which our Lord, in loving, brings to birth. / For that living Light, which so streams forth / from its shining Source that it neither parts from it / nor from the Love that is intrined with them, / of its own goodness gathers its own shining, / as though it were a mirror, in nine subsistences, / and yet eternally endures as one. / From that height light descends to the lowest

Again, speaking about the countless angels, Beatrice shows Dante that the divine light is reflected by them, preserving its unity (*Par.* 29.142–45):

> *Vedi l'eccelso omai e la larghezza*
> *de l'etterno valor, poscia che tanti*
> *speculi fatti s'ha in che si spezza,*
> *uno manendo in sé come davanti.*[30]

Ascending to God is accomplished by following his degrees of illumination given to the world. It is not possible to be confused on this path, because we are brought to him by a hierarchical progression, as related in *De caelesti hierarchia* 3.1–2:

> In my opinion a hierarchy is a sacred order, a state of understanding and an activity approximating as closely as possible to the divine. And it is uplifted to the imitation of God in proportion to the enlightenments divinely given to it. The beauty of God—so simple, so good, so much the source of perfection—is completely uncontaminated by dissimilarity. It reaches out to grant every being, according to merit, a share of light and then through a divine sacrament, in harmony and in peace, it bestows on each of those being perfected its own form. The goal of a hierarchy, then, is to enable beings to be as like as possible to God and to be at one with him. A hierarchy has God as its leader of all understanding and action. It is forever looking directly at the comeliness of God. A hierarchy bears in itself the mark of God. Hierarchy causes its members to be images of God in all respects, to be clear and spotless mirrors reflecting the glow of primordial light and indeed of God himself. It ensures that when its members have received this full and divine splendor they can then pass on this light generously and in accordance with God's will to beings further down the scale. It would be quite wrong for those granting initiation in the sacred things, as indeed for those sacredly initiated, ever to do anything or even to exist against the sacred orderings of him who is after all the source of all perfection. This would certainly be wrong, particularly if they themselves desire the splendor of God, if they are forever gazing on this splendor in a way appropriate to its sacred character, and if it is to this splendor that they are conformed, proportionately to each mind.[31]

---

elements, / passing down from act to act, becoming such / that it produces nothing more than brief contingencies.

30 "See now the height and breadth of the Eternal Worth, / one light, which shines dispersed among / so many mirrors yet remains / in Itself one, just as It was before."

31 Pseudo-Dionysius, *Complete Works*, 153–54. Pseudo-Dionysius, *Dionysiaca*, 2:785–90:

> *Est quidem hierarchia (secundum me) ordinatio sancta et scientia et operatio, ad Deiforme (sicut est possibile) assimilata, et ad inditas ipsi a Deo illuminationes iuxta proportionem ad Dei imitativum sursumacta. Deo autem conveniens pulchritudo, sicut simplex, sicut bona, sicut teletarchica, munda quidem est universaliter ab omni dissimilitudine, distributiva autem proprii luminis secundum dignitatem uniuscuiusque, et perfectiva in perfectione divinissima secundum*

Illumination given to everyone according to each one's merits is the form into which the hierarchy is made visible to mankind, as Dante says at the end of his journey (*Par.* 31.22–24): "ché la luce divina è penetrante / per l'universo secondo ch'è degno, / sì che nulla le puote essere ostante."[32] It is the manifestation of the order established by God. It is now clear that the presence of light is not something additional, unessential, or ornamental, used only because it is common knowledge that God is light; instead, it is something useful and essential to the representation of the Neoplatonic and Pseudo-Dionysian idea that God acts through light, being light himself.

Light also brings union, thus establishing a perfect blend and match of purposes and wills between the creator and the creatures, as in Piccarda's explanation of the essence of being blessed (*Par.* 3.70–84):

> *Frate, la nostra volontà quïeta*
> *virtù di carità, che fa volerne*
> *sol quel ch'avemo, e d'altro non ci asseta.*
> *Se disïassimo esser più superne,*
> *foran discordi li nostri disiri*
> *dal voler di colui che qui ne cerne;*
> *che vedrai non capere in questi giri,*
> *s'essere in carità qui necesse,*
> *e se la sua natura ben rimiri.*
> *Anzi è formale ad esto beato esse*
> *tenersi dentro a la divina voglia,*
> *per ch'una fansi nostre voglie stesse;*
> *sì che, come noi sem di soglia in soglia*
> *per questo regno, a tutto il regno piace*
> *com'a lo re che 'n suo voler ne 'nvoglia.*[33]

---

perfectorum convenienter ad ipsam intransmutabilem formationem. Intentio igitur hierarchiae est ad Deum (sicut est possibile) assimilatio et unitio; ipsum habens omnis sanctae et scientiae et operationis ducem, et ad ipsius divinissimum decorem indeclinabiliter quidem videns et sicut est possibile formata et ipsius chorum agentes insignia divina faciens specula clarissima et immaculata, susceptiva principis luminis et thearchici radii; indita quidem claritate sancte impleta, hanc autem rursus copiose ad ea quae sequuntur cum spendore emittentia secundum thearchicas leges. Non enim fas sanctorum perfectoribus aut sancte perfectis operari aliquid universaliter praeter proprias perfectionis principis sanctas ordinationes; sed neque exsistere aliter, nisi Deificam ipsius claritatem desiderant, et ad ipsam ut decet sanctos respiciant, et reformentur secundum uniuscuiusque sanctarum mentium proportionem.

32 "For the light of God so penetrates the universe, / according to the fitness of its parts to take it in, / that there is nothing can withstand its beam."

33 Brother, the power of love subdues our will / so that we long for only what we have / and thirst for nothing else. / If we desired to be more exalted, / our desires would be discordant / with His will, which assigns us to this place. / That, as you will see, would not befit these circles / if to be ruled by love is here required / and if you consider well the nature of that love. / No, it is the very essence of this blessèd state / that we remain within the will of God, / so that our

The ultimate enlightenment occurs in the Empyrean, where light, in addition to being pure, is also intellectual (*Par.* 30.39–40). With a slight but significant change, Dante defines as intellectual not the Empyrean, as we are used to from Capella onward, but its light.[34] In so doing, Dante follows Pseudo-Dionysius, who thinks of God as intellectual light, following, in turn, the Neoplatonic mindset and terminology.[35] The aim is to fill every intellectual and rational being (angels and men) to bring them to knowledge and, therefore, union with God (*De divinis nominibus* 4.6):

> So then, the Good which is above all light is given the name "light of the mind," "beam and spring," "overflowing radiance." It crams with its light every mind which is above and beyond the world, or around it or within it. It renews all the powers of their minds. It steps beyond everything inasmuch as it is ordered beyond everything. It precedes everything inasmuch as it transcends everything. Quite simply, it gathers together and supremely anticipates in itself the authority of all illuminating power, being indeed the source of light and actually transcending light. And so it assembles into a union everything possessed of reason and of mind. For just as it is ignorance which scatters those in error, so it is the presence of the light of the mind which gathers and unites together those receiving illumination. It perfects them. It returns them toward the truly real. It returns them from their numerous false notions and, filling them with the one unifying light, it gathers their clashing fancies into a single, pure, coherent, and true knowledge.[36]

> wills combine in unity. / Therefore our rank, from height to height, / throughout this kingdom pleases all the kingdom, / as it delights the King who wills us to His will.

34 The history of the Empyrean was written by B. Nardi, *Saggi di filosofia dantesca* (Florence, 1967), 167–214. See also *Enciclopedia Dantesca*, s.v. "Empireo."

35 The poet uses the same expression in Dante Alighieri, *Convivio*, in *Opere minori* 1.2, ed. C. Vasoli and D. De Robertis (Milan and Naples, 1988), 3.12.7: "così Dio prima sé con luce intellettuale allumina, e poi le [creature] celestiali e l'altre intelligibili." The English translation is Dante Alighieri, *Dante's Il convivio (The Banquet)*, trans. R. H. Lansing (New York, 1990): "therefore God illuminates with intellectual light first himself and then the celestial creatures and all other intelligent beings." On the Empyrean and intellectual light, as well as on the various manifestations of light, see C. Moevs, *The Metaphysics of Dante's "Comedy"* (New York, 2005), 15–35 and *passim*; Susanna Barsella, *In the Light of the Angels: Angelology and Cosmology in Dante's "Divina Commedia"* (Florence, 2010), 36–44 and *passim*.

36 Pseudo-Dionysius, *Complete Works*, 76. Pseudo-Dionysius, *Dionysiaca*, 1:174:

> *Igitur lumen intelligibile dicitur, quod est super omne lumen bonum, sicut radius fontanus et supermanans luminis effusio, omnem supermundanam et circamundanam et immundanam mentem ex plenitudine ipsius illuminans et intellectuales ipsarum totas virtutes renovans et omnes excedens, eo quod superextendatur, et omnia comprehendens, eo quod superiaceat; et simpliciter omnem illuminativae virtutis dominationem, sicut principaliter lucens et superlucens, in seipsa coassumens et superhabens et praehabens et intellectualia et rationalia omnia congregans et indestructibilia faciens. Etenim, sicut ignorantia divisiva est eorum qui in errorem ducti sunt, ita intelligibilis luminis praesentia congregativa et unitiva est eorum qui illuminantur, et perfectiva et adhuc conversiva ad vere existens, a multis opinionibus convertens et varias visiones aut, ut*

To my knowledge, the presence of intellectual light is very rare. It is not found in any of the aforementioned visions, not even in those that end in the Empyrean, such as the *Visio Godeschalci,* which might have referred the quality of being intellectual at least to the Empyrean. Intellectual light does not appear in cosmogonic poems rooted in a deep Neoplatonic background, either, although it plays an important role in shaping the landscape; this is the case for Alan of Lille's *Anticlaudianus*, in which a progressive illumination and the Empyrean are also mentioned.[37] A similar example is that of Bernardus Silvestris's *Cosmographia*,[38] which contains many Dionysian influences—a progressive illumination (although descending) is present; God is called superessential, a typical Pseudo-Dionysian term; the abode of God is populated by a hierarchy of creatures; God's brightness produces the very Dionysian luminous darkness; and God expands into the Trinity without losing his unity. However, no mention is made of intellectual light, not even in reference to the Empyrean, where it is clear that God is present even though not explicitly named. The poets simply stress the fact that light in the abode of God is extremely bright, strong, and beyond human vision, yet it is still physical and natural light. Also interesting is what we find in an anonymous author from the twelfth century: "a Platonist to the utmost degree."[39] In the ascent to God, the author imagines a ten-fold happiness for the soul: "The seventh [joy] is that the soul feels the light flowing from the divine essence through intellectual perception."[40] An intellectual perception is necessary in order to feel and understand light coming from the divine essence, yet the author does not mention intellectual light. In a Neoplatonic environment, some of God's features are similar to those described by Dante: he is the "first and pure light of the utmost purity."[41]

For the blessed or the angels, union brought by God seems to entail loss of identity, as they are no longer individuals. As Dante ascends to God, they appear to become just light because they are deprived of their bodies (*Par.* 5.127–129); they move and sing together, as in the dance of the learned souls (*Par.* 12.1–21); and they blend together, as is the case of the eagle in the heaven of Jupiter, whose unanimous speech amazes the poet (*Par.* 19.7–12). In other words, they seem to act like an anonymous body without personality. However, this is not really the case, because light is not a reduction of vision, just as harmony is not anonymity. Once asked by Dante to reveal themselves, the blessed display their personalities; each light is not the same and can be distinguished, as in the third heaven where the poet sees the different lights (*Par.* 8.16–21):

---

magis proprie dicatur, phantasias ad unam veram et mundam et uniformem congregans cognitionem et uno et unitivo lumine implens.

37 Alan of Lille, *Viaggio della Saggezza*, trans. C. Chiurlo (Milan, 2004), 4, p. 189; 5, p. 199ff.

38 Bernardus Silvestris, *Cosmographia*, ed. P. Dronke (Leiden, 1978), 2.5.1–5, pp. 127–28.

39 Marie-Thérèse D'Alverny, "Les pérégrinations de l'âme dans l'autre monde d'après un anonyme de la fin du XIIe siècle," *Archives d'histoire doctrinale et littéraire du Moyen-Age* 13 (1942): 239–99, esp. 254. Quotations from the text are from pp. 289 and 293.

40 *Septima est ut sensu intellectibili sentiat anima fluxum luminis a diuina essentia.*

41 *Lumen primum et purum in fine puritatis.*

E come in fiamma favilla si vede,
e come voce in voce si discerne,
quand'una è ferma e altra va e riede,
vid'io in essa luce altre lucerne
muoversi in giro più e men correnti,
al modo, credo, di lor viste interne.[42]

In the light of the planet Venus, *luce*, it is possible to see other lights moving, namely, "Lucerne," the blessed. In the fifth heaven, that of Mars, the blessed appear in a luminous cross so that Dante can say that "m'apparvero splendor dentro a due raggi" (*Par* 14.95).[43] In the following verses, he underlines that it is possible to identify the lights of the blessed within the rays of the cross, in the same way that different stars can be seen in the Galaxy (*Par.* 14.97–102):

Come distinta da minori e maggi
lumi biancheggia tra 'poli del mondo
Galassia sì, che fa dubbiar ben saggi;
sì costellati facean nel profondo
Marte quei raggi il venerabil segno
che fan giunture di quadranti in tondo.[44]

In the above-mentioned eagle, Dante can see a "distinto foco" (*Par.* 18.108),[45] a specific group of souls forming the shape of the bird's head and neck. Even angels are recognizable. They never speak to or interact with Dante, yet they are not just a mass of light. They are in a hierarchy, meaning that there are differences between them (*Par.* 29.136–141):

La prima luce, che tutta la raia,
per tanti modi in essa si recepe,
quanti son li splendori a chi s'appaia.
Onde, però che a l'atto che concepe
segue l'affetto, d'amar la dolcezza
diversamente in essa ferve e tepe.[46]

42 "And, as one sees a spark within a flame / or hears, within a song, a second voice, / holding its note while the other comes and goes, / so I saw within that light still other lights, / swifter and slower in their circling motions, / it seemed in measure to their inner sight."

43 "Splendors . . . / appeared to me within two beams."

44 "As the Milky Way, arrayed with greater and lesser lights, / glows white between the universal poles, / making even sages wonder how and why, / these rays, thus constellated, made, deep within Mars, / the venerable sign that the crossing / of its quadrants fixes in a circle."

45 "Overlay of fire."

46 "The Primal Light that irradiates them all / is received by them in just as many ways / as there are splendors joined with It. / Therefore, since affection follows / the act of conceiving, love's sweetness glows / with differing radiance, more brightly or subdued."

Beatrice argues that the first light, God, illuminates every angel, but they receive light in many different ways; therefore, the knowledge of, love for, and degree of beatitude of God are different. Looking at the point of light surrounded by nine shining circles, Dante had noticed that the closer a circle was to the point, the brighter it was, the result of being closer to truth (*Par.* 28.37–39): *e quello avea la fiamma più sincera / cui men distava la favilla pura, / credo, però che più di lei s'invera.*[47]

In the ninth heaven, after Beatrice's explanation of the relationship between angels and heavens, "L'incendio suo seguiva ogne scintilla" (*Par.* 28.91),[48] every single spark, or angel, could be spotted, in each of the nine flaming rings, even though they were countless in number (*Par.* 28.92–93); the glory of the Virgin is a triumph of angels "ciascun distinto di fulgore e d'arte" (*Par.* 31.132).[49] It is important to point out that union through light does not involve the annulment of individuality, following Pseudo-Dionysius's notion of the "separate union" (*De divinis nominibus* 2.4):

> Let me resort here to examples from what we perceive and from what is familiar. In a house the light from all the lamps is completely interpenetrating, yet each is clearly distinct. There is distinction in unity and there is unity in distinction. When there are many lamps in a house there is nevertheless a single undifferentiated light and from all of them comes the one undivided brightness. I do not think that anyone would mark off the light of one lamp from another in the atmosphere which contains them all, nor could one light be seen separately from the others since all of them are completely mingled while being at the same time quite distinctive. Indeed if somebody were to carry one of the lamps out of the house its own particular light would leave without diminishing the light of the other lamps or supplementing their brightness. As I have already explained, the total union of light, this light that is in the air and that emerges from the material substance of fire, involved no confusion and no jumbling of any parts. But turn now to that unity above being. I say that it surpasses not only the union of things corporeal, but also the union of souls, and even that of minds themselves. These minds purely, supernaturally, and thoroughly possess the godlike and celestial lights, but they do so in a participation proportionate to their participations in the unity which transcends all things.[50]

47 "And that one least removed from the blazing point of light / possessed the clearest flame, because, I think, / it was the one that is the most intruthed by it."

48 "Each spark keeping to its flaming ring."

49 "Each distinct in brightness and in motion."

50 Pseudo-Dionysius, *Complete Works*, 61–62. Pseudo-Dionysius, *Dionysiaca*, 1:78:

> *Quemadmodum lumina luminarium, ut sensibilibus et propriis utar exemplis, existentia in domo una et tota in se invicem totis sunt et diligentem habent ad se invicem discretionem proprie subsistentem unita discretione et unitione discreta. Et quidem videmus in domo multis existentibus luminaribus ad unum quoddam lumen unita omnium lumina et una claritate indiscreta resplendentia; et non aliquis, ut arbitror, possit huius luminaris lumen ab aliis ex aëre omnia lumina continente discernere et videre sine altero alterum totis in totis sine mixtione concretis.*

As we have seen before, Dante becomes aware of the Trinity and Christ's Incarnation within God's unity. The Trinity and the Incarnation do not deprive God of his supreme and ultimate unity. The souls and the intelligences share in their union with God this very feature, namely, that being united with God means to have a separate union, because God's unity is beyond every union with others.

After these considerations, I find it useful to look back at opinions expressed by scholars who believe that the last *cantica* is monotonous and repetitive, as compared to the two previous sections, one reason being the pervasive presence of light. I would like to mention at least two of these scholars. Momigliano states:

> *Il passaggio da un cielo all'altro, nonostante il crescere della luce, è meccanico, e non si può paragonare alla salita da un girone all'altro del purgatorio. . . . Il paradiso Dantesco è un complesso di sfere concentriche: la sua architettura è tutta qui; ed essendo mutuata, non ad uno spettacolo naturale, ma ad una costruzione scientifica, ha un fondo di rigidezza che si tradisce nelle nostre impressioni di relativa monotonia e di slegatura.*[51]

Cosmo is quite harsh as well: "Negli effetti artistici quello sfolgorio era come una nebbia che agguaglia ogni contorno, sfuma ogni individualità."[52] Light is not a device Dante uses to cover up or to embellish lack of inspiration, an element misused or abused and made to represent an extremely difficult, or abstract, matter; rather, light and its features are the essence of heaven, according to Neoplatonic thought, and Dante gives prom-

---

> *Sed si unum aliquis luminarium educat a domo, coëgredietur et proprium universum lumen, nihil aliorum luminum in seipso coavellens aut sui ipsius aliis derelinquens. Erat enim ipsorum, quod dixi, totorum ad tota perfecta unitio, non mixta universaliter et nulla parte confusa; et haec totaliter in corpore aëre et ex materiali igne pendente lumine. Ibi autem supersubstantialem unitionem collocari dicimus, non super solas unitiones, quae sunt in corpore, sede et super illas quae sunt in animabus ipsis et in ipsis mentibus, quas habent non mixte et supermundane tota per tota deiformia et supercaelestia lumina, secundum partecipationem unitionis ab omnibus supersegregatae proportionalem participantibus.*

I think it is interesting to point out a seeming coincidence: commenting on this passage, the scholiast Maximus the Confessor says that Pseudo-Dionysius calls souls and intelligences celestial/supercelestial lights and observes that they are united, as in the example of the lamps in the house, insofar as they are deiform and share in a proportioned way the unity of God. Maximus, whose notes were translated into Latin by Anastasius the Librarian, considers souls and angels as lights in the very same way as Dante will do afterward: one is left to speculate whether the poet may have read the works by Pseudo-Dionysius enriched by the notes of Maximus.

51 A. Momigliano, *Dante, Manzoni, Verga* (Messina, 1965), 31:

> Going from one heaven to the next, in spite of increased light, is repetitive and cannot be compared with the ascent through the terraces in the purgatory. . . . Dante's paradise is a complex of concentric spheres: this is all there is to it; and since it comes from a scientific model, rather than from a natural one, it follows a rigid pattern that gives us the impression of monotony and disconnectedness.

52 U. Cosmo, *L'ultima ascesa: Introduzione alla lettura del Paradiso* (Florence, 1965), 17: "As for the artistic outcomes, that blazing light was like fog that makes every edge fuzzy, blurring every individual."

inence to them while representing heaven. While it may be true that the *Paradiso* is more predictable and monotonous, and less dynamic and varied, than the *Inferno* and *Purgatorio,* this can be explained by the different topics treated in the three *cantiche*, an earthly reality that mirrors the variety of humankind, set in an earthly environment under or above the earth, versus a heavenly kingdom made uniform by the beatitude experienced by all, and where the only diversity is in the degree of its intensity. Given that, I would argue that it was perhaps Dante's intention to create such an effect of uniformity in depicting his ascent to God in order to prepare the reader to meet him.

Scazzoso considers Pseudo-Dionysus an inspirer of Byzantine art, and he parallels Dionysius's style with the features of the icon, an object that leads the believer into a contemplative mindset through its repetitiveness, monotony, and uniformity (features also found in Dionysius's style). These very features may appear to give the impression of an aloof, mechanical, and indifferent art. More generally, Scazzoso attributes three qualities to Byzantine art, and therefore to the icons: royal, because of its precious material; hieratic, because of the liturgy-like dignity and composure; mystic, because it inspires contemplation.[53] Considering also that the Greek Father was a source of inspiration for Dante, it is not far-fetched to apply the categories of Byzantine art to the exegesis of *Paradiso*: in this case, too, the contemplative atmosphere is conveyed by the repetition, monotony, and uniformity of elements, such as light, relations between characters, and situations. The *Paradiso* is also precious because of the mention of precious materials such as "argento" (silver) and "oro" (gold), and precious stones such as "ambra" (amber), "balasso" (splendid ruby), "gemma" / "gemme" (jewel / jewels), "margarita" / "margherite" (pearl / pearls), "rubin" / "rubinetto" (ruby / single ruby), "topazio" / "topazi" (topaz / topazes), and "zaffiro" (sapphire). These terms are used to indicate the blessed, planets, and angels, and the precious stones themselves are a source of light; the last *cantica* is also hieratical and mystical, as Dante creates locations, scenes, movements, and attitudes of the blessed and angels that are inspired by liturgical, dignified composure, leading the pilgrim toward contemplation.

53 P. Scazzoso, *Ricerche sulla struttura del linguaggio dello Pseudo-Dionigi Areopagita* (Milan, 1967), 133–49. Also by the same scholar is another very interesting study for the topic addressed in this paper: P. Scazzoso, "I nomi di Dio nella *Divina Commedia* e il *De Divinis Nominibus* dello Pseudo-Dionigi," *La scuola cattolica* 86 (1958): 193–213.

Cartographic Dante

A Note on Dante and the Greek Mediterranean

THEODORE J. CACHEY JR.

DANTE CARRIES OUT AN ASSERTIVE and thoroughgoing marginalization of the Greeks in the *Commedia,* the extent and implications of which have not been fully appreciated for their impact on the poem's "map of the world." It has been noted that Dante ostracizes the Greeks from a temporal point of view: he knows of the existence of the Byzantine Greeks but shows little or no interest in them.[1] He considers the ancient Greeks on a par with the Saracens as unredeemable pagans who competed with Christian Rome and had to be defeated by Providence so that Rome, and Christianity, might prevail.[2] To sail to Byzantium was to be headed in the wrong direction from the point of view of Dante's theory of history, "contr'al corso del ciel" (counter to Heaven's course), as he writes at the beginning of *Paradiso* 6, that is, "ch'ella seguio dietro a l'antico che Lavina tolse" (the course it took / behind the ancient one who wed Lavinia; *Par.* 6.1–3).[3] A Roman and Italocentric "projection,"

1 G. W. Most, "Dante's Greeks," *Arion* 13, no. 3 (winter 2006): 15–48, p. 23. Agostino Pertusi suggests, in the entry for "Bizantina Civiltà" in the *Enciclopedia Dantesca*, 1:638–42, that Dante's knowledge of the modern Greeks was limited: "Il primo problema che ci dobbiamo porre è se D. ebbe una conoscenza concreta e precisa della cultura Greco-bizantina. La risposta è in gran parte negativa. However, in the context of Dante's anti-Byzantine perspective that the entry goes on to describe, and that is touched upon elsewhere in this volume (see the essay by William Caferro), one has to wonder whether lack of evidence of Dante's knowledge of the Byzantine civilization, including complete silence regarding the Latin Empire that lasted from 1204 to 1261, is the result of intentional suppression and not just lack of access to information.

2 Most, "Dante's Greeks," 21.

3 Dante Alighieri, *La Commedia secondo l'antica vulgata*, ed. G. Petrocchi, 4 vols. (Florence, 1994). Translations of the *Commedia* are from Dante Alighieri, *Paradiso,* trans. R. Hollander and J. Hollander (New York, 2007); and *Inferno,* trans. R. Hollander and J. Hollander (New York, 2000). The commentary tradition on *Paradiso* 6.1–9 is unanimous in its understanding of these lines as a criticism of Constantine for the transfer of the capital of the empire to Constantinople in 324, thereby establishing what came to be known as the Byzantine Empire or Byzantium. The movement from west to east was contrary to the "course of the heavens," namely, from east to west, as was Aeneas's journey (the "ancient one who wed Lavinia") from Troy to Rome.

to use a cartographic term, fundamentally informs Dante's map of the world, which rhetorically expresses, as all maps inevitably do at one level or another, an underlying cultural-political theory.[4]

Indeed, the anti-Greek attitude of the *Commedia* is rooted in the fact that Dante's poetic pilgrimage is fundamentally modeled on the journey to Italy of Aeneas, "quel giusto figliuol d'Anchise che venne di Troia, poi che 'l superbo Iliòn fu combusto" (that righteous son of Anchises who had come from Troy / when flames destroyed the pride of Ilium; *Inf.* 1.73–75). The marginalization of the Greeks in the poem goes well beyond simply condemning Ulysses and Diomedes to hell in *Inferno* 26 and can be documented throughout the work. It is pursued even at the level of an ostensibly minor detail, as exemplified by a passage from *Inferno* 28 in which the prophesied murder by drowning of Guido del Cassero and Angiolello di Carignano off the promontory of Focara on the Adriatic coast is compared to the worst crimes of the Greeks. Neptune is figured there as a witness to criminal acts that issue from Argos, the home of Sinon, and no less importantly, the home port of the Argo, the first ship of history: "Tra l'isola di Cipri e di Maiolica / non vide mai sì gran fallo Nettuno, / non da pirate, non da gente Argolica" (Between the isles of Cyprus and Maiorca Neptune has never seen so cruel a crime committed by pirates or the Argives; *Inf.* 28.82–84). As Hollander, among others, has noted, the phrase "da gente Argolica" derives from Virgil's "neque me Argolica de gente negabo," where the speaker Sinon, the same "falso Sinon, Greco di Troia," condemned by Dante among the falsifiers (*Inf.* 30.98), confesses to the fact that he is one of the Greeks who fought against Troy.[5]

I propose to return to this passage in the second part of this essay, which will be concerned with a cartographic reading of *Inferno* 28. There my focus will be on the way in

4 An important genealogical link exists between Dante and contemporary Mediterranean theorists of European identity currently debating the competing cultural projections, claims, and legacies of north vs. south / east vs. west. In the first chapter of his provocative book, Roberto Dainotto describes the processes by which the originators of the idea of Europe, the Greeks, came to occupy a position at its margins. He remarks in passing that "Dante's casting of Ulysses and Diomedes in hell is a chapter in this marginalization of Greece. For its re-Europeanization we need to wait until the 1820s, when the Greek wars of national liberation against the Ottoman Empire will fuel the Romantic generation of Lord Byron"; R. Dainotto *Europe (in Theory)* (Durham, NC, 2007), 27. The current debate about European and southern European identities offers a potentially useful context within which to reconsider Dante and the Greek Mediterranean. See F. Cassano, *Pensiero meridiano* (Bari, 1996), esp. 23, and idem, *Paeninsula: L'Italia da ritrovare* (Bari, 1998); M. Cacciari, *Arcipelago* (Venice, 1997); F. Saffioti, *Geofilosofia del mare: Tra oceano e Mediterraneo* (Reggio Emilia, 2007). For a very helpful overview, see C. Fogu, "From Mare Nostrum to Mare Aliorum: Mediterranean Theory and Mediterraneanism in Contemporary Italian Thought," *California Italian Studies Journal* 1, no. 1, http://escholarship.org/uc/item/7vp210p4 (accessed 22 July 2013).

5 The Greeks are understood to be "cruel people" by Dante, who follows Virgil (*Aen.* 2.78). See A. Ronconi "Parole di Dante, per una semantica dei virgilianismi," *Lingua nostra* 11 (1950): 81: "i Greci sono qui, virgilianamente intesi, dal punto di vista di Priamo, cui Sinone si rivolge, e poi di Enea che racconta, dei 'nemici di Guerra.'" See also A. Roncaglia, "Parole di Dante, 'Gente Argolica'," *Lingua nostra* 8 (1947): 8.

which the tercet's first verse, "Tra l'isola di Cipri e di Maoilica,"[6] represents a synecdoche for the Greek Mediterranean and plays a key structural role in a broader cartographic program that maps both the world and the poem. In general, we might say that Dante uses the Greeks to chart, between the pillars of Hercules in the west and Argos in the east, not only the boundaries of the Mediterranean on the horizontal plane of the earth's surface, but also the journey of the poet on a vertical axis that passes from the depths of hell to as far as the sublime heights of the vision of God, where Neptune and the Argonauts are again famously evoked at the culminating moment of the poet's experience:[7] "Un punto solo m'è maggior letargo / che venticinque secoli a la 'mpresa / che fé Nettuno ammirar l'ombra d'Argo" (That one moment brings more forgetfulness to me than twenty-five centuries have brought to the endeavor that startled Neptune with Argo's shadow; *Par.* 33.94–96).

Cartographic Dante

From the perspective of the new history of cartography, inaugurated by J. B. Harley and David Woodward and canonized in the monumental volumes of the *History of Cartography*, we have come to recognize that all mappings represent "projections" of one form or another, constructions of the world and our place in it that are embedded in and express the cultures that produce them.[8] This insight has led to a new understanding of the map and, in particular, its rhetorical power. Indeed, one of the best books in the field, by Denis Wood, is simply titled: *The Power of Maps*.[9] These developments in the history of cartography have led to a new appreciation for premodern maps and a better understanding of medieval maps in particular. This new perspective on cartographic traditions that until fairly recently had been judged according to rationalist and modern scientific criteria as deficient motivates a renewed attention to the cartographic impulse in Dante. While the trope of calling the *Commedia* a kind of mappamundi is fairly commonplace, I think it is fair to say that Dante studies has yet to fully explore the implications of the new history of cartography for the light it might shed on Dante as a cartographic author, and that there are significant discoveries in this area yet to be made.

6 Dante probably derives the notion that Cyprus and Maiolica mark the east and west of the Mediterranean, respectively, from Orosius (1.2). See Dante Alighieri, *Commedia*, vol. 1, *Inferno*, ed. A. M. Chiavacci Leonardi (Milan, 1991), 844.

7 The soaring verticality and plummeting depths of the map of the poem can be seen to correspond in an inverse relation to the limits that Dante establishes on a horizontal plane through his suppression of the Fortunate–Canary Islands in the west and the Marcopolean marvels of the east in the poem's geography. See T. J. Cachey Jr., "Dante e le isole fortunate: Un locus deperditas nella geografia del poema," *Le isole fortunate: Appunti di letteratura italiana* (Rome, 1995), 17–81; and B. Deen Schildgen, *Dante and the Orient* (Urbana, IL, and Chicago, 2002), 18–44. For the shift from a vertical to a horizontal temporal paradigm as signaling the onset of modernity, see M. Bakhtin, *The Dialogic Imagination: Four Essays*, ed. M. Holquist, trans. C. Emerson and M. Holquist (Austin, 2006), 84–258.

8 *The History of Cartography*, ed. J. B. Harley and David Woodward (Chicago, 1987–). For a collection of Harley's influential essays, see J. B. Harley, *The New Nature of Maps: Essays in the History of Cartography*, ed. P. Laxton (Baltimore, 2001).

9 D. Wood, *The Power of Maps* (New York, 1992).

There is a well-known and lengthy tradition of studying Dante's geography and, in connection with this, his knowledge and use of maps, in particular as source materials for geospatial aspects of the poem.[10] Yet there is a difference between approaching the theme of Dante and cartography in terms of intellectual history and source criticism,[11] and adopting a hermeneutical attitude that considers Dante's writing in relation to a general shift in the history of the spatial imagination of Europe that took place during the Duecento and Trecento.[12] Beyond the question of the depth of Dante's knowledge of sailing charts and their direct use in the poem,[13] a more fundamental point bears emphasizing for its interpretive implications: Dante's poem expresses the same mapping impulse that produced the first modern maps, also known as nautical or portolan charts, that first appeared during the Duecento, such as the *Carta Pisana* or "Chart of Pisa," the oldest of these highly accurate manuscript sea charts of the Mediterranean to have survived (Fig. 1).

The *Carta Pisana* dates from the end of the thirteenth century. The map's charting of coastlines and coastal toponyms is characteristic of this new, modern genre of mapping and is remarkably detailed.[14] In its intensive distribution of toponyms throughout its three *cantiche*, the *Commedia* represents a written form of mapping parallel to that of the "Chart of Pisa" or to the somewhat later map of Angelino Dulcert, the first sailing chart to be signed by its author and the first to be dated (1339) that has come down to us (Fig. 2). The Dulcert chart documented, for the first time, the rediscovery of the Fortunate or Canary Islands, which Petrarch recorded in the *Vita Solitaria* and Boccaccio in the *De Canaria*—islands that later became the staging ground for Columbus's discovery of the New World.[15] The rediscovery of these islands and their subsequent conquest would eventually lead to the suppression of an assortment of mythical islands of the Atlantic traditionally located beyond the pillars of Hercules: Dante's Mount Purgatory stands as a last vestige of these islands, at the same time that Ulysses' journey in *Inferno* 26 represents a harbinger of New World discoveries to come. In its

10 For example, E. Coli, *Il paradiso terrestre dantesco* (Florence, 1897); E. Moore, "The Geography of Dante," in his *Studies in Dante: Third series; Miscellaneous Essays* (Oxford, 1968; orig. ed. 1903), 109–43; P. Revelli, *L'Italia nella Divina commedia, con la riproduzione diplomatica del planisfero vaticano-palatino di Pietro Vesconte del 1320–21, e una cartina "L'Italia di Dante"* (Milan, 1922).

11 P. Armour, "Dante e *l'imago mundi* del primo Trecento," in *Dante e la scienza*, ed. P. Boyde and V. Russo (Ravenna and Longo, 1995), 191–202.

12 A. Murray, "Purgatory and the Spatial Imagination," in *Dante and the Church: Literary and Historical Essays*, ed. P. Acquaviva and J. Petrie (Dublin, 2007), 61–92.

13 A question worth exploring at greater length, and resolving in another context, is the diversity of opinion about Dante's awareness and use of Mediterranean sailing charts. The positions range from the firmly convinced (Baldacci) to the agnostic (Armour). O. Baldacci, "Carte geografiche," *Enciclopedia Dantesca* (Rome, 1978), 1:852–54; and P. Armour, "Dante e *l'imago mundi*."

14 See T. Campbell, "Portolan Charts from the Late Thirteenth Century to 1500," in *The History of Cartography*, vol. 1, *Cartography in Prehistoric, Ancient, and Medieval Europe and the Mediterranean*, ed. J. B. Harley and D. Woodward (Chicago, 1987), 371–463.

15 See T. J. Cachey Jr., "Petrarca, Boccaccio e le isole Fortunate: 'Lo sguardo antropologico'," in *Boccaccio geografico*, ed. R. Morosini (Florence, 2010), 205–28.

cartographic depictions of the sea "between Cyprus and Maiorca" (*tra l'isola di Cipri e di Maiolica*), the *Commedia* can be said to articulate and translate in poetic form the same cartographic impulse that inspired contemporary late medieval maps, for example in Ulysses' tour of the Mediterranean basin: "L'un lito e l'altro ... infin la Spagna, / fin nel Morrocco, e l'isola d'i Sardi, / e l'altre che quel mare intorno bagna" (from one shore and the other ... as far as Spain, Morrocco—the island of Sardegna, and other islands set into that sea; *Inf.* 26.103–5). As we will see, this terrestrial geospatial reality is represented in a maplike manner in the Malebolge (or evil-pouches) cantos of the eighth circle of hell, from which it is projected into paradise, where it ultimately serves as a framework for the extraterrestrial extension of the poet's journey and the space of the poem as artifact.

A related but somewhat different set of issues exists with regard to Dante's knowledge and use of medieval world maps. That there is some deep kinship between the encyclopedic, historical, and sacred aspects of late medieval mappaemundi and Dante's poetic geography has been recognized for some time.[16] Nonetheless, further interpretive opportunities remain, particularly in light of the greater range of primary sources that has become better known through recent studies of medieval maps.[17] For example, Evelyn Edson has discussed an eighth-century world map, one of the oldest to have survived, which presents a configuration that closely parallels that of Dante in *Inferno* 14, with the island Crete at the center of the ecumene or inhabited world,[18] at the intersection of the three continents, and in juxtaposition to Jerusalem. (In this map, special city symbols highlight Jerusalem, distinguished by a starlike shape, as well as Rome and Carthage; Fig. 3).

16 John Demeray has been a pioneer in the use of the mappamundi as a hermeneutical key to a reading of the poem; see J. G. Demaray, *The Invention of Dante's Commedia* (New Haven, 1974); idem, *Dante and the Book of the Cosmos* (Philadelphia, 1987); and idem, in *The Dante Encyclopedia,* ed. R. Lansing (New York and London, 2000), 232–35, s.v. "Cosmology." Scholars such as Peter Hawkins, Brenda Schildgen, and, most recently, Alessandro Scafi have underscored this aspect of Dante's poetics: P. S. Hawkins, "'Out upon Circumference': Discovery in Dante," in his *Dante's Testaments: Essays in Scriptural Imagination* (Stanford, 1999), 265–88. B. Deen Schildgen, *Dante and the Orient* (Urbana, IL, and Chicago, 2002), esp. 18–44; A. Scafi *Mapping Paradise: A History of Heaven on Earth* (Chicago, 2006); idem, "Onesto Riso e Dolce Gioco: Dante, L'Eden e la Cartografia Medievale," *Letture classensi: Dante e l'arte* 35–36 (2007): 59–82.

17 In particular, see the studies of Evelyn Edson, including *Medieval Views of the Cosmos,* with E. Savage-Smith (Oxford, 2004); *Mapping Time and Space: How Medieval Mapmakers Viewed their World* (London, 1997); and *The World Map, 1300–1492: The Persistence of Tradition and Transformation* (Baltimore and Santa Fe, 2007). Among areas worthy of further investigation in connection to Dante are traditions of mapping associated with Lucan, as well as potential connections between Dante and the world maps studied by Edson that were included in calendar or Computus manuscripts devoted to computing the date of Easter.

18 According to the commentator Benvenuto da Imola, in fact, Crete was a kind of microcosm of the ecumene itself embedded in the surrounding sea: "Est ... hic bene notandum quod autor per istam insulam figurat nobis mundum istu, sive terram habitabilem, quia ista insula est circumcincta mari sicut terra tota oceano ... et est quasi in medio mundi et quasi omnia maria et confinia partum terrae terminantur ibi"; P. Toynbee, *A Dictionary of Proper Names and Notable Matters in the Works of Dante,* rev. C. S. Singleton (Oxford, 1968), 204, s.v. "Crete."

Fig. 1. Carta Pisana, thirteenth century, BnF, Rés. Ge. B. 1118

While one needs to exercise caution before arguing that Dante had any particular map in mind when he "invented" the Mediterranean mapping of Crete,[19] consideration of the traditions of medieval world maps can provide a revealing interpretive lens through which to view the poem as a form of verbal mapping or "cartographic writing."

A third and final genre of mapping that surely ought to be considered in relation to Dante's *Commedia* is the chorographic or regional map of the Italian peninsula.[20]

19 Ambrogio Camozzi has recently characterized the poem's mapping of Crete as "inusitata, inventata, e precedentemente sconosciuta," in A. Camozzi, "Il Veglio di Creta alla luce di Matelda: Una lettura comparativa di *Inferno* XIV e *Purgatorio* XXVIII," *The Italianist* 29 (2009): 3–49.

20 The distinction between geography and chorography derives from Ptolemy, for whom geography

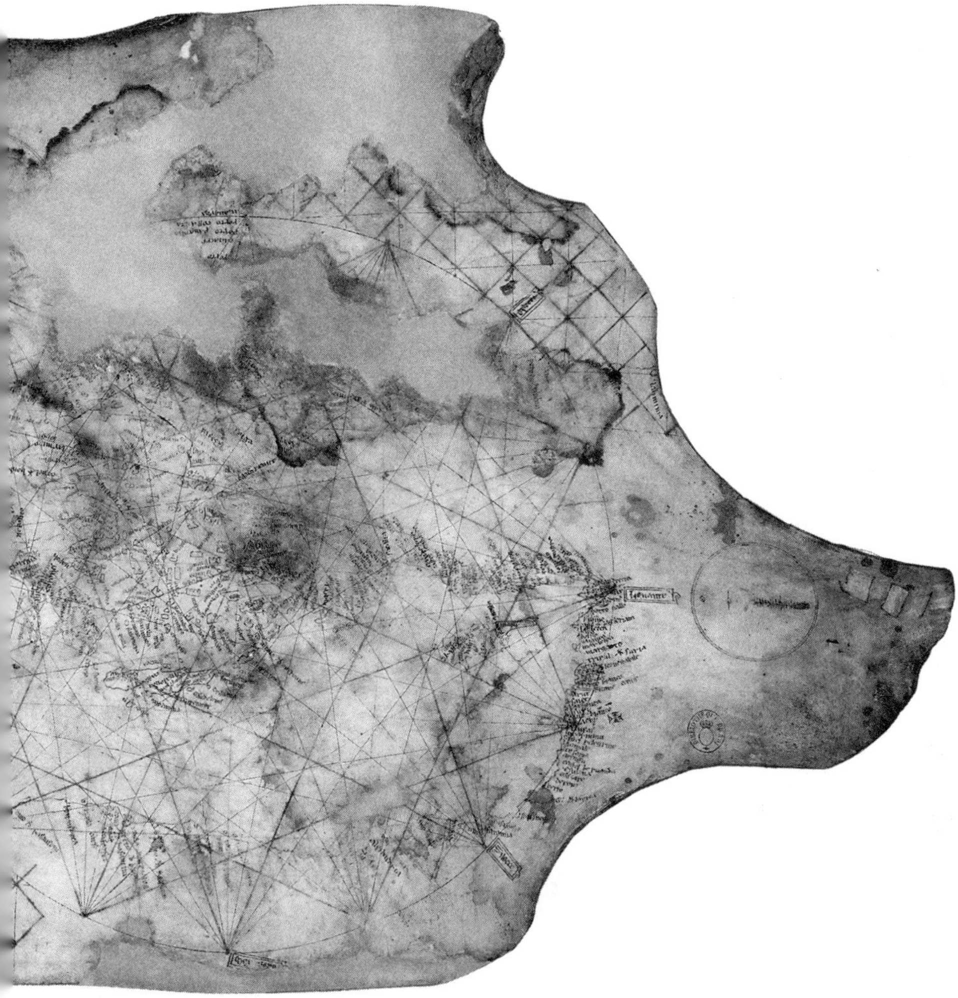

Unfortunately, nothing directly contemporary, as far as I know, survives. Slightly later than Dante are the maps of Pietro Vesconte and Paulinus Venetus, whose cartography has been discussed on occasion in connection with the *Commedia*. But what stands out when one compares the surviving maps of these cartographers and the poem is the intensity and the specificity of Dante's own verbal mappings of the peninsula.

was the study of the entire world or large sections or countries of it, while chorography was the study of its smaller parts—provinces, regions, cities, or ports: "The goal of regional cartography is an impression of a part, as when one makes an image of just an ear or an eye; but the goal of world cartography is a general view, analogous to making a portrait of the whole head."; J. Lennart Berggren and A. Jones, eds., *Ptolemy's Geography: An Annotated Translation of the Theoretical Chapters* (Princeton and Oxford, 2001), 57.

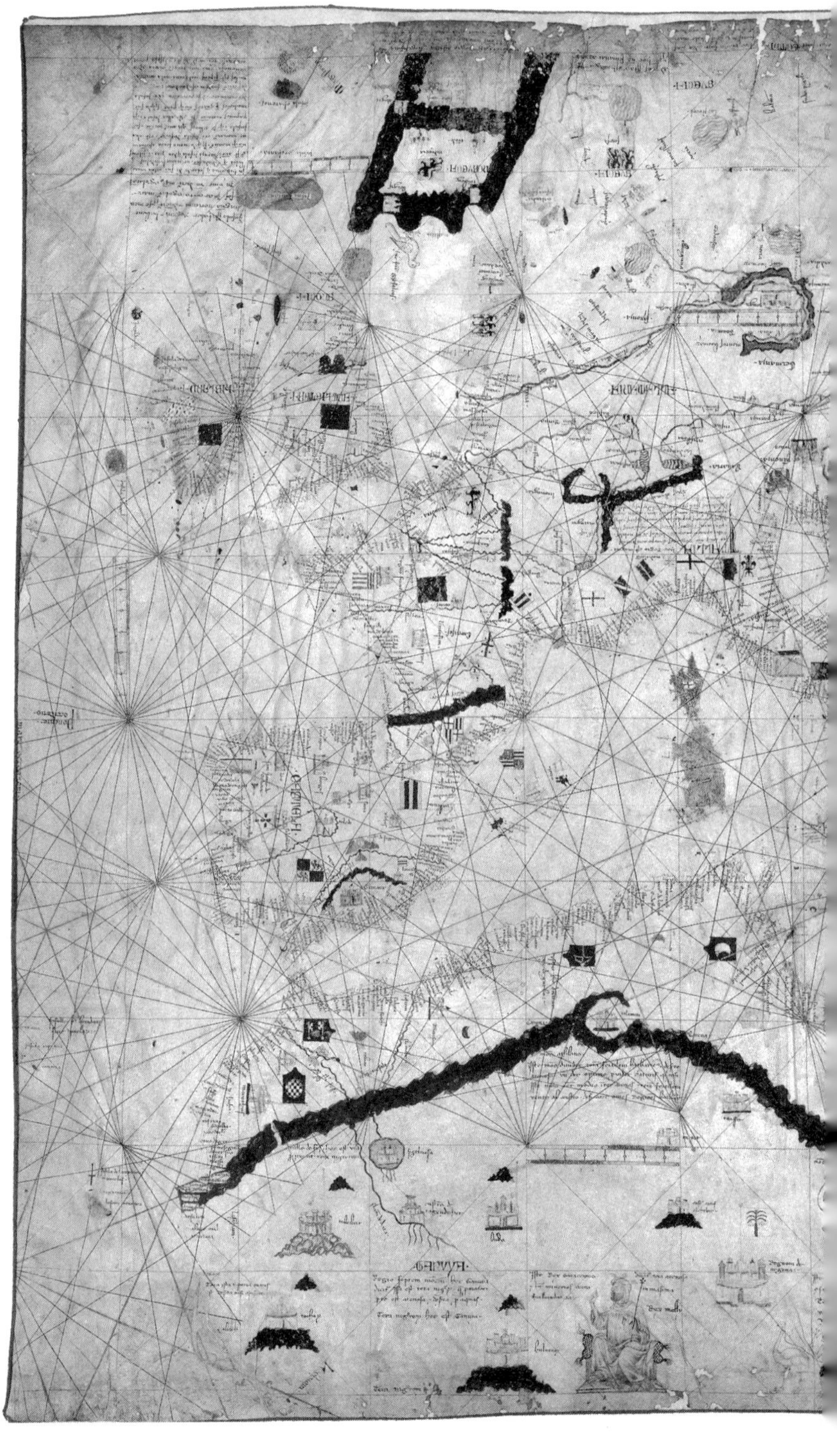

Fig. 2. Dulcert Chart, BnF, Rés. Ge. B 696

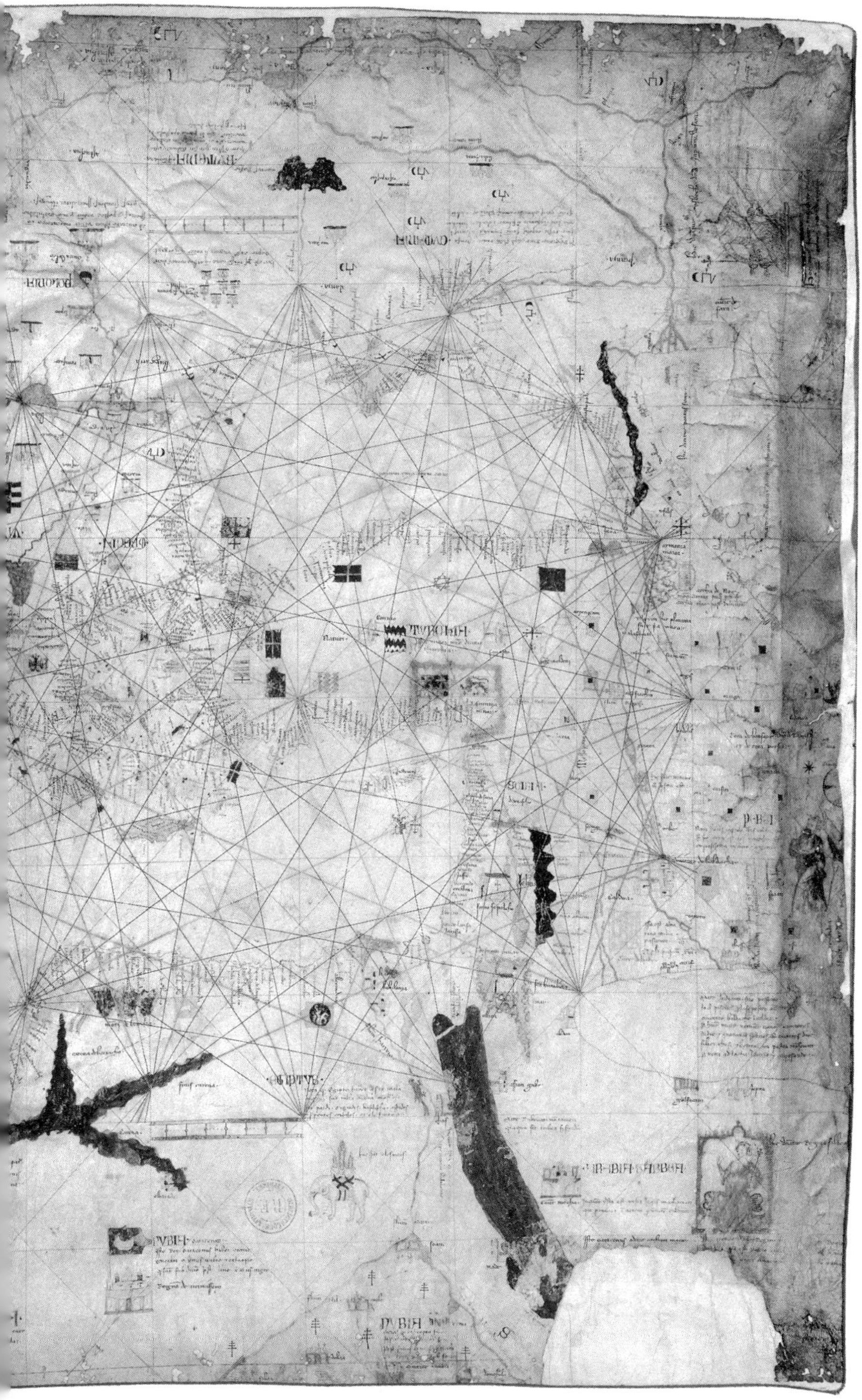

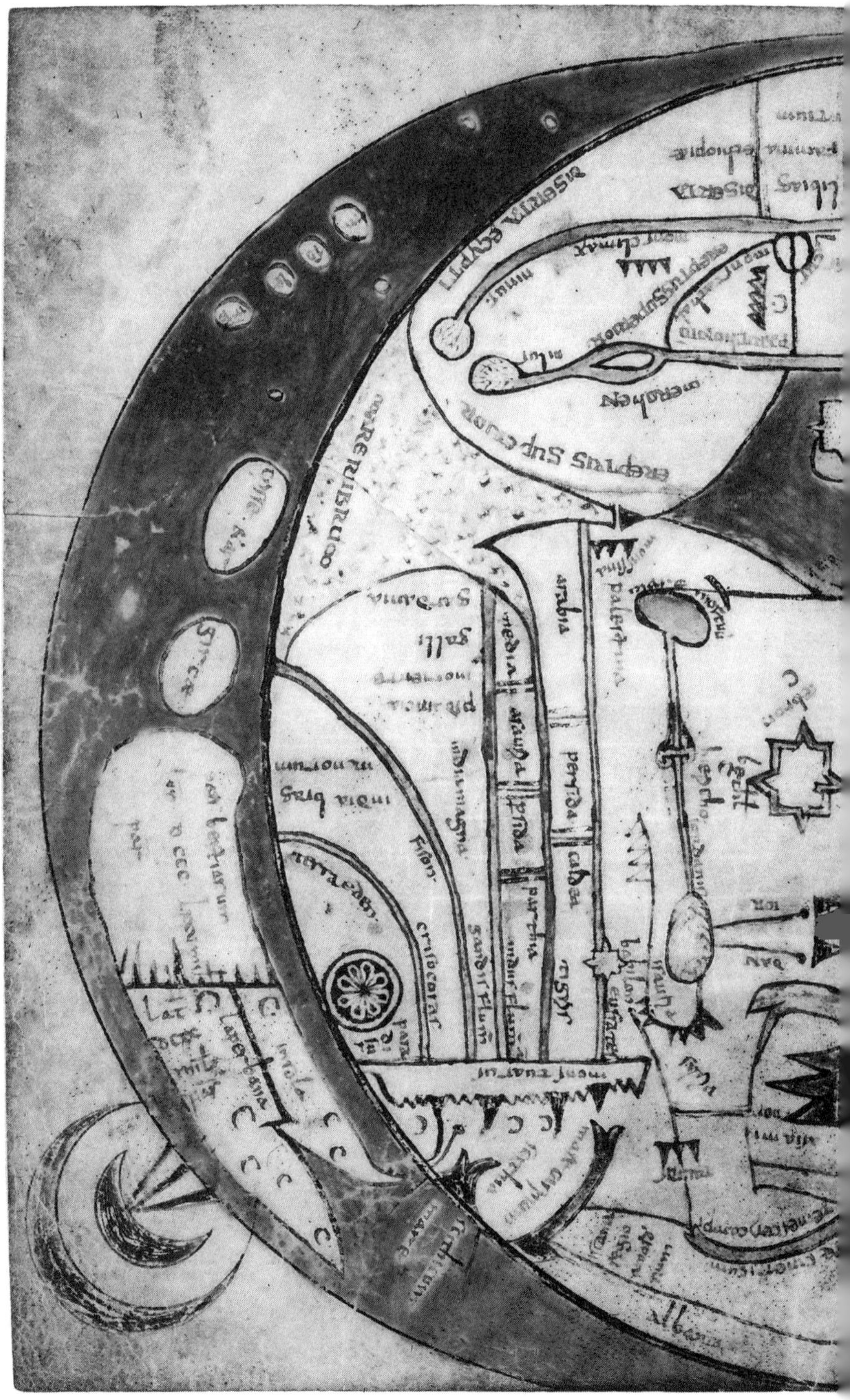

Fig. 3. Mappamundi from an eighth-century manuscript, Vat. lat. 6018, 63v–64r

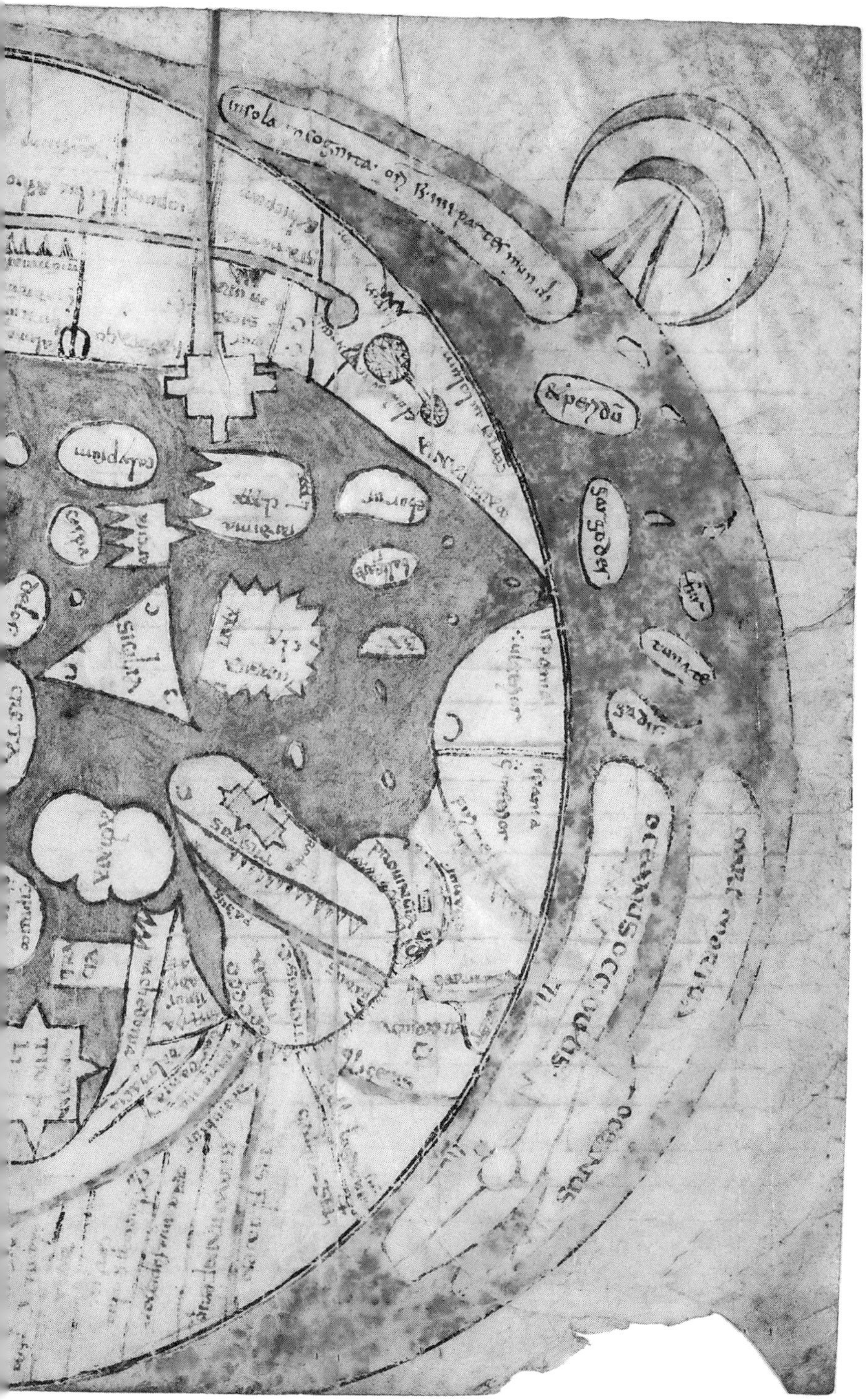

Indeed, it would be fair to say that Dante's cartography of Italy offers one of the most important and most detailed representations of the peninsula to survive from the period. To begin with, the mapping of Italy in the *De vulgari eloquentia* presented an incipient national-territorial cartographic ambition that was remarkably precocious for the period.[21] Yet despite the evident cartographic interest of Dante's treatment of the peninsula in the minor works and in the poem, Dante scholars have, generally speaking, given scant attention to Dante's cartography of Italy,[22] and the critical implications of Dante's cartographic descriptions of Italy have yet to be explored.[23]

To suggest the kind of discoveries that are yet to be made, and to illustrate briefly what I mean by Dante's cartographic writing, let us take an example from the *Inferno* that will have implications for our reading of *Inferno* 28. As far as I know, it has not been previously noted that Dante very clearly traces the cartographic outline of Italy in a series of structurally key similes that articulate the stages of the descent into hell. It begins in *Inferno* 9, just within the gates of Dis. The first simile of the series renders the passage of the ethical border into lower hell tantamount to descending into Italy from the north. Dante describes the burial ground of the heretics at the same time that he evokes the northwest and northeast borders of the peninsula:

> *Sì come ad Arli, ove Rodano stagna,*
> *sì com' a Pola, presso del Carnaro*
> *ch'Italia chiude e suoi termini bagna*
> *fanno i sepulcri tutt'il loco varo,*
> *così facevan quivi d'ogne parte* (Inf. 9.112–16)
>
> As at Arles, where the Rhone makes its delta, as at Pola, near the Carnaro that encloses Italy and bathes its boundaries, tombs variegate the place, so they did here on every side, except that the manner was more bitter

21 As the geographer Franco Farinelli pointed out not long ago in a stimulating essay concerned with the history of the cartographic image of Italy. Farinelli reads the *De vulgari eloquentia* as a precursor of modernity's "cartographic ethos." For Farinelli, Dante foreshadows in the ideal of the "illustrious vernacular" a national political perspective erected on the foundation of reason (constituting a "bird's-eye" perspective on the peninsula conceived as a territorial unity, although not yet the perspective from the early modern national and "zenitale" perspective of a Tasso [above Jerusalem] or a Manzoni [above Lake Como]). See F. Farinelli, "L'immagine dell'Italia," in *Geografia politica delle regioni italiane*, ed. P. Coppola (Turin, 1997), 33–59.

22 At least since the studies of Basserman and Revelli at the end of the 19th century: see Revelli, *L'Italia nella Divina commedia* (above, n. 10), and A. Bassermann, *Dantes Spuren in Italien: Wanderungen und Untersuchungen* (Munich and Leipzig, 1898); Italian trans., *Orme di Dante in Italia; opera tradotta da Egidio Gorra* (Bologna, 1902).

23 Although a recent essay by William Franke on "The Place of the Proper Name in the Topographies of the *Paradiso*," in *Speculum* 4 (2012): 1089–1124, suggests that this situation may be changing. Precise and very useful information regarding Dante's chorographic treatment of the Italian peninsula is also to be found in the commentary tradition and in the *Enciclopedia Dantesca*.

Following the longest interval in the poem without a simile,[24] as if to draw attention to the map he is constructing, Dante introduces a simile to an Alpine landscape at the beginning of the first of the three subdivisions of violence:

Qual è quella ruina che nel fianco
di qua da Trento l'Adice percosse,
o per tremoto o per sostegno manco,
che da cima del monte onde si mosse,
al piano è sì la roccia discoscesa,
ch'alcuna via darbbe a chi su fosse;
cotal di quel burrato era la scesa; (*Inf.* 12.4–10)

The place where we came to descend the bank was mountainous, and, because of what else was there, such that every sight would shun it. Like the landslide which struck the flank of the Adige this side of Trento, because of an earthquake or the falling of support, where from the summit of the mountain, whence they fell, down to the plain, the rocks lie so strewn that they would provide a path for one who was above; such was the descent into that valley.

Progressing deeper into hell and farther down in the geography of the peninsula, the poet evokes an Apenninic terrain on the eve of the encounter with Geryon, and from the seventh circle of violence to the eighth of fraud, in *Inferno* 16:

Io lo seguiva, e poco eravam iti,
che 'l suon de l'acqua n'era sì vicino,
che per parlar saremmo a pena uditi.
Come quel fiume c' ha proprio cammino
prima dal Monte Viso 'nver' levante,
da la sinistra costa d'Apennino,
che si chiama Acquacheta suso, avante
che si divalli giù nel basso letto,
e a Forlì di quel nome è vacante,
rimbomba là sovra San Benedetto
de l'Alpe per cadere ad una scesa
ove dovea per mille esser recetto;
così, giù d'una ripa discoscesa,
trovammo risonar quell'acqua tinta,
sì che 'n poc'ora avria l'orecchia offesa (*Inf.* 16.91–105)

24 Hollander notes in his commentary that the space between *Inferno* 9.112–14 to *Inferno* 12.1–10 represents "the longest stretch in the poem between similes except for that between *Paradiso* 6.1 and 8.15 (unless we were to count the brief comparison at *Par.* 7.8–9 as a simile)." Cited from the Dartmouth Dante Project, ad loc. (accessed 22 July 2013).

Fig. 4. Pietro Vesconte, Mappamundi, ca. 1320, BAV, MS Pal. lat. 1362A, cc. 1v–2r

> Like that river which is first to take its own course toward the east, after monte Viso, on the left side of the Apennines, which is called Acquacheta above, before it falls down into the low bed and loses that name at Forlì, as it thunders there above San Benedetto de l'Alpe, when falling in one cascade where it usually descends by a thousand: so down from a steep cliff we found that dark water resounding, such that in a short while it would have harmed our ears.

The sequence of verbal mappings constitutes a system that, as will be suggested below, culminates in Malebolge in the famous opening simile of *Inferno* 28 that compares the gruesome bloody "filth" of the ninth "bolgia" of the sowers of discord to the battlefields of Puglia or southern Italy.[25]

In effect, any of the three genres or categories of cartography mentioned in this brief survey of Dante's cartographic context, including regional or chorographic maps of Italy, medieval mappaemundi, and contemporary sailing charts, might individually provide a useful interpretative perspective on Dante's poem. But what has not been tried is a reading of the *Commedia* as a form of cartographic writing or verbal mapping that brings all three of them together in an inspired poetic synthesis. Indeed, one would not expect Dante's procedure vis-à-vis his contemporary cartographic context to have been any less original and cumulative than was his approach to the inherited system of literary genres or literary sources. Although it should be noted that by combining diverse cartographic strata, as in the kind of cartographic palimpsest we are about to examine in *Inferno* 28, Dante parallels to some extent coeval cartographic procedures. For example, in his world maps, which are nearly contemporary to Dante, Pietro Vesconte brought together Mediterranean sailing charts and regional cartography within the traditional mappamundi framework. There we encounter, for the first time,[26] the empirically based nautical chart of the Mediterranean embedded within a mappamundi scheme (Fig. 4).

But, finally, the marvelously combinatory dimension of Dante's poetic cartography suggests a corollary issue that cannot be developed fully in this context but is worth mentioning, namely, the question of the relationship between cartography (and geography) and the truth claim of the poem.[27] I can only suggest here that Dante's cartographic

25 For discussion of this system, see T. J. Cachey Jr., "Cartographic Dante," *Italica* 86, no. 3 (2010): 325–54, and in an expanded Italian version, "Cartografie dantesche," in *Critica del testo* 14, no. 2 (2011): 229–59, in which the idea that Dante effectively rewrites the map of Italy of the *De vulgari eloquentia* in the *Inferno* is more fully developed.

26 As Michelina da Cesare has had occasion to point out, "Il sapere geografico di Boccaccio tra tradizione e innovazione: *L'imago mundi* di Paolini Veneto e Pietro Vesconte," in *Boccaccio geografo: Un viaggio nel Mediterraneo tra le città, i giardini Ea il "mondo" di Giovanni Boccaccio,* ed. R. Morosini and A. Cantile (Florence, 2010), 67–88.

27 Dante's marvelous invention Geryon, upon which the poet stakes the truth claim of his *comedia* (*Inf.* 16.124–39), is an apt figure for the fabulously synthetic but nonetheless truthful revelations of Dante the cartographer. For the Mediterranean geographical aspect of Dante's metaliterary monster Geryon, in which the poet can be said to concentrate all of the marvels of the East and more, see T. J. Cachey Jr., "Dante's Journey Between Truth and Fiction: Geryon Revisited," in *Atti del*

descriptio of the earth might be considered one of the pillars of the poet's rhetorical program in support of the truth claim of the poem. As the cartography historians Denis Wood and John Fels observe in *The Natures of Maps*: "Insisting that something is *there* is a uniquely powerful way of insisting that something *is*. Mapped things—no matter how conceptually daunting—possess such extraordinary credibility that they're capable of propelling into popular discourse abstruse abstractions cantilevered from abstruse abstractions: high pressure cells, El Niño, seafloor spreading, thermohaline circulation."[28] In the variety of cartographic dimensions it presents, the poem comes to possess something of the extraordinary credibility of maps, through the density and specificity of the toponyms that in certain passages render the poem like a contemporary Mediterranean sailing chart; in the poem's Global Positioning System that tags and triangulates the locations of Crete, Jerusalem, and Purgatory; and in the *sermo humilis* mapping of the Italian peninsula, featuring even the humblest and most obscure of places. Such places include a hot spring near Viterbo, called the Bulicame (*Inf.* 14.79); "Gaville" (*Inf.* 25.151), a village in the upper Valdarno not far from Figline (registered, in turn, in *Par.* 16.50), and "Marcabò" (*Inf.* 28.75), a castle built by the Venetians in the territory of Ravenna on the Po di Primaro in order to protect the navigation of the river toward Ravenna and Ferrara;[29] and "Focara" (*Inf.* 28.89), a lofty headland on the Adriatic, between Cattolica and Fano in the Marches, where Guido del Cassero and Angiolello di Carignano, two noblemen of Fano, of opposing parties, were to be cast overboard and drowned according to the prophecy of Pier da Medicina in *Inferno* 28.

Inferno 28 as Map of Italy, the Greek Mediterranean, and as Mappamundi

Dante scholars have come to consider *Inferno* 28, dedicated to the "sowers of discord" of the ninth and penultimate Malebolge of fraud, to be a structural and thematic focal point in the development of the first canticle of the poem for a variety of reasons. In the canto's last verse, the Provençal poet Bertran de Born holds out his severed head like a lantern to the pilgrim and famously announces for the first time the key ethical and rhetorical principle of the *contrapasso*: "Così s'osserva in me lo contrapasso" (Thus you observe in me the *contrapasso; Inf.* 28.142). The explicit statement by Bertran of the law by which the punishments of hell are fashioned to match the sins, so that sinners

---

Seminario Dantesco Internazionale 2000, ed. M. Picone (Florence, 2001), 75–92. Peter Armour and Brenda Schildgen, cited earlier, have observed in their respective treatments of Dante's geography how the marvels of the East are largely absent from the geographical gazetteer of the poem, although Schildgen has noted that some aspects of these marvels can be seen to inform the monsters that populate hell. In fact, Dante's Geryon presents a kind of summa of such mirabilia. See Z. G. Baranski, "Il 'meraviglioso' e il 'comico' (*Inferno* XVI)," in *"Sole nuovo, luce nuova": Saggi sul rinnovamento culturale in Dante* (Turin, 1996), 153–82.

28 D. Wood and J. Fels, *The Natures of Maps: Cartographic Constructions of the Natural World* (Chicago, 2008), 7.

29 I. Baldelli, "'Lo dolce piano che da Vercelli a Marcabò dichina,' *Inferno* XXVIII 74–75," *Lettere Italiane* 47 (1995), 2:193–202.

can be said to "reap what they have sown," has led some scholars to focus attention on the canto's key role in defining the ethical and poetic system of Dante's hell.[30] More recently, critics have based claims for the canto's structurally significant role on numerological considerations, beginning with the fact that the number 28 is the next perfect number after 6.[31] The prevalence of the figure of *accumulatio* that rhetorically characterizes the canto also contributes to its distinctly climactic or cumulative quality.[32] Yet, as far as I know the figure of *accumulatio* has not been related to the way in which Dante brings together various cartographic elements that had been introduced earlier in the poem and recapitulates them in a forceful and climactic manner in *Inferno* 28. In fact, the canto represents a watershed in the poet's deployment of cartographic writing as an innovative mode of poetic expression.

To begin with, the battlefield setting of the famous hypothetical simile that opens the canto is geographically located in "la fortunata terra / Di Puglia" (the fortune-tossed land of Puglia; *Inf.* 28.8–9). While today Puglia denotes a region in the southeastern part of Italy that forms the "heel" of the peninsula, in the Middle Ages the toponym was used to indicate the medieval kingdom of Naples, which included the whole of the south of Italy, stretching from the "heel" and "toe" as far north as the Tronto and Garigliano rivers on either coast (near modern Ascoli and Gaeta).[33] The opening simile of *Inferno* 28 thus completes, within the realm of the Malebolge of fraud, the cartographical outline of the peninsula that the poet had started to sketch in the circle of violence in the series of similes that were discussed earlier:

S'el s'aunasse ancor tutta la gente
che già, in su la fortunata terra
di Puglia, fu del suo sangue dolente
per li Troiani e per la lunga guerra
che de l'anella fé sì alte spoglie,
come Livïo scrive, che non erra,
con quella che sentio di colpi doglie
per contastare a Ruberto Guiscardo;

30 See M. Cogan, *The Design in the Wax: The Structure of the Divine Comedy and Its Meaning* (Notre Dame, IN, 1999), 36–38; Giuseppe Mazzotta has dedicated important pages to *Inferno* 28, where "repeated statements of a measurable bond between a crime and its punishment are put to the test," in "Metaphor and Justice," *Dante's Vision and the Circle of Knowledge* (Princeton, NJ, 1993), 75–95, p. 83.

31 O. Liberknecht, "Dante's Historical Arithmetics: The Numbers Six and Twenty-Eight as 'numeri perfecti secundum partium aggregationem' in *Inferno* XXVIII," paper given at the 32nd International Congress on Medieval Studies, 8–11 May 1997, http://www.lieberknecht.de/~diss/papers/p_np_txt.htm (accessed 22 July 2013); V. Kirkham, "Contrapasso: The Long Wait to *Inferno* 28," in *Tra Amici: Proceedings of a Symposium in Honor of Giuseppe Mazzotta, Modern Language Notes,* Italian Issue Supplement, 127, no. 1 (January 2012), 1–12.

32 E. Sanguineti, *Interpretazione di Malebolge* (Florence, 1961), 284–85.

33 Dante Alighieri, *The Divine Comedy of Dante Alighieri*, ed. and trans. R. M. Durling, intro and notes R. L. Martinez and R. M. Durling (New York, 1996–2011), 1:441, n. 8.

e l'altra il cui ossame ancor s'accoglie
a Ceperan, là dove fu bugiardo
ciascun Pugliese, e là da Tagliacozzo,
dove sanz'arme vinse il vecchio Alardo;
e qual forato suo membro e qual mozzo
mostrasse, d'aequar sarebbe nulla
il modo de la nona bolgia sozzo. (*Inf.* 28.7–21)

Could all the wounded troops again assemble: first from Apulia, land laid low by war, who grieved for their lost blood shed by the Trojans, then all those of the long war, whose corpses were despoiled of piles of rings—as Livy writes, who does not err—together with the ones who felt the agony of blows fighting in the fields against Guiscard, and those whose bones still lie in heaps at Ceprano, where each Apulian played it false, and those near Tagliacozzo, where old Alardo conquered without force of arms: and should one show his limb pierced through, another his, where it has been cut off, it would be nothing to the ninth pit's filth.

The exordium of *Inferno* 28 marks the infernal climax of the cartographic treatment of Italy as a sacred and contested territory in need of redemption, which Dante introduced at the very beginning of the poem when he provided a first glimpse of the Italian peninsula from the same perspective of Aeneas's ship arriving at its shores, and remembered both the Trojan and Latins who died in battle for its conquest: "di quella umile Italia . . . per cui morì la vergine Camilla, Eurialo e Turno e Niso di ferute" (of low-lying Italy . . . for which the maid Camilla died of wounds, and Euryalus, Turnus, and Nisus; *Inf.* 1.106–8).[34] But it is not only the map of the Italian peninsula that is completed in this canto. The map of the Greek Mediterranean is also recapitulated there: "Tra l'isola di Cipri e di Maiolica" (Between the isles of Cyprus and Maiorica; *Inf.* 28.82). And both of these chorographic or regional cartographies are embedded, as I intend to show, within the broader geographical and ethical framework of a mappamundi.

As far as the cartography of the Italian peninsula is concerned, the central episodes of the "body" of *Inferno* 28 (28.55–60, 28.73–90) recapitulate the same mappings of Alpine and Apenninic Italy that we already encountered in the series of chorographic similes of the seventh circle, that is, upon entering the first ring where are punished

34 The Virgilian intertext for *Inferno* 1.106–8 has not been fully explained by the commentary tradition. Dante's echo of *Aeneid* 3.522–23, "cum procul obscuros collis humilemque videmus / Italiam" (when from afar we saw the dim hills of Italy lying low on the horizon), glimpses Italy at the poem's outset from the perspective of a ship arriving at its shores. Dante is a new Aeneas and a Columbus *ante litteram*. It is in the new world of the poem that he undertakes the Christian conversion and reform of Italy, and at the same time the remapping of the Italian peninsula in the wake of the abandoned cartographic experiment of the *De vulgari eloquentia*. For further discussion of the relationship between the respective mappings of the *De vulgari eloquentia* and the poem, see Cachey, "Cartographic Dante" (above, n. 25).

those who were violent against others (*Inf.* 12.4–10) and before exiting the last subcircle of the seventh circle dedicated to the usurers (16.91–105). *Inferno* 28, for its part, features Fra Dolcino de' Tonielli of Novara, the head of a heretical sect, which was condemned to be suppressed by Clement V in a papal bull of 1305. Fra Dolcino fled with his brethren to the Alps between Novara and Vercelli, where he defied the authorities for more than a year before he was eventually captured and burned at the stake in June 1307. He is introduced by his fellow schismatic Muhammad, who addresses Dante the pilgrim:

> *"Or dì a fra Dolcin dunque che s'armi,*
> *tu che forse vedra' il sole in breve,*
> *s'ello non vuol qui tosto seguitarmi,*
> *sì di vivanda, che stretta di neve*
> *non rechi la vittoria al Noarese,*
> *ch'altrimenti acquistar non saria leve."* (*Inf.* 28.55–60).

> "You, who perhaps will shortly see the sun warn Fra Dolcino to provide himself—unless he'd like to join me here quite soon—with stocks of victuals, lest the siege of snow hand the Novarese the victory not otherwise so easy to attain."

Fra Dolcin is paired in the canto's central panels with the obscure Pier da Medicina, a figure about whom we know little except that he apparently hailed from Medicina, a large village between Imola and Bologna,[35] and reportedly sowed discord between the Malatesta and Polenta families of the Romagna. The pairing of Fra Dolcino and Pier da Medicina repeats the same characterizing Italian topographies referenced earlier in the Malebolge in the two most extensive and famous carto-chorographic passages of the eighth circle of fraud. In his account of the foundation of Mantua in *Inferno* 20, Virgil describes the Alpine territory around the city. Dante the pilgrim subsequently describes the "dolce terra latina" of the Romagna to Guido da Montefeltro in *Inferno* 27. Dante locates these key passages of chorographic description in highly sensitive contexts from a metaliterary and ideological point of view. Through their placement in those "evil pouches" of the eighth circle of fraud that are dedicated to the punishment of false prophets and false counselors, respectively, they underscore the special connection between geography and the truth claim of the poem.

Pier da Medicina, meanwhile, in *Inferno* 28, continues to sow discord even from hell, and exhorts the pilgrim:

> *"rimembriti di Pier da Medicina,*
> *se mai torni a veder lo dolce piano*
> *che da Vercelli a Marcabò dichina.*
> *E fa sapere a' due miglior da Fano,*
> *a messer Guido e anco ad Angiolello,*

35 See Baldelli, "'Lo dolce piano'" (above, n. 29).

che, se l'antiveder qui non è vano,
gittati saran fuor di lor vasello
e mazzerati presso a la Cattolica
per tradimento d'un tiranno fello.
Tra l'isola di Cipri e di Maiolica
non vide mai sì gran fallo Nettuno,
non da pirate, non da gente argolica.
Quel traditor che vede pur con l'uno,
e tien la terra che tale qui meco
vorrebbe di vedere esser digiuno,
farà venirli a parlamento seco;
poi farà sì, ch'al vento di Focara
non sarà lor mestier voto né preco." (*Inf.* 28.73–90)

"should you ever see that gentle plain again that slopes from Vercelli down to Marcabò, for Pier da Medicina spare a thought. And let the two chief men of Fano know, both messer Guido and Angiolello, that, unless our foresight here is vain, through a brutal tyrant's treachery near La Cattolica they shall be heaved out of their ship with weights to sink them down. Between the islands of Cyprus and Majorca Neptune never witnessed so terrible a crime, whether one committed by pirates or by Greeks. That traitor, who sees through one eye only and rules the city that another down here with me would take delight in never having seen, will have the men of Fano come to parley and he will so deal with them that, to control Focara's wind, they'll need no vows or prayers."

Pier da Medicina gives a memorable, densely chorographic prophecy that evokes the entire valley of the Po, from Vercelli in the Alps down to near Ravenna. Dante, in fact, makes a point of linking the Alpine and Apenninic settings of the Fra Dolcino and Pier da Medicina episodes in the latter's speech. As noted above, Vercelli is where Fra Dolcino was executed, and Pier's reference to the Piedmontese village at the western end of the Po river basin serves to connect the two episodes spatially. The linkage of episodes and sinners in terms of geographical territory is a distinctive characteristic of the canto, which also, by means of geography, links episodes and sinners that are asynchronic from a historical perspective, as when Pier indirectly introduces the ancient Roman Curio by declaring that "another down here with me" wishes he had never seen the same Romagna controlled by the Malatesta: "e tien la terra [Malatestino, lord of Rimini] che tale qui meco [Curio] vorebbe di vedere esser digiuno" (he rules the city that another down here with me would take delight in never having seen; *Inf.* 28.86–87). By means of these topographic connections Dante insinuates, in subtle contrast to the canto's surface reality of fragmented geographical vistas and mangled and dismembered bodies, the vision of an underlying ideal Christian unity of the body and the land. Pier concludes with a warning addressed to high-ranking nobles of Fano (Guido del Cassero and Angioello da Carignano) that they will be cast overboard and drowned en route to a parlay treacherously arranged by Malatestino, lord of Rimini, described here as "Quel traditor che vede pur con l'uno" (that traitor who sees with only one eye; *Inf.* 28.85). In its implicit allusion to Polyphemus, the prophecy reinforces for the reader the Greek Mediterranean frame of reference evoked by the first verse of the preceding tercet, "tra l'isola di Cipri e di Moailica." According to Pier di Medicina, not just Italy but the whole of the Mediterranean world had never witnessed such an egregiously fraudulent crime as the one prepared by the Cyclops Malatestino, for to say Cyprus in the east and Majorca in the west is to encompass, by synecdoche, the entire Mediterranean.

The canto, therefore, not only recapitulates the previously outlined cartographic parameters of Italy, but by means of this synecdoche reiterates the eastern and western ends of the map of the Greek Mediterranean that had recently been traversed in earlier cantos of the eighth circle. In fact, Jason had appeared in the first canto of the Malebolge in *Inferno* 18, in the first bolgia dedicated to pimps and seducers; while Dante encounters Ulysses, who ventured beyond the pillars of Hercules in the farthest west, in the eighth bolgia, as recounted in *Inferno* 26. The synthetic allusion to the Greeks in the Mediterranean of *Inferno* 28.82–84: "Between the islands of Cyprus and Maiorca, Neptune never witnessed so terrible a crime," serves at one level to contrast the crimes of the ancient Greeks and the crimes of the modern Italians in a bitterly ironic manner.[36] This rhetorical expression serves also to recapitulate the same cartographic and ethical structure that has previously ordered the space of the poem according to a chiasmus of rhetorically tragic and comic examples, whereby ancient Greek and modern Italian sinners are juxtaposed. Thus, the modern Italian Venedico Caccianemico is contrasted with the ancient Greek Jason in *Inferno* 18, just as the ancient Greek Ulysses in *Inferno* 26 is contrasted with the modern Italian Guido da Montefeltro in *Inferno* 27. The same ethical structure informs the summative comparison of the Adriatic crimes of modern Italians with those of the ancient Greeks. Within the Malebolge, three structurally and thematically linked passages, therefore, cumulatively map the Mediterranean basin in its specifically geospatial aspect, and the last one in the sequence, which provides a fleeting glimpse of the entire Mediterranean from the perspective of the promontory of Focara, evoked as is Marcabò in the manner of a toponym on a contemporary map, represents the recapitulation and climax of the series.

The Mediterranean passages of the *Inferno* have implications for the map of the poem that extend to the *Paradiso*. The first encounter with the Greeks in Malebolge had portrayed Jason, who "per cuore e per senno / li Colchi del monton privati féne" (who with heart and head / deprived the men of Colchis of their ram; *Inf.* 18.86–87) is punished among the seducers for his abandonment of Hypsipyle on the island of Lemnos: "Ello passò per l'isola di Lenno / poi che l'ardite femmine spietate / tutti li maschi loro

36 Cf. Most, "Dante's Greeks" (above, n. 1), 29: "In such cases, the ancient figure explains and dignifies the modern one: Dante seems to be saying that his age too has its villains who are not unworthy to be put alongside their more celebrated predecessors . . . . Of course, Dante's elevation of his own 'modernity' is bitterly ironic: what is involved are invariably not saints but sinners."

a morte dienno" (He made landfall on the isle of Lemnos after its women, bold and pitiless, had given all their males to death; *Inf.* 18.88–90).

The voyage of Jason and the Argonauts, whose first adventure during their quest for the Golden Fleece took place in the north Aegean island of Lemnos, is central to Dante's myth-making about his poetic enterprise. The poet will compare the composition of the poem to the voyage of the Argonauts in a famous address to the readers near the beginning of the third canticle: "Que' gloriosi che passaro al Colco / non s'ammiraron come voi farete, / quando Iasón vider fatto bifolco" (Those men of glory, those who crossed to Colchis, when they saw Jason turn into a ploughman were less amazed than you will be; *Par.* 2.16–18). The "men of glory" referred to in *Paradiso* 2 are the Argonauts who accompanied Jason on the first voyage made by ship, in the thirteenth-century BC, to Colchis.[37]

The first reference to Jason and the Argonauts at the beginning of Malebolge is thus echoed at the beginning of the *Paradiso.* The allusion to Neptune in Pier da Medicina's prophecy in the last of Malebolge's three cartographical views of the Mediterranean, "non vide mai sì gran fallo Nettuno" (Neptune never saw so great a crime), is accordingly re-evoked and reversed in a complementary passage at the end of the *Paradiso.* There the marvel of the god of the sea at the voyage of the Argonauts is connected to no less than the poet's failing memory of his vision of God: "Un punto solo m'è maggior letargo / che venticinque secoli a la 'mpresa / che fé Nettuno ammirar l'ombra d'Argo" (That one moment brings more forgetfulness to me than twenty-five centuries have brought to the endeavor that startled Neptune with the Argo's shadow; *Par.* 33.94–96).

Between these evocations of the voyage of the Argonauts at the beginning of the Malebolge, and the beginning and the end of the *Paradiso,* respectively, Dante's major treatment of the Mediterranean in the Malebolge cantos of the *Inferno* was, of course, the voyage of Ulysses, whose doomed extra-Mediterranean journey in *Inferno* 26 offered a counterpoint to the successful voyages of the Argo and of Dante:

Io e' compagni eravam vecchi e tardi
quando venimmo a quella foce stretta
dov'Ercule segnò li suoi riguardi
acciò che l'uom più oltre non si metta;
da la man destra mi lasciai Sibilia,
da l'altra già m'avea lasciata Setta. (*Inf.* 26.106–11)

37 Piero Boitani has studied in detail the sublime image of the sea that dominates the *Paradiso* and has written a marvelous chapter about it. He observes how at the beginning of the third canticle in *Paradiso* 2, we find ourselves "on the open seas . . . now there is no port. . . . We are, so to speak, at the Pillars of Hercules that separate the Mediterranean from the Atlantic." (Just as, we might add, we are about to undertake again, metaphorically speaking, the first voyage of history made by the Argo.) P. Boitani, *Il tragico e il sublime nella letteratura medievale* (Bologna, 1992), 370. But see also E. R. Curtius, "The Ship of the Argonauts," in *Essays on Euorpean Literature* (Princeton, NJ, 1973), 485–96; and M. Picone, "Dante argonauta: La ricezione dei miti ovidiani nella *Commedia,*" in *Ovidio redivivus: Von Ovid zu Dante,* ed. M. Picone and B. Zimmermann (Stuttgart, 1994), 173–202.

> And I and my companions were already old and slow, when we approached the narrow strait where Hercules set up his boundary stones that men might heed and never reach beyond; upon my right I had gone past Seville, and on the left already passed Ceuta.

This passage from Malebolge is also recapitulated from the transcendent heights of the perspective of the sphere of the fixed stars, in *Paradiso* 27, where Dante views the Mediterranean basin, as if looking down upon a contemporary sailing chart (or a globe), including the trajectory of Ulysses' "mad flight" beyond the pillars of Hercules: "sì ch'io vedea di là da Gade il varco / folle d'Ulisse, e di qua presso il lito / nel qual si fece Europa dolce carco" (So that beyond Cadiz I saw Ulysses' mad course and, to the east, could almost see that shoreline where Europa was sweet burden; *Par.* 27.82–84).

Beneath the kaleidoscopic and fragmentary surface of the cartographic writing of the eighth circle a coherent and comprehensive mapping of the Greek Mediterranean emerged, one that corresponded to a cartographic logic and consistency that was capable of extension and ramification into the *Paradiso*. The two ends of the Mediterranean frame both the narrative and textual space of the Malebolge and the *Paradiso*. The contemporary sailing chart of the Mediterranean informs the map of the poem that is limited within the parameters of the Greek Mediterranean, that is, between the setting out to sea of the first ship of history from Argos in the east and the pillars of Hercules in the west. These boundaries are extended and projected poetically to provide a framework, or to use a cartographic term, a kind of cartouche, for the otherwise unmappable and oceanic experience of the utopic space of paradise, in the sense that the function of the cartouche in cartography is, in addition to conveying information, "to fill up empty spaces or distract the viewer's attention from missing but needed geographical data."[38] Dante's own oceanic experience beyond the pillars of Hercules on an extraterrestrial journey to paradise found its archetypal terrestrial framework and point of departure in the Greek Mediterranean of Jason and the Argonauts, and the first ship of history, the Argos.

But returning back to earth, we find that the Mediterranean also provided a cartographic framework for *Inferno* 28 that is articulated structurally in the canto's disposition of the figures of Muhammad and Alì in the east at the beginning of the canto and Bertran de Born at the end of the canto in the west. These paradigmatic fomenters of religious schism and political discord are associated with either end of the Mediterranean so as to bracket *Inferno* 28 in both figural (two bodies in one versus one body in two parts) and geographical terms. The canto's verbal mappings are therefore not exhausted by the chorographic mappings of Italy and the Mediterranean that we have just been discussing. These chorographic descriptions are ultimately embedded within the map of the world, just as in the Vesconte world map, although in this instance by allusion to the T-O type, which was the most common of medieval world maps.

38 "Cartouche" (Munich, n.d.), http://www.kettererkunst.com/dict/cartouche.shtml (accessed 22 July 2013).

T-O maps, in fact, figured the inhabited part of the earth as a circle divided into the three known continents. The horizontal bars of the T correspond to the Don or Tanais and the Nile, which are represented as if on the same axis, while the vertical bar corresponds to the Mediterranean (Fig. 5).[39] This canonical format of the T-O map, which, as early as the ninth century was associated with the crucifix of Christ, is recapitulated in the figural program of *Inferno* 28. At the beginning of the canto, the vertical slash on the body of Muhammad from "his chin to where we fart" is continued on the body of his son-in-law Alì "from chin to forelock":

Già veggia, per mezzul perdere o lulla,
com'io vidi un, così non si pertugia,
rotto dal mento infin dove si trulla.
Tra le gambe pendevan le minugia;
la corata pareva e 'l tristo sacco
che merda fa di quel che si trangugia.
Mentre che tutto in lui veder m'attacco,
guardommi e con le man s'aperse il petto,
dicendo: "Or vedi com'io mi dilacco!
vedi come storpiato è Mäometto!
Dinanzi a me sen va piangendo Alì,
fesso nel volto dal mento al ciuffetto. (*Inf.* 28.22–33)

No barrel, even though it's lost a hoop or end-piece, ever gapes as one whom I saw ripped right from his chin to where we fart: his bowels hung between his legs, one saw his vitals and the miserable sack that makes of what we swallow excrement. While I was all intent on watching him, he looked at me, and with his hands he spread his chest and said: "See how I split myself! See now how maimed Muhammad is! And he who walks and weeps before me is Alì, whose face is opened wide from chin to forelock.

At the end of the canto, we encounter the corresponding and complementary horizontal slash that separates Betran de Born's head from his body:

Io vidi certo, e ancor par ch'io 'l veggia,
un busto sanza capo andar sì come
andavan li altri de la trista greggia;
e 'l capo tronco tenea per le chiome,
pesol con mano a guisa di lanterna:
e quel mirava noi e dicea: "Oh me!" (*Inf.* 28.118–23)

39 See E. Edson, *Mapping Time and Space* (above, n. 17), 4–7; and *The World Map* (above, n. 17), 11–32. But for the T-O map as a symbol of the passion of Christ, see D. Woodward, "Medieval Mappaemundi," in *History of Cartography* (above, n. 8), 1:286–370, esp. 334–42.

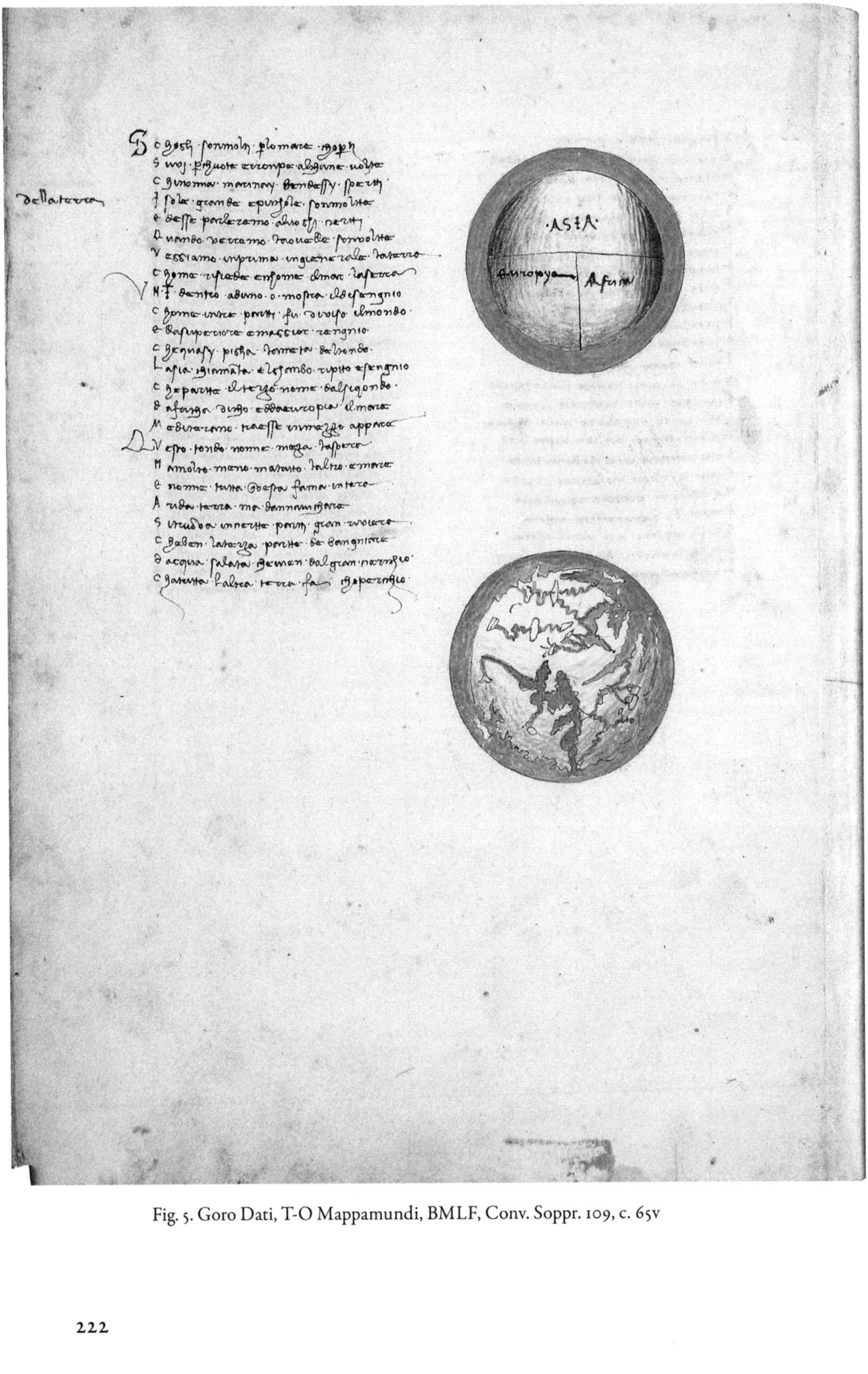

Fig. 5. Goro Dati, T-O Mappamundi, BMLF, Conv. Soppr. 109, c. 65v

I surely saw, and it still seems I see, a trunk without a head that walked just like the others in that melancholy herd; it carried by the hair its severed head, which swayed within its hand just like a lantern; and that head looked at us and said: "Ah me!"

The cuts on the bodies of Muhammad and Alì and Bertran de Born at either end of the canto are intended to evoke, at either end of the Mediterranean, the vertical and horizontal bars of the T of the T-O map of a medieval mappamundi. The circular figuration of the punishment or *contrapasso*, meanwhile—the sinners process in a circle and are slashed by a demon in an endless cycle of closing and opening of wounds—recapitulates the figure of the O of the circling ocean as represented by the T-O map. Dante's mappamundi in *Inferno* 28, however, turns Christ's cross upside down on the map of the world, as the horizontal bar of the decapitated Bertran is located in the west and the vertical cut on the body of Muhammad and Alì is in the east. Dante's poetic map, thus, represents an infernal parody of the T-O map at the same time that it evokes antiphrastically in its images of dismemberment the notion of the unity of the body of Christ as projected on the unity of the body of the world, according to another cartographic model, famously exemplified by medieval mappaemundi such as the Ebsdorf map and the English Psalter (Figs. 6–7).

According to Daniel Birkholz, the Ebsdorf map is "one of a number of compositions in variations to be found across the spectrum of medieval illuminated books which share a loose thematic affiliation.... Their common element is that they blend, juxtapose or otherwise bring together a bodily representation of the divine—typically God as world's creator and/or Christ as a world redeemer with a more or less map-like disk."[40] Evelyn Edson notes that several medieval world maps are drawn with Christ embracing or presiding over the world. For example, on the often-reproduced thirteenth-century English Psalter map, Christ, flanked by incense-bearing angels, stands over the world and astride it. In the version of the map on the opposite side of the folio, featuring the English Psalter map, Christ embraces the earth.

By means of this cartographic frame of reference, Dante causes the wounds on the bodies of the sowers of discord to evoke both the wounds on the body of Christ, which is, in turn, taken as the body of the world. Thus, in a manner analogous to Vesconte's cartographic procedure in his mappamundi, that of Dante merges diverse cartographic traditions in *Inferno* 28, including the chorography of Italy, the Greek Mediterranean, and medieval mappaemundi. The map of Italy can be said to anchor the Italocentric and Roman ideological frame of the poem, while the mappamundi, appropriately enough, describes the poem's moral and ethical parameters with regard to this life within the confines of the inhabited world or ecumene. Dante's mapping of the Greek Mediterranean, on the other hand, provides the model for charting the poem's metaphysical and poetic

40 D. Birkholz, *The King's Two Maps: Cartography and Culture in Thirteenth-Century England* (New York, 2004), xxiii.

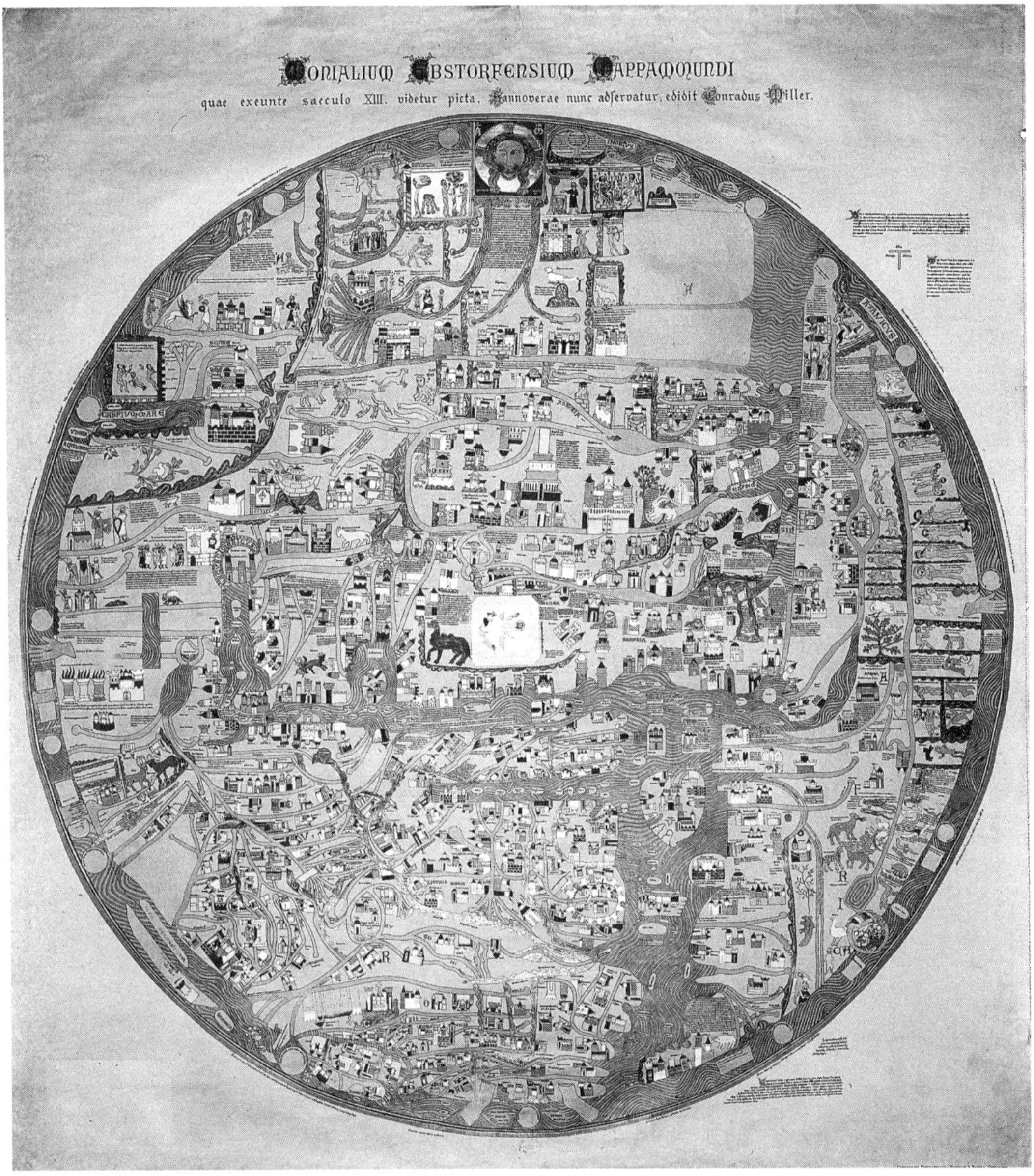

Fig. 6. The Ebsdorf Mappamundi, ca. 1235–39 (destroyed during WWII)

parameters, that is, across the twenty-five centuries of the human journey that would ultimately transcend time and space. Thus, the Greeks, originally marginalized in keeping with Dante's theory of history, are appropriately re-evoked at the end of the journey. To the extent that the Greek Mediterranean serves as a frame or cartouche for the unmappable utopic space of the *Paradiso,* it can be said to transcend not only the ideological home of Italy as a historical and political territory but also the mappamundi of

Fig. 7. Mappamundi in the English Psalter, thirteenth century, BL, Add. Ms. 28681, c. 9

the terrestrial world itself. At the same time that Dante "others" the Greeks (a gesture apparently essential to any kind of European identity), he takes a Greek Mediterranean mapping of the journey of time and space, between the limit of the pillars of Hercules and Argos, as the space within which to imagine a transcendence (not a transgression, as in Ulysses) of the spatial-temporal limit of the terrestrial world. In figuring his own spiritual and poetic transcendence in terms of the original journey of the pagan Greek

Jason and the Argonauts, Dante expressed more than a medieval Christian desire for religious transcendence of this world. His identification of the first ship of history with the ship of the poem expresses a perennial literary and cultural aspiration to transcend the limits of the spatial-temporal world that is perhaps no less compelling to us today in a postmodern and secular age.

Dante, Byzantium, and the Italian Chronicle Tradition

WILLIAM CAFERRO

THIS ESSAY SEEKS TO EVALUATE Dante's treatment of Byzantium in the *Commedia* in terms of contemporary Italian chronicles. It takes as its starting point the thesis that Dante's "idea of Rome," as Charles Till Davis famously called it, created an inherent "problem" with respect to Byzantium.[1] The divine choice of the Romans for world rule and the association of them with classical and Christian notions of justice left little room for the inclusion of contemporary Byzantines, who were at once Romans (*Romaioi*, as they called themselves) and heirs of the empire, but also Greeks and religious schismatics, owing to the split between the churches in 1054. In this reading, Emperor Justinian (*Par.* 6), whom Dante visually encountered in the mosaics at San Vitale in Ravenna, is a wholly Roman figure, who brought the eagle ("uccel di dio") back west from the bounds of Europe ("stremo d'Europa") and transformed divine justice into earthly justice through codification of Roman law. Conversely, Emperor Constantine, who founded Byzantium and brought the Roman Eagle east "against the course of heaven," is "Greek" ("fece il greco, con le legge e meco"; *Par.* 20.6–57). The equation of justice with Rome, grounded in Virgil, is so strong that figures like Ripheus, from book 2 of the *Aeneid,* is in paradise.[2] Conversely, the

1 This was the subject of my doctoral prospectus and an enthusiastic, but flawed and inadequate first professional essay. W. Caferro, "Dante and the Problem of Byzantium," in *The Unbounded Community*, ed. W. Caferro and D. G. Fisher (New York and London, 1996), 93–111. On the idea of Rome, see C. T. Davis, *Dante and the Idea of Rome* (Oxford, 1957), and "Dante and Empire," in *The Cambridge Companion to Dante*, ed. R. Jacoff (Cambridge, 1993): 257–69; N. Lenkeith, *Dante and the Legend of Rome* (London 1952). On the political nature of Dante's thought, see J. Ferrante, *The Political Vision of the Divine Comedy* (Princeton, 1984), and J. A. Scott, *Dante's Political Purgatory* (Philadelphia, 1996). This essay uses *The Divine Comedy of Dante Alighieri*, ed. and trans. R. M. Durling and R. L. Martines, vols. 1–3 (Oxford, 1996–2011), and *The Dante Encyclopedia*, ed. R. Lansing (New York, 2000).

2 Robert Hollander wrote that "if one were to epitomize the central concern of the poem in a single word, justice might embody the best choice." The word occurs as a noun thirty-five times and as an adjective thirty-six times. R. Hollander, *Dante: A Life in Works* (New Haven and London, 2010), 106.

association of Greek with falsehood is such that Sinon, "falso" and "greco da Troia," is in the pit of hell (*Inf.* 30). The depiction of Rome is, as Rachel Jacoff has emphasized, a "fragile" construct, which runs counter to Augustine's depiction of the Romans in *City of God*.[3]

The thesis does not deny the echoes and important intellectual and structural influences of Byzantium adduced by scholars. But the *Commedia* contains little overt reference to contemporary Byzantine historical persons and events, an omission that, as John Sinclair said of the absent King Louis IX of France, seems "strange."[4] The theological harmony of *Paradiso* (10–13), in which Thomas praises the Franciscans and Bonaventura the Dominicans, does not include reconciliation with the schismatic Byzantines, although the Council of Lyons (1274) that temporarily brought the Greek and Latin Churches together occurred in Dante's lifetime. Dante would seem to allude to the council in his accusation in *Purgatorio* 20 that Charles of Anjou drove Aquinas ("rispinse al ciel, Tommaso") back to heaven, repeating the rumor that Thomas, who died while traveling to the council, was killed by Anjou to forestall the union, which would undo his planned invasion of Byzantium. Moreover, Dante deals substantially with political issues involving southern Italy, including Charles of Anjou and the Sicilian Vespers, in which the Byzantines played a very prominent role. The main protagonists—Peter of Aragon, Popes Nicholas III and Martin IV, Marquis William VII of Montferrat—are in the *Commedia*, but not Michael VIII Palaiologos (r. 1261–1282), emperor of a revived Byzantium who retook Constantinople in 1261 and, according to several accounts, conspired with Peter of Aragon and Pope Nicholas III to initiate the Vespers. Michael was excommunicated by Martin IV and accused of paying Nicholas to betray Anjou. Dante appears to refer to the latter in *Inferno* 19 when describing how Nicholas, condemned for avarice, received *mal tolta moneta* that made him *ardito* against Anjou.

It is thus with a historian's instinctive caution that this essay attempts to account for silences in Dante. It does so acknowledging that as poet and visionary, Dante need not be held liable for recording the many and varied political events of his day. But the effort is worthwhile, because Byzantium was the subject of misunderstanding and mistrust in the medieval West and negative stereotypes among contemporary Western writers.[5] The

3 R. Jacoff, "Sacrifice and Empire: Thematic Analogies in San Vitale and the Paradiso," in *Renaissance Studies in Honor of Craig Hugh Smyth*, ed. A. Morough et al. (Florence, 1985), 1:317–32, 322. See Davis, *Dante and the Idea of Rome*, 46.

4 *The Divine Comedy of Dante Alighieri: The Purgatorio,* ed. and trans. J. D. Sinclair (New York, 1961), 2:269.

5 Bishop Liutprand of Cremona described the Byzantines during his embassy to Constantinople in AD 968 as "Greeks" who were "faithless, greedy, and obsequious." The Catalan chronicler Ramon Muntaner (1265–1336) called the Byzantines "worthless people" who nevertheless believed that they were "worth more than any other people in the world" and exhibited "no charity toward their neighbors." A. Kaldellis, *Hellenism in Byzantium: The Transformations of Greek Identity and the Reception of the Classical Tradition* (Cambridge, 2007), 334–45; K. Ciggaar, *Western Travellers to Constantinople: The West and Byzantium 962–1204* (Leiden, 1996), 26, 95, 97–98; *The Chronicle of Muntaner*, trans. Lady Goodenough (London, 1921), 2:492; T. Shawcross, "Re-inventing the

events treated in the *Commedia* coincide with heightened interaction between East and West, with strong anti-Latin feelings in Byzantium arising from the "unholy" crusade of 1204 and with what some scholars have argued was a time of increased "Greek" sentiment among Byzantines, closer identification with their Hellenic classical past, self-definition in opposition to the Latins, and even the precocious stirrings of Greek nationalism.[6] Upon retaking Constantinople in 1261, Michael Palaiologos called himself the "new" Constantine, an appellation he projected at home and used in his correspondence with the West.[7] Thus, during Dante's youth, there was quite literally a "Greek" Constantine. During Dante's adulthood, an anonymous Genoese poet devoted a brief vernacular work to contemporary Byzantines, calling them "thieves, wicked and haughty" ("lairaor, neco e soperbo").[8] In the next generation, Petrarch, who admired ancient Greece and sought to learn the Greek language, described Byzantines as "deceitful" and "indolent" ("fallax," "iners") in one of the letters in his *Rerum familiarum* (book 14.5).[9] In his epistle to Boccaccio (*Rerum senilium* 3.6), Petrarch ridiculed Leontius Pilatus, the first chair of Greek of the Florentine studio, for calling himself Thessalian rather than Calabrian, as "if Greek was more noble than Italian," and for suggesting that Constantinople was another Rome, with greater riches, when it was inferior with respect to "arms, virtues, and glory."[10]

Homeland in the Historiography of Frankish Greece: The Fourth Crusade and the Legend of the Trojan War," *BMGS* 27 (2003): 120–53, and eadem, *The Chronicle of Morea: Historiography in Crusader Greece* (Oxford, 2009).

6 Contemporary Byzantine writers such as George Pachymeres and Manuel Hobolos, court orator of Michael Palaiologos, expressed anti-Latin sentiment. According to Deno Geanakoplos, the Byzantines considered the Latins heretical, supercilious, and culturally inferior. D. J. Geanakoplos, *Michael Paleologus and the West, 1258–1282* (Cambridge, MA, 1959), 131, 271, and "Greco-Latin Relations on the Eve of the Byzantine Restoration: The Battle of Pelagonia 1259," *DOP* 7 (1953): 99–141; D. Nicol, *The Last Centuries of Byzantium: 1261–1453* (Cambridge, 1993). On Greek nationalism, see A. E. Vacaloupolus, *The Origins of the Greek Nation: The Byzantine Period (1204–1261)* (New Brunswick, NJ, 1970).

7 Michael's predecessor John III Vatatzes (1222–1254) also associated himself and his rule with Constantine, in opposition to the Latin "usurpers" in Constantinople. M. Angold, "Byzantine Nationalism," *BMGS* (1975): 56, and "After the Fourth Crusade," in *The Cambridge History of Byzantine Empire, 500–1492* (Cambridge, 2008), 751; R. Macrides, "The New Constantine," *BMGS* 6 (1980): 13–41; A. E. Laiou, *Constantinople and the Latins: The Foreign Policy of Andronicus II, 1282–1328* (Cambridge, MA, 1972), 1.

8 "Quasi ogni Greco per comun/ e lairaor, neco e soperbo." L. Cocito, *Anonimo Genovese: Poesie* (Rome, 1970), 208 (poem 26.1–2); S. A. Epstein, *Genoa and the Genoese, 958–1528* (Chapel Hill and London, 1996), 166–71.

9 Francesco Petrarca, *Le familiari*: *Edizione critica*, ed. V. Rossi (Florence, 1937), 3:120; Francis Petrarch, *Letters on Familiar Matters (Rerum familiares libri IX–XVI)*, trans. A. S. Bernardo (Baltimore and London, 1982), 239. On Petrarch's negative attitude toward Byzantium, see N. Bisaha, "Petrarch's Vision of the Muslim and Byzantine East," *Speculum* 76, no. 2 (2001): 284–314.

10 "Greci enim Constantinopolim alteram Romam vocant quam non parem modo antique sed maiorem corporibus ac divitiis effectam dicere ausi sunt . . . certe viris armis ac virtutibus et gloria parem dicere, quamvis impudens Graeculus non audebit." *Epistole di F. Petrarca*, ed. U. Dotti (Turin, 1978), 110; Francis Petrarch, *Letters of Old Age (Rerum senilium libri I–XVIII)*, trans. A. S. Bernardo, S. Levin, and R. A. Bernardo (Baltimore and London, 1992), 101.

My intention is to gain perspective on Dante and the *Commedia* by looking at accounts of contemporary writers to judge the extent of their knowledge of Byzantium and ascertain their views. The essay begins in Tuscany, the subject of much study with regard to Dante, and proceeds north and south, seeking regional coverage throughout the peninsula, including Sicily, a selection that Dante himself would have appreciated.[11] The approach is not without problem; any choice of sources may be deemed arbitrary and is necessarily bound by the availability of modern editions.[12] The purpose is not to hide this, but to move forward in the hope of expanding the historical discourse, too often centered on Florence, and stress the challenges inherent in tracing the transmission of medieval texts and ideas, about which little is in fact known, even with regard to Dante.[13] In this respect, a certain arbitrariness is not entirely undesirable, as it reflects the scholarly status quo.

The common element in the sources is that they all deal with Angevin politics and the "ambiguous" events (East/West) and persons noted above in the *Commedia*. The sample includes vernacular and Latin works: the former, like (Florentine) Giovanni Villani's *Nuova cronica*, have already been studied in terms of Dante, and the latter, like (Roman)

11 Dante described Sicily as the seat of the imperial throne in *De vulgari eloquentia*. Dante, *De vulgari eloquentia*, ed. and trans. S. Botterill (Cambridge, 1996), 29.

12 On the Italian chronicle tradition, see the still useful U. Balzani, *Le cronache Italiane nel medio evo* (Milan, 1884). Balzani deals with a wide range of works, many of which have still not received adequate attention in English. More recent scholarship has had a largely regional focus: see G. Arnaldi, *Studi sui cronisti della Marca Trevigiana nell' etá di Ezzelino da Romano* (Rome, 1963); G. Arnaldi and L. Capo, "Cronisti di Venezia e della Marca Trevigiana dalle origini alla fine del secolo XIII," in *Storia della cultura veneta: Dalle origini al Trecento* (Vicenza, 1975), 404–5; G. Fasoli, *Cronache medievali di Sicilia: Note d'orientamento* (Bologna, 1995). An attempt to deal with the lacuna on the subject in English language scholarship is *Chronicling History: Chroniclers and Historians in Medieval and Renaissance Italy*, ed. S. Dale, A. Williams Lewin, and D. Osheim (University Park, PA, 2007).

13 The well-worn discourse on Dante and the Florentine chronicle tradition has focused on whether Villani used Dante or vice versa, or whether they used a third source—the so-called Malispini question. R. Morghen, "Note malispiniane," *Bullettino dell'Istituto Storico Italiano per il Medio Evo e Archivio Muratoriano* 40 (1920): 105–26, and "Dante, il Villani e Ricordano Malispini," *Bullettino dell'Istituto Storico Italiano per il Medio Evo e Archivio Muratoriano* 41 (1921): 171–94; M. C. De Matteis, "Ancora su Malispini, Villani, e Dante: Per un riesame dei rapporti tra cultura storica e profezia etica nell'Alighieri," *Bullettino dell'Istituto Storico Italiano per il Medio Evo e Archivio Muratoriano* 82 (1970; published 1973): 329–90, and "Malispini da Villani o Villani da Malispini? Una ipotesi sui rapporti tra Ricordano Malispini, il 'Compendiatore,' e Giovanni Villani," *Bullettino dell'Istituto Storico Italiano per il Medio Evo e Archivio Muratoriano* 84 (1973; publ. 1978): 145–221. N. Rubinstein believed that Dante read the first book of Giovanni Villani. N. Rubinstein, "The Beginnings of Political Thought in Florence," *JWarb* 5 (1942): 198–227. Charles Till Davis believed that Villani used Dante and that Malaspini was a later work; Davis, *Idea of Rome* (above, n. 1), 244–62, and "Recent Work on the Malispini Question," in *Dante's Italy and Other Essays* (Philadelphia, 1984), 290–99; Giovanni Aquilecchia, "Dante and The Florentine Chronicles," *The Bulletin of John Rylands Library* 48 (1965–66): 30–55. The more recent wok on the Florentine tradition includes G. Porta, "La costruzione della storia in Giovanni Villani," in *Il senso della storia nella cultura medievale italiana (1100–1350)* (Pistoia, 1995), 125–38; F. Ragone, *Giovanni Villani e i suoi continuatori: La scrittura delle cronache a Firenze nel Trecento* (Rome, 1998).

Saba Malaspina's *Liber gestorum* and (Sicilian) Bartolomeo da Neocastro's *Historia sicula*, have largely not been studied.[14] The sources frame the years of Dante's life. The earliest, the anonymous *Chronicon Marchiae tarvisinae et Lombardiae*, was written at about the time of Dante's birth, and the last, Marino Sanudo Torsello's *Istoria del Regno di Romania*, was written just after Dante's death.[15] The writers were clerics, merchants, and government officials, categories of professions that should not be viewed as exclusive. They were, like Dante, mobile men concerned with and often involved in the political events of the day. They include the renowned Franciscan chronicler Salimbene de Adam of Parma, adherent of Joachim of Fiore, and the Dominican Ptolemy of Lucca, pupil of Aquinas and writer on republicanism, who was in Florence during the upheavals that led to Dante's banishment.[16] Ptolemy worked for Pope Nicholas III, Malaspina for Pope Martin IV, and Bartolomeo served as procurator of Peter of Aragon. The essay also uses the *Annali Genovesi di Caffaro*, whose authors were, like the Venetian Sanudo, from the ruling merchant elite of a state closely connected to Byzantium.[17] Finally, I include Brunetto Latini, Dante's teacher, mentioned in *Inferno* 15. According to Julia Holloway

14 Giovanni Villani, *Nuova cronica*, ed. G. Porta (Parma, 1990–2007), vols. 1–3; *Die Chronik des Saba Malaspina*, ed. W. Koller und A. Nitschke, in *Monumenta Germaniae historica: Scriptores* 35 (Hanover, 1999); Bartolomeo da Neocastro, *Historia sicula, 1250–1293*, ed. G. Paladino, in *Rerum italicarum scriptores* 13.3 (Bologna, 1921–22). According to Louis Green, Giovanni Villani (1280–1348) began his chronicle in the 1320s, redacting it between 1333 and 1341 and until his death in 1348. Malaspina (d. 1297/98?) most likely wrote from 1283 to 1285. Bartolomeo da Neocastro (1250–1294) wrote in 1292. L. Green, *Chronicle into History* (Cambridge, 1972), 164–69; L. Genuardi, "Saba Malaspina e le fonti del suo 'Liber gestorum'," *Congresso per il progresso delle scienze tenutosi a Catania, 1923* (Palermo, 1925), 3–11.

15 *Chronicon Marchiae tarvisinae et Lombardiae*, ed. L. A. Botteghi, in *Rerum italicarum scriptores* 8.3 (Città di Castello, 1914); Marino Sanudo Torsello, *Istoria del Regno di Romania*, in *Chroniques gréco-romanes*, ed. K. Hopf (Paris, 1873; repr. Brussels, 1966). The authorship of the *Chronicon* is unknown. It deals with the years 1207–70. Arnaldi and Capo, "Cronisti di Venezia" (above, n. 12), 404–5; Marino Sanudo Torsello (1270–1343) wrote the *Istoria* from 1328 to 1333. A. E. Laiou, "Marino Sanudo Torsello, Byzantium and the Turks: The Background of the Anti-Turkish League of 1332–1334," *Speculum* 45 (1970): 374–92.

16 Salimbene (1221–1287) wrote his chronicle from 1283 to 1288; *The Chronicle of Salimbene de Adam*, ed. and trans. J. L. Baird, G. Baglivie, and J. R. Kane (Binghamton, NY, 1986). Ptolemy (1236–1327) wrote numerous works during his long life. I have used here *Historia eccleciastica nova*, his most extensive and least studied work, which starts with the advent of Jesus and continues until 1316. There is dispute about the authenticity of the later sections of the work. James Blythe has argued that the balance of *Historia* was likely written from 1313 to 1316. There is need for a new critical edition, which has been announced by Ludwig Schmugge. Ptolemy of Lucca, *Historia eccleciastica nova*, ed. L. A. Muratori, in *Rerum italicarum scriptores* 11 (Milan, 1727; repr. Bologna, 1977). J. Blythe, *The Life and Works of Ptolemy Fiadoni* (Turnhout, 2009), 208; C. T. Davis, "Ptolemy of Lucca and the Roman Republic," *Proceedings of the American Philosophical Society* 118 (1974): 254–89; Ferrante, *Political Vision* (above, n. 1), 15–16.

17 *Annali Genovesi di Caffaro e suoi continuatori*, ed. C. Imperiale, vol. 4 (Rome, 1926), vol. 5 (Rome, 1929). The Genoese writers were government bureaucrats, whose chronicle was approved by the *podestà* and council of elders. Among the identified writers of the *Annali* at this time was Jacopo Doria, active in the 1280 and 1290s. J. Dotson, "The Genoese Civic Annals: Caffaro and His Continuators," in *Chronicling History* (above, n. 12), 55–70.

Bolton, Latini was a key figure in the Sicilian Vespers, serving as an envoy in negotiations with Byzantium and author of an account of the event in a single manuscript copy in an Italian version of his *Trésor* (1260–66). The authenticity of that account has been disputed, and therefore I have focused instead on the French *Trésor*.[18]

The results are preliminary and intended as a starting point for further research. There is much that can be done with chronicles of individual city-states and, above all, with the pre-humanist tradition, particularly the works of Riccobaldo of Ferrara and Ferreto Ferreti of Vicenza.[19] Nevertheless, even this limited inspection of contemporary writers and consideration of the "problem of Byzantium" is useful as impetus toward better contextualizing Dante. Moving beyond Tuscany, I found early in my research echoes of Dante in the chronicle of the fifteenth-century Venetian writer Antonio Morosini, who took his description of Charles of Anjou and the battle of Tagliacozzo from Jacopo della Lana's gloss (1324–28) of Dante's *Commedia*, which for this study emphasizes the importance of Dante's rendering of Angevin politics.[20] The sources of the chronicle of Dante's Roman contemporary, Malaspina, align closely with those of the poet, particularly his use of the *Aeneid*, which is frequently quoted and, indeed, embedded in its language.[21] Like Dante, Malaspina emphasizes the role of justice, in both biblical and classical terms, and offers an "idea of Rome" centered on the figure of Charles of Anjou. Malaspina begins book 6, detailing the transformation of Anjou from a man of "virtue and justice" to one of "greed and avarice" during the Sicilian crisis and Vespers, with the quote from *Aeneid* 3 against lust for gold ("quid non mortalia pectoria cogis / auri sacra fames?"), which appears in *Purgatorio* 20 and is stated directly by Statius in *Purgatorio* 22.[22]

18 J. Bolton Holloway, *Twice-Told Tales: Brunetto Latino and Dante Alighieri* (New York, 1993), 57–60, 112. Sicardi published Latini's account of the Vespers taken from an Italian version of the *Trésor* of which a lone manuscript (from 1375) has survived in the Florentine Biblioteca nazionale. See *Due cronache del Vespro in volgare siciliano del secolo XIII,* ed. E. Sicardi, in *Rerum italicarum scriptores* (Bologna, 1917), lxxvi. On Latini, see also C. T. Davis, "Brunetto Latini and Dante," in *Dante's Italy*, 166–97; R. Witt, *In the Footsteps: The Origins of Humanism from Lovato to Bruni* (Leiden, 2000), 178–79.

19 A comprehensive assessment of the prehumanist tradition is in Witt, *In the Footsteps* (see previous note). For the works of Riccobaldo of Ferrara and Ferreto Ferreti of Vicenza, see A. T. Hankey, *Riccobaldo of Ferrara: His Life, Works and Influence* (Rome, 1996); Riccobaldo of Ferrara, *Compilatio chronologica*, ed. A. T. Hankey (Rome, 2000); A. F. Masséra, "Dante e Riccobaldo da Ferrara," *Bulletino della Societá dantesca italiana* 23 (1915): 168–200. Ferreto, a poet, worked for Can Grande della Scala and wrote *Historia rerum in Italia gestorum, 1250 to 1317*, from 1329/30 until his death in 1337. C. Cipolla, *Le opere di Ferreto de Ferreti Vicentino* (Rome, 1908); G. Maniera, *Ferreto dei Ferreti: Preumanista Vicentino* (Vicenza, 1949); Witt, *In the Footsteps*, 113–14, 163–64.

20 Jacopo della Lana (1278–1358) and his family settled in Venice, after his career at Bologna. Antonio Morosini, *The Morosini Codex*, ed. M. P. Ghezzo, J. R. Melville-Jones, and A. Rizzi (Padua, 1999), 1:63.

21 Interestingly, Ugo Balzani dismissed the language of Malaspina's work as "bloated and coarse" ("gonfio e rozzo") with respect to style. Recent historians have used Malaspina primarily for information on battles. Balzani, *Le cronache Italiane* (above, n. 12), 220.

22 Malaspina, *Die Chronik* (above, n. 14), 241.

Allowing for the different vantages, scope, and intentions of the writers and their works, what is clear from all the sources is that Byzantium was part of the political and diplomatic landscape of Italy. Where there is mention of Charles of Anjou and Angevin politics, there is inevitably mention of Byzantium and, in particular, the deeds of Michael Palaiologos. The Byzantines are identified as "Greeks," a term that, as Anthony Kaldellis has argued, was pejorative in the West, "even if it did not evince odium on every occasion."[23] They are compared to the Greeks of antiquity, but the references are both positive and negative, ranging from Bartolomeo's invocation of "amicos Danaos" and an attempt to trace Byzantine Greek roots for his native Sicily, to the anonymous chronicler of Treviso's depiction of Byzantine Greek civilization as fallen precipitously "ab illo florido statu" that it had reached during the conquest of Troy and under Alexander the Great.[24] Writers were particularly interested in contemporary religious issues. They indicted Byzantine civilization as heretical for splitting from the Roman Church and connected Byzantium's religious error to its military decadence. As in Petrarch's letter to Boccaccio, writers saw Constantinople, the "New" Rome, as inferior to the old Rome with respect to "arms, virtue, and glory," coupling in several cases Byzantine martial weakness with its (alleged) fiscal riches. Above all, Michael Palaiologos emerges as a prominent and problematic figure who associated himself through Constantine with the Roman tradition, held the title Roman emperor (*basileius Romaion*), but was seen by writers as Greek and "emperor of the Greeks."[25] There was, however, considerable disagreement and discussion of the issue, indicative of a still greater unease evoked by Michael and Byzantium with regard to the Roman imperium, which appears in the sources as a complicated issue, with an East-West component in addition to the pope-emperor dimension. This is most apparent in Sanudo's *Istoria*, in which Michael Palaiologos appears as a central character who helps unite the imperium when corrected in his faith, a depiction with strong echoes of Dante's Justinian. Such ambiguity made it difficult to reconcile Michael and Byzantium with the political agenda of the *Commedia*, for which the imperium was wholly Roman, made manifest by feat of arms, virtue, and correct faith. The evidence reveals how "fragile" Dante's idea of Rome was in its contemporary context.

The "universal" works of the Tuscan writers Brunetto Latini, Ptolemy of Lucca, and Giovanni Villani trace events back to the time of Constantine and Justinian, and thus allow comparison with Dante's treatment of the two men. They make clear the distinctiveness of the poet's construct.

23 Kaldellis, *Hellenism in Byzantium* (above, n. 5), 337.

24 Bartolomeo, *Historia sicula* (above, n. 14), 10; *Chronicon Marchiae* (above, n. 15), 47–48.

25 Michael's title rendered in Latin was "Christo Deo fidelis imperator et moderator Romaeorum, ducas, semper Augustus." Laiou, *Constantinople and the Latin* (above, n. 7), 1.

Chapter 87 of Brunetto Latini's *Trésor* resembles the beginning of *Paradiso* 6. Justinian and Constantine appear together, separated by the same temporal span (two hundred years) as in Dante, followed by a history of the Roman imperium (chaps. 88–94).[26] Like Dante, Latini presents Justinian as a man of "great wisdom" ("mult sages" and "grant sapiense") and as a lawgiver, corrected in his faith by Pope Agapetus.[27] In chapter 17, Latini even connects Justinian to Moses and the Jewish tradition of law, as Dante does for Justinian at the beginning of *Paradiso 7*. But unlike Dante, Latini presents Justinian as one of several lawgivers, giving examples also from Ancient Egypt and Greece. Latini ties Justinian directly to Constantine in the Roman tradition. Constantine "began the laws," and Justinian completed them.[28] Thus, in Latini, Constantine and Justinian work together; in Dante, the men quite literally move in opposite directions. Latini's account of the history of the Roman imperium is more "Greek" than Dante's and includes consideration of the Byzantine tradition post-Justinian. Latini makes note of the reign of Emperor Heraclius (610–641) and the iconoclast controversy under Emperor Leo (717–741).

Like Latini, Ptolemy of Lucca and Giovanni Villani also present Justinian and Constantine in contrasting ways to Dante, and allow more space to the Byzantine tradition. In both, Justinian is a less singular figure and Belisarius, his general, is a more prominent one. In *Historia ecclesiastica nova*, Ptolemy claims that Justinian's conquests occurred *before* he was freed of heresy and accuses the emperor of "dishonesty" in his treatment of Belisarius. As a result of his military victories, Belisarius earned a share of the Roman imperium as "patrician/protector" of Rome, a distinction that appears nowhere in Dante's work.[29] In *Nuova cronica*, Villani follows Ptolemy in granting Belisarius a share of the imperium, but Villani follows Dante more closely in portraying Justinian as a "man of wisdom." He also retains the poet's distinction in *Paradiso* 6 that Belisarius did the fighting, while Justinian focused on compiling and correcting Roman law. Nevertheless, Villani describes Belisarius in similar fashion to Justinian, calling him a "wise man."[30]

Like Latini, Ptolemy and Villani link the reigns of Justinian and Constantine thematically. They do so, however, not with respect to Roman law but religious heresy, namely, the Arian controversy, which occurred at the end of Constantine's rule and continued into that of Justinian. Ptolemy, the cleric, gives considerable space to Constantine. He dwells on his actions on behalf of the Church and, in sharp contrast to Dante, praises his Donation of secular authority as an instance of "divine virtue" ("divinam virtutem").[31] When Constantine moved the capital east and established the city he named for himself, he left the Roman imperium under the protection of

26 Brunetto Latini, *Li livres dou trésor*, ed. S. Baldwin and P. Barrette (Tempe, AZ, 2003), 50.

27 Ibid., 49.

28 Ibid., 13–14.

29 Ptolemy, *Historia* (above, n. 16), cols. 885–89, 891.

30 Villani, *Nuova cronica* (above, n. 14), 1:106–8.

31 Ptolemy, *Historia*, cols. 823–825, 833.

Pope Sylvester and secular patricians. Villani introduces Constantine in terms of the Donation, but gives no opinion of it or of the emperor more generally.[32] Interestingly, however, Villani's Constantine is, like Dante's, "Greek." The identification is implicit rather than explicit, the result of Constantine's transfer of the capital of the empire to Constantinople, after which subsequent rulers in the East were known as "imperatori greci."[33] Villani does not follow Dante in associating the term Greek with falseness. Instead, he connects it to a divided and "damaged" imperium, which caused wars among Constantine's sons and their successors.[34] The division is evident in the different symbols of Roman authority. Constantine and rulers in the East used as their symbol a golden eagle on a vermillion background, which had been first employed by Julius Caesar. The eagle had two heads, representing the imperium's divided nature. The emperors in the West took as their symbol a black eagle on a gold background, first adopted by Caesar's son Octavian. This eagle had one head and alone represented, Villani tells us, Roman authority "above all temporal lords."[35] The western claim to authority was therefore superior to the eastern one. Thus Villani indicates that from its inception, the Eastern Byzantine empire created problems with respect to notions of Roman imperium, an interpretation that we will see in other contemporary works, but not in Dante.

Taken together, the evidence from Ptolemy and Villani, along with that from Brunetto Latini, makes clear the singularity of Dante's depiction in the *Commedia* of Justinian and Constantine. The two figures stand in stark contrast (Greek/Roman) to each other in Dante, but not in the works of the other writers. For Dante, Justinian is the embodiment of a unified Roman imperium. In Ptolemy and Villani, the imperium is not wholly united under Justinian, and Belisarius is not as generic a figure, but shares in the imperium. Dante's Justinian loses any Greek connotation, as does the imperium he represents.

Ptolemy and Villani follow Latini in including discussion of Byzantine "Greek" activities after Justinian. They recount the deeds of Emperor Heraclius and various church councils in the East and West.[36] Latini's *Trésor* proceeds no further historically than the battle of Tagliacozzo in 1266, but Ptolemy and Villani continue to Dante's day. Many of the (famous) passages adduced by scholars connecting Villani to Dante, and vice versa, relate to contemporary Angevin politics and events in southern Italy.[37] Villani, unlike the poet, was an ardent supporter of Charles of Anjou and, as

32 Villani, *Nuova cronica*, 1:38, 65, 86–88, 91.

33 Ibid., 1:38, 65.

34 "guastarono lo imperio di Roma"; ibid., 1:87–88.

35 Ibid., 1:65. Dante's eagle(s) has gold feathers in *Purgatorio* 9.20 and is on a gold background as a symbol of the imperial Roman army in *Purgatorio* 10.80–81.

36 Ptolemy, *Historia*, cols. 947–48.

37 On Dante and the Angevins, see P. Brezzi, "Dante e gli Angioini," in *Atti del II Congresso nazionale di studi danteschi: Dante e l'Italia meridionale* (Florence, 1966): 149–62, and A. Tanzarella, "Dante e gli Angioini," *Archivio storico pugliese* 16 (1963): 150–62.

Laura K. Morreale has recently argued, may even have arranged the basic structure of his chronicle around his rendering of Angevin politics.[38] Villani's account of the Sicilian Vespers covers a full thirty-one chapters, almost half of those devoted to the years 1281 to 1287. In addition to the echoes of Dante already cited by scholars, Villani includes a play on the word nose—"naso"—relating to the Vespers. In *Purgatorio 7*, Dante identifies Charles of Anjou in the Valley of Princes as "maschio naso" (113) and "nasuto" (124). Villani describes Anjou as "grande naso" and, later, when recounting the conversation between Anjou and Pope Martin IV regarding Peter of Aragon's betrayal that led to the Vespers, recites a popular proverb for which "naso" is the centerpiece. Villani chides Charles for forgetting the adage "tu hai meno il naso, ponviti la mano," that is, he did not abide the warning signs about Peter and thus fell victim to his betrayals in Sicily.[39] Ptolemy of Lucca also references a body part, the tongue, in his account of the Vespers. This occurs, as in Villani, in the context of a discussion of betrayal among the principal players at the start of the war, here Pope Martin IV and Peter of Aragon regarding Charles of Anjou. Ptolemy has Peter say that he would "rather cut out his tongue" than to reveal his secret plans against Anjou.[40]

It is, however, with respect to Byzantium that the differences between Villani and Dante are most clear. While Dante is silent about the Byzantines, Villani is well informed and speaks at length about them. Villani follows Dante (*Inf.* 19) in accusing Pope Nicholas III of taking money to betray Charles of Anjou, but he specifically says that the money came from Michael Palaiologos, who bribed the pope.[41] Villani confirms the poisoning of Thomas Aquinas prior to the Council of Lyons and attributes the deed to a physician in Charles of Anjou's employ.[42] Villani reports the activities of Byzantium throughout his chronicle. Indeed, Villani's famous description of Dante's personality and death is directly preceded by an account of the internal political struggles in Byzantium in 1320 and Byzantine support for exiles in Genoa. This is followed by a description of a "grande tempesta" (great storm) in the Black Sea (October 1323), in which ships and merchandise belonging to the Byzantines lost, an incident that Villani says was relayed to him by Florentine merchants operating in the region.[43]

Ptolemy of Lucca pays similarly close attention to Byzantium. He notes Michael Palaiologos's recapture of Constantinople and the ongoing political and military machinations involving Charles of Anjou.[44] Ptolemy claims to have personally witnessed

38 Morreale also emphasizes Villani's use of French sources and French words and turns of phrase. L. K. Morreale, "French Literature, Florentine Politics, and Vernacular Historical Writing, 1270–1348," *Speculum* 85, no. 4 (2010): 885–91. Teresa Shawcross has noted similarities among the accounts of Charles of Anjou and Angevin events in the chronicles of Villani, Muntaner, and Morea, and wonders whether they used a common source. Shawcross, *The Chronicle of Morea* (above, n. 5), 76.

39 Villani, *Nuova cronica*, 1:406, 509.

40 Ptolemy, *Historia*, col. 1187.

41 Villani, *Nuova cronica*, 1:495.

42 Ibid., 2:402.

43 Ibid., 2:333–34, 410.

44 Ptolemy, *Historia*, cols. 1147, 1166–67, 1179–84.

("ego vidi") the conspiracy that led to the Vespers. He accuses Michael Palaiologos and his allies Giovanni de Procida and Benedetto Zaccaria of making a pact to initiate the uprising.[45] Ptolemy, however, gives a more positive assessment than either Villani or Dante of Pope Nicholas III, for whom he worked. He does not implicate the pope in the Vespers and makes no mention of his receiving bribes, but instead praises his pontificate and the building projects he undertook in Rome. Ptolemy focuses a great deal of attention on the Council of Lyons and Thomas Aquinas, his teacher. He does not blame Aquinas's death on Anjou or treachery.[46] He depicts the council as a critical moment in East-West relations, which brought with it widespread hope for peace in anticipation of a crusade to the Holy Land.[47] He links the failure of Lyons directly to the Vespers, blaming Pope Martin IV for repudiating the union and excommunicating Michael. The mistaken act and the wars that followed damaged the Church and the Angevin cause.[48] Ptolemy accused Martin of using the crusade money collected at Lyons to fund his political and military activities in Italy, rendering him a more sinister character than Dante's gluttonous Martin, with his eels cooked in wine (*Purg.* 24.23–24). More pointedly, Ptolemy places the Council of Lyons and the failed East-West union at the center of his discussion of Angevin politics, while Dante, who cared so much about the latter, fails to make any direct mention of Lyons. The difference highlights the distinctiveness of Dante's construct and its wholly Western aspect.

Angevin politics and the Vespers play a less prominent role in the sprawling chronicle (1212–86) of the Franciscan monk from Parma, Salimbene de Adam. For the fateful year 1281, Salimbene gives equal attention to the Vespers and Pope Martin IV's designs on the Romagna.[49] Nevertheless, Salimbene shows great interest in Byzantium, which, as in Villani and Ptolemy, appears in his chronicle as a fundamental part of the diplomatic and political world of Italy.[50] Indeed, Salimbene ties contemporary Italy closely to Byzantium, relaying the details of dynastic unions of East and West, including the marriage in 1284 of Michael Palaiologos's son to the daughter of William VII of Montferrat (*Purg.* 7.134). He traces Byzantine relations with the house of Montferrat back to the time of Manuel I (1118–1180), emperor during the crusade of the German ruler Conrad I, who girded Dante's ancestor Cacciaguida with his knighthood

45 Ibid., cols. 1186–87.

46 Ibid., cols. 1168–73.

47 Ibid., cols. 1166, 1176–77.

48 "Sed post illam sententiam contra Paleologam promulgatam nec sibi [Charles of Anjou] nec ecclesia bene cessit"; ibid., col. 1190.

49 *Chronicle of Salimbene* (above, n. 6), 550–52. On Salimbene, see A. W. Lewin, "Salimbene de Adam and the Franciscan Chronicle," in *Chronicling History* (above, n. 12), 87–112.

50 Salimbene de Adam recounts the Byzantine conquest of Constantinople (p. 474), the Council of Lyons (pp. 498, 504–5), and the Vespers (pp. 550–52). He viewed the Byzantines as Greeks (pp. 304–5, 474).

(*Par.* 15.139–40). Salimbene pays close attention to Michael Palaiologos, noting his conquest of Constantinople and his role in the Vespers. He describes Palaiologos as less an operative force during the Vespers and more a victim, "afraid" of the designs of Charles of Anjou and Pope Martin.[51] Like his Dominican counterpart Ptolemy, the Franciscan Salimbene devoted particular attention to the Council of Lyons. He emphasizes the importance of the religious union with the Byzantines, whom he compares in one place to "wandering Argives" (Isa. 49:4) and in another to errant Jews. Salimbene weaves out the comparison between Greek and Jew for a whole chapter, citing Joachim da Fiore and his glosses on Scripture.[52] Salimbene takes the long view of Byzantine interest in religious reconciliation prior to Lyons, dating it back to Emperor John III Vatatzes (r. 1221–1254), who was attracted to the Roman faith by the example of the holiness of the minister general of the Franciscan order, John of Parma. Vatatzes asked the pope to send John to Constantinople.[53] Salimbene follows Ptolemy in linking the failure of negotiations, and of the subsequent Council of Lyons, to the dire political and military events that occurred afterward.[54]

Salimbene's Sicilian contemporary, Bartolomeo da Neocastro, a judge from Messina in the employ of Peter of Aragon, gives substantial space to Byzantium in his *Historia sicula*, but offers a different vantage and perspective. He is overtly anti-Angevin and blames the Vespers on Charles of Anjou. He cites Charles's excessive taxation in Sicily and his attack on Byzantium in 1279, which he launched in the guise of a crusade, taking up "the cross of the thief."[55] Bartolomeo calls the Byzantines "praiseworthy people" and presents Michael Palaiologos as an unwilling participant in the Vespers who became involved only after the people of Messina appealed to him directly. Bartolomeo's Michael is—in sharp contrast to his antagonist Charles of Anjou—a genuinely holy man who received guidance for his actions from God. Bartolomeo compares contemporary Byzantines to the Greeks of Troy without Virgilian pejorative and connects Byzantium directly to his native Sicily, claiming that the two sprang from "the same root," dating back to Emperor Heraclius. Heraclius and his general, George Maniaces (Danai Maniach), liberated Sicily from the heathen Arabs.[56]

The evidence from the *Historia sicula* makes clear the very different opinions that existed among contemporaries about Byzantium. Salimbene's "wandering Argives" and errant Jews become Bartolomeo's "amicos Danaos." The writers disagree about Michael's status as ruler. Salimbene refers to Michael as "imperator Graecorum," emperor of the Greeks, and carefully distinguishes the title from that of Baldwin of Flanders, the Latin ruler Michael had deposed, who was "imperator Constantinopolitanus."[57] Similarly,

51 *Chronicle of Salimbene*, 517–18.

52 Ibid., 505–6.

53 Ibid., 304–5.

54 Ibid., 498–99, 505.

55 "latronis crucem assumpsit." Bartolomeo, *Historia sicula* (above, n. 14) 10–11.

56 Ibid., 36–37.

57 *Chronicle of Salimbene*, 304.

Villani calls Michael emperor of the Greeks, in contrast to Baldwin, who was emperor of Constantinople.[58] Ptolemy of Lucca calls Michael "prince of Constantinople" ("principem Constantinopolitanum"), a title which appears to acknowledge Michael's rights to that city, but falls short of the title granted Baldwin, who is referred to as "Latin emperor" ("imperator latinus").[59] Bartolomeo stands alone in allowing Michael the title he himself favored, "imperator Romaeorum," the Latinized version that Michael used in documents. Bartolomeo even credits the Byzantine Greeks, by dint of Heraclius's conquest of Sicily, with bringing "justice and correct faith" to Italy. The role that Bartolomeo gives Heraclius is not unlike that which Dante gives Justinian. Heraclius traveled from the East to the West, brought with him justice and peace, while freeing Italy from its heathen overlords. Bartolomeo's Maniaces may be said to resemble in this regard Dante's Belisarius, acting as the instrument of the emperor's military might. And like the historical Belisarius, Maniaces fell into dispute with his employer.[60]

Bartolomeo's positive classical allusions and beneficent attitude toward Byzantium are reversed in the anonymous *Chronicon Marchiae tarvisinae et Lombardiae*. The author, most likely a monk from Padua, took a decidedly negative view of Byzantium.[61] He ends the work in 1270, before the Council of Lyons or the Vespers, but focuses considerable attention on Michael Palaiologos and his conquest of Constantinople in 1261. The *Chronicon* compares the capture of Constantinople to that by the ancient Greeks of Troy. Both were achieved by means of subterfuge, the latter with bribes paid to local citizens to open the gates. Michael is described as "crafty and astute" ("callidus et astutus"), the species of false Greek who won the city by corrupting "impious people" within with money.[62] The account is followed by an extended comment on contemporary Byzantine civilization. The *Chronicon* describes Byzantium as fallen with respect to its ancient counterpart: "It was a long time since the Greeks were in that flowering state, when they captured Helen and Alexander the Great seized the 'imperium' of the East."[63] In those days, the Greeks were supreme in philosophy, the arts, and science, and under Alexander, the greatest in terms of military might. But Greek civilization had lost its preeminence, above all its strength on the battlefield, as a result of religious error and repudiation of the Roman Church. This rendered Byzantium militarily

58 Villani, *Nuova cronica*, 1:500.

59 Ptolemy, *Historia*, cols. 1147, 1186.

60 Bartolomeo got his history wrong. George Maniaces did not live at the time of Heraclius but three centuries later. He died in 1043. "Sicialia conversa ad fidem et nomen Heracle Imperatoris." Bartolomeo, *Historia sicula*, 64.

61 Little is known of the authorship and intention of the *Chronicon*, which deals with the years 1207 to 1270. The work is, however, sophisticated, and its author draws on the *Aeneid*, most notably in his description of Marquis Azzo VII d'Este. Arnaldi and Capo, "Cronisti di Venezia" (above, n. 12), 39.

62 *Chronicon Marchiae* (above, n. 15), 47.

63 "Longe quippe sunt Greci ab illo florido statu, in quo decenna libello troiana menia in ultionem rapte helene subverterunt, nec non a strenuitate qua sub Alexandro invictissimo rege Macedonium, regnis Asie subiugatis, totius obtinuerunt imperium Orientis." Ibid., 47–48.

weak and thus "prey to all" people, especially its barbarous neighbors, the Saracens and Turks.[64] The *Chronicon* makes clear that Palaiologos was able to consolidate his hold on Constantinople only with the help of his more powerful Genoese allies.

The sentiments recall those expressed by Petrarch a generation later in his letter to Boccaccio, which derided Constantinople as unequal to Rome with respect "to arms, virtues, and glory." The *Chronicon* equates Byzantine religious error with its loss of military power and imperium, which was "torn asunder."[65] The equation represents the reverse image of Dante's "idea of Rome," in which the imperium and Rome's chosen status depend on correct faith, in conjunction with nobility and justice. That the *Chronicon* treats the imperium in terms of Byzantium suggests that for contemporaries the issue involved an Eastern component.

The connection between correct faith, military prowess, and the imperium plays a central role in the *Istoria del regno di Romania* by the Venetian writer Sanudo. An "expert in Eastern affairs," Sanudo knew Byzantium well and quotes the Greek language in several places in his chronicle.[66] He includes all the major events of the day—the conquest of Constantinople, the Vespers—as well as details of the numerous intervening struggles between Michael and his Western enemies. Although not a cleric, Sanudo devotes much space to religious issues. He divided the Christian world into two basic parts, one that followed the Greek rite (or "sect," as he called it), and one that followed the Latin rite, the former being larger than the latter.[67]

Sanudo pays particularly close attention to Michael Palaiologos and, indeed, as with Justinian in the *Commedia,* no single individual has more space in the work.[68] The discussion of Michael occurs in the context of consideration of the imperium ("impero romano") and its transfer ("translatio") from the East to the West, from the "Greeks to Germans" at the time of Charlemagne. Sanudo notes that after this the Greeks had little to do with the Latins. Sanudo portrays Michael's religious reconciliation with the West at the Council of Lyons as healing the imperium. Sanudo compares Palaiologos's actions to the Corpus Christi ceremony of the Latin mass: when they raise the body of Christ, they chant, "Sanctus Sanctus Deus Sabahot," which is the equivalent of saying, "Lord of armies, virtues, and wars" (Dominus exercituum, virtutum et bellorum), he is blessed, and will receive help from God in his struggles, because God demonstrates his preference by miracles in war, into which go both body and soul, shame and honor, not just of a single man but of a whole people.[69]

64 Ibid., 48.

65 Ibid.

66 Sanudo, son of the ruler of the Venetian colony on Naxos, traveled extensively and knew Byzantium well. Sanudo, *Istoria* (above, n. 15), 121; Laiou, "Marino Sanudo Torsello" (above, n. 15), 374–92.

67 Sanudo, *Istoria*, 139–44.

68 Ibid., 134–37.

69 Ibid., 137.

The depiction is striking. It echoes Dante's portrayal of Justinian and even includes part of the prayer spoken by Justinian at the beginning of *Paradiso* 7. Like Justinian, Michael Palaiologos succeeds when he returns to the "grace and favor" of the Roman Church.[70] As with Dante's Roman Empire, divine favor is made manifest by "miracles in war." The coincidence is close enough to wonder whether Sanudo took from Dante or whether the two used a common source. The Venetian writer cites as the basis of his Corpus Christi metaphor verses from "il Provenzal," after which the manuscript breaks off.[71] Dante may not have known Sanudo's *Istoria*, written after his death, but it is perhaps possible that he knew the Provençal source.

In any case, Sanudo follows the *Chronicon Marchiae tarvisinae et Lombardiae* in emphasizing the importance of religion to the imperium. The Venetian writer seems to respond directly to the *Chronicon*, having Michael at Lyons repair the prior damage done to the imperium by religious error that had left Byzantium "prey to its enemies." In an earlier work, Sanudo had portrayed the Byzantines as "uncooperative schismatics," who lacked military might. Michael's actions in the *Istoria*, however, fortified Byzantium against its foes, notably the Turks. As with Dante's Justinian, religious rectitude and correction of previous error is the starting point of success and God's choice. Sanudo even describes Michael, in the manner of Dante's Romans, as "noble" and turns him into an Italian, comparing him to Castruccio Castracane, the lord of Lucca.[72] Sanudo contrasts Michael with his enemy, Charles of Anjou, whose attack on Michael and Constantinople and hope for world monarchy lead directly to his downfall.

The problem for any further connection between Sanudo's Michael and Dante's Justinian is that for all their similarities, Michael was, for the Venetian writer, undeniably Greek. Sanudo refers to him as emperor of the Greeks, the same title used by the writers of the *Annali Genovesi*, rivals of the Venetians in the East and the state most closely allied to Byzantium during much of the period.[73] Like Sanudo's *Istoria,* the *Annali* are particularly well informed about Byzantium and relay all the events of the day, including the intriguing detail that Michael sent a Florentine merchant to convey the news to the West about his capture of Constantinople.[74] It is from the *Annali* that we know that Michael projected himself at home and abroad as a "new" Constantine, the name he used in documents and placed on official seals, and that a *peplos* hung at Hagia Sofia.[75] Like Sanudo, the Genoese writers stress Michael's piety and nobility. He

70 Ibid., 135.

71 Ibid., 137.

72 Ibid., 138.

73 The Genoese had, in Angeliki Laiou's words, "a special relationship" and "restrained friendship" with Byzantium in these years. Laiou, *Constantinople and the Latins* (above, n. 7), 205, 260.

74 *Annali Genovesi* (above, n. 17), 4:45.

75 Ibid., 4:45; Macrides, "The New Constantine" (above, n. 7), 22–23; D. M. Nicol, *Byzantium and Venice* (Cambridge, 1988), 197.

is in one place described as a "vir illustrissimus" and in another as the "sanctissimus imperator."[76] But Michael is also always "imperator Grecorum," the same title used also by Villani and Salimbene, and carefully contrasted with that of the Latin emperor Baldwin, who is "imperator Constantinopolitanus."[77]

The evidence makes clear that Michael Palaiologos projected a strong but ambiguous image in the West. Taken together, the Venetian and Genoese accounts depict Michael as noble and pious, but also as a second Constantine and a Greek. Ptolemy of Lucca and Salimbene de Adam describe Michael as a political usurper, "dominated by ambition," who seized political control in Byzantium by blinding the sons of his predecessor.[78] The *Chronicon Marchiae tarvisinae et Lombardiae* portrays Michael as winning Constantinople by "money and fraudulent promises,"[79] but it adds its own element of ambiguity by noting that he succeeded also on account of "probi labor," a description closer to Sanudo. Villani emphasizes the role of money in Michael's success. His discussions of both Michael and Byzantium revolve around the word "tesoro." Palaiologos recaptured Constantinople by means of "molto tesoro" paid to his Genoese allies and gained support for the Vespers by giving allies "ricchi gioelli e di moneta gran tesoro." Villani traces the practice back to the days of Charlemagne, who was offered "tesoro" by the Byzantines in return for his help in defeating enemies in the East. Charlemagne refused the gifts.[80] The association of Byzantium with treasure also appears in Salimbene. The chronicler describes how Emperor John Vatatzes was so impressed by the piety of John of Parma that he offered him "treasure" and gifts. At the same time, Salimbene notes how the Byzantines helped allies in Lombardy by sending them "thousands of bezants."[81]

Such depictions reflect perhaps long-standing notions of a rich Byzantium, Western Europe's wealthy trading partner for much of the Middle Ages. But the reconstructed empire under Michael Palaiologos was, in fact, impoverished and poor. It is notable that the allusions to Byzantine wealth in the sources are often coupled with reference to military weakness. Villani contrasts Michael Palaiologos's "tesoro" with his military and personal weakness. He paid his allies prior to the Vespers because he was a weak, desperate man, "ridotto piu che altro signor," with little hope against the more powerful

76 *Annali Genovesi*, 4:107, 115.

77 Ibid., 4:41, 55, 65–66, 107, 115, 171; 5:16, 29, 37.

78 Ptolemy, *Historia* (above, n. 16), cols. 1147, 1149.

79 "Igitur cum vehementer laboraret, ut propositum suum effectui manciparet, sciens vir callidus et astutus, quia labor probi omnia vincit pariterque cognoscens quod pecunie obedient omnia, maximeque homines necessariis indigentes, per idoneas personas mediante pecunia et promissionibus fraudolentis corrupuit quosdam impios homines in urbe constantinopolitana habitantes: qui firmiter promisuerunt ei tempore opportune tradere civitatem." *Chronicon Marchiae*, 47.

80 Villani, *Nuova cronica* (above, n. 14), 1:364, 503.

81 *Chronicle of Salimbene* (above, n. 6), 304, 550.

Charles of Anjou. This same theme appears in all the accounts of Sicilian Vespers published by Enrico Sicardi, including that attributed to Brunetto Latini. Latini speaks of "secreto tesoro" possessed by Byzantium and how Michael offered 100,000 ounces of gold for military help against Charles of Anjou. As in Villani, Michael is a "desperate man," unable to resist his enemy.[82] The portrait is starkest in the Sicilian chronicle *Lu Ribellamentu di Sichilia*, which has Michael again paying 100,000 ounces of gold for martial support, but he is presented as so desperate and weak that he is reduced to crying at his plight.[83]

The evidence suggests additional parallels with Petrarch's letter to Boccaccio, which contrasts Constantinople's wealth with its lack of military prowess. The notion was clearly widespread among Dante's contemporaries. It did little, however, to commend Michael or Byzantium to Dante, for whom the connection between treasure and military might was evocative of French imperial claims rather than Roman ones. But Michael Palaiologos was still more problematic, owing to his alleged piety. This image, as we have seen, runs throughout the sources. For Sanudo, it was Michael's reintegration into the Roman faith at Lyons that empowered him. Palaiologos followed this by doing good works, "with the help of God," including building a beautiful tower in the Holy Land at Acri and arranging marriage alliances with Western princes.[84] Bartolomeo's Michael is profoundly pious and is depicted on the eve of the Vespers looking up to the heavens, communicating directly with God and effecting his will in Sicily.[85] In the *Annali Genovesi*, Michael is the "most holy emperor," and even Ptolemy and Salimbene, who relay Michael's political treachery, acknowledge that it was on account of his pious participation at Lyons that Michael paid the price at home, opposed by his own clergy and left unburied at his death.[86]

The confusion caused by Michael and Byzantium is palpable. If, as Sanudo says, Palaiologos's piety allowed him to repair the imperium, and if, as the author of the *Chronicon* says, lack of piety lost the imperium for Byzantium in the first place, the question arises: what exactly was the contemporary Byzantine claim to imperium? Sanudo asserts that despite the "translatio" and Michael's conversion at Lyons, the Latin West remained "incomparabile migliore" to the Greek East with respect to arms.[87] Whatever claim the East had to the Roman imperium, it was, as Villani had noted in his description of Constantine and the inception of Byzantium, inferior to that of the West.

Concern about the issue is evident in the various titles applied to Michael in the sources. The terms were carefully chosen, and contemporaries were well aware of the distinctions and imperial implications embedded in them. Sanudo, for example, refers to Michael as "imperadore Greco" and the deposed Baldwin as "imperadore

82 *Due cronache del Vespro* (above, n. 18), 107.

83 Ibid., 7.

84 Sanudo, *Istoria* (above, n. 15), 135–36.

85 Bartolomeo, *Historia sicula* (above, n. 14), 37.

86 Ptolemy, *Historia*, cols. 1198–99; *Annali Genovesi*, 5:16, 29.

87 Sanudo, *Istoria*, 143.

Latino." But he reserves the term "Roman Emperor" ("Re Augusto de Romani") for the German Rudolf of Habsburg, whom the pope affirmed at Lyons as the legitimate heir of the Roman imperium.[88] Salimbene refers to both Michael Palaiologos and John Vatatzes as Greek emperors. But in the more distant past, before the Latin conquest of Constantinople, he calls Emperor Manuel I "emperor of Constantinople," the same title as Baldwin.[89] Villani depicts Michael as emperor of the Greeks in his account of Lyons and the Vespers, but after Baldwin's death he refers to Michael's son Andronikos as emperor of Constantinople.[90] Even the overtly pro-Byzantine Bartolomeo appears to draw a distinction. Michael Palaiologos was "imperator rom*aeo*rum," mirroring Michael's own usage. But Bartolomeo used the term "imperator rom*ano*rum" in his chronicle for the Hohenstaufen ruler Frederick II and his immediate successors. The distinction suggests that for Bartolomeo, Michael's title was restricted and perhaps referred to Palaiologos's rule over Romania, the name Westerners used for Byzantine territories in the East (see Sanudo).[91]

The careful delineation emphasizes the complexity of the issues surrounding Michael and Byzantium. Sanudo's Corpus Christi metaphor, as noted above, is embedded in discussion of the "translatio imperii," which the writer saw as the root of the problems between East and West. He claimed that when the "impero romano" was transferred from the Greeks to the Germans ("l'Impero Romano fu trasferito da Greci a Tedeschi") there was "no love left between the Latins and Greeks." This split was what Michael sought to heal at Lyons. Indeed, a basic task of the historical Council of Lyons was to settle the Roman imperium, for which there had been competing claims and no real successor since Frederick II's death in 1250. Salimbene put the issue directly in his chronicle when he wrote that the aim at Lyons was to "renew the Empire." Religious reconciliation with Byzantium was part of the "renewal," which sought to bring all sides together for a crusade against the infidel. In any case, the discussion of the imperium in Dante's day clearly included not only issues of Church and State, but also consideration of Eastern claims, the exact nature of which is unclear. In his account, Villani stressed the competing aims at Lyons. Palaiologos sought confirmation of himself as emperor of Constantinople, while German ruler Rudolf sought confirmation as Roman emperor. Rudolf was then to go to Italy to assume his crown and from there on crusade east, with the Byzantines.[92] The *Annali Genovesi* stresses the confirmation of Rudolf as "rex Romanorum" at Lyons and the attempts by the king of Castile, Alfonso X, to contest Rudolf's election and press his own claim to the office.[93]

88 Ibid., 99, 118, 139, 142.

89 *Chronicle of Salimbene*, 304, 550.

90 Villani, *Nuova cronica*, 1:500, 481–82, 501; 2:333.

91 Bartolomeo, *Historia sicula*, 1:36–37, 82.

92 Villani, *Nuova cronica*, 1:481–82. As Dante notes, this did not happen. Rudolf "aver negletto cio che far dovea," *Purgatorio* 7.92.

93 *Annali Genovesi*, 4:171–73.

Given the stakes, it is no surprise that the Council of Lyons was so important in the sources. Writers treated it as a key moment for Christendom, one which brought hope for peace and harmony but whose failure led directly to chaos and war. Salimbene attributed the death of Pope Gregory X, who had called out the council, to the "divine will" that "did not desire for there to be another Roman emperor after Frederick II."[94] Ptolemy blamed Pope Martin IV for repudiating the union and for excommunicating Michael, which he saw as leading to the wars that ultimately harmed the Church and the Angevin cause. Sanudo also denounced Martin's actions and saw the failure at Lyons as weakening all Christendom and leaving it open to attack from the Turks. He noted that Byzantium had, as a result, lost its "best province," Paphlagonia, which in ancient times was the home of the Eneti, who had aided Troy during the Greek siege and later helped build Venice, which, Sanudo pointed out, resembles Paphlagonia in terms of topology.[95]

The importance of Lyons was stated most forcefully by the Roman writer Malaspina in *Liber gestorum*. Malaspina is silent about Martin IV, for whom he worked. But he portrays the council as representing widespread hope and stresses the significance of bringing the Byzantines, "graecos scismaticos," back into the fold to create "one pastor and one flock."[96] The failure of the union was the turning point of the career of Charles of Anjou, the focus of Malaspina's chronicle, and, by implication, the turning point for Christendom (as well as the turning point of Malaspina's chronicle). Charles repudiated the council, worked to undo the union, and in his desire for world monarchy prepared an attack against Byzantium. As a result, Malaspina says, Charles, who had fought with the "arms of justice" and been victorious in war, now was "greedy and avaricious" and unsuccessful on the battlefield.[97] All the Regno, Italy, and Christendom became inflamed by war. Malaspina even reversed the classical metaphor, equating Anjou and the French with the Greeks of antiquity. He compared Anjou's fleet sent against Reggio Calabria during the Vespers to that sent by "magna Graecia contra Troyanam civitatem."[98]

Malaspina's account takes us full circle. His portrait of a greedy Anjou, whose avarice denied him world monarchy, would surely have appealed to Dante, as would have Malaspina's comparison of the French to the Greeks. As we have seen in this essay, the Byzantine Greeks possessed qualities similar to those imputed by Dante to the Capetians and Angevins, most notably their (alleged) use of wealth to buy military might. Salimbene and Sanudo, in fact, record direct connections between contemporary Byzantines and French ruling houses though marriage alliances.

For all their twists and turns, what is nevertheless clear from our sources is that Byzantium and Michael Palaiologos were unsuited to the *Commedia*. The association of Greeks with Jews, of Michael and the Byzantines with the Roman imperium, the

94 *Chronicle of Salimbene*, 499, 505.

95 Sanudo, *Istoria*, 144–45.

96 Malaspina cites John 10:16 about "one pastor and one flock." Sanudo used the same biblical quote in his account of Lyons.

97 Malaspina, *Die Chronik* (above, n. 14), 290, 246–47.

98 Ibid., 302–10.

Council of Lyons with universal peace, were themes contrary to Dante's political aims. For Dante, the imperium was a subject about which there was no ambiguity. It was Roman, and the empire was the source of universal peace. Jews resembled Romans in their chosen status, not Greeks in their mutual need for conversion to the proper faith.

Whether we may indict Dante for willful silence with regard to Byzantium is perhaps to allow modern scholars psychological insight beyond their due. But the case is persuasive. At the very least, Byzantium raised questions for contemporary writers about the imperium. Dante appears to have consciously stripped from the *Commedia* all Greek connotation from those issues and figures (Justinian) related to the Roman imperium, while adding it to Constantine, who damaged the imperium by means of his Donation. Dante's evocation of Raymond IV Berengar's daughters and the Provençal dowry at the end of his account of the Roman imperium in *Paradiso* 6 is important in this context. It recalls the spurious French claim to the imperium through money rather than by justice and divine choice and, willy nilly, reinforces the unsuitability to the *Commedia* of the Byzantines, whose imperial claim was not unlike the French one. In any case, the many-sided Michael Palaiologos—pious, weak, wealthy, crafty, astute, Greek, and Roman—created a confusion that warranted his exclusion. The same may be said of the Council of Lyons and Pope Gregory X, who convoked it. Neither appear in the *Commedia*, even though Gregory traveled to Florence (1273) just before the council began and even made peace in the city, albeit temporarily, between the Guelphs and Ghibellines, in a public ceremony that Dante may, according to one scholar, have personally witnessed.[99] In the end, Gregory shares with Michael Palaiologos the "silent" fate of French King Louis IX, another problematic figure who challenged the political agenda of the *Commedia*.

99 Giuseppe Mazzotta, "Life of Dante," in *The Cambridge Companion to Dante,* ed. R. Jacoff, 2nd ed. (Cambridge, 2007), 5.

Angels, Monsters, and Hybridity in the *Divine Comedy*

Ancient Greek Cultural Legacies and Dante's Critique of the Church

GEORGE DAMERON

At the end of canto 16 of the *Inferno,* the half-man, half-serpent creature, Geryon, dramatically ascends from a dark abyss to the cliff edge on which Dante and his guide, Virgil, are perched. Virgil has summoned Geryon by dropping the cord from Dante's waist from the top of the waterfalls into the dark pit below. Dante calls Geryon nothing less than the filthy image of fraud (*quella sozza imagine di froda*; *Inf.* 17.7).[1] At the beginning of canto 17, Virgil hails him as the wild beast (*fiera*) that causes the whole world to stink (*Ecco colei che tutto 'l mondo appuzza!*; *Inf.* 17.3). In Greek mythology, Geryon was usually portrayed as a monster with either three heads or the body of three men from the waist down. His father Chrysaor sprang from the blood of the slain gorgon Medusa.[2] According to Greek mythical tradition, Geryon possessed a herd of cattle that he entrusted to a shepherd, Eurytion, and his two-headed dog. Hercules killed both Eurytion and the dog, and dispersed the cattle in one of his famous labors. Dante may well have known about Geryon from many sources, but one source is prominent. In book 6 of Virgil's *Aeneid,* at the entrance to the underworld in the realm of Dis, Aeneas sees Geryon, "the triple-bodied ghost" (*tricorporis umbrae*; *Aen* 6.289),[3] among the harpies, gorgons, and other monsters gathered at the entrance to hell. Dante's own description differs from Virgil's, however. For Dante, Geryon has the face of a man, hairy paws, and the body of a serpent. Dante's Geryon has been the subject of lively scholarly commentary for more than seven hundred years, and he is rich

1 All quotes from the *Commedia* come from the standard authoritative edition by G. Petrocchi (Milan, 1966–68), reproduced in Dante Alighieri, *The Divine Comedy,* trans. C. S. Singleton, Bollingen Series 80, 6 vols. (Princeton, NJ, 1970–75).

2 *The Oxford Companion to Classical Literature* (Oxford, 1969), s.v. "Geryon."

3 *Aeneidos 6,* in *P. Vergili Maronis Opera,* ed. R. A. B. Mynors (Oxford, 1969), 236. The English translation is from *Aen.* 6.395, trans. R. Fitzgerald (New York, 1990), 170. Subsequent references will come from the Mynors OCT edition and the English translations will come from Fitzgerald. Geryon is mentioned several times in the *Aeneid* (Fitzgerald translation): *Aen.* 6.395, 7.910, 8.271. Dante's image of Geryon was also inspired by Rev. 9:7–10.

with symbolic possibilities. For John Freccero, Geryon's descent with Dante and Virgil into the Malebolge recalls "flights of the soul in Plotinus, Ambrose, or Augustine." John Block Friedman argued a generation ago that Geryon is the Antichrist, the symbol of a corrupted papacy.[4] Whatever the perspective, this human-beast-serpent Geryon is the controlling image of the seventh circle—the circle of fraud— and it is here where those who have sinned by misuse of intellect are punished. Among those sinners are the corrupt and avaricious popes in canto 19, the bolgia of the simoniacs. And like Geryon, as with beasts, the popes emit a nasty stench.

Throughout the *Commedia*—not just here in cantos 16 and 17—Dante draws upon a wide array of figures and images from ancient Greek mythology, such as Geryon, to convey on a symbolic level his critical views regarding the temporal or carnal Church, particularly the papacy.[5] Imagery from Greek mythology associated with serpents, giants, dragons, sirens, and hybrid creatures is particularly useful to Dante. These images, specifically those of the hybrid creatures, vividly and visibly portray the extent to which avarice and cupidity have debased, dehumanized, and distorted clerical motivations and desires, particularly regarding the papacy. Hybrid creatures, unlike normal beasts, are composites whose two natures often come from two separate spheres (e.g., air, land, or water). Consequently, they constitute synergized beings with the combined and greatly enhanced powers of their two natures. For Dante, these monsters symbolically embody the very worst traits of the contemporary materialistic Church and its leadership.[6] Serpents, animal-human hybrid shepherds, and beasts are figures often used by Dante to refer either to a particular pope, such as Boniface VIII (d. 1303), or, more generally, to the papacy itself. Other half-human hybrids, such as sirens, appear in the *Commedia* to embody vanity, desire, and the temptations for worldly goods and knowledge. Dante also links the corrupt papacy with giants, figures traditionally connected in Greek mythology with rebellion against the gods and the flaw of pride.[7] Other hybrid figures from Greek mythology,

4 J. Freccero, "Allegory and Autobiography," in *The Cambridge Companion to Dante*, ed. R. Jacoff, 2nd ed. (Cambridge, 2007), 164, 168; J. Block Friedman, "Antichrist and Iconography of Dante's Geryon," *JWarb* 35 (1972): 108–22, esp. 108–10, 113–14; L. Pertile, "Introduction to *Inferno*," in Jacoff, *Cambridge Companion to Dante*, 79–80. See also *The Dante Encyclopedia*, ed. R. Lansing (New York, 2000; repr. 2010), s.v. "Geryon"; J. Ferrante, *The Political Vision of the Divine Comedy* (Princeton, NJ, 1984), 166.

5 For the purposes of this essay, "Church" is defined as ecclesiastical institutions, their respective clergies, and the papacy. In the sense used here, "Church" does not refer to the entire community of the faithful.

6 N. Havely, *Dante* (Maldon, MA, and Oxford, 2007), 160. As Joan Ferrante observed, for Dante, the Church needed to destroy the "monster" it had become (*Political Vision*, 131). For information about hybrids and snakes, see *The Continuum Encyclopedia of Animal Symbolism in Art*, ed. H. B. Werness (New York, 2004), 230–31, 376–79.

7 W. Stephens, *Giants in Those Days: Folklore, Ancient History, and Nationalism* (Lincoln, NE, 1989), 1–6, 67–70; *Dante Encyclopedia*, s.v. "Giants." According to J. A. Scott, *Dante's Political Purgatory* (Philadelphia, 1996), 201, giants in *Inferno* "rebelled against Empire, opposing the will of heaven." For sirens and Geryon, see C. Rose, *Giants, Monsters, and Dragons: An Encyclopedia of Folklore, Legend, and Myth* (Denver and Oxford, 2000), 135, 336.

such as griffins and angels, convey very different, more positive messages regarding the possibilities of the fourteenth-century Church, in contrast to the debased papacy. Dante's knowledge of these Greek mythological creatures came primarily from Roman texts, most importantly Virgil's *Aeneid,* Ovid's *Metamorphoses*, and Statius's *Thebaid*. Hebrew and Christian mythologies—particularly the books of Ezekiel, Job, and Revelation—were also sources of inspiration for Dante's monstrous creatures. Scholars have certainly noticed the prominence of these hybrid creatures in the *Commedia*, particularly as enforcers and guardians of the various circles of hell.[8] Nevertheless, critics have largely underestimated, if not ignored, how Dante mobilizes these figures inspired by Greek mythology to criticize both the papacy and other corrupt members of the clergy.[9]

An exploration of these classical allusions may not only enrich our understanding of Dante's views regarding ecclesiastical corruption, but they may also provide us with a useful case study of the poet's indebtedness to Greek learning. Like scholarship on the figure of Geryon, studies regarding Dante's assessment of the contemporary Church and his debt to classical learning in the *Commedia* are extensive and complex. Three examples illustrate this point quite well. Building on themes developed earlier by Raoul Manselli and Charles Davis, Nick Havely's *Dante and the Franciscans* explores the strong impact of Franciscan views on Dante regarding evangelical poverty. It also offers a useful overview of the previous historiography. Kevin Brownlee, in his essay "Dante and the Classical Poets," describes and explains the "profound ambivalence" that Dante brings to his portrayals of Virgil, Statius, Lucan, and Ovid. This ambivalence arises from the tension between the pagan classical, non-Christian principles of these poets and the "Christian truth" that Dante wants them to elucidate. In an essay on the *Inferno*, examining another topic associated with ancient traditions, Lino Pertile observes that classical mythology, especially book 6 of the *Aeneid,* is, indeed, the source of Dante's demons. Pertile also argues that some of these figures—half-human, half-beast—function as guardians of hell and represent "the moral features of the sinners they rule over and torment."[10] Dante's allusions to classical literature and his Franciscan-influenced critique

8 Pertile, "Introduction to *Inferno*," 79. Ovid was a particularly important source of Greek myths for Dante; see A. Robson, "Dante's Reading of the Latin Poets and the Structure of the *Commedia*," in *The World of Dante*, ed. C. Grayson (Oxford, 1980), 86.

9 R. Jacoff and J. Schnapp, "Introduction," in *The Poetry of Allusion: Virgil and Ovid in Dante's Commedia*, ed. R. Jacoff and J. Schnapp (Stanford, 1991), 1–11, 290. Ovid's *Metamorphoses* was an obvious model for "Dante's depiction of the transformative consequences of sin within a Christianized Aristotelian moral scheme." Moreover, "Sin disfigures and deforms, and its result is the sort of downward ontological drift marked by the *Inferno*'s pervasive imagery of bestiality, monstrosity, and reification" (p. 9). For Dante's indebtedness to Virgil, Lucan, Ovid, and Statius, see also K. Brownlee, "Dante and the Classical Poets," in *Cambridge Companion to Dante* (above, n. 4), 141–60. *Auctores maiores* (Virgil, Ovid, Lucan, Horace) were common in syllabi of the 11th and 12th centuries. They became less common in the course of the 13th century; however, they returned to the syllabus by the turn of the 14th century (Dante's lifetime); R. Black, *Education and Society in Florentine Tuscany* (Leiden and Boston, 2007), 48–49.

10 N. Havely, *Dante and the Franciscans: Poverty and the Papacy in the Commedia* (Cambridge, 2004); Robson, "Dante's Reading," 81–114; Brownlee, "Dante and the Classical Poets," 141–60 (quote

of the Church are therefore well-trodden fields of scholarly inquiry. Nevertheless, these two thematic strains deserve to be brought together in a more comprehensive and cogent fashion. How and why did Dante draw upon his knowledge of Greek myths and images in the *Commedia* to communicate his critique of the "carnal" Church? What can his use of particular Greek images and figures tell us about his assessment of contemporary ecclesiastical life?

We will narrow our attention to those cantos that focus particularly on the clergy, particularly *Inferno* 17, 19, 24, and 25; *Purgatorio* 29–33; and *Paradiso* 16, 17, 27–28.[11] In the *Commedia,* the poet draws on Greek myths to demonstrate that many within the major ecclesiastical institutions and their elite clergies, particularly the papacy, were venal and corrupt. Dante's extensive reading of classical authors and Franciscan apocalyptic writings, probable attendance at lectures at the Franciscan friary of Santa Croce, visit to the papal court as an envoy of the commune of Florence, and early intellectual development as evident in his first poetical works all had a significant impact on the later development of his ideas regarding the institutional Church. His mature views regarding the Church seem to be in place by the time he writes the first cantos of *Paradiso* (after 1315) and *Monarchia* (ca. 1318). The memory of his own political experiences is also a key factor in the generation of these views. During his exile in the years following 1302, Dante reflects on the divisive legacy of Florentine politics, the state of the Florentine Church before his expulsion, and the disappointing failure of the mission of Henry VII into Italy in 1310.[12] They not only lead Dante to an uncompromising assessment of the

at 142), and Pertile, "Introduction to *Inferno,*" both in *Cambridge Companion to Dante*, 67–90 (esp. 76, 86, and quote at 79); Jacoff and Schnapp, "Introduction," 1–11. For a short overview of previous scholarship on Franciscan influences on Dante by Felice Tocco, Raoul Manselli, and Charles Davis, see Havely, *Dante and the Franciscans*, 6–7.

11 Each of these cantos has been the subject of sustained scholarly debate and discussion since the early 14th century. Among those works that have particular resonance for our purposes here are Havely, *Dante and the Franciscans*; Scott, *Dante's Political Purgatory*; P. Dronke, *Dante and Medieval Latin Traditions* (Cambridge, 1986); Ferrante, *Political Vision*; P. Armour, *The Door of Purgatory: A Study of the Multiple Symbolism in Dante's Purgatorio* (Oxford, 1983); R. E. Kaske, "Dante's Purgatorio XXXII and XXXIII: A Survey of Christian History," *University of Toronto Quarterly* 43, no. 3 (1974): 193–214; Friedman, "Antichrist and Iconography"; and for the closing cantos of *Purgatorio*, L. Pertile, *La puttana e il gigante: Dal Cantico dei Cantici al Paradiso Terrestre di Dante* (Ravenna, 1998).

12 Havely, *Dante and the Franciscans,* chaps. 1–4; C. Davis, "Poverty and Eschatology in the *Commedia,*" and "Education in Dante's Florence," both in his *Dante's Italy and Other Essays* (Philadelphia, 1984), 42–70, and 137–65. Nick Havely observes Dante was finishing the last cantos of *Paradiso* between 1317 and 1321 (*Dante and the Franciscans,* 161), and the second edition of the *Cambridge Companion to Dante* dates *Monarchia* as early as 1310 and as late as 1317 (p. xiii). However, scholarship now apparently situates the text to about 1318; R. Kay, "Review of A. K. Cassell, *The Monarchia Controversy* (Washington, 2004)," *The Catholic Historical Review* 90, no. 4 (2004): 772. An anonymous reader for this essay suggests the dates 1318–21 for its composition. For Henry's expedition in Italy, see W. Bowsky, *Henry VII in Italy: The Conflict of Empire and City-State, 1310–1313* (Westport, CT, 1974; orig. ed. 1960). For a brief and succinct overview of Dante's politics, see

institutional Church of his day, but they also help give him the tools to create a masterwork of profound beauty.

For his epic poem, Dante takes much of the animal imagery associated with Greek mythology from his readings of the *Aeneid* and Ovid's *Metamorphoses*. Like the *Commedia*, the *Aeneid* has been subject to several competing interpretations, especially in the last century. For example, is the killing of Turnus at the end of book 12 an act of reason and duty (*pietas*) or frenzy and passion (*furor*)?[13] Regardless of one's view on the matter, one can certainly recognize that Virgil is promoting the values of duty and restraint, while simultaneously describing the negative consequences of passionate intensity. The imagery of monsters taken from Greek mythology plays a major role in Virgil's poem, just as it does thirteen centuries later for Dante. Among the most important monsters from Greek mythology are serpents, and the large serpents or dragons (Greek, *drakon*; Latin, *draco*) often serve as guardians of shrines. Romans later associate them with the guardian spirits of a place, the *genius loci*.[14] In Virgil's *Aeneid*, serpents or snakes are closely associated with malevolent forces involving anger, passion, rage, madness, and an unrestrained appetite to destroy. They appear frequently in the poem as physical manifestations of the *furor* or *ira* that mark the presence of malevolent forces. They stand in opposition to the values Virgil praises in his poem, exemplified in one word: *pietas*.[15] A principal theme of the *Aeneid* is, therefore, Aeneas's struggle to resist *furor* and embrace *pietas*. Virgil exploits the imagery associated with serpents and snakes to describe characters that harm, destroy, and otherwise cause disorder. References to snakes appear repeatedly whenever the forces of disorder and passion are present. We see snake imagery linked with Juno and her anger in book 1, Pyrrhus (the murderer of Priam) in book 2, the burning of Troy and the death of Laocoön in book 2, Allecto (who rouses the anger of Amata against the Trojans) in book 7, and the rising fury of Turnus at the beginning of book 12.

Not only is serpent or snake imagery thematically important in the *Aeneid*, but Virgil also draws heavily upon the Greek myth of the hybrid half-man, half-beast creature highlighted in Pertile's previously mentioned essay. Perhaps the best example is Cacus, whom we encounter in book 8. Evander, king of the Arcadians, recounts the

---

R. Hollander, *Dante: A Life in Works* (New Haven, CT, 2001), 129–43. For the political significance of Dante's letters, see L. Pertile, "Dante Looks Forward and Back: Political Allegory in the Epistles," *Dante Studies* 115 (1997): 1–17.

13 See S. Morton Braund, "Virgil and the Cosmos: Religious and Philosophical Ideas," in *The Cambridge Companion to Virgil*, ed. C. Martindale (Cambridge, 1997), 204–21, esp. 214–15. For a summary of the debates about the meaning of book 12, see W. R. Johnson, *Darkness Visible: A Study of Virgil's Aeneid* (Berkeley and Los Angeles, 1976).

14 *Oxford Companion to Classical Literature*, s.v. "Monsters." I credit a comment made during the discussion after the presentation of my paper at the Dumbarton Oaks conference for reminding me that serpents did not always carry negative connotations for the Romans.

15 C. Burrow, "Virgils, from Dante to Milton," in *Cambridge Companion to Virgil*, 83; R. J. Tarrant, "Poetry and Power: Virgil's Poetry in Contemporary Context," in *Cambridge Companion to Virgil*, 181.

story of Cacus to Aeneas. Cacus lived in a cave in the Aventine Hill and stole some of the cattle of Geryon that Hercules had dispersed. Cacus was,

semihominis Caci facies quam dira tenebat
solis inaccessam radiis; semperque recenti
caede tepebat humus, foribusque adfixa superbis
ora virum tristi pendebant pallida tabo. (*Aen.* 8.194–97)

. . . a bestial form, half man,
And the ground reeked forever with fresh blood,
While nailed up in vile pride on his cave doors
Were men's pale faces ghastly in decay.

For Virgil, Cacus exemplifies the destructive forces of barbarism and is a character who seems to prefigure the early medieval Anglo-Saxon Grendel and his mother. Cacus's theft of cattle, animals that are often symbols of civilized society, represents an undermining of the forces of order and civilization. His death at the hands of Hercules portrays on an allegorical level the triumph of civilization and civilizing values over barbarism and bloodthirsty savagery. In book 8, Evander explains to Aeneas why his people annually perform the ritual that commemorates Hercules' triumph:

saeuis, hospes Troiane, periclis
seruati facimus meritosque nouamus honores. (*Aen.* 8.188–90)

we carry out these rites,
Renewed each year, as men saved from the barbaric
Dangers in the past.

This reenactment of the purging of Cacus from the Aventine therefore marks the triumph of *pietas* over *furor*, of civilization over barbarism, of order and reason over chaos and passion. Cacus is indeed apparently Roman, not Greek, in legend, but he is inspired by the figure of the hybrid half-man, half-beast so common in Greek mythology. And the central theme of Virgil's retelling of the story is rooted in the Greek literary traditions that inspired him. Significantly and explicitly in book 8 of the *Aeneid*, the story of Cacus is also directly connected to that of Geryon. Here Geryon makes his second appearance in the poem. He is identified as a "triple-bodied giant" whose herds Hercules had taken and which grazed in the marshy valley where the Arcadians lived: the future site of Rome. In answer to the prayers of the Arcadians, Hercules (*tergemini nece Geryonae spoliisque superbus / Alcides aderat taurosque hac victor agebat*; *Aen* 8.202–4) "appeared, still flushed with pride / In spoils he took when slaughtering Geryon, / The triple-bodied giant". Dante's reading of the *Aeneid,* therefore, shapes the meaning, characters, and structure of the *Commedia*, and he understands the significance of the imagery of the hybrid monsters like Geryon and Cacus in Virgil's masterpiece.[16] We can see this quite well in cantos 17–19 and cantos 24–25. In canto 17, the flight of Geryon brings Dante and Virgil to the eighth circle, the circle of the fraudulent. The figure of this man-beast-serpent creature dominates all ten levels of the entire circle of the Malebolge, and he embodies the bestial, appetite-driven passions of man. His countenance is human (*La faccia sua era faccia d'uom giusto*; *Inf.* 17.10), his paws are hairy (*due branche avea pilose insin l'ascelle*; *Inf.* 17.13), and his trunk is that of a snake (*e d'un serpente tutto l'altro fusto*; *Inf.* 17.12).[17] Here are punished those who subjected their intellects to the satisfactions of their passions and bartered their humanity to satisfy their worldly appetites. In bolgia 3, canto 19, we encounter the simoniacs, and among them in particular is Pope Nicholas III (r. 1277–1280). Turned upside down in a receptacle that is the mockery of a baptismal font, Nicholas announces that two successors, Boniface VIII (r. 1294–1303) and Clement V (r. 1305–1314), will later take his place in that very spot. In what will be a consistent theme throughout the *Commedia*, Dante lashes out at Nicholas III (and presumably at his successors) for the destructive consequences of their avarice: the good are pushed down, the bad are raised up (*ché la vostra avarizia il mondo attrista, / calcando i buoni e sollevando i pravi*; *Inf* 19.104–5). Quite cleverly, Dante alludes to the bestiality of Pope Nicholas III by making a pun of his name, Giovanni Gaetano Orsini. Nicholas observes that he was the son of a she-bear (*orsa*), eager to promote the worldly interests of his bear-cubs (*orsatti*).[18] For an early commentator on Dante, L'Ottimo Commento (3) (1338), the bear is the greediest animal (*la quale è animale cupidissimo*). For Jacopo Alighieri (1322), the greedy Pope Nicholas was truly son of the bear, the most avaricious of animals (*il quale per sua cupidezza, veramente figliuolo dell'orsa si come d'animal cupidissimo si figura*).[19] This beastly nature of Nicholas III and, by extension, his papal successors, is reaffirmed later in the canto in the reference to the vision of Saint John in the Book of Revelation. John describes seeing the hybrid, seven-headed, she-beast fornicate with kings. We should note here that Dante explicitly identifies Nicholas III as a shepherd and accuses him

16 See, for example, Brownlee, "Dante and the Classical Poets" (above, n. 9), 143–47; Jacoff and Schnapp, *Poetry of Allusion* (above, n. 9), 1–11; Robson, "Dante's Readings of the Latin Poets" (above, n. 8). For Dante's assessment and reverence for Virgil, see *The Virgilian Tradition: The First Fifteen Hundred Years*, ed. J. Ziolkowski and M. J. Putnam (New Haven, 2008), 130–32, 448–51.

17 Dante actually gives him several natures: the paws of a beast, the face of a human, and the body and tail of a dragon. Its biblical references include Rev. 9:2–11, 11:7 or 13, and Job 40:20; Havely, *Dante* (above, n. 6), 160.

18 *e veramente fui figliuol de l'orsa, / cupido sì per avanzar li orsatti* (*Inf.* 19.70–71).

19 L'Ottimo Commento (3) (1338), *Inf.* 19.64–87; Jacopo Alighieri (1322), *Inf.* 19.69–72; For L'Ottimo Commento (1333), commenting on *Inf.* 19.67–72, *l'orsa è un animale cupido; prima divora, che senta e essamini quello, che mangia. E dice, che fu sì avaro per avanzare a' suoi, che su, cioè in vita, si misse in borsa li danari, e misse sè qui, cioè in Inferno, che è etterna dannazione. Onde è da sapere, che costui fatto Papa fue corrotto per pecunia, della quale elli era vago, da Messer Jan di Procida, trattatore della ribellione di Sicilia.* All citations from the online Dartmouth Dante Project http://dante.dartmouth.edu/ (accessed 22 February 2011).

of avarice. He states that Saint John was thinking of shepherds (*pastor*) exactly like Nicholas III when he saw that woman sitting upon the waters copulating with kings (*Di voi pastor s'accorse il Vangelista, / quando colei che siede sopra l'acque / puttaneggiar coi regi a lui fu vista*; *Inf.* 19.106–8). Many commentators on *Inferno* 19 have seen here a direct allusion to the great whore (*meretrix magna*) mentioned in Revelation 17. Medieval commentators, including Bonaventure, saw her as a personification of avarice. And for many modern critics, she represents the corrupted, carnal Church, the *ecclesia carnalis*.[20] Perhaps this identification of the avaricious Pope Nicholas III as a shepherd recalls other beastlike herdsmen mentioned in the two previous cantos: the half-man, half-serpent Geryon and Cacus.[21] Like Cacus and Geryon, Nicholas III and his successors are failed shepherds whose bestial appetites (twisted by avarice) have placed their flocks in danger.

Dante's use of snake and beast imagery as well as human-beast hybridity to illustrate misdirected, unrestrained worldly appetites and passions is also apparent in cantos 24 and 25, the seventh bolgia of the eighth circle. Here we find the thieves punished by writhing reptiles that tie their hands and legs together and bite them in the neck. The most prominent among them is Vanni Fucci, the thief who stole the treasure of Saint Jacopo from the cathedral in Pistoia. Like the popes in canto 19, he steals from the Church. Vanni Fucci identifies himself to the poet and his guide as "the beast." He even compares himself to a mule, a hybrid of a horse and an ass. Indeed, he is a human-beast hybrid whose reason, as L'Ottimo Commento, the fourteenth-century commentator on the *Commedia* notes, is subject to his appetites. The bestial life pleased him, he said, not the human life: *Vita bestial mi piacque e non umana, / sì come a mul ch'i' fui; son Vanni Fucci / bestia, e Pistoia mi fu degna tana* (Bestial life pleased me, not human, mule that I was; I am Vanni Fucci the beast, and Pistoia was a worthy lair for me; *Inf.* 24.124–26).[22] After he blasphemes God with an obscene gesture, Vanni Fucci is then set upon by none other than Cacus himself, on whose back are serpents and a fire-breathing dragon. Virgil identifies Cacus as the one who fraudulently stole the herd of Hercules and was, in turn, killed by him. He is a centaur, a hybrid creature from Greek mythology, half-horse, half-man. Centaurs first appear in canto 12, the circle of the violent. According to a fourteenth-century commentary on the poem, these hybrid beasts are associated with theft and violence. And like Pope Nicholas III in canto 19, Cacus is a fraudulent pastor or shepherd whose bestial appetites to steal were disruptive and corrupting. Cacus is the symbolic link between Pope Nicholas III and Vanni Fucci. Like Cacus, both are thieves. Significantly, Dante chooses at this

20 Regarding the *meretrix magna*, see Havely, *Dante and the Franciscans* (above, n. 10), 112–14; Kaske, "Dante's *Purgatorio*" (above, n. 11), 195.

21 Throughout their history, popes portrayed themselves as shepherds. Dante uses the image ironically to underscore the failures of the papacy of his day; Ferrante, *Political Vision* (above, n. 4), 112–14.

22 All translations from Dante are those of Martinez and Durling. Nick Havely discusses the bestial imagery with regards to Vanni Fucci in *Dante* (above, n. 6), 164. On the human-beast hybrid see L'Ottimo Commento (1333), *Inf.* 24.122–26, Dartmouth Dante Project.

point in the canto to introduce the prophecy regarding the factional split between the White and Black Guelphs, a civil war that had dire personal consequences for the poet. In 1302, once the Blacks had seized power with the help of Charles of Valois and Pope Boniface VIII, the leaders of the commune of Florence expelled Dante and his sons.[23] The bestial side of man—his unrestrained passions and appetites for worldly pleasures, his avarice, enabled by fraud—leads not only to simony and theft, Dante seems to be saying, but, on a grander scale, papal corruption and civil war. Dante has therefore drawn upon several images and themes associated with Greek mythology—communicated to him primarily through Virgil and Ovid—to explore the bestial, dark side of the human character. From Virgil and from his own experiences after 1302, Dante has learned that the ultimate social consequence of the bestial nature of man can be chaos and, for both Aeneas and Dante, the loss of their home.

In canto 31, the poet draws upon another major figure from Greek and Hebrew mythology: the rebellious giant. Of the four giants described in the ninth circle, the circle of traitors, three are from Greek mythology: Antaeus, Ephialtes, and Tityus. One (Nimrod) is from the Old Testament.[24] These giants (*orribili giganti*; *Inf.* 31.44) are the monstrous projections of the worst human sin for Dante: pride or arrogance, exemplified in an act of defiance against divine authority. As Walter Stephens has argued, Dante sees them as evil and "mentally deficient."[25] These are "failed tyrants," humans "on a monumental scale." The first giant to be identified is Nimrod. According to Dante's interpretation of Genesis 11, out of his arrogance and vanity (*per lo cui mal coto*; *Inf* 31.77) he led the effort to build a tower that would reach to heaven. God punished mankind for this sin of hubris by multiplying the number of languages in the world, each one incomprehensible to the other (Gen. 11:1–9). Dante here explicitly links the Virgilian theme of *furor* and *ira*, the destructive power of passion, with Nimrod. When the giant sees Dante and Virgil, he begins to shout words that are incomprehensible to the two poets. Virgil admonishes him: use your horn when rage and anger overtake you (*quand' ira o altra passïon ti tocca!*; *Inf.* 31.72).[26] A figure associated with arrogance and vanity, Nimrod is linked directly with the papacy as the poet compares the proportions of his face to the size of the giant, sculpted pinecone at Saint Peter's in Rome: *La faccia sua mi parea lunga e grossa / come la pina di San Pietro a Roma, / e a sua proporzione eran l'altre ossa*; *Inf.* 31.58–60).[27] Dante's association of the papacy with these symbols of pride

23 J. Najemy, "Dante and Florence," in *Cambridge Companion to Dante* (above, n. 4), 237–38; idem, *A History of Florence* (Maldon, MA, and Oxford, 2008), 88–95; G. Holmes, *Florence, Rome, and the Origins of the Renaissance* (Oxford, 1986), chap. 7. For the commentary on *Inf.* 25, see L'Ottimo Commento (3) (1338), *Inf.* 25.29–33, Dartmouth Dante Project.

24 Giants are common in Greek and Roman literature and Hebrew mythology (Old Testament); *Dante Encyclopedia* (above, n. 4), s.v. "Giants"; Stephens, *Giants* (above, n. 7), 5.

25 Stephens, *Giants*, 67–88, 98.

26 Dronke, *Dante and the Medieval Latin Traditions* (above, n. 11), 54. R. Durling and R. Martinez, "Notes on Canto 31," in *The Divine Comedy of Dante Alighieri*, vol. 1, *Inferno* (New York, 1997), 493.

27 Nimrod is highlighted in this canto for his infamous opposition to God (also described by Augustine), as Stephens, *Giants*, 67–68, points out. This is all the more reason why the allusion to

becomes even more explicitly visual in *Purgatorio*. Here, again, he mobilizes figures from Greek mythology to develop his critique of a corrupted clerical hierarchy.

Purgatory is the site of renewal and rebirth.[28] Just as Geryon and snakes, taken from Greek mythology, are the principal figures in the *Inferno,* the griffin appears to be the central organizing figure from the Greek tradition in the *Purgatorio*.[29] In one of the most commented-upon series of cantos in the *Commedia*, cantos 29 through 32, the griffin appears in the heavenly pageant at the end of the canticle, pulling the chariot that represents the Church. In the Greek tradition, the griffin appears first in Hesiod, and later, for Herodotus, it guards Scythian gold.[30] This ancient animal hybrid—part eagle, part lion—may represent justice and fortitude. For many commentators on the *Purgatorio*, however, the griffin stands for Christ, the hybrid man-God. For L'Ottimo Commento (1333), for example, the hybridity of the griffin represents the union of the humanity and the divinity of Christ. Unlike Cacus, or Geryon, however, he is not a man-beast hybrid, with all its connotations of the bestial qualities in man. Rather, the griffin leads the chariot of the Church in triumph in the earthly paradise. At its sides are the three theological virtues (Faith, Hope, and Love) and the four cardinal virtues (Prudence, Fortitude, Temperance, and Justice). The griffin is an example of the positive use of a hybrid figure from Greek mythology to represent constructive attributes and virtues, such as divinity and justice.[31]

The chariot is also guarded by four animals, representing the Four Evangelists, each with three pairs of wings and full sets of eyes. Dante adds that their eyes remind him of Argus, the many-eyed herdsman sent by Hera (the Roman Juno) to guard Io, beloved of Zeus (the Roman Jove). Jove had transformed Io into a cow to protect her from Hera.[32]

---

the papacy is meant to underscore what Dante perceives to be papal disobedience to God. Beccheria, papal legate of Alexander IV and abbot of Vallombrosa, is in this circle because he treacherously worked with the Ghibellines against the Guelphs.

28 J. T. Schnapp, "Introduction to *Purgatorio,*" in *Cambridge Companion to Dante*, 91–93.

29 Seven hundred years of commentary on this figure have led to numerous interpretations of its symbolic significance. For a brief review of the different viewpoints, see P. Armour's article in *Dante Encyclopedia* (above, n. 4), s.v. "Griffin." For Armour's detailed analysis of the figure (and the closing cantos of *Purgatorio*), see his *Dante's Griffin and the History of the World: A Study of the Earthly Paradise (Purgatorio XXIX–XXXIII)* (Oxford, 1989). The traditional view identifies the griffin with Christ. Peter Dronke suggests, however, that it more accurately represents aspects of Dante's own soul or *daimon*; Dronke, *Dante and Medieval Latin Traditions,* 61. For Pertile's approach to the griffin, *La puttana e il gigante* (above, n. 11), 143–62.

30 See *Oxford Companion to Classical Literature* (above, n. 2), s.v. "Monsters." R. Kaske, "The *Seven Status Ecclesiae* in *Purgatorio* XXXII and XXXIII," in *Dante, Petrarch, and Boccaccio: Studies in the Italian Trecento in Honor of Charles S. Singleton*, ed. A. S. Bernardo and A. L. Pellegrini (Binghamton, NY, 1983), 89–113, argues that *Purgatorio* 32 represents the classic formulation of the seven "conditions of the Church." A recent interpretation of the closing cantos of *Purgatorio* (30–33), which sees these cantos as focusing on an exegetical and religious reading of the Song of Songs, is Pertile, *La puttana e il gigante*, 61.

31 L'Ottimo Commento (1333), *Purgatorio* 29.106–14. See also Ferrante, *Political Vision* (above, n. 4), 93, and Armour, *Dante's Griffin*, 4.

32 The story of Argus and Io comes from Ovid's *Metamorphoses*, book 1. See Ovid, *The Metamorphoses*, trans. H. Gregory (New York, 2001), 20–25.

In the *Purgatorio*, unlike the allusions to Cacus and Geryon in the *Inferno*, the connection to the herdsman, Argus, seems to underscore the positive, constructive role that the Gospels play. After all, they lead men and women to salvation (and not to its perverted opposite, bestiality). Beatrice, standing in the chariot, is compared to Minerva, the Greek Athena, the goddess of wisdom and crafts. In cantos 30 and 31, she reprimands Dante for having fallen short in his quest for truth and enlightenment. A weeping Dante admits that when she died he became obsessed with present-day matters and their false pleasures (*Piangendo dissi: "Le presenti cose / col falso lor piacer volser miei passi, / tosto che 'l vostro viso si nascose"*; *Purg.* 31.34–36). This lapse, Beatrice exclaims, is the result of having fallen prey to the siren's song, the temptation to become enmeshed in things of the flesh. Beatrice rebukes Dante. Her death, she says, should have spurred him on to higher things: *"Tuttavia, perché mo vergogna porte / del tuo errore, e perché altra volta, / udendo le serene, sie più forte"* ("Still, so that you may now bear the shame of your error, and so that another time, hearing the sirens, you may be stronger"; *Purg.* 31.43–44). This is an allusion to *Purgatorio* 19, where the siren first makes her appearance. She is another hybrid image from Greek mythology, albeit one with negative connotations, and she is most famously associated with the voyage of Ulysses. In the *Commedia*, the siren represents the love of worldly things and the desire for temporal knowledge. In the *Purgatorio,* Virgil strips off some of her clothes and a noxious stench is released (*puzzo*; *Purg.* 19.33), which recalls the *puzzo* of Geryon in *Inferno* 17. He urges Dante to resist her lure. This is the stink of beast-human hybrids, symbolic of worldly appetites and pleasures. Beatrice warns Dante to resist the seductive wiles of the siren, but she also presents *herself* implicitly as a Christian siren, luring Dante to things divine not mundane: *Ben ti dovevi, per lo primo strale / de le cose fallaci, levar suso / di retro a me che non era più tale* (After the first arrow from deceptive things, you should have risen up after me, for I was no longer such; *Purg.* 31.55–57).[33] Dante uses the siren in both negative and positive senses, representing alternately worldly concupiscence on one hand and divine love on the other.

In canto 32, the Argus and the giant return to underscore Dante's allegorical condemnation of the material Church and its corrupt papacy.[34] The canto begins with the griffin tying the chariot to the tree of good and evil. The branches flower, and Dante hears a hymn and falls asleep. He is reminded of Argus, as described by Ovid, who also fell asleep. If only he could be like a painter, muses the poet, and portray how the eyes of Argus grew heavy with sleep as he was listening to the tale told by Mercury about the nymph Syrinx, then he (Dante) could successfully describe how he also fell asleep listening to that hymn. Nevertheless, he notes that no one can portray sleepiness (*l'assonar*; *Purg.* 32.69) well, so he will not try. Argus was supposed to keep Io away from Jove,

33 Sirens are also hybrid creatures, often portrayed as birds with the heads of women; *Oxford Companion to Classical Literature*, s. v. "Sirens."

34 For discussions about the various interpretations of Argus and the giant in canto 32, see R. Durling and R. Martinez, "Notes to Canto 29" and "Notes to Canto 32," in *The Divine Comedy of Dante Alighieri*, vol. 2, *Purgatorio* (New York, 2004), 507, 561. Scott, *Dante's Political Purgatory* (above, n. 7), 194–212, 211–12; Kaske, "Dante's *Purgatorio*" (above, n. 11), 194–98, 202–6.

who had fallen in love with her. Instead, Hermes (the Roman Mercury), the messenger of Jove, beheaded Argus after he fell asleep listening to the story about Syrinx, another sirenlike figure. The image of the drowsy Argus harks back to the previous passage in *Inferno* 19, when Dante compared Pope Nicholas III to a shepherd watching "she who sits on the waters" (*colei che siede sopra l'acque*; *Inf.* 19.107) fornicate with kings. The allusion to Argus seems to foretell the great event about to unfold in canto 32: the allegorical pageant of the material, corrupted Church. Argus's drowsiness reminds us of Dante's own heeding of the hybrid siren, an experience that lulled him into a focus on present things. In the narrative that follows, the poet, as prophetic visionary, develops an elaborate allegory.[35] An eagle attacks the chariot and the tree. An attack by a fox follows. The eagle returns, leaving its feathers to cover the chariot. The earth then opens up and a dragon (*drago*; *Purg.* 32.131) emerges. With its tail, which is compared to the stinger of a wasp (*e come vespa che ritragge l'ago*; *Purg.* 32.133), it tears apart the base of the chariot. The chariot turns into a many-headed monster on which sits a whore (*puttana*; *Purg.* 32.160), and she is accompanied by a jealous giant who beats her when she turns her lascivious eyes toward Dante. The giant thereupon pulls the chariot into the forest.

Dante mobilizes these familiar images taken from the Greek and early Chistian mythological traditions—the dragon, the giant, the whore—to construct an allegory of a corrupt, fallen, materialistic Church and papacy. The dragon, or large serpent, represented for the Greeks (and later the Romans) the forces of unrestrained cupidity, passion, and disorder. Some commentators on the *Commedia* have traditionally associated the dragon with the devil, the Antichrist, or Muhammad. For L'Ottimo Commento (1333), the dragon is the most powerful of all the serpents on the earth, the symbolic embodiment of those forces in the world that persecute the Church. For Jacopo della Lana (1324–28), the dragon is more explicitly a representation of Muhammad himself. The inclusion of the image of the whore again calls to mind the passage in *Inferno* canto 19, in which Pope Nicholas III is compared to the shepherd who watches a prostitute fornicate with kings. Commenting on *Purgatorio* 32.148–50, L'Ottimo Commento (1333) and Jacopo della Lana (1324–28) identify the *puttana* with the papal court and the papacy (the "shepherd" of the Church), respectively. Dante had firsthand experience with the papal court, as he was serving as a Florentine envoy to Rome when he was exiled in 1302 during the Black Guelph takeover of the city. The image of the *puttana,* therefore, takes us back to the figure of the great whore (*meretrix magna*) of Revelation. Just in case the connection between papal corruption as portrayed in *Inferno* 19 and *Purgatorio* 33 is not clear enough, the use of the words *puttaneggiar* in the former and *puttana* in the latter underscores the fact that Dante is here referring in both to the worldly Church and its corrupted papacy.[36]

35 Kaske, "Dante's *Purgatorio,*" 202–8; Dronke, *Dante and Medieval Latin Traditions* (above, n. 11), 61–63.

36 Dronke, *Dante and Medieval Latin Traditions*, 70–73; Pertile, *La puttana e il gigante* (above, n. 11), 203–25. Pertile argues that the events portrayed here involving the *puttana* come straight from

Beatrice, who implicitly presents herself in canto 31 as a pure and saintly "siren" whom Dante should see as the embodiment of divine truth, now compares herself to a prophet whose impenetrable prophecies are like those of the Greek goddess Themis and her oracle the Sphinx. This is another Greek myth that Dante found in Ovid's *Metamorphoses* (book 7). According to Ovid, when Themis learned that Oedipus had solved her Sphinx's riddle, she punished the Thebans by destroying their livelihoods: their flocks, their fields, and their food. Beatrice assures Dante that no such disasters will occur when her own prophecy is revealed: (*ma tosto fier li fatti le Naiade, / che solveranno questo enigma forte / sanza danno di pecore o di biade*; *Purg.* 33.49–51) "but soon events will be the Naiads who will solve this hard enigma, without loss of sheep or grain". The corrupted Church will soon be no more. The attacking eagle, perhaps a symbol of empire, will have an heir, a new emperor, and God will destroy both the whore (the sinning papacy) and the giant (identified by Jacopo della Lana [1324–28] as the French monarchy). Most likely, the new emperor is Henry VII. Beatrice admonishes Dante to recall her words and write them down accurately, acknowledging the meaning and purpose of the tree of the knowledge of good and evil. She compares the vain desires of his own past slothful thoughts, prompted by his listening to the siren's song, to Ovid's mulberry tree, stained red with the blood of Pyramus and Thisbe. Just as blood stains the tree and hides its true color, so, too, do self-centered thoughts obscure Dante's own view of an underlying, divine truth.[37]

Dante's journey culminates in the third canticle, *Paradiso*. Although it includes, as Rachel Jacoff has observed, "more didactic and doctrinal materials than the previous canticles," it contains some of the loftiest poetry in the entire *Commedia*.[38] Cantos 15, 16, 17, 27, and 28 are briefly worth exploring here. Here again we have references to dragons, shepherds, and the stink of hybrid beasts, all of which underscore disgust at the greediness among many in the clergy. Cantos 15, 16, and 17 are among the most celebrated

---

the Song of Songs (p. 204). He also acknowledges that there is indeed a correspondence between *Inferno* 19 and *Purgatorio* 33, but the precedence for the kiss in *Purgatorio* is the incipit in the Song of Songs ("Osculetur me osculo oris sui"; p. 214). For early commentators, see L'Ottimo Commento (1333), *Purg.* 32.130–35 and 32.148–50, and Jacopo della Lana, *Purg.* 32.130–35 and 32.148–53, both Dartmouth Dante Project. L'Ottimo Commento (1333) makes a direct reference to Revelation 12: "And another portent appeared in heaven; behold, a great red dragon, with seven heads and ten horns, and seven diadems upon his heads. His tail swept down a third of the stars of heaven, and cast them to the earth" (Rev. 12:3–4). Dronke, however, argues for a nontraditional interpretation in which these figures have both an inner and an outer meaning. They actually represent, he argues, the inner drama within Dante himself (p. 72). Dante was a special ambassador to the papal court in 1302 when he was exiled along with 559 other men by the Blacks. He stood accused of "fraud, extortion, and obstructing the peace-making efforts of Charles and Boniface"; Najemy, *History of Florence* (above, n. 23), 92.

37 Vain desires, like stain on the mulberry tree, had "encrusted his mind," preventing him from seeing the tree for what it was: divine justice; Dronke, *Dante and Medieval Latin Traditions* (above, n. 11), 78. Hollander, *Dante: A Life in Works* (above, n. 12), 139, argues that this passage probably refers to Henry VII, as he most likely wrote these lines in 1312. For the identification of the giant with the French monarchy, see Jacopo della Lana (1324–28), *Purg.* 32.148–53. Dartmouth Dante Project.

38 R. Jacoff, "Introduction to *Paradiso*," *Cambridge Companion to Dante* (above, n. 4), 108.

cantos in the *Commedia*. Here Dante meets his illustrious ancestor, Cacciaguida (d. 1147), in the fifth sphere of heaven, the level of the warriors. Cacciaguida complains about the decline of Florence and its illustrious families as inferior immigrants swelled the city. This hybridization of Florence as the noble "old" is merged with the degraded "new" is a cause for complaint. Cacciaguida also offers a trenchant critique of three families with close ties to the Florentine bishopric: the Visdomini, Tosinghi, and Adimari:

> *Oh quali io vidi quei che son disfatti*
> *per lor superbia! e le palle de l'oro*
> *fiorian Fiorenza in tutt' i suoi gran fatti.*
> *Così facieno i padri di coloro*
> *che, sempre che la vostra chiesa vaca,*
> *si fanno grassi stando a concistoro.* (*Par.* 16.109–114)

> Oh how great they seemed to me, those who have been undone by their pride! And the golden balls made Florence flourish in all her great deeds. Such were the fathers of those who whenever your church is vacant, make themselves fat in consistory.

Whenever the bishopric of Florence fell vacant, as it did between 1275 and 1286, the Visdomini *consorteria* had the traditional privilege of administering the temporal holdings of the bishopric until the cathedral chapter and papacy chose a new prelate. As a young man in Florence during this long episcopal vacancy, Dante witnessed the extent to which these families avariciously enriched themselves with the income of the bishopric. He compares them to animals fattening themselves at the trough (the trough here is compared to a church consistory).[39] The next family to receive Cacciaguida's condemnation is another lineage with close ties to the Florentine Church: the Adimari. The Adimari increasingly came to dominate the chapter of one of the wealthiest ecclesiastical institutions in the city, the church of San Lorenzo. For much of the third quarter of the thirteenth century, the Adimari were locked in a power struggle with the Tosinghi over access to Church offices and properties. As a young man, Dante was in a position to take note of the greed of these two Florentine lineages. Drawing again upon a figure from Greek and Hebrew mythology, Dante compares the ways of the Adimari to those of a dragon, consistently the symbol of malevolent greed and disorder: *L'oltracotata schiatta che s'indraca / dietro a chi fugge, e a chi mostra 'l dente / o ver la borsa, com' agnel si placa* (The presumptuous clan that is like a dragon against those who flee, but is placated like a lamb by those who show their teeth or their purse; *Par.* 16.115–17). His criticism of these families quite possibly stemmed from his own observations of their behavior in ecclesiastical offices. Canons in both cathedral chapter and the church of San Lorenzo were quite publicly and consistently involved in property disputes with

39 Singleton, *Divine Comedy* (above, n. 1), 2:280. See also G. Dameron, *Florence and Its Church in the Age of Dante* (Philadelphia, 2005), 68; idem, *Episcopal Power and Florentine Society, 1000–1320* (Cambridge, MA, 1991), 1–2.

other ecclesiastical institutions and Florentine citizens in the second half of the thirteenth century.[40]

In canto 17, Cacciaguida foretells the tragedy of Dante's exile by order of Pope Boniface VIII in Rome, but he also offers him hope for a future vindication. Like the Greek mythological figure Hippolytus, whose story is recounted in Ovid's *Metamorphoses,* book 15, and Virgil's *Aeneid,* book 7, Dante will be forced to leave home because of treachery. In Dante's case, it is through the political machinations of a man (Pope Boniface VIII) who lives in Rome, where Christ is "bought and sold every day" (*Questo si vuole e questo già si cerca, / e tosto verrà fatto a chi ciò pensa / là dove Cristo tutto dì si merca*"; *Par* 17.49–51). Just as Phaedra, the lascivious daughter of King Minos of Crete, falsely accused her stepson Hippolytus of having attempted to seduce her, forcing him into exile at the order of his father, so, too, did Corso Donati and Pope Boniface VIII unjustly accuse Dante and many White Guelph lineages of serious crimes, forcing them into exile as well. Phaedra was the daughter of Pasiphaë, whose lust was so great that she mated with a bull. She gave birth to the hybrid minotaur, half-beast, half-man. Phaedra's lineage, and by symbolic association, Boniface's as well, is therefore enmeshed in bestiality and concupiscence. As is true for Florence itself, hybridization has led to decadence and vice. Dante, on the other hand, as Cacciaguida implies, will be a new Hippolytus, a twice-man (*virbius*) who returns in triumph to tell his tale. According to Ovid, Hippolytus dies, but Diana and Aesculapius restore him to life, renaming him Virbius. Virgil also has him brought back to life by the goddess Diana and Aesculapius, as recounted in the seventh book of the *Aeneid.* In canto 17, Cacciaguida compares Dante to Hippolytus: both men suffer libelous accusations, go into exile, but later find themselves vindicated.[41] Regarding this same passage in *Paradiso* (17.46–48), L'Ottimo Commento (1333) suggests a parallel between Phaedra and Theseus, on one hand, and Corso Donati and Pope Boniface VIII, on the other. Just as Phaedra falsely accused Hippolytus to his father to have him exiled, Corso Donati had gone to the court of the pope, with money in hand, to convince him to send Charles of Anjou to Florence to help expel the White Guelphs (including Dante). The expulsion order came in 1302.[42]

40 Singleton, *Divine Comedy,* 2:280. For the most recent assessment of the connection between the Adimari and San Lorenzo, see W. Bowsky, "Pietà e proprietà nella Firenze medievale: Una casa in San Lorenzo," in *La chiesa di San Lorenzo a Firenze nel medioevo,* ed. R. Nelli (Florence, 1999), 1–90, especially 42–44. Dameron, *Florence and Its Church,* 118–21, explores the property interests of the major ecclesiastical institutions of the city before 1330.

41 The story of Hippolytus appears in *Metamorphoses* 15.424–426; *Aen.* 7.1048–1076 (trans. Fitzgerald). See J. T. Schnapp, "Dante's Ovidian Self-Correction in *Paradiso* 7," in *The Poetry of Allusion* (above, n. 9), 214–23; *Oxford Companion to Classical Literature* (above, n. 2), s.v. "Hippolytus"; *Dante Encyclopedia* (above, n. 4), s.v. "Hippolytus." For the direct connection drawn by Cacciaguida between Hippolytus and Dante, see the comments of the 14th-century commentator Jacopo della Lana (1324–28) on *Par.* 17.46–48. Dartmouth Dante Project.

42 *E tacitamente vuole che si intenda, che cacciato anzi il MCCC messer Corso [e] i suoi Neri di Firenze, elli se n'andò a corte a papa Bonifazio, e con prieghi e con amici, con moneta o con senno*

In canto 18, Beatrice explicitly calls upon heaven to unleash its wrath on the see of Rome. In canto 21, the church reformer Peter Damian (d. 1027) rails against bishops, whom he calls false pastors. They resemble man-horse hybrids as they ride their horses in their fine robes:

> *Or voglion quinci e quindi chi rincalzi*
> *li moderni pastori e chi li meni,*
> *tanto son gravi, e chi di rietro li alzi.*
> *Cuopron d'i manti loro i palafreni,*
> *sì che due bestie van sott' una pelle.* (*Par.* 21.130–34)

> Now the modern shepherds need someone on each side to hold them up and lead them, they are so fat, and someone to lift them up behind. They cover their palfreys with their mantles, so that two beasts go beneath one skin.

In the following canto, Beatrice assures Dante that God's vengeance on them will come in time. By canto 27, in the eighth sphere of the fixed stars, Saint Peter himself unleashes his wrath against contemporary popes (particularly Boniface VIII). He implicitly links them to greedy wolves dressed like shepherds (*In vesta di pastor lupi rapaci*; *Par.* 27.55), recalling again the image of failed pastors. Boniface VIII is the usurper who made the tomb of Saint Peter a sewer of blood and stink:

> *Quelli ch'usurpa in terra il luogo mio,*
> *il luogo mio, il luogo mio che vaca*
> *ne la presenza del Figliuol di Dio,*
> *fatt' ha del cimitero mio cloaca*
> *del sangue e de la puzza; onde 'l perverso*
> *che cadde di qua sù, là giù si placa.*[43] (*Par.* 27.22–27)

> He who on earth usurps my place, my place, my place, which is vacant in the presence of the Son of God, has made my burial place a sewer of the blood and stench that placate the perverted one down there, who fell from up here.

> *fece sì, che 'l detto Papa mandò per messer Carlo fratello del re di Franca, per lo cui vigore il detto messer Corso ritornòe in Firenze, e caccióne l'Autore e li Bianchi*

L'Ottimo Commento (1333), *Par.* 17.46–48. Dartmouth Dante Project. For an account of the appeal made to the pope by Corso Donati, see Najemy, *A History of Florence* (above, n. 23), 91.

43 See Jacoff, "Introduction to *Paradiso*" (above, n. 38), 116, 122. Dante and Saint Bernard of Clairvaux also shared common ideas regarding their notions of an ideal Christian community, but there is no proof that Saint Bernard exerted any direct influence on the poet; see S. Botterill, "Ideals of the Institutional Church in Dante and Bernard of Clairvaux," *Italica* 78, no. 3 (Autumn 2001): 297–313, esp. 297–98, 309–10.

We have returned, indeed, at the end of the *Paradiso* to an image of a Geryon-like figure, a stinking man-beast hybrid, a false shepherd, a failed protector of his flock, a pope.

In contrast to the negative imagery taken from Greek mythology marshaled against the institutions of the papacy and clerical families like the Visdomini, Dante employs positive imagery taken from the Greek cultural tradition in canto 28. For example, the poet places the hierarchically arranged angels of Pseudo-Dionysius the Areopagite in the fourth sphere among the Doctors of the Church.[44] They act as movers of the spheres of the universe. In canto 10, he credits Dionysius, who was probably a sixth-century Syrian monk who wrote in Greek, for knowing more about angels and the ministry than anyone else: *Appresso vedi il lume di quel cero / che giù in carne più a dentro vide / l'angelica natura e 'l ministero* (Next you see the light of that candle which below, in the flesh, saw deepest into the nature and the ministry of angels; *Par.* 10.115–117). As Piero Boitani has argued, the creation of the angels by God is a "reflection of light, an opening out of Love into new loves." In the vocabulary of the Neoplatonism of the Areopagite, they represent the manifestations of the outward emanation of the divine.[45] These angels of a light-radiating deity, themselves human-bird hybrids, like the griffin and the twice-man Hippolytus, are positive counterparts to the hybrid beast-shepherds, serpents, dragons, giants, and animal stink that Dante associates with a degraded and debauched Church.

In conclusion, one may ask why the images taken from Greek mythology associated with bestiality and man-beast hybridity resonated so well with Dante and were so important to his critique of the Church hierarchy. For one, the Greeks and Hebrews were among the first in literature to probe the darkest, as well as the most promising, aspects of the human condition. They consequently created a robust reservoir of images, figures, and vocabulary that vividly illustrated man's basest animalistic passions as well as his highest aspirations. Roman and early Christian writers continued to draw upon this rich cultural legacy for centuries to come. Although Dante knew no Greek, he was familiar with that tradition through Latin classics. Indeed, Dante drew upon this reading of Virgil, Ovid, and Statius to express his harsh judgments regarding the papacy and clergy, and he recognized resonances between this Greek-inspired mythology and Franciscan apocalyptic literature. Even in modern popular culture, Dante's vision of hell and purgatory, with some of its richest imagery inspired by the ancient Greeks, still inspires modern writers and artists as they continue to explore the darkest aspects of the human condition.

44 Dante's familiarity with this work probably stemmed from his knowledge of Hugh of Saint Victor's commentary on *De angelica hierarchia* of Pseudo-Dionysius, to which he most likely had access at Santa Croce; Davis, "Education in Dante's Florence" (above, n. 12), 15.

45 J. A. Mazzeo, *Medieval Cultural Tradition in Dante's Comedy* (Ithaca, 1960), chap. 1; Jacoff, "Introduction to *Paradiso,*" 113; P. Boitani, "The Poetry and Poetics of the Creation," in *Cambridge Companion to Dante* (above, n. 4), 226–27.

I wish to acknowledge with gratitude the comments, corrections, and suggestions that I received from Antonello Borra, Louisa Burnham, Thomas Cachey, William Caffero, Marcia Colish, Will Marquess, Kristina Olson, Bill Stephani, Nancy Vickers, and the three anonymous reviewers of this essay. I also wish to express my special appreciation to Jan Ziolkowski for having invited me to participate in the extremely stimulating interdisciplinary gathering on Dante and the Greeks at Dumbarton Oaks.

Ulysses and the Three Traditions

PIERO BOITANI

As Leigh Hunt tells us, John Keats maintained that as far as Ulysses was concerned, Dante's authority was on a par with Homer's. "Talking with a friend about Dante," Hunt recalled,

> he [Keats] observed that whenever so great a poet told us anything in addition or continuation of an ancient story, he had a right to be regarded as a classical authority. For instance, said he, when he [Dante] tells us of that characteristic death of Ulysses in one of the books of the *Inferno,* we ought to receive the information as authentic, and be glad that we have more news of Ulysses than we looked for.[1]

1 L. Hunt, "More News of Ulysses," in *The Indicator: A Miscellany for the Fields and the Fireside* (New York, 1845), pt. 1: 65. A short bibliography on the figure of Ulysses and its "Nachleben," including Dante, would now have to include at least the following: B. Andreae, *L'immagine di Ulisse: Mito e archeologia* (Turin, 1983); *Ulisse: Il mito e la memoria*, ed. B. Andreae and C. Parisi Presicce (Rome, 1996); *Ulisse da Omero a Pascal Quignard,* ed. A. M. Babbi and F. Zardini (Verona, 2000); *Odysseus/Ulysses,* ed. H. Bloom (New York, 1991); P. Boitani, *The Shadow of Ulysses* (Oxford, 1994); idem, *Sulle orme di Ulisse* (Bologna, 2007); *Ulisse: Archeologia dell'uomo modern,* ed. P. Boitani and R. Ambrosini (Rome, 1998); P. Boitani, "The Shadow of Ulysses beyond 2001," *Comparative Criticism* 21 (1999): 3–19; F. Brommer, *Odysseus: Die Taten und Leiden des Helden in antiker Kunst und Literatur* (Darmstadt, 1983); M. Corti, *Scritti su Cavalcanti e Dante* (Turin, 2003); F. Ferrucci, *L'assedio e il ritorno: Omero e gli archetipi della narrazione* (Milan, 1991); P. H. Damon, "Dante's Ulysses and the Mythic Tradition," in *Medieval Secular Literature: Four Essays,* ed. W. Matthews (Berkeley, 1965), 25–45; J. Freccero, *Dante: The Poetics of Conversion*, ed. R. Jacoff (Cambridge, MA, 1986); *Lange Irrfahrt—grosse Heimkehr: Odysseus als Archetyp—zur Aktualität des Mythos,* ed. G. Fuchs (Frankfurt am Main, 1994); E. Hall, *The Return of Ulysses: A Cultural History of Homer's Odyssey* (London and New York, 2008); F. Hartog, *Mémoire d'Ulysse: Récits sur la frontière en Grèce ancienne* (Paris, 1996); *Ulisse nel tempo: La metafora infinita,* ed. S. Nicosia (Venice, 2003); G. Padoan, *Il pio Enea, l'empio Ulisse: Tradizione classica e intendimento medievale in Dante* (Ravenna, 1977); A. Perutelli, *Ulisse nella cultura romana* (Florence, 2006); *The Oxford Guide to Classical Mythology in the Arts, 1300–1990s,* ed. J. D. Reid (New York and Oxford, 1993), s.v. "Odysseus"; *Da Ulisse a Ulisse,* ed. G. Revelli (Pisa and Rome, 2001); J. A. Scott, *Dante Magnanimo: Studi sulla "Commedia"*

Keats's opinion is that of a poet, and we should therefore regard it as supremely authoritative, especially as it concerns two of the greatest poets ever, and two of the poets Keats himself loved most. It is, I think, highly significant that in his "On First Looking into Chapman's Homer," Keats thought fit to insert at least one Dantean reminiscence into a sonnet that basically revisits the *Odyssey*.[2]

This might not tell us much about Dante and the Greeks, although Keats, one of the foremost Hellenists of his age, would have seen no contradiction in coupling the Florentine poet with the deep-browed Ionian bard. But I think it actually tells us more than we as philologists might be inclined to believe. It seems to indicate Dante's total independence from Homer and, at the same time, invite us to take his account of Ulysses as an "addition" to or "continuation" of ancient myth.

In this sense, Keats's pronouncement strangely agrees with that of the ancient commentator Benvenuto da Imola. Benvenuto is acquainted with the plot of the *Odyssey* (and perhaps a bit more), as well as with Dares and Dictys. He can hardly believe, he writes, that Dante was unaware of what even children and the ignorant know, namely, that both "poetic" and "historical" authorities had given very different accounts of Ulysses' death from that of *Inferno* 26. Far from reproaching Dante, however, he praises him for his "industry" and "invention," his "new" fiction (*fingere de novo*), which have the precise aim of revealing Ulysses as the example of the *vir magnanimus, animosus* who had spared no toil, no danger, nor even life itself to acquire *experientia rerum*, and who "had chosen to live gloriously for a short time rather than ignominiously for a long one." In other words, Benvenuto understands the novelty of Dante's Ulysses and appreciates it. Even he, however, when it comes to glossing the famous *altrui* (another) of the penultimate line of *Inferno* 26, tries to let himself off the hook, adopting concepts from antiquity that were common currency in the Middle Ages, but giving them as alternatives: he glosses the crucial hemistich, *deo, fato vel fortunae*.[3] The agent of Ulysses' shipwreck could thus be, according to Benvenuto, God or fate or fortune. This is, of course, a nice way of getting out of the stumbling block of *com'altrui piacque* (as pleased another), but, as the subsequent six centuries have shown, it simply does not work.

Yet one thing Benvenuto does see clearly, namely, that Dante could not have ignored the plot of Homer's story of Ulysses, and that, if he had chosen to write a different tale, it must have been because he wanted to invent a *new* story, one from which the magnanimity of the hero, and his quest for *experientia rerum*, would emerge fully.

The question is, is this true? Did Dante deliberately set aside Homer and the Greeks in composing *Inferno* 26? The question is complex, not so much because we know that

---

(Florence, 1977); W. B. Stanford, *The Ulysses Theme: A Study in the Adaptability of a Traditional Hero*, 2nd ed. (Ann Arbor, 1968); D. Thompson, *Dante's Epic Journeys* (Baltimore, 1974); *Odysseen*, ed. H. Wagner and B. Wolf (Berlin, 2008); F. Zardini and G. Lana, *La morte di Ulisse: Riflessioni dall'antico al barocco* (Verona, 2006).

2 The "pure serene" of line 7 is a reminiscence, via Cary's translation, of *Purg.* 1.14–15, and *Par.* 15.3.

3 Benvenuto da Imola, *Comentum*, ed. G. W. Vernon and J. P. Lacaita, 5 vols. (Florence, 1887), 5:293.

Dante had no direct access to Greek texts, but because it implies looking at the entire Ulysses tradition to approach an answer. Let me, therefore, simplify matters by saying that three mythical and literary traditions, all equally authoritative, were available to Dante when he embarked on his account of Ulysses.

In the first, the Greek hero is a trickster, a teller of tall stories, and a sharp talker. This feature is present in the *Iliad* and the *Odyssey*, but it acquires particular poignancy in the great Attic plays of the fifth century, especially Sophocles' *Philoctetes* and Euripides' *Hecuba* and *Cyclops*, and it then passes to Roman imperial times, as in Philostratus's *Heroicus*. Yet even Sophocles gives a slightly more sympathetic view of Ulysses in his *Ajax*, and Euripides shows himself to be more neutral in his *Rhesus*.[4] Ulysses the trickster is, of course, the character that eventually passes into the hands of Virgil in the *Aeneid* and Ovid in the *Metamorphoses*, then into Statius's *Achilleis* and into a score of later writers, such as Dictys, Benoît de Sainte-Maure, and Guido delle Colonne.[5] And Dante duly has Ulysses condemned to hell on account of his deceit: as Virgil clarifies in his presentation of the ancient flame, it was for the "agguato del caval," and for the stratagems by means of which, with Diomedes, he took Achilles from Deidamia and stole the Palladium.[6]

However, a second venerable tradition exists in which Ulysses is the embodiment of virtue and wisdom, and the noble pursuer of knowledge. He is the "classical" ideal of the magnanimous hero who, according to Benvenuto, wants to gain "experience of the world." Again, this feature is already present in Homer's portrait. The protagonist of the *Odyssey* is undoubtedly condemned by Poseidon to sail the seas for ten years, but it is Ulysses who, when urged by his companions not to go farther in the land of the Cyclops, absolutely insists that he wants to explore it and find out what kind of people live there. He does exactly the same when they reach Circe's island, Aeaea, and again when they sight the sirens.[7]

These Homeric hints form the basis on which Dante builds his own portrait of the indomitable explorer. Furthermore, the Greek tradition is itself full of praise for Ulysses. Herodotus clearly takes him as the model for the historian, and Polybius later identifies the historian (*historein* means to search, research) with Ulysses *tout court*.[8] In his *Republic,* Plato presents Ulysses at the very end of the myth of Er as the man who, having now learned true wisdom, chooses the persona of a common individual for his reincarnation.[9] Neoplatonic exegesis extols Ulysses: Plotinus for his desire to return to the Father, spurning all temptations of the flesh; Porphyry, in *The Cave of the Nymphs*,

4 See Stanford, *Ulysses Theme*, 102–17, 149–52.

5 See Ibid., 146–58.

6 *Inf.* 26.8–63: *Aeneid* 2.165ff.; for this tradition, see Padoan, *Il pio Enea* (above, n. 1), 170–204.

7 *Odyssey* 9.172–76, 10.190–97, 12.154–200.

8 D. Asheri, "Introduzione generale," in *Erodoto, Le Storie* (Milan, 1988), 1: xxv; Polybius, *Histories* 12.27.

9 Plato, *Republic* 10.620c–d; see also Proclus, *Commentaire sur la Republique*, trans. A. J. Festugière (Paris, 1970), 3:279–80.

turning him into a prototype of the mystic. By the time of Eustathius in the twelfth century, Ulysses has become *the* philosopher and, more precisely, the ἀποτελεσματικός φιλόσοφος, the "astrologian philosopher," the scientist of astrology.[10]

Almost every thinker in late antiquity, and many among the early Church Fathers, provides favorable interpretations of Ulysses. His figure is present in Stoics, Cynics, and Gnostics, and in Heraclitus as well as in Plutarch, Numenius, Philo, Maximus of Tyre, Clement of Alexandria, Hippolytus of Rome, Ambrose, and Maximus of Turin.[11] The emperor Tiberius—who often asked his scholars what the sirens really sang[12]—consecrates Ulysses' image and adventures to promote the legend that the Greek hero is the ancestor of his own Claudian family and celebrate his own wisdom as man and politician in a grotto by the sea in his villa at Sperlonga, just overlooking Mount Circeo, the mountain of Circe. Nero, Hadrian, and the Roman bourgeoisie all celebrate Ulysses in statues and painting. The iconography reaches all shores of the Mediterranean, from Tunisia to Palestine.[13]

Cicero, Horace, and Seneca, but also Fulgentius, Boethius, and, in the Middle Ages, Bernardus Silvestris and Giovanni del Virgilio, Dante's friend and contemporary, all speak of Ulysses in these terms.[14] Dante himself makes his hero remind his companions (so that he becomes a paragon of man's "passion . . . to gain experience of the world," *l'ardore . . . a divenir del mondo esperto*; *Inf.* 26.97–98):

> *Considerate la vostra semenza:*
> *fatti non foste a viver come bruti,*
> *ma per seguir virtute e canoscenza.*[15]

> Consider how your souls were sown: you were not made to live like brutes or beasts, but to pursue virtue and knowledge.

10 Plotinus, *Enneads* 1.6.8; Porfirio, *L'antro delle ninfe*, ed. L. Simonini (Milan, 1986), 247–49; Eustathius, *Commentarii ad Homeri Odysseam* (Hildesheim and New York, 1970), A 18.39 (1390.4), 17: the commentary touches here on *Odyssey* 5.270–75.

11 See Stanford, *Ulysses Theme* (above, n. 1), 118–27; J. Pépin, "The Platonic and Christian Ulysses," in *Odysseus/Ulysses* (above, n. 1), 228–48. One should add the passage against unholy wandering from Augustine's *De vita beata* (1.1), first recalled by Freccero, *Poetics of Conversion* (above, n. 1), 20–23, and the many quoted by P. Boyde, *Human Vices and Human Worth in Dante's Comedy* (Cambridge, 2000), 231–72.

12 Suetonius, book 3, *Tiberius*, chap. 70.

13 See *Lexicon Iconographicum Mythologiae Classicae* (Zurich and Munich, 1992), 6:943–83, s.v. "Odysseus."

14 Cicero, *De officiis* 1.31.113, 3.26; Horace, *Epistles* 1.2; Seneca, *De constantia sapientis* 2.1; Boethius, *De consolatione philosophiae* 4, m. 3; Fulgentius, *Mitologiarum liber*, 8, ed. R. Helm (Stuttgart, 1970), 48; *The Commentary on the First Six Books of the Aeneid of Vergil Commonly Attributed to Bernardus Silvestris*, ed. J. W. Jones and E. F. Jones (Lincoln, NE, and London, 1977), 3, 383 (see references in notes, p. 21, to Bernardus Silvestris's commentary on Martianus Capella, William of Conches, and the Vatican Mythographers); F. Ghisalberti, "Giovanni del Virgilio espositore delle 'Metamorfosi'," *Giornale Dantesco* 34, n.s. 4 (1933): 99.

15 *Inf.* 26.118–20.

At this point, let me observe that while the Dante, who begins the *Convivio* with the memorable Aristotelian sentence "All men by nature desire to know,"[16] would have agreed whole-heartedly with Ulysses' passion, and Dante the character is undoubtedly drawn to Ulysses by an overwhelming *desio*: *vedi che del desio ver' lei mi piego,* as he tells Virgil (you see how eagerly I lean in its direction; *Inf.* 26.69), Dante the poet senses the extreme danger Ulysses represents for him, as he enigmatically announces at the beginning of the canto:

> *Allor mi dolsi, e ora mi ridoglio*
> *quando drizzo la mente a ciò ch'io vidi,*
> *e più lo 'ngegno affreno ch'i non soglio,*
> *perché non corra che virtù nol guidi;*
> *sì che, se stella bona o miglior cosa*
> *m'ha dato 'l ben, ch'io stessi nol m'invidi.*[17]

> I grieved then and now I grieve again as my thoughts turn to what I saw, and more than is my way, I curb my powers lest they run on where virtue fails to guide them, so that, if friendly star or something better still has granted me its boon, I don't refuse the gift.

Lastly, Dante the poet has his hero drowned by God, Dante the judge condemns him to hell, and even Dante the character and author will later repeat that Ulysses' *varco* (crossing) was indeed *folle* (mad).[18]

And, as if this were not enough, Dante the writer out-Ulysses Ulysses and plays a trick on his hero worthy of his own wiles. A third exegetic tradition exists, equally venerable and time-honored, in which Ulysses, tied to the mast before the sirens, is a "prefiguration of Christ."[19] Now, in the account of *Inferno* 26, neither Ulysses nor Dante nor Virgil makes any mention of the sirens. In *Purgatorio* 19, however, Dante himself dreams of *una femmina balba, / ne li occhi guercia e sovra i piè distorta, / con le man monche, e di colore scialba* (a female, stuttering, cross-eyed, and crooked on her feet, with stunted hands, and pallid in color; *Purg.* 19.7–9), whom his own gaze transforms into a beautiful siren, and who immediately begins to sing in such a way that the listener is rapt:

> *"Io son," cantava, "io son dolce serena,*
> *che' marinari in mezzo mar dismago;*
> *tanto son di piacer a sentir piena!*
> *Io volsi Ulisse del suo cammin vago*
> *al canto mio; e qual meco s'ausa,*
> *rado sen parte; sì tutto l'appago!"*[20]

16 *Conv.* 1.1.1: Aristotle, *Metaphysics*, 1.1.980a.21.

17 *Inf.* 26.19–24.

18 *Par.* 27.82–83.

19 H. Rahner, *Symbole der Kirche: Die Ekklesiologie der Väter* (Salzburg, 1964), 234–71.

20 *Purg.* 19.19–24.

> "I am," she was singing, "I am a sweet siren, who enchant the sailors on the deep sea, so full of pleasure am I to hear! I turned Ulysses from his course, desirous of my song, and whoever becomes used to me rarely leaves me, so wholly do I satisfy him!"

Here, again, is the irresistible call of the open sea from the *Odyssey,* but this time the siren manages to divert Ulysses from his wandering way (*cammin vago*) or, as others have it, turns him off track, enamored as he is of traveling. The two readings, dividing over the *vago*, are subtly different, the second reemphasizing the desire for travel and knowledge evinced in *Inferno* 26. There is inevitable, and fierce, critical debate over this passage. Quite validly drawing on other passages in the *Commedia* and a respectable iconographic and allegorical tradition, the majority maintains that the siren stands for pleasure, lust, avarice, and gluttony: in a word, that the siren and the *femmina balba* represent the imperfect pleasures of this world and the fatal attraction they exert over unwary mortals. Others, following the "moralization" of the character already established in the Middle Ages, identify the siren-woman with Circe (her intemperate swine becoming a distinctive feature of the signified), or even with Calypso.[21] There is, lastly, a vocal minority that reads the siren as *cupiditas sapientiae* (desire for wisdom), based on a passage in Cicero's *De finibus bonorum et malorum,* a work that Dante cites in the *Convivio.* Homer, Cicero says after translating the relevant lines of *Odyssey* 12, realized that his narrative would have appeared less than plausible if a man as great as Ulysses could be ensnared by a mere snatch of song (*si cantiunculis tantus irretitus vir teneretur*): "it is knowledge the sirens offer, and it is not to be wondered at if to a lover of knowledge this is dearer than his fatherland and his home" (*né dolcezza di figlio, né la pieta / del vecchio padre,* Dante will have Ulysses say, *vincer potero dentro a me l'ardore / ch'i' ebbi a divenir del mondo esperto / e de li vizi umani e del valore*).[22]

What does the siren mean? I think Dante is more complex than his interpreters. He conjures up a "holy" woman (*donna santa e presta*) to expose the beauty projected on to the "femmina balba" by his own subconscious. At her request, Virgil rends the siren's garments, revealing to Dante the belly, the smell of which wakes him. In other words, Dante changes the ancient story of Ulysses and the sirens almost beyond recognition (it will take a Kafka to go further than this), making Ulysses succumb to extreme desire, be it of the flesh, mind, or even poetry.[23] He is also teaching us a lesson in interpretation. The nightmare of the "femmina balba" turns into an enthralling erotic dream when the protagonist's own gaze, "as the sun strengthens cold limbs that the night weighs down . . . gave color to her wan face, just as love desires" (*come 'l sol conforta / le fredde membra che la notte aggrava . . . com' amor vuol, così le colorava*; *Purg* 19.10–11). It is the dreamer's desire that reads beauty into the siren, straightening the crippled body of the woman and endowing

21 See Padoan, *Il pio Enea* (above, n. 1), 200–204.

22 Cicero, *De finibus* 5.18.49.

23 F. Kafka, "The Silence of the Sirens," in *Parables and Paradoxes* (New York, 1961), 88–93.

her with a tongue to speak and sing. The appearance of the enchantress then changes once more when the dream becomes an allegory, that is, when reason and wisdom emerge from Dante's sleeping consciousness to reveal the creature's ultimate ugliness.

If, then, as we could conclude from *Inferno* 26 and *Purgatorio* 19, poetry begins with a projection of *desio* toward its object and is able to burn the poet's tongue, it is still desire, the reader's, that succumbs to temptation. But interpreting, "rending the garments," forces us to project these desires onto a rational reflection, a re-cognition.

Finally, I would like to recall two details that might establish indirect links between Dante and Homer. The first is Ulysses' indication that after his speech to the companions, they made *de' remi . . . ali al folle volo* ("in our mad flight . . . oars to wings"; *Inf.* 26.125). This goes back to the *Odyssey*, where Tiresias prophesies to Ulysses his last voyage and his having to find a land that knows no sea, no salted food, no oars, "which are wings to ships" (τά τε πτερὰ νηυσὶ).[24] A tradition that goes through Virgil comes all the way to Dante.[25] The second detail emerges from a passage in the *Iliad*, in which Diomedes has to choose a companion for his spying expedition to the Trojan camp. Diomedes, of course, chooses Ulysses: "if he were to come with me," he says, "we could both escape even a burning flame, for he can understand (because he knows)" (τούτου γ' ἑσπομένοιο καὶ ἐκ πυρὸς αἰθομένοιο / ἄμφω νοστήσαιμεν, ἐπεὶ περίοιδε νοῆσαι).[26] I have always wondered if this "burning flame" might not find a way to become, in ironical *contrapasso* fashion, the "*fiamma*" with two "horns" of *Inferno* 26.85. Of course, I know that the *fiamma antica* comes from Virgil. And indeed, here is one of the *Commedia*'s conundrums, because the very same expression is used later for Dante's love toward Beatrice at the climactic moment of their reunion: *Conosco i segni de l'antica fiamma* (I recognize the signs of the ancient flame), following Dido's *adgnosco veteris vestigia flammae* (I recognize traces of the former flame).[27] Just a minimal inversion in the word order signals the difference: *fiamma antica* for Ulysses, *antica fiamma* for Beatrice.[28] Ulysses and Beatrice are the two poles of desire in the poem—the same flame, but. . . .

Benvenuto da Imola and John Keats were right, then. Homer, Virgil, and Dante are linked in a series of authorities we should simply accept. We should also recognize that from Homer onward the Ulysses tradition is split, and that these divisions are clearly reflected in Dante's story. Dante begins the episode by asking Virgil who is inside the *foco diviso*, the cloven fire that goes back to Statius's *Thebaid*, and remains silent at the end. He begins with curiosity and wonder, and ends, significantly, in total silence. Equally significant, however, is his mentioning Ulysses throughout the *Commedia*, all the way to the threshold of the Empyrean. Ulysses is indeed his ancient flame. Soon, he will become the flame of European civilization.[29]

24 *Odyssey* 11.25.
25 *Aeneid* 1.301, 3.529.
26 *Iliad* 10.246–47.
27 *Aeneid* 4.23.
28 *Inf.* 26.85: *Purg.* 30.48.
29 See Boitani, *The Shadow of Ulysses* (above, n. 1), 44–68.

ABBREVIATIONS

AB	*Analecta Bollandiana*
AFP	*Archivum Fratrum Praedicatorum*
ArtB	*Art Bulletin*
BAR	*British Archaeological Reports*
BMGS	*Byzantine and Modern Greek Studies*
BZ	*Byzantinische Zeitschrift*
CAG	Commentaria in Aristotelem Graeca
CCSG	Corpus Christianorum, Series Graeca
CCSL	Corpus Christianorum, Series Latina
CFHB	Corpus Fontium Historiae Byzantinae
ChHist	*Church History*
CLCAG	Corpus Latinum Commentariorum in Aristotelem Graecorum
DOP	*Dumbarton Oaks Papers*
DOS	Dumbarton Oaks Studies
EO	*Echos d'Orient*
Ἐπ.Ἑτ.Βυζ.Σπ	*Ἐπετηρὶς ἑταιρείας βυζαντινῶν σπουδῶν*
GBA	*Gazette des Beaux Arts*
ICS	*Illinois Classical Studies*
JÖB	*Jahrbuch der Österreichischen Byzantinistik*
JWarb	*Journal of the Warburg and Courtauld Institutes*
OCP	*Orientalia Christiana Periodica*
OCT	Oxford Classical Texts
ODB	*The Oxford Dictionary of Byzantium*, ed. A. Kazhdan et al. (New York–Oxford, 1991)
OED	*Oxford English Dictionary*
OKS	*Ostkirchliche Studien*
PG	Patrologiae cursus completus, Series Graeca, ed. J.-P. Migne (Paris, 1857–66)

PLP	*Prosopographisches Lexikon der Palaiologenzeit*, ed. E. Trapp et al. (Vienna, 1976–)
RE	*Paulys Real-Encyclopädie der classischen Altertumswissenschaft*, new rev. ed. by G. Wissowa and W. Kroll (Stuttgart, 1894–1978)
REB	*Revue des études byzantines*
RSBN	*Rivista di studi bizantini e neoellenici*
ST	Studi e testi

ABOUT THE AUTHORS

TEODOLINDA BAROLINI, Da Ponte Professor of Italian at Columbia University, is author of *Dante's Poets* (1984; Italian 1993), *The Undivine Comedy: Detheologizing Dante* (1992; Italian 2003), *Dante and the Origins of Italian Literary Culture* (2006; Italian 2012), and a new commentary on Dante's lyrics, *Rime giovanili e della "Vita Nuova"* (2009; English 2014).

PIERO BOITANI teaches Comparative Literature at Rome "Sapienza" University and at the University of Italian Switzerland. He is a Fellow of the British Academy, of the Medieval Academy of America, and the Accademia dei Lincei, and the editorial director of the Greek and Latin Classics series of Fondazione Valla. His latest books are *Il grande racconto delle stelle* (Mulino 2012), *The Gospel according to Shakespeare* (Notre Dame University Press, 2013), and *Dante e il suo futuro* (Storia e Letteratura, 2013).

THEODORE J. CACHEY JR. is Professor of Italian in the Department of Romance Languages and Literatures at the University of Notre Dame. His research focuses on Italian literature and culture of the Middle Ages and the Renaissance, in particular Dante, Petrarch, the "Questione della lingua," cartography and literature, and travel literature.

WILLIAM P. CAFERRO is the Gertrude Conaway Vanderbilt Professor of History at Vanderbilt University, where he teaches medieval European and economic history. He authored most recently *Contesting the Renaissance* (Blackwell, 2010) and is finishing a book called *Petrarch and the Meaning of Florentine Wages at the Time of the Black Death.*

MARCIA L. COLISH, Frederic B. Artz Professor of History emerita at Oberlin College, is Lecturer in History at Yale University. Her publications include *The Mirror of Language* (2nd ed. 1983), *Peter Lombard* (1994), *Medieval Foundations of the Western Intellectual Tradition* (1997; Italian 2003; Chinese 2009), and *Ambrose's Patriarchs* (2005).

GEORGE DAMERON is Professor and Chair of History and Director of the Humanities Center at Saint Michael's College. He is the author of two books on the Florentine Church as well as several articles and essays on medieval Tuscany. His current interest focuses on food (grain) provisioning and politics in Tuscan city-states before 1350.

ELIZABETH A. FISHER is Professor of Classics at George Washington University. She is editor of *Michaelis Pselli orationes hagiographicae* (Teubner 1994), co-editor with Denis Sullivan and Stratis Papaioannou of *Byzantine Religious Culture: Studies in Honor of Alice-Mary Talbot* (Brill 2012) and author of numerous articles on Byzantine literary topics.

RÉKA FORRAI received her PhD in Medieval Studies at the Central European University in Budapest in 2008 and is currently a Postdoctoral Fellow at the Centre for Medieval Literature at the University of Southern Denmark, Odense (2012–2015). She has published extensively on questions related to medieval Greek-Latin translation theory and practice. Her current research focuses on papal involvement in the spreading of Greek culture in the West during the Middle Ages.

FILIPPO NAITANA completed a PhD in Italian at Yale University, and is currently Assistant Professor at Quinnipiac University. His research interests include Dante and the classical tradition and the Renaissance in a Mediterranean context. He is currently working on a manuscript entitled *Dante and the Question of Happiness.*

DIEGO SBACCHI is currently a secondary school teacher of Italian and Latin Language and Literature in Macerata, Italy. He earned a PhD in Italian Studies from the University of Toronto. He studies the influence of Pseudo-Dionysius on Dante's work in particular, and he is author of articles on Dante, Petrarch, Ariosto and Tasso.

MICHELE TRIZIO is a Post-Doctoral Research Fellow at the University of Bari (Italy). He has published several articles on philosophical literature and the philosophers in Byzantium, in particular on philosophy in the middle Byzantine period, and on the Greek-Latin philosophical interaction in the Middle Ages. He is currently preparing the critical edition of Robert Grosseteste's medieval Latin translations of the *Suda Lexicon* and of the Greek-Byzantine commentaries on Aristotle's *Nicomachean Ethics* (books V and VI).

VERA VON FALKENHAUSEN is professor emerita of Byzantine History at the Università di Roma-Tor Vergata. She has also taught at the universities of Pisa, Potenza, and Chieti. Her research is focused on Byzantine and post-Byzantine southern Italy and Byzantine hagiography. Her bibliography is accessible online at www.studibizantini.it.

INDEX